445

THE KINGDOM OF GOD
AND PEACE ESSAYS

Oxford University Press, Ely House, London W. 1

GLASGOW   NEW YORK   TORONTO   MELBOURNE   WELLINGTON
CAPE TOWN   IBADAN   NAIROBI   DAR ES SALAAM   LUSAKA   ADDIS ABABA
DELHI   BOMBAY   CALCUTTA   MADRAS   KARACHI   LAHORE   DACCA
KUALA LUMPUR   SINGAPORE   HONG KONG   TOKYO

THE
KINGDOM OF GOD
AND
PEACE ESSAYS

BY
LEO TOLSTÓY

Translated with an
Introduction by
AYLMER MAUDE

LONDON
OXFORD UNIVERSITY PRESS
NEW YORK   TORONTO

LEO TOLSTÓY

Born: Yásnaya Polyána, Túla
28 August (Old style) = 9 September (New style) 1828

Died: Astápova, Riazán
7 November (Old style) = 20 November (New style) 1910

The Kingdom of God is Within You *was first published in* 1893, *and the Essays between* 1894 *and* 1909. *In* The World's Classics *they were first published in* 1936 *and reprinted in* 1942, 1946, 1951, 1960, *and* 1974

ISBN 0 19 250445 2

*Printed in Great Britain
at the University Press, Oxford
by Vivian Ridler
Printer to the University*

CONTENTS

INTRODUCTION

THESE articles on patriotism and war, now retranslated and collected into one volume, represent Tolstóy's final and considered opinion on war, and on the belief in violence which makes wars possible and popular.

A house divided against itself cannot stand, and the truth of Tolstóy's statement that no society can permanently endure half militarist and half Christian, seems to be recognized by Stálin, Mussolini, and Hitler, who have realized that teachings such as those of Jesus are dangerous to a dictatorship relying on physical force, and have therefore banned these works.

The 180,000,000 inhabitants of the U.S.S.R. are not even allowed to import any one of the sixty-six books of the Bible, and in that country all religion is officially condemned.

In Germany Hitler's régime is actively concerned that the 65,000,000 people under its sway, if they retain any sort of Christianity shall have one that will include patriotism (which Jesus omitted from among the virtues he commended) and that in its moral code will allot high honour to the practice of physical violence.

Tolstóy's protests against the suppression of personal freedom, and of liberty of the press and of speech, as well as his protest against the employment of mass-hypnotism to obliterate the workings of conscience, are if possible more topical to-day than when these articles were written some forty years ago. They deal with a most vital problem of to-day, for man's mastery over matter and the extent to which material achievements now eclipse moral considerations render the destruction of our civilization a not improbable prospect of the near future.

Should some Chinese survivor of that catastrophe, searching amid the ruins of the British Museum, chance upon a copy of this book, he will probably marvel that contemporaneously with such barbarism there lived a man who so clearly discerned the moral weakness of the age, foresaw the impending disaster, and living under a ruthless and despotic government dared to speak out so boldly.

In England, and in western Europe generally, Christianity is not as yet officially denounced or derided, but it seemed to Tolstóy to have been sterilized by the Church Creeds which divert men's attention from those teachings of Jesus which conflict with the tendencies of patriotic governments. Tolstóy held that it is this intrusion of dogmas, elaborated by angry theologians at the time when the Church was first submitting to State control, that renders it wellnigh impossible for educated and intelligent Hindus, Chinese, or Mohammedans, to regard Christianity as other than a grossly superstitious and irrational religion.

In one of his essays he tells us that: 'To understand any book one must choose out the parts that are quite clear, dividing them from what is obscure or confused. And from what is clear we must form our idea of the drift and spirit of the whole work. Then, on the basis of what we have understood, we may proceed to make out what is confused or not quite intelligible. That is how we read all kinds of books.'

This advice is particularly apposite when we are reading the works of a writer who belongs neither to our race nor to our generation, and whose mind moved forward from one position to another so considerably that an acquaintance with his earlier works may sometimes set the reader on a wrong track for appreciating what he says in a later volume, and vice versa.

His disapproval of war, incidentally expressed in his early stories *The Raid* and *Sevastopol*, is but little in evidence in *War and Peace*, but became prominent when he devoted himself to the study of religion in 1878 to 1884. The text 'Resist not him that is evil: but whosoever smiteth thee on thy right cheek turn to him the other also', impressed him greatly, and he was amazed to notice how generally that precept is ignored both in preaching and in practice.

At that time the fact that those words are attributed to Jesus weighed more with him than it did later, when referring to attempts made to deny the historicity of Jesus he once wrote: 'They are attacking the last of the outworks, and if they carry it and demonstrate that Christ never was born, it will be all the more evident that the fortress of religion is impregnable. Take away the Church, the traditions, the Bible, and even Christ himself—the ultimate fact of man's knowledge of goodness, that is of God, directly through reason and conscience, will be as clear and certain as ever; and it will be seen that we are dealing with truths that can never perish —truths humanity can never afford to part with.'

But though he no longer attached special importance to the fact that the words are attributed to Jesus, the idea they express still appeared profoundly true and lost none of its significance for him. He regarded it as showing the way by which the world may be saved from approaching destruction and men's souls saved from the taint of participating in wholesale and premeditated murder, and he continued to employ the words: 'Resist not him that is evil' or the abbreviated form 'Resist not evil' and the phrase 'non-resistance'.

It is curious to note that those words of Christ's had not attracted much scorn or denunciation as long as they slumbered in the obscurity to which they were relegated by the prominence the Church gave to Creeds unrelated to conduct. But as soon as Tolstóy began to repeat them and apply them to real life, the precept attracted both scorn and denunciation. He was himself excommunicated by the Most Holy Synod, placed under police supervision, and had many of his works suppressed by the censor. Dean Farrar referred scornfully to the words as a 'divine paradox', and numerous writers cited the imaginary case of a burly brigand outraging a woman or kicking a baby to death in the presence of someone who could have knocked him down in such a way that he would have stayed put till the woman or baby had been removed—but refrained from doing so owing to the pernicious influence of those words of Christ's. Tolstóy's reply, given in this volume in his Introduction to a *Life of Garrison*, deserves consideration. That reply is practical and pertinent, though it does not prove that the rule admits of no exceptions.

In my *Life of Tolstóy* I have dealt carefully and at length with the exception I think can reasonably be taken to the wording of Tolstóy's proposition, especially in relation to its application to civil government. I need not therefore pursue the matter here, beyond saying that it is not reasonable to allow a question of precise phrasing to divert attention from Tolstóy's courageous and powerful indictment of an enormous evil no one else of his standing had dared or been able so to challenge.

Belief in the efficacy of physical violence is still very general, as anyone may see who notices how regularly on the films a man's readiness to knock down his opponents marks him out as the proper person for the heroine to marry with full assurance of living happily ever after. And any attempt to substitute goodwill for violence in dealing with foreign countries or subject-races still meets with much disapproval.

It cannot be claimed that Tolstóy's statement of the case is indubitably and completely sound, but he aims in the right direction and scores many important points. Life, however, is so complex that it is difficult to state any moral principle emphatically, briefly, and clearly, yet so that it shall be applicable in all cases. For instance, at first it seems a sound rule to say that you should 'always tell the truth'. But if an old man on his death-bed asks what his much-loved daughter is doing, it might be very cruel to tell him that she had just eloped with a chauffeur he strongly disapproved of. That objection to the principle is not readily met, but does not afford sufficient reason for rejecting the general injunction to tell the truth. Similarly the popular objections to the abandonment of physical violence as a means of settling human affairs, do not prove that the injunction to which Tolstóy attaches such importance is not one mankind will have to reckon with if it is to escape destruction, and individuals will have to reckon with if they are to save their souls alive.

Christianity and Patriotism is a very remarkable essay. Tolstóy's many-sidedness shows itself in the excellent fun he makes of the worked-up enthusiasm of the Kronstadt-Toulon naval festivities, but this in no way lessens his moral indignation at the whole affair, or his clear perception—twenty years before the outbreak of the Great War—of the direction in which matters were tending.

We have here a good example of how the gift of prophecy works. A wise man, acquainted with what is happening in the world, is strongly moved by moral indignation against what he recognizes as false and wrong in what goes on around him. Convinced that such conduct must lead to a great calamity, his common sense indicates from what direction that calamity is to be expected. His contemporaries neglect his warnings and consider him a visionary whom practical men may disregard, but his vision of what is coming is clearer and truer than that of the men of the world who despise him.

Finally we should not overlook the courage required to face the odds that were against Tolstóy when he delivered his message. Arrayed against him were the Church, the State, the censor, the militarists, the patriots, all who sought honours, distinctions, and material prosperity, all the old-fashioned folk, and several members of his own family, including his wife. To write such works knowing that publication in Russia would be prohibited, having no copyright abroad, declining payment for his work even when that was offered, and encountering obloquy and abuse from those who curried favour from the powers that be—needed a man of Tolstóy's heroic, inflexible, and profoundly religious nature.

AYLMER MAUDE

May 1936.

THE KINGDOM OF GOD IS
WITHIN YOU

*Christianity not as a mystical doctrine but as a new
understanding of life*

Ye shall know the truth, and the truth shall make you free.
JOHN iii. 32.

Fear not them which kill the body, but are not able to kill the
soul; but rather fear him which is able to destroy both soul
and body in hell. MATT. x. 28.

Ye were bought with a price; become not bondservants of
men. I COR. vii. 23.

PREFACE

IN 1884 I wrote a book called *What I Believe*,
in which I gave an account of what I do
believe.

When giving an account of my belief in Christ's
teaching I could not avoid a statement of why I
disbelieve, and regard as erroneous, the Church
doctrine which is usually called Christianity.

Among the many divergences of that doctrine
from the teaching of Christ, I pointed out as the
chief one its omission to acknowledge the law of
non-resistance to evil by violence which, more
evidently than other differences, indicates how
the Church doctrine perverts the teaching of
Christ.

Like most people I knew very little of what had
previously been done and preached and written
on the subject of non-resistance to evil. I knew
what had been said on the subject by the Fathers
of the Church—Origen, Tertullian, and others—

and I knew that the so-called sects of Mennonites, Herrnhuters, and Quakers, who do not allow a Christian to use weapons and do not accept military service, have existed and still exist; but of what these so-called sects had done towards elucidating this question I knew but little.

My book was, as I expected, suppressed by the Russian censorship but, partly owing to my reputation as a writer and partly because the book interested people, it circulated in manuscript and lithographed copies in Russia and in translations abroad, and brought me on the one hand, from people sharing my convictions, much information concerning works written on the subject, and on the other hand a series of criticisms of the opinions expressed in my book.

These criticisms, both hostile and friendly, together with the historical events of the last years, cleared up many things for me and led me to fresh deductions and conclusions which I now wish to express.

First I will speak of the information I received as to the history of the question of non-resistance to evil, then of the opinions expressed on the subject by unworldly critics—that is, by professed believers in the Christian religion—and also by secular critics, that is, by people who do not profess the Christian religion; and lastly I will speak of the conclusions to which I have been brought by all this and by the historical events of recent years.

LEO TOLSTÓY

I

From the very foundation of Christianity the doctrine of not resisting evil by violence has been professed, and still is professed, by a minority of men.

AMONG the first responses to my book were letters from American Quakers. In those letters, expressing their sympathy with my views as to the unlawfulness of war or the use of violence for a Christian, the Quakers gave me details of their so-called sect, which for more than two hundred years has professed and practised the teaching of Christ as to non-resistance of evil by violence, and does not make use of weapons in self-defence. Together with these letters the Quakers sent me their pamphlets, journals, and books, from which I learnt how, already many years ago, they had irrefutably demonstrated that it is a Christian's duty to fulfil the command of not resisting evil by violence, and how fully they had exposed the error of the Church's teaching which allows of capital punishment and war.

Having proved by a whole series of argument and texts that a religion based on peacefulness and goodwill towards men is incompatible with war—that is, with mutilating and killing men—the Quakers maintain and prove that nothing has contributed so much to obscure Christian truth in the eyes of the heathen, or has so hindered the spread of Christianity in the world, as the sanctioning and practice of war and violence by Christians.

'Christ's teaching,' they say, 'having reached men's consciousness not by means of violence and the sword, but by non-resistance to evil, gentleness, meekness, and peacefulness—can only be diffused through the world by the example of peacefulness, concord, and love, among its followers.'

'A Christian, according to the teaching of God Himself, can be guided in his relation to men only by love of peace, and therefore no authority can bind a Christian to act contrary to God's teaching and to the chief attribute of a Christian in his relation to his neighbours.'

'Those who for the sake of worldly advantage try to reconcile the irreconcilable, may be compelled by the law of State Necessity to betray the law of God, but for a Christian who sincerely believes that the fulfilment of Christ's teaching gives him salvation, such considerations of State can be of no significance.'

An acquaintance with the Quakers' activity and with their works: with Fox, Penn, and especially with a book by Dymond published in 1827—showed me not only that the impossibility of reconciling Christianity with violence and war had long ago been recognized, but that this incompatibility had long since been so clearly and indubitably proved that one could only wonder how this impossible combination of Christianity and war, which has been and still is preached by the Church, can continue to exist.

Besides what I learned from the Quakers, I also received from America about the same time information on the subject from quite another source, previously entirely unknown to me.

The son of William Lloyd Garrison, the famous champion of the emancipation of the negroes, wrote me that having read my book, in which he found ideas similar to those expressed by his father in 1838, and thinking that it would interest me to know this, he was sending me a declaration or proclamation of 'non-resistance' drawn up by his father nearly fifty years before.

This declaration was drawn up under the following circumstances: in America, in 1838, William Lloyd Garrison took part in a discussion in a Society for the Establishment of Peace among men—on means of preventing war. He came to the conclusion that the establishment of universal peace can only be founded on the open acknowledgement of the doctrine of non-resistance to evil by violence (Matt. v. 39) in its full significance, as it is understood by the Quakers with whom he was in friendly relations. Having come to this conclusion, Garrison drew up and laid before the Society the following declaration, which was signed at the time—in 1838—by many members:

'Declaration of Sentiments adopted by the Peace Convention.

Boston 1838.

'We, the undersigned, regard it as due to ourselves, to the cause which we love, to the country in which we live, and to the world, to publish a Declaration expressive of the principles we cherish, the purposes we aim to accomplish, and the measures we shall adopt to carry forward the work of peaceful and universal reformation.

'We cannot acknowledge allegiance to any human government. . . . We recognize but one King and Lawgiver, one Judge and Ruler of mankind. . . . Our country is the world, our countrymen are all mankind. We love the land of our nativity only as we love all other lands. The interests and rights of American citizens are no more dear to us than those of the whole human race. Hence we can allow no appeal to patriotism to revenge any national insult or injury. . . . We conceive that a nation has no right to defend itself against foreign enemies or to punish its invaders, and no individual possesses that right in his own case, and the unit cannot be of greater importance than the aggregate. If soldiers thronging from abroad with intent to commit rapine and destroy life may not be resisted by the people or the magistracy, then ought no resistance to be offered to domestic troublers of the public peace or of private security.[1]

'The dogma that all the governments of the world are approvingly ordained by God, and that THE POWERS THAT BE in the United States, in Russia, in Turkey, are in accordance with His will, is not less absurd than impious. It makes the impartial Author of our existence unequal and tyrannical. It cannot be affirmed that the Powers that be, in any nation, are actuated by the spirit or guided by the example of Christ in the treatment of enemies; therefore they cannot be agreeable to the will of God; and therefore

---

[1] Tolstóy has considerably abbreviated Garrison's Declaration, and in so doing has not always followed the exact wording of the original.—A.M.

their overthrow by a spiritual regeneration of
their subjects is inevitable.

'We regard as unchristian and wrong not only
war itself, whether offensive or defensive, but all
preparations for war: the building of any naval
ship, any arsenal, or any fortification: we regard
as unchristian and wrong the existence of any
standing army, all military chieftains or soldiers,
all monuments commemorative of victory over
a fallen foe, all trophies won in battle, all celebrations in honour of military exploits, all annexa-
tions acquired by armed force; and we regard as
unchristian and wrong every edict of government
requiring military service of its subjects.

'In consequence of all this we consider it unlawful to bear arms or to hold any office that
obliges us to compel men to do right on pain
of imprisonment or death. We therefore voluntarily exclude ourselves from every legislative
and judicial body, and repudiate all human politics, worldly honours, and stations of authority.

'If we cannot occupy a seat in the legislature
or on the bench, neither can we elect others to
act as our substitutes in any such capacity.

'It follows that we cannot sue any man at law
to compel him by force to restore anything which
he may have wrongly taken from us or others;
but if he has seized our coat, we shall surrender
up our cloak rather than subject him to punishment.

'We believe that the penal code of the old
covenant, an eye for an eye and a tooth for a
tooth, has been abrogated by Jesus Christ, and
that under the new covenant the forgiveness

instead of the punishment of enemies has been
enjoined upon all his disciples in all cases whatsoever. To extort money from enemies, to confine them in prison, to exile them, or hang them
on a gallows, is obviously not to forgive but to
take retribution.

'The history of mankind is crowded with evidence proving that physical coercion is not
adapted to moral regeneration; that the sinful
disposition of men can be subdued only by love;
that evil can be exterminated only by goodness;
that we should not trust to the strength of an arm
to preserve us from harm, but that real security
dwells in gentleness, long-suffering and mercy;
that it is only the meek who shall inherit the
earth, but that the violent who resort to the sword
are destined to perish with the sword.

'And therefore both for the safety of life, property, liberty, public quietude and private welfare, and in order to fulfil the will of Him who is
King of kings and Lord of lords, we cordially
adopt the non-resistance principle, being confident that it provides for all possible consequences and, expressing the will of God, must
ultimately triumph over every evil force. We
advocate no revolutionary doctrines. The spirit
of revolutionary doctrine is the spirit of retaliation, violence, and murder, and neither fears
God nor regards man. We would be filled with
the spirit of Christ. Following the fundamental
rule of not resisting evil by evil, we cannot engage
in plots, riots, disturbances, or violence. We shall
submit to every ordinance and every requirement of government except such as are contrary

to the commands of the Gospel, and in no case resist the operation of law, except by meekly submitting to the penalty of disobedience. But while we shall adhere to the doctrine of non-resistance and shall passively endure all attacks directed against us, we intend for our part, in a moral and spiritual sense, unceasingly to assail iniquity in high places and in low places, in civil, political, legal and ecclesiastical institutions, and to strive to hasten the time when the kingdoms of this world will have become the Kingdoms of our Lord Jesus Christ.

'It appears to us a self-evident truth that whatever the gospel is designed to destroy at any period of the world, being contrary to it, ought now to be abandoned. If, then, the time is predicted when swords shall be beaten into ploughshares and spears into pruning-hooks and men shall not learn the art of war any more, it follows that all who manufacture, sell, or wield those deadly weapons, do thus array themselves against the peaceful dominion of the Son of God on earth.

'Having stated our principles, we will now say how we propose to attain our purpose. We hope to prevail through the "foolishness of preaching".

'We shall try to spread our views among all people, to whatever nation, creed, or class of society they may belong. For that purpose we shall organize public lectures, circulate printed announcements and pamphlets, form societies, and petition our State and national governments. In general we shall try by all means in our power to effect a radical change in the views, feelings, and practices of society respecting the sinfulness of war and the treatment of enemies.

'Entering upon this great work we fully realize that our sincerity may be exposed to cruel tests. It may subject us to insult. We expect outrage, suffering, and even death itself. We anticipate misunderstanding, misrepresentation, and calumny. Tumults may arise against us. The proud and pharisaical, the ambitious and tyrannical, the rulers and the authorities, may all unite to crush us. So they treated the Messiah, whose example we are humbly striving to imitate. But we shall not be afraid of those terrors. We trust not in man but in the Lord Almighty. Having withdrawn from human protection, what can sustain us but that faith which overcomes the world? We shall not be surprised by the trials to which we are exposing ourselves, but shall rejoice to be partakers of Christ's sufferings.

'Therefore we commit the keeping of our souls to God, believing what is written, that he who forsakes houses, or brethren, or sisters, or father, or mother, or wife, or children, or lands, for Christ's sake, shall receive a hundredfold, and shall inherit everlasting life.

'Firmly relying upon the certain and universal triumph of the sentiments contained in this Declaration, however formidable may be the opposition arraigned against them, we hereby affix our signatures, commending it to the reason and conscience of mankind, and above all resolving, in the strength of the Lord God, calmly and meekly to abide the issue.'

Immediately after this Declaration a Society for Non-Resistance was founded by Garrison, and a journal called *The Non-Resistant* was started, in which the doctrine of non-resistance was advocated in its full significance and with all its consequences, as it had been expounded in the Declaration. I obtained information as to the subsequent fate of the society and the journal from the excellent biography of W. L. Garrison written by his sons.

Neither society nor journal existed long. Most of Garrison's fellow-workers in the movement for the emancipation of the slaves, fearing that the too-radical programme of *The Non-Resistant* might keep people away from the practical work of negro-emancipation, gave up the profession of the principle of non-resistance as expressed in the Declaration, and both society and journal ceased to exist.

Garrison's declaration so strongly and eloquently professed a faith of such importance to men that one would have expected it to make a strong impression, to be known the world over, and to excite general discussion. But nothing of the kind happened. Not only is it unknown in Europe, but even to Americans who esteem Garrison's memory highly that declaration is almost unknown.

A similar disregard befell another champion of non-resistance—an American, Adin Ballou, who died recently after preaching that doctrine for fifty years. How remarkably little is known of all that relates to the question of non-resistance may be seen from the fact that—replying to my inquiry whether any society of non-resistance now exists and whether the doctrine has any followers—Garrison's son, who had written an excellent four-volume biography of his father, informed me that as far as he knew the society had broken up and there were no followers of the teaching, while at the very time he was writing to me, Adin Ballou—who had taken part in Garrison senior's labours and had devoted fifty years of his life to advocating the doctrine of non-resistance both orally and in print—was living at Hopedale in Massachusetts. Subsequently I received a letter from Wilson, a pupil and assistant of Ballou's, and entered into correspondence with Ballou himself. I wrote to him and he replied and sent me his works. Here are some extracts from them:

'Jesus Christ is my Lord and Master,' says Ballou in one of the articles in which he arraigns the inconsistency of Christians who recognize a right of self-defence and war. 'I have covenanted to forsake all and follow Him through good or evil report, until death. But I am nevertheless a Democratic-Republican citizen of the United States, implicitly sworn to bear true allegiance to my country and to support its Constitution, if need be with my life. Jesus Christ requires me to do unto others as I would that they should do unto me. The Constitution of the United States requires me to do unto two million slaves [there were slaves then, now in their place we may put workmen] the very contrary of what I would have them do to me, namely, assist to keep them in their present condition of slavery.... But I am quite easy. I help the government. I am willing to hold any office I may be elected to under the Constitution. And I am still a Christian. I go on professing. I find no difficulty in keeping my covenant both with Christ and the Constitution. . . .

'Jesus Christ forbids me to resist evildoers by taking an eye for an eye, a tooth for a tooth, blood for blood, and life for life.

'My government requires the very reverse, and depends for its own self-preservation on the halter, the musket, and the sword, seasonably employed against its foreign and domestic enemies. Accordingly the land is well-filled with gibbets, prisons, arsenals, train-bands, soldiers, and ships of war.

'In the maintenance and use of this expensive and life-destroying apparatus, we can exemplify to the full the virtues of forgiving those who injure us, loving our enemies, blessing them that curse us, and doing good to those that hate us. For this reason we have regular Christian chaplains to pray for us and call down God's blessing on our holy murders. . . .

'I see it all [that is, the contradiction between our profession and our life], and yet I insist that I am as good a Christian as ever. I assent to it all; I go on voting, I go on helping govern, I go on professing; and I glory in being at once a devoted Christian and a no less devoted adherent to the existing government. I will not give in to those miserable non-resistant notions. I will not throw away my political influence and leave unprincipled men to carry on government alone. . . .

'The Constitution says: "Congress shall have power to declare war." I agree to this. I endorse it. I swear to help carry it through. . . . What then, am I less a Christian? Is not war a Christian service? Is it not perfectly Christian to murder hundreds of thousands of fellow-human beings, to ravish women, sack and burn cities, and exact all the other cruelties of war? Out upon these new-fangled scruples! This is the very way to forgive injuries and love one's enemies! If we only do it all in true love, nothing can be more Christian than wholesale murder!'

In another article entitled *How Many Does it Take?* he says, 'How many does it take to metamorphose wickedness into righteousness? One man must not kill. If he does it is murder. Two, ten, one hundred men acting on their own responsibility must not kill. If they do it is still murder. But a state or nation may kill as many as it pleases and it is no murder. It is just, necessary, commendable, and right. Only get people enough to agree to it, and the butchery of myriads of human beings is perfectly innocent. But how many men does it take? That is the question. Just so with theft, robbery, burglary, and other crimes. . . . A whole nation may commit them. . . . But how many does it take? Why may not one, ten, or a hundred men, violate God's law, when a great number may do so?'

And now here is Ballou's catechism, composed for his flock.

A Catechism of Non-Resistance[1]

Question. Where is the term 'Non-resistance' taken from?

Answer. From the injunction: Resist not him that is evil. Matt. v. 39.

Q. What does the term signify?

A. It expresses the lofty Christian virtue enjoined by Christ.

Q. Is the word 'resistance' to be taken in its widest meaning, that is, as showing that no resistance whatever is to be shown to evil?

A. No, it is to be taken in the strict sense of the Saviour's injunction; that is, we are not to resist evil with evil. Evil is to be resisted by all just means, but never with evil.

Q. What is there to show that Christ prescribed non-resistance in that sense?

A. From the words which he then used: He said: 'Ye have heard that it was said, An eye for an eye, and a tooth for a tooth. But I say unto you, Resist not him that is evil: but whosoever smiteth thee on thy right cheek, turn to him the other also. And if any man would go to law with thee, and take away thy coat, let him have thy cloke also.'

Q. Of whom was Jesus speaking when he said: 'Ye have heard that it was said by them of old time'?

A. Of the patriarchs and prophets and what they said—as contained in the Old Testament,

---

[1] This translation is made freely with some omissions.—L.T. (Apparently Tolstóy compiled this Catechism from various passages in one of Ballou's works.—A.M.)

and which the Hebrews generally call the Law and the Prophets.

Q. What injunctions did Christ refer to when he used the words: 'It was said'?

A. The injunctions by which Noah, Moses, and other prophets, in order to destroy evil, authorized the infliction of personal injury on those who inflict injury.

Q. Quote those injunctions.

A. 'Whoso sheddeth man's blood, by man shall his blood be shed.' Gen. ix. 6.

'He that smiteth a man, so that he die, shall be surely put to death. . . . And if any mischief follow, then thou shalt give life for life, eye for eye, tooth for tooth, hand for hand, foot for foot, burning for burning, wound for wound, stripe for stripe.' Exodus xxi. 12. 23–5.

'And he that killeth any man shall surely be put to death. . . . And if a man cause a blemish in his neighbour, as he hath done, so shall it be done to him: breach for breach, eye for eye, tooth for tooth.' Lev. xxiv. 17, 19, 20.

'And the judges shall make diligent inquisition: and, behold, if the witness be a false witness, and hath testified falsely against his brother, then shall ye do unto him as he had thought to have done unto his brother. So shalt thou put the evil away from among you. . . . And thine eye shall not pity: but life shall go for life, eye for eye, tooth for tooth, hand for hand, foot for foot.' Deut. xix. 18, 21.

These are the precepts of which Jesus spoke.

Noah, Moses, and the prophets, taught that he who kills, maims, or injures his neighbours, does evil. To resist such evil and destroy it, the doer of evil is to be punished by death or maiming or some personal injury. Injury must be met by injury, murder by murder, torture by torture, evil by evil. So Noah, Moses, and the prophets, taught.

But Christ rejects all this. 'But I say unto you' —is written in the Gospels—'that ye resist not him that is evil.' Do not resist an insult with an insult, but rather bear the repeated insult from the doer of evil.

What was authorized is prohibited. If we understand what kind of resistance was taught, we clearly see what we are taught by Christ's non-resistance.

Q. Did the ancients authorize the resistance of injury by injury?

A. Yes. But Jesus prohibited this. A Christian has not the right under any condition to deprive of life or to subject to insult him who does evil to his neighbour.

Q. May a man kill or maim another in self-defence?

A. No.

Q. May he enter a court with a complaint, to have this injurer punished?

A. No, for what he does through others he really does himself.

Q. May he fight in an army against enemies, or against domestic rebels?

A. Of course not. He cannot take any part in war or warlike preparations. He cannot use death-dealing arms. He cannot resist injury with injury, no matter whether he be alone or with others, through himself or through others.

Q. May he voluntarily choose or fit out military men for the government?

A. He can do nothing of the kind, if he wishes to be true to Christ's law.

Q. May he voluntarily give money to aid the government, which is supported by military forces, capital punishment, or violence in general?

A. No, unless the money is intended for some special object, just in itself, where the aim and means are good.

Q. May he pay taxes to such a government?

A. No, he must not voluntarily pay the taxes, but he must also not resist their collection. The taxes imposed by the government are collected independently of the will of the subjects. It is impossible to resist the collection without having recourse to violence; but a Christian must not use violence, and so he must give up his property to the violence which is exercised by the powers.

Q. May a Christian vote at elections and take part in a court or in the government?

A. No. Participation in elections, in the law-court, or the government, is participation in governmental violence.

Q. In what does the chief significance of the doctrine of non-resistance consist?

A. In that it alone makes it possible to tear out evil by the root, both out of our own hearts and those of our neighbours. The teaching forbids the doing of that by which evil is multiplied in the world. He who attacks another and insults him, engenders in him the sentiment of hatred, the root of all evil. To offend another because he has offended us, on the specious pretext of removing an evil, is really to repeat an evil deed, both against him and against ourselves—to beget, or at least to free and to encourage, the very demon we wish to expel. Satan cannot be driven out by Satan, untruth cannot be cleansed by untruth, and evil cannot be vanquished by evil.

True non-resistance is the one true resistance to evil. It crushes the serpent's head. It kills and finally destroys the evil sentiment.

Q. But even if the idea of the doctrine be right, is it practicable?

A. It is as practicable as any good prescribed by the Law of God. The good cannot under all circumstances be executed without self-renunciation, privation, suffering, and in extreme cases the loss of life itself. But he who values life more than the fulfilment of God's will is already dead to the one true life. Such a man, in trying to save his life, shall lose it. And in general, where non-resistance demands the sacrifice of one life, or the sacrifice of some essential good of life, resistance demands thousands of such sacrifices.

Non-resistance preserves; resistance destroys.

It is incomparably safer to act justly than to act unjustly; to bear an insult than to resist it by violence. It is safer even in relation to the present life. If no man resisted evil with evil, our world would be blessed.

Q. But if only a few should act thus, what will become of them?

A. If only one man acted thus, and all the others agreed to crucify him, would it not be

more glorious for him to die in the triumph of
non-resisting love, praying for his enemies, than
to live wearing the crown of Caesar, bespattered
with the blood of the slain? But one man or a
thousand who have firmly determined not to resist evil with evil—whether among enlightened
people or savage neighbours—are much safer
from violence than those who rely on violence.
The robber, murderer, or deceiver, will more
quickly leave them alone than those who resist
with weapons. They who take the sword perish
with the sword, and those who seek peace, who
act in a friendly manner, inoffensively, who forget and forgive offences, for the most part enjoy
peace, or, if they die, die blessed.

Thus if all kept the commandment of non-
resistance, it is evident that there would be no
offences and no evil deeds. If these formed a
majority, they would establish the reign of love
and goodwill, even towards the ill-disposed, by
never resisting evil with evil and never using
violence. If there were a considerable minority
of such, they would have such a corrective moral
effect upon society that every cruel punishment
would be abolished, and violence and enmity
would be changed to peace and love. If there
were but a small minority of them, they would
rarely experience anything worse than the contempt of the world, and the world in the meanwhile, without noticing it and without feeling
itself under obligation, would become wiser and
better for this secret influence. And if, in the very
worst case, a few members of the minority should
be persecuted to death, these men, dying for the

truth, would leave behind them their teaching, sanctified by their martyr's death.

Peace be with all who seek peace, and may all-conquering love be the imperishable inheritance of every soul that voluntarily submits to the Law of Christ—not to resist by violence him that is evil.

Adin Ballou.

For fifty years Ballou wrote and published books dealing principally with the question of non-resistance to evil men by violence. In those works, admirable in clearness of thought and beauty of exposition, the question is considered from every possible angle, and the binding nature of this command on every Christian who acknowledges the Gospel as the revelation of God is established. All the ordinary objections to the doctrine of non-resistance are cited, both from the Old and New Testaments, such, for instance, as the expulsion of the money-changers from the Temple, and so on; and he refutes them all. Independently of Scripture, he shows the practical reasonableness of this rule, and all the objections usually made against its practicability are stated and refuted. Thus one chapter treats of non-resistance in exceptional cases, and he admits that if there were any cases in which it is impossible to apply it, that would prove the law in general to be invalid. Citing these exceptional cases he shows that it is precisely in them that the application of the rule is both necessary and reasonable. There is no aspect of the question, either in support of or in opposition to the rule, which is not examined in these works.

I mention all this to show the unquestionable interest such works ought to have for those who profess Christianity, and that consequently Ballou's work ought to have become well known and the ideas he expressed either accepted or refuted; but nothing of the sort occurred.

The activity of W. L. Garrison in founding the Society of Non-Resistants, and his Declaration, more even than my relations with the Quakers, convinced me that State-Christianity's abandonment of Christ's law of non-resistance by violence had been observed and pointed out long ago, and that men have laboured and still labour to expose it. Ballou's work convinced me of this still more. But the fate of Garrison and Ballou—especially the latter, who remained quite unrecognized in spite of fifty years of constant and persistent work in one and the same direction—confirmed me in the idea that a kind of tacit, but obstinate, conspiracy of silence exists concerning all such efforts.

Ballou died in August 1890, and on August 23rd the American *Religio-Philosophical Journal*, a magazine with a Christian tendency, published an obituary notice of him.

In this laudatory notice it is mentioned that Ballou was the spiritual director of a parish, that he delivered between eight and nine thousand sermons, married a thousand couples, and wrote some five hundred articles; but not a single word is said of the object to which he devoted his life, and the word 'non-resistance' is not even mentioned!

So that all that has been preached by the

Quakers for the last two hundred years, as well as the efforts of W. L. Garrison, the foundation of his Society and journal and his Declaration, as well as the whole of Ballou's life-work, are as though they did not exist and never had existed.

A striking example of works directed to the elucidation of non-resistance and the arraignment of those who do not accept that law, being similarly ignored, is provided by the fate of the work written by the Czech Chelčický, which has only recently become known and has not yet been printed.

Soon after a German edition of my book had appeared, I received a letter from a professor of the University at Prague[1] informing me of the existence of *The Net of Faith*, a work never yet printed, by Chelčický, a fifteenth-century Czech. In that work, the professor told me, Chelčický some four centuries ago had put forward the same view as to true and false Christianity that I expressed in *What I Believe*. He also mentioned that Chelčický's work was to be published for the first time, in the Czech language, in the Journal of the Petersburg Academy of Science. Being unable to obtain the work itself, I tried to acquaint myself with what was known of Chelčický, and obtained the following information from a German book sent to me by that same Prague professor, and from Pýpin's history of Czech literature. This is Pýpin's account:

'*The Net of Faith* is the teaching of Christ, which should draw man from the dark depths of

[1] This was T. J. Masaryk, now President of the Czech Republic.—A.M.

the sea of worldliness and falsehood. True faith consists in believing God's word, but a time has now come when men have mistaken true faith for heresy, and therefore it is for reason to indicate wherein faith consists. Darkness hides it from men and they do not recognize the law of Christ.

'To make that law plain Chelčický points to the primitive organization of Christian society— an organization which, he says, is now considered by the Roman Church to be an odious heresy.

'This primitive Church was his own ideal of social organization, founded on equality, freedom, and brotherhood. Christianity, in Chelčický's opinion, still preserves these foundations, and it is only necessary for society to return to its pure doctrine to render unnecessary every other social order, in which kings or popes are necessary. The law of love alone would suffice in all cases.

'Historically Chelčický attributes the degeneration of Christianity to the time of Constantine the Great, whom Pope Sylvester admitted into the Christian Church with all his heathen morals and life. Constantine in turn endowed the Pope with worldly riches and power. From that time these two authorities have constantly aided one another and striven for nothing but outward glory. Divines, ecclesiastical dignitaries and the clergy, concerned themselves only about subduing the whole world to their authority, and armed men to kill and rob one another and, in creed and life, have quite destroyed Christianity. Chelčický completely denies the right to make war or inflict the punishment of death; every soldier, even the "knight", is only a violent evil-doer and murderer.'

The same, with some biographical details and extracts from Chelčicky's correspondence, is said in the German book.

Having thus learnt the essence of Chelčicky's teaching, I awaited with still greater impatience the appearance of *The Net of Faith* in the Academy's Journal. But a year, two years, three years passed, and still the book did not appear. Not till 1888 did I learn that the printing of it, which had been begun, had been stopped.[1] I obtained proof-sheets of what had been printed, and read them, and found it to be in all respects a wonderful book.

Its tenor is quite correctly given by Pýpin. Chelčicky's fundamental idea is that Christianity having allied itself with temporal power in Constantine's time and continuing to develop in those conditions, became completely perverted and ceased to be really Christian. Chelčicky entitled his book *The Net of Faith* because—having taken for epigraph the verse of the Gospel about Christ calling his disciples to be fishers of men— he says, continuing that metaphor: 'Christ by means of his disciples caught the whole world in his net of faith, but the big fish burst the net and escaped from it, and through the holes they made the other fish got out, so that the net has been left almost empty.'

The big fish that burst the net are the rulers, emperors, popes, and kings, who, without

[1] It was at last published in 1893.—A.M.

renouncing power, accepted not Christianity but only its mask.

Chelčický teaches what is taught to-day by the non-resistant Mennonites and Quakers, and was taught in former times by the Bogomiles, Paulicians, and many others. He says that Christianity—demanding of its followers meekness, humility, kindness, forgiveness of injuries, turning the other cheek when smitten, and the love of one's enemies—is incompatible with the use of violence which is an indispensable condition of power.

A Christian, according to Chelčický, not only cannot be a ruler or a soldier; he cannot take any part in the government, nor be a merchant, or even a landowner; he can only be an artisan or a husbandman.

This book is one of the few exposing official Christianity that have survived the *autos-da-fé*. All such books, which were pronounced heretical, were burnt, together with their authors, so that ancient works exposing the errors of official Christianity are very rare. This work is therefore especially interesting.

But besides being of interest from whatever point of view one regards it, this book is a most remarkable production of human thought, both from the profundity of its contents, the wonderful force and beauty of its popular language, and its antiquity.

Yet for more than four centuries it has been left unprinted, and it is still unknown except to some learned specialists.

One would have thought that all such works,

whether of the Quakers, Garrison, Ballou, or Chelčický, asserting and demonstrating, on the basis of the Gospel, that our world understands Christ's teaching wrongly, ought to arouse interest, agitation, emotion, and discussions, both among pastors and their flocks.

Works of that kind, touching the very essence of Christian teaching, should, one would think, be examined, and either accepted as true or else refuted and rejected.

But nothing of the kind happens. The same fate befalls all such works. Men of most diverse opinions, both believers and—surprisingly—unbelieving liberals also, as though by agreement, preserve the same persistent silence about them, and all that has been done by people to explain the true meaning of Christ's teaching remains unknown or forgotten.

But still more startling is the general neglect of two other books of which I also learnt when my book appeared. These are Dymond's *On War*, first published in London in 1824, and Daniel Musser's *On Non-resistance*, written in 1864. It is particularly astonishing that these books should not be known, because—not to speak of their worth—they both treat not so much of the theory as of the practical application to life of the relation of Christianity to military service, which is particularly important and interesting now in view of the universal liability to military service.

People will perhaps ask: How should a subject behave who believes war to be incompatible with his religion, but from whom the Government demands that he should join the army? That

would seem to be a very vital question, a reply to
which is particularly important in view of the
general military conscription of to-day. All, or
the immense majority, of our people are Christians, and they are all called on to perform
military service. How should a man, as a Christian, meet this demand? Dymond's reply is as
follows:

'His duty is mildly but firmly to refuse to serve.

'There are people who, without any definite
reasoning, simply conclude that responsibility
for Government measures rests entirely on those
who enact them; or that the rulers and kings
decide what is right and wrong for their subjects
and that the duty of the subjects is to obey. Such
considerations, I believe, often serve as opiates
to men's consciences. "I have no part," it is said,
"in the councils of the Government and am
therefore not responsible for its misdeeds." We
are indeed not responsible for the crimes of our
rulers, but we are responsible for our own actions.
And the crimes of our rulers are our own if, knowing them to be crimes, we promote them by our
co-operation. . . . Those who suppose that obedience in all things is required, or that in political
affairs responsibility is transferred from them to
their rulers, deceive themselves.

'They say: "We submit our conduct to the will
of others, and act wickedly or well without merit
for virtue or responsibility for crime, since our
actions are not done of our own will."

'It is remarkable that just this is expressed in
the instructions to soldiers which they are made
to learn by heart, in which it is said that the

officer is solely responsible for the consequences of his orders.

'But this is not true. A man cannot shift the responsibility for his own actions. And this is seen by the following example:

'If your officer orders you to kill your neighbour's child, or to kill your father or your mother, will you obey him? If you will not, there is an end of the argument, for if you may reject his authority in one case, where is the limit of rejection? There is no rational limit but that assigned by Christianity, and that is both rational and practicable.

'We think, then, that it is the business of every man who believes that war is inconsistent with Christianity respectfully but steadfastly to refuse military service. And let those whose lot it is to act thus remember that a great obligation rests upon them. On their fidelity, as far as it depends on man at all, depends the cause of peace for mankind. Let them avow their opinions and maintain them, not in words only but also, if need be, by sufferings. If you believe that Jesus Christ forbade murder, pay no heed to the arguments or to the commands of those who call on you to take part in it. By such a firm refusal to take part in violence, you will call down on yourselves the blessings promised to those who hear the word of God and keep it, and the time will come when even the world will honour you as having contributed to the reformation of mankind.'

The book by Musser is called: *Non-resistance Asserted: or The Kingdom of Christ and The Kingdom of this World Separated* (1864).

This is devoted to the same question and examines it in relation to the demands for military service made by the American Government on its citizens at the time of the Civil War. It, too, is of contemporary importance, elucidating as it does the question how, in such circumstances, people should and can refuse military service. In his introduction the author says:

'It is known that in the United States there are many people who conscientiously reject war. They are called "non-resistant" or "defenceless" Christians. They refuse to defend their country or to bear arms and at the demand of the Government make war on its enemies. Till now this religious cause has been respected by the Government, and those who professed it were excused from service. But since the beginning of our Civil War public opinion has been agitated by this state of affairs. It was natural that people who considered it their duty to bear all the hardships and perils of army life for the defence of their country should feel resentment against those who have long shared with them the protection and the advantages of government, but in time of necessity and danger would not share in bearing labour and danger in its defence. It is even natural that they should declare the attitude of such men to be irrational, monstrous, and suspicious.

'Many speakers and writers', says our author, 'have raised their voices against this attitude, and have tried to prove the injustice of non-resistance, both on common-sense grounds and from Scripture. And this is quite natural, and in many cases these writers are right—right, that is, in regard to persons who, while refusing the hardships of army service, do not decline the benefits they receive from the Government. But they are not right in regard to the principle of "non-resistance" itself.'

Above all, our author proves the binding nature of the rule of non-resistance for a Christian, and that this command is quite clear and is indubitably enjoined by Christ upon every Christian.

Bethink yourselves, whether it is right to obey man more than God, said Peter and John. And this is precisely what every man who wishes to be a Christian should say to demands for military service, when Christ has said: Resist not him that is evil by force.

The question of the principle itself our author regards as decided. But he considers in detail the other question, whether people have a right to refuse military service who do not renounce the benefits conferred by a Government that employs violence, and he comes to the conclusion that a Christian following the law of Christ, since he does not go to war, can just as little take part in any of the institutions of Government—either the courts of law or the elections—and similarly in personal concerns must not have recourse to the authorities, the police, or the law. Farther on in the book he treats of the relation of the Old Testament to the New, and the importance of a government for non-Christians. The objections to the doctrine of non-resistance are stated and refuted. The author concludes his book as follows: 'Christians do not need a government, and therefore cannot submit to it in what is contrary to Christ's teaching. Still less can they take part in it.'

'Christ', he says, 'took his disciples out of the world. They do not expect worldly advantage and worldly happiness, but they expect eternal life. The spirit in which they live renders them contented and happy in any situation. If the world tolerates them, they are always contented. If the world will not leave them in peace, they will go elsewhere, since they are pilgrims on the earth and have no fixed abode. They believe that "the dead may bury their dead", but they need only one thing—to follow their Master.'

Leaving aside the question of the correctness or otherwise of the statement given in both these books of a Christian's duty in regard to war, one cannot but perceive the practical importance and urgency of a decision on this question.

There are people—hundreds of thousands of Quakers, Mennonites, our Doukhobórs, Molokans, and others unattached to any definite sect —who consider that violence, and therefore military service, is incompatible with Christianity. Every year in Russia, therefore, some of those called up for military service refuse it on the ground of religious conviction. What does the Government do? Does it let them off? No! Does it compel them to serve, and in case of refusal punish them? No. . . . In 1818 the Government acted in this way. Here is an extract from the diary of N. N. Muravëv-Kúrski,[1] which was not

[1] N. N. Muravëv-Kúrski, 1794–1866, was Viceroy of the

passed by the censor and is known to hardly anyone in Russia.

'*Tiflis.   October 2nd, 1818.*

'In the morning the Commandant told me that five peasants belonging to a landowner in Tambóv province had lately been sent to Georgia. These men had been sent for soldiers, but would not serve. They had already been knouted several times and made to run the gauntlet, but they submitted readily to the most cruel punishments, and were even prepared for death, rather than serve. "Let us go," they said, "and leave us alone, and we will not hurt anyone. All men are equal, and the Tsar is a man like ourselves. Why should we pay him taxes? Why should we expose our lives to danger in order to kill in battle someone who has done us no harm? You can cut us to pieces, but we will not change our opinion or put on a soldier's cloak or eat rations. Those who pity us will give us charity, but we have not had, and will not have, anything from the Crown." These were the words of those peasants, who declare that there are many like them in Russia. They were taken before the Committee of Ministers four times, and it was at last decided to refer the matter to the Tsar. He gave orders that they should be sent to Georgia for correction, and he instructed the Commander-in-Chief to report to him monthly on the gradual success he might have in bringing these peasants to a proper state of mind. . . .'

Caucasus and Commander-in-Chief of the Army of the Caucasus. During the Crimean War he captured Kars from the Turks.—A.M.

How this correction ended is unknown, just as nothing is known of the whole episode, which was kept a profound secret.

That is how the Government acted seventy-five years ago, and so it has acted in a great number of cases, which are always carefully concealed from the public. And that is how it acts now, except in relation to the German Mennonites settled in the province of Khersón, whose refusal of military service is accepted and who are made to serve their term as labourers in the forests.

But with others than the Mennonites, in recent cases of refusal of military service on religious grounds, the Government authorities have acted in the following manner:

First they apply all the methods of coercion that are employed in our times to 'correct' the refuser and bring him to 'a proper state of mind', and these methods are kept profoundly secret. I know that in the case of one man who declined to serve in 1884 in Moscow, a very thick portfolio about the matter had accumulated at the Ministry two months after his refusal, and was kept in strict secrecy.

They usually begin by sending the man to the priests, and they—to their shame be it said—always admonish him. But since admonitions in Christ's name to renounce Christ are generally fruitless, he is then sent to the gendarmes, and they, usually finding nothing of a political nature to charge him with, send him back again, and then he is sent to learned men, to the doctors, and to an insane asylum. During all these recommitments the refuser is deprived of liberty and has to endure all kinds of indignities and suffering, like a convicted criminal. (This was repeated in four cases.) The doctors dismiss the refuser from the insane asylum, and then all sorts of cunning shifts are practised to avoid releasing him (and run the risk of encouraging others to refuse as he has done) and at the same time not to leave him among the soldiers, lest they should learn from him that the levy for military service is not in accord with the law of God as they have been assured, but is contrary to it.

The most convenient thing for the Government to do would be to execute the refuser, by flogging him to death or in some other way, as used to be done. But it is impossible to put a man openly to death for being true to a teaching we all profess, and it is equally impossible to let a man alone if he refuses to serve. And so the Government tries either by ill treatment to compel him to renounce Christ, or to get rid of him unnoticed without openly putting him to death, and in some way to conceal both his action and the man himself from other people. And all kinds of shifts and wiles and torturings of the man are begun. Either he is sent to some distant place, or he is provoked to insubordination and then tried for breach of discipline and sent to prison or to the disciplinary battalion where he can be ill-treated in secret, or they declare him to be mad and lock him up in a lunatic asylum. They sent one man to Tashként on the pretext of transferring him to the Tashként Army, another was sent to Omsk, a third was tried for insubordination and shut up in prison, while a fourth was confined in a lunatic asylum.

Everywhere one and the same thing is repeated. Not only the Government but also the majority of so-called liberal and advanced people, as though by agreement, carefully turn away from everything that has been or is being said, written, and done, to show the incompatibility of violence in its most terrible, coarse, and glaring form (in the form of troops of soldiers ready to kill anyone) not only with the teaching of Christianity, but even of the humanitarianism which society is supposed to profess.

So the information I received concerning the extent to which the true significance of Christ's teaching has been elucidated (and is being more and more elucidated), and of the attitude of the upper and ruling classes, not only in Russia but in Europe and America, towards this elucidation and the performance of the teaching, has convinced me that there exists among these ruling classes a consciously hostile relation to true Christianity, which expresses itself chiefly by the way in which they studiously ignore all its manifestations.

II

Pronouncements on Non-Resistance by Churchmen and Unbelievers

FROM the criticisms of my book I received a similar impression of a desire to conceal and hush up what I had tried to express.

On its appearance the book was prohibited, as

I had anticipated, and according to law it should have been burnt. But instead of being burnt copies of it were appropriated by the officials themselves, and it circulated widely in written and lithographed copies, as well as in translations published abroad.

Criticisms, clerical and lay, began to appear, and were not only allowed, but even encouraged, by the Government; so that the refutation of a book supposed to be unknown was even set as a theme for theological essays in the academies.

The critics of my book, Russian and foreign alike, may be divided into two classes: the religious ones who regard themselves as believers, and lay critics who are free-thinkers.

I will begin with the first:

In my book I accuse the Churchmen of teaching contrary to Christ's commandments clearly and definitely expressed in the Sermon on the Mount, and especially contrary to his command concerning resistance to him that is evil, and that they thus deprive Christ's teaching of its significance. The Church authorities accept as a divine revelation the Sermon on the Mount, including the command about not resisting the evil man by violence, and therefore one would have thought that if they felt called upon to write about my book, they ought first of all to answer this chief point of my charge against them and say plainly whether they do or do not acknowledge as obligatory on a Christian the Sermon on the Mount and the commandment not to resist the evil man. And they should have answered this question, not as is usually done by saying

that though, on the one hand, one cannot absolutely deny... yet, on the other hand, one cannot
directly affirm . . . especially as . . . &c., &c.
They should have replied to the question as it is
presented in my book: Did Christ actually demand of his disciples that they should carry out
what he taught in the Sermon on the Mount?
And, therefore, can a Christian, remaining a
Christian, go to law to have people sentenced, or
seek for legal protection by means of violence?
And can a Christian, remaining a Christian, take
part in a government that employs violence
against his neighbours? And—most important
of all, and a question presented to everyone in
these days of universal military service—can a
Christian while remaining a Christian, contrary
to Christ's direct instruction, promise future obedience to commands directly opposed to Christ's
teaching? And can he, by accepting army service, prepare himself to murder men and actually
murder them?

The questions were put clearly and frankly and
seemed to require a clear and frank answer. But
nothing of the kind was forthcoming in any of
the criticisms; just as nothing of the kind has been
done with all those exposures of the teachers of
the Church for their defection from Christ's law,
of which history has been full since the time of
Constantine. In connexion with my own book
much was made of my having incorrectly interpreted this or that passage of the Gospel, of my
error in not acknowledging the Trinity, the redemption, and the immortality of the soul. Very
much was said about that, but nothing about the

one thing that is for every Christian the most essential question of actual life—how to reconcile the duty of forgiveness, meekness, patience, and love for all men whether neighbours or enemies, which is clearly expressed in the words of our Teacher and is in the heart of every one of us—with the demand to use military violence against men of our own or another nation.

Everything that in any way resembled an answer to this question can be classed under the following five heads. I have tried to collect all the material I could, not only from criticisms of my book but also what has been written on this subject in former times.

The first and crudest way of answering consists in boldly asserting that violence does not run counter to Christ's teaching but is permitted and even enjoined on Christians in the Old and New Testaments.

Assertions of this kind proceed chiefly from men who occupy the highest positions in the governing or ecclesiastical hierarchy, and who consequently feel fully assured that no one will dare to contradict their assertions, or that should anyone do so they will hear nothing about it. These men, as a result of their intoxication by power, have for the most part so lost the conception of what Christianity—in the name of which they hold their position—is, that everything of a Christian nature in Christianity presents itself to them as sectarianism, while everything in the Old or New Testaments that can be interpreted in an anti-Christian and pagan sense seems to them to be basic Christianity. In support of their assertion that Christianity is not opposed to the use of violence, these men usually cite with the greatest confidence the most questionable passages from the Old and New Testaments and interpret them in the most unchristian manner: the cases, for instance, of Ananias and Sapphira, of Simon the Sorcerer, and so forth. They quote all the sayings of Christ which can possibly be misinterpreted as justifications of cruelty: the expulsion from the Temple, 'It shall be more tolerable for the land of Sodom than for this city', and so on.

According to these men's conceptions a Christian government is not at all bound to be guided by the spirit of peace, forgiveness of injuries, and love of enemies.

It is useless to refute such assertions, for the men who make them refute themselves, or rather renounce Christ and invent a Christ and a Christianity of their own in place of that in whose name the Church itself, and the positions which they occupy in it, exist. If all men were to learn that the Church preaches a punishing, unforgiving, and warring Christ, no one would believe in that Church and it could not prove to anyone what it is trying to prove.

A second form of argument, rather less gross, consists in declaring that, although Christ did preach that we should offer our cheek and give up our coat, and although this is a very lofty moral demand, yet there are malefactors in the world, and if these evil men are not curbed by force the whole world will perish and the good men with it. I first encountered this argument in St. John Chrysostom, and pointed out its incorrectness in my book, *What I Believe*.[1]

This argument is invalid because, in the first place, if we allow ourselves to regard some men as specially evil (*raca*), we thereby annul the whole meaning of the Christian teaching, according to which we are all equal and brothers, sons of one Father in heaven; and secondly because, even if God permitted the use of violence against evil-doers, it is quite impossible to find a sure and indubitable indication that unerringly distinguishes the wicked from the good—and so all men, or societies of men, may mutually regard one another as malefactors, as occurs now. In the third place, even if it were possible unerringly to distinguish the wicked from the good, it would still be impossible in a Christian society to execute, injure, or shut up in prison, these evil-doers, for in a Christian society there would be no one to do this, since to every Christian, as a Christian, an injunction has been given not to do violence to him that is evil.

A third form of argument, even more subtle than the preceding, consists in asserting that though the commandment not to resist him that is evil by violence is obligatory on a Christian when the evil is directed against him personally, it ceases to be obligatory when the evil is directed against his neighbours, and that then a Christian is not merely not bound to fulfil the commandment, but is even bound, in defence of his neighbours, to employ violence against the evil men.

[1] See *What I Believe*, pp. 365–8, in the volume containing *A Confession* and *The Gospel in Brief*.—A.M.

This assertion is quite arbitrary and no confirmation of such an interpretation can be found anywhere in Christ's teaching. Such an interpretation is not a limitation merely, but a direct contradiction and negation of the commandment. If each man has a right to use violence when another is threatened with danger, the question of the use of violence is reduced to the question of defining what constitutes danger for another person.

If one's personal judgement is to decide the question of what constitutes danger for other people, there is no case of violence that cannot be justified on the ground of danger threatening somebody. The Girondists were themselves executed, and executed their enemies, because those in authority considered them dangerous to the people.

If this important limitation, which fundamentally undermines the commandment, was in Christ's mind, there ought somewhere to be a reference to it. But no such limitation is indicated in his whole life or in his teaching; on the contrary a precise warning is given against this false and seductive limitation nullifying the commandment. The error and impossibility of such limitation is shown with particular clearness in the Gospel in connexion with the advice given by Caiaphas, who made this very limitation. He admitted that it was not good to execute the innocent Jesus, but saw in him a source of danger not for himself but for the whole nation, and therefore said: 'It is expedient for us that one man should die for the people, and that the whole nation perish not.' And Jesus expressed his rejection of such a limitation very clearly in the words he addressed to Peter when the latter attempted to resist by violence the evil directed against his Master (Matt. xxvi. 52). Peter was not defending himself but his beloved and divine Teacher. And Christ reproved him, saying that he who takes the sword shall perish with the sword.

Besides that, the justification of violence used against one's neighbour to defend another neighbour from worse violence is always unsound, for when violence is used against one who has not yet committed his evil deed it is never possible to know which will be the greater evil—my violence, or that which I wish to prevent. We execute a criminal that society may be rid of him, but never know whether the man who was a criminal would not have been a changed man to-morrow and whether his execution is not a useless cruelty. We imprison a man whom we consider a dangerous member of society, but next day this man might cease to be dangerous and his imprisonment may be useless. I see that a man I know to be a robber is pursuing a young girl, and I have a gun in my hand. I shoot the robber and save the girl. But the robber has certainly been killed or wounded, while I cannot know what would have happened had I not shot him. And what an immense amount of evil must result, and does result, from people arrogating to themselves the right to prevent an evil which may occur but has not yet occurred! Ninety-nine per cent. of the evil in the world results from such reasoning, from the Inquisition to high-explosive bombs, executions, and the sufferings of tens of thousands of so-called political offenders.

A fourth and yet more ingenious way in which people deal with the question of a Christian's attitude towards Christ's commandment not to resist evil men by violence, consists in declaring that they do not deny this commandment but recognize it like all the others, only they do not ascribe any special and exclusive significance to it as the sectarians do. To regard this command as an invariable condition of Christian life, as Garrison, Ballou, Dymond, the Quakers, the Mennonites, and the Shakers do, and as the Moravian Brethren, the Waldenses, the Albigenses, the Bogomiles, and the Paulicians did in the past, is one-sided sectarianism. This command has neither more nor less importance than any other and a man who through weakness infringes any of the commandments, including that of non-resistance, does not therefore cease to be a Christian, provided that he holds the true faith.

That subterfuge is very artful, and men who wish to be deceived are easily deceived by it. The subterfuge consists in treating a direct and conscious negation of the command as a casual breach of it. But we have only to compare the attitude of Church teachers towards this and towards other commands which they do really acknowledge, to be convinced that their attitude to this one is quite different from their attitude to the others.

They recognize the command against adultery and under no circumstances therefore do they cease to regard it as wrong. They never point out any cases in which the command against adultery ought to be broken, and always teach that allurements leading men to commit adultery should be avoided. But it is not so with the command about non-resistance.

All the Church preachers know cases in which this law should be broken, and they teach men so. And not merely do they not teach men to avoid temptations to a breach of this law—the chief among which is the oath—but they themselves administer that oath. The clergy never advocate the violation of any other commandment, but in regard to the law of non-resistance they openly teach that it is not necessary to take it too literally, and that not merely is it unnecessary to fulfil it always, but that there are conditions when just the contrary should be done—that is, that men should go to law, wage war, and execute people. So that regarding the law of non-resistance by violence to him that is evil, what is usually taught is how not to fulfil it. Fulfilment of this command, they say, is very difficult, and characteristic only of perfection. But how can it help being difficult when its infringement is not merely condoned but directly encouraged, and law-courts, prisons, guns, armies, and battles are blessed by the Church itself?

So it is not true that this command is recognized by the preachers of the Church as of equal significance with the other commandments. The Church preachers simply do not recognize it, and only try to conceal their non-recognition of it because they dare not confess it openly.

Such is the fourth kind of reply.

A fifth method, the most subtle, the most generally used, and most effective, consists in evading the question and pretending that it was long ago decided by someone in a clear and satisfactory manner, and that it is not worth talking about. This method is employed by all the more or less cultured religious writers, that is to say, those who have some respect for the laws of logic. Knowing that the contradiction existing between Christ's teaching, which we verbally profess, and the whole order of our lives cannot be solved by words, and that touching on it can only make it more obvious, they evade it with more or less agility—making it appear that the problem of reconciling Christianity with the use of violence has either been decided already or does not really exist at all.[1]

The majority of the ecclesiastical critics of my book employ this fifth method. I could cite dozens of such criticisms in which without excep-

[1] I know only one work—not a criticism strictly speaking, but a pamphlet—(dealing with this subject and having my book in view) which stands to some extent outside this general statement. This is Bishop Troýtsky of Kazán's *The Sermon on the Mount*. The author evidently recognizes Christ's teaching in its true significance. He says that both the commandment about non-resistance and the prohibition of the taking of oaths mean just what they say. He does not, as others do, deny the significance of Christ's teaching, but unfortunately does not draw the inevitable deductions which present themselves in our life when we understand Christ's teaching in that way. If we must not resist evil by violence or bind ourselves by oaths, men will naturally ask: But how about military service and oaths of allegiance? To this question the bishop gives no answer; but it must be answered. And if he cannot answer it, it would be better not to speak on the subject at all, for such silence conduces to error.—L.T.

tion the same thing is repeated: everything is discussed except the chief subject of the book. As a characteristic example of such criticism I will quote an article by the famous and refined English author and preacher, Canon Farrar, who, like many learned theologians, is a great master of circuitous evasion. His article appeared in the American *Forum* in October 1888.

Having given a conscientious summary of my book, Canon Farrar says:

'Tolstóy came to the conclusion that a coarse deceit was palmed upon the world when these words were held by civilized society to be compatible with war, courts of justice, capital punishment, divorce, oaths, national prejudices, and indeed most of the institutions of civil and social life. He now believes that the Kingdom of God would come if all men kept those five commandments: (1) Live in peace with all men; (2) be pure; (3) take no oaths; (4) never resist evil; (5) renounce national distinctions.

'Tolstóy', he says, 'rejects the divine inspiration of the Old Testament and of the Epistles; hence he rejects the dogmas of the Church: that of the Atonement by blood, that of the Trinity, that of the descent of the Holy Ghost upon the Apostles, and his transmission through the priesthood . . . and he recognizes only the words and commandments of Christ.[1] But is this interpreta-

---

[1] It would be more correct to say that Tolstóy accepted whatever he found in the Bible or elsewhere that he could understand and agree with, but attributed no supernatural authority to any book. Canon Farrar is right to this extent, that Tolstóy found little or nothing to disagree with in the words or conduct of Jesus, but found much to disagree with

tion of Christ a true one?' asks Canon Farrar
'Are all men bound, or is any man bound, to act
as Tolstóy has taught, that is, to fulfil the five
commandments of Christ?'

So one expects that on that essential question
which alone could have incited a man to write
an article about my book, he will say that this
interpretation of Christ's teaching is correct and
should be followed, or that it is not correct, and
will show why and give some other, correct,
interpretation of the words I interpret incorrectly. But nothing of the kind is done. Canon
Farrar only expresses a 'conviction' that 'though
actuated by the noblest sincerity, Count Tolstóy
has been misled by partial and one-sided interpretations of the meaning of the Gospel and the
mind and will of Christ'.

No explanation is given of what this error consists in. It is only said that 'to enter into the
proof of this is impossible in this article, for I have
already exceeded the space at my command'.

And he concludes, with a tranquil mind:

'Meanwhile the reader who feels troubled lest
it should be his duty also to forsake all the conditions of his life and to take up the position and
work of a common labourer, may rest for the
present on the principle, *securus judicat orbis terrarum.*[1] With few and rare exceptions', he concludes, 'the whole of Christendom, from the days
of the Apostles down to our own, has come to the
firm conclusion that it was the object of Christ to

in the rest of the Bible and even in some parts of the Gospels.
—A.M.

[1] The judgement of the whole world is sure.

lay down great, eternal principles, but not to disturb the bases of, and revolutionize the institutions of, all human society, which themselves rest on divine sanction as well as on inevitable conditions. Were it my object to prove how untenable is the doctrine of communism,[1] based by Count Tolstóy upon the divine paradoxes (*sic*) which can be interpreted only on historical principles in accordance with the whole method of the teaching of Jesus, it would require an ampler canvas than I have here at my disposal.'

What a pity he had not that ampler canvas! And how strange it is that space has been lacking for fifteen centuries to prove that Christ, whom we profess, did not say at all what he actually did say! They could prove it if they wished to, but it is not worth while to prove what everybody knows. It is enough to say: *Securus judicat orbis terrarum.*

And such without exception are the criticisms of the educated believers who understand the instability of their position. For them the only way out lies in the hope that by asserting the authority, antiquity, and holiness of the Church, they will succeed in bewildering the reader and draw him away from the idea of reading the Gospel for himself and thinking the question out in his own mind. And in this they succeed.

Who indeed would suppose that all that has been repeated from century to century with such

---

[1] The use of the word 'communism' in this connexion is confusing. Tolstóy had no sympathy at all with political Communism such as prevails in Soviet Russia, but in the Gospel sense of having all things in common, there is some justification for Canon Farrar's use of the word.—A.M.

assurance and solemnity by all these deans, bishops, archbishops, Most Holy Synods, and Popes—is all an odious lie and calumny foisted on Christ by them to secure the money they need to lead a comfortable life sitting on other people's backs; and that it is a lie and calumny so obvious, especially in these days, that the only possibility of maintaining it consists in bewildering people by their assurance and shamelessness?

It is just what has been occurring of late years in the military tribunals. Behind a table with a Mirror of Justice upon it, and under a life-size portrait of the Emperor, dignified old officials sit in their regalia, conversing freely and easily, noting down, giving orders, and summoning. Here also, with a pectoral cross and a silk cassock, his grey hair flowing over his stole, stands a prosperous-looking old priest in front of a desk on which lies a gold cross and a copy of the Gospels bound in gold.

They call up Iván Petróv. A young man comes forward in poor and dirty clothes, the muscles of his face twitching with fear, his eyes bright and restless, and in a breaking voice, almost a whisper, he says: 'I . . . according to the Gospel . . . as a Christian . . . I cannot . . .'

'What's he muttering about?' asks the President, frowning impatiently and raising his head from his book to listen.

'Speak up!' shouts a colonel with shining epaulettes.

'I . . . I . . . as a Christian . . .'

At last it appears that the young man is refusing to serve in the army because he is a Christian.

'Don't talk nonsense! Stand over there to be measured! Doctor, be so good as to take his height. Is he suitable?'

'He is.'

'Reverend Father, administer the oath.'

No one is at all perturbed or even pays any attention to what the frightened and pitiful young man is muttering. 'They all mutter something, but we've no time to spare—there are so many of them still to be enrolled.'

The recruit still tries to say something.

'It is against the law of Christ.'

'Get along, get along! We know without you what is according to law and what is not. And you get away from here. Reverend Father, admonish him. Next . . . Vasíli Nikítin.'

And the trembling youth is led away. And to which of the guards, or Vasíli Nikítin who is brought in, or of those who witness this scene, does it occur that these few indistinct words uttered by the young man and so promptly suppressed by the authorities, contain the truth, while the loud words solemnly pronounced by the calm, self-confident officials and the priest, are a lie and a deception?

A similar impression is produced not only by Canon Farrar's article but by all those solemn sermons, articles, and books, which come out on all sides the moment the truth peeps out and exposes the ruling lie. At once long, clever, elegant, and pretentious discourses and writings appear about questions nearly related to the subject, though shrewdly avoiding contact with the subject itself.

In this consists the fifth and most effective means of circumventing the contradiction in which Church Christianity has enmeshed itself by professing Christ in words while abjuring his teaching in practice and teaching others to do so.

Those who justify themselves by the first method, simply and crudely asserting that Christ sanctioned violence, wars, and murder—abjure Christ's teaching. Those who justify themselves by the second, third, and fourth methods, get entangled, and it is easy to point out their falsity; but this fifth class, who do not discuss, do not condescend to discuss, but shelter themselves behind their dignity, and pretend that the whole question has long ago been decided by them or by someone else and is no longer open to any doubt—appear invulnerable, and will be invulnerable as long as men remain under the influence of the hypnotic suggestion exercised by governments and the Churches, and until they shake it off.

Such has been the attitude of the clergy—of men professing belief in Christ—to my book. Nor could they treat it otherwise. They are bound by the contradiction in which they live—belief in the divinity of their Teacher and unbelief in his most explicit utterances—from which they have in some way to extricate themselves, and so one cannot expect from them a free consideration of the essential question concerning the change in men's lives which must result from the application of Christ's teaching to the existing order of the world. Such a consideration I expected only from secular and free-thinking critics who are in no way bound by Christ's teaching, and can therefore consider it freely. I thought that free-thinking writers would regard Christ not as Churchmen do—as the founder of a religion of worship and personal salvation—but, to put it in their own language, as a reformer who destroyed the old and laid new foundations of life—a reform which has not yet been completed but is still going on.

Such a view of Christ and his teaching follows from my book. But to my surprise, out of the many criticisms of my book that appeared, not one, either Russian or foreign, treated the subject from the aspect in which it was presented—that is (to use their learned terminology), considered Christ's teaching as a philosophical, moral, and social doctrine. Not a single critic did that.

The Russian lay critics conceived the whole substance of my book to lie in the theory of non-resistance, and understanding that theory to forbid any kind of conflict against evil (this probably for greater facility of refutation), furiously attacked it and for some years very successfully demonstrated that Christ's teaching is erroneous, since he forbids resistance to evil. Their refutations of that imaginary doctrine of Christ's were all the more successful because they knew in advance that their argument could be neither refuted nor corrected, since the censor not having passed the book would also not pass articles defending it.

It is remarkable in this connexion that in Russia where not a word may be said about the Holy Scripture without incurring the censor's prohibition, the distinct and explicit command of Christ (Matt. v. 39) has been perverted, criticized, condemned, and ridiculed for several years past in all the periodicals.

The Russian secular critics, evidently unaware of all that has been done in developing the principle of non-resistance, and sometimes even seeming to imagine that I personally invented it, attacked the idea itself with great ardour, refuting and perverting it and advancing arguments that have long ago been analysed from every side and refuted, and pointed out that a man is bound to defend by violence all who are wronged and oppressed, and that therefore the teaching of non-resistance to evil by violence is immoral.

The whole significance of Christ's preaching presented itself to all the Russian critics in the fact that, as though to spite them, it hampers active opposition to what they, at the given moment, considered to be an evil; so that it turned out that the principle of non-resistance to evil by violence has been attacked by two opposite camps—by the conservatives, because this principle interferes with their activity in resisting the evil perpetrated by the revolutionaries and hunting them down and executing them; and by the revolutionaries, because this principle interferes with their resistance to the evil produced by the conservatives and with their overthrow. The conservatives were indignant that the teaching of non-resistance to evil by violence forbids the suppression by violence of the revolutionary elements who may imperil the welfare of the nation;

while the revolutionaries were indignant because
the same principle forbids the overthrow of the
conservatives who destroy the welfare of the
people.

What is remarkable is that the revolutionaries
attacked the principle of non-resistance, though
it is a most terrible and most dangerous doctrine
for every despotism; for ever since the world began, the opposite principle—that of resisting evil
by violence—has lain and still lies at the basis of
all violence, from the Inquisition to the Schlüssel-
burg Fortress.[1]

Besides this the Russian critics pointed out that
the application to life of the command of non-
resistance would side-track humanity from the
path of civilization along which it is marching;
and the path of civilization on which European
civilization is marching is in their opinion the one
on which all humanity must always march.

Such was the general standpoint of the Russian
critics.

Foreign critics started from the same platform,
but their discussions of my book differed somewhat from those of the Russian critics not only
by being less irritable and more cultured, but also
in the essential matter.

Discussing my book and the Gospel teaching
generally as it is expressed in the Sermon on the
Mount, the foreign critics maintained that such
a doctrine is not strictly Christian (Christian
teaching, in their view, is Catholicism and Pro-

---

[1] A terrible prison for political offenders. Many of the
Decembrists were there incarcerated, and Lénin's brother was
hanged there in 1887.—A.M.

testantism) but the teaching of the Sermon on
the Mount is only a series of very nice, unpracti-
cal reveries *du charmant docteur*, as Renan puts it,
suitable for the naïve and semi-savage inhabitants of Galilee who lived 1,800 years ago and
for semi-savage Russian peasants such as Sutáev[1]
and Bóndarev[2] and the Russian mystic Tolstóy,
but quite inapplicable to a high stage of European culture.

The foreign free-thinking critics, in a delicate
manner without being offensive to me, tried to
let it be felt that my opinion that humanity could
be guided by such a naïve doctrine as that of the
Sermon on the Mount proceeds partly from my
lack of knowledge, my ignorance of history and
of all the vain attempts that have been made to
apply those principles to life, which are recorded in
history but which have led to nothing; and partly
to my lack of understanding of the full value of the
lofty civilization to which we have now attained,
with its Krupp guns and smokeless powder, its
colonization of Africa and coercion of Ireland,
its parliamentary governments, its journalism,
strikes, constitutions, and Eiffel Towers.

So wrote de Vogüé and Leroy Beaulieu and
Matthew Arnold, as well as the American writers
Talmage and Ingersoll (a popular American
free-thought preacher) and many others.

'Christ's teaching will not do, because it does

---

[1] Sutáev was a peasant acquaintance of Tolstóy's mentioned
in *What Then Must We Do?* and also in *The Life of Tolstóy* in
this edition.—A.M.

[2] Bóndarev was a peasant sectarian and agriculturist, of
whose opinions and writings Tolstóy wrote and spoke in high
terms.—A.M.

not harmonize with our industrial age,' says Ingersoll, ingenuously expressing, with complete precision and *naïveté*, just what highly educated people of our day think of the teaching of Christ. The teaching is unsuitable for our industrial age —just as though what constitutes an industrial age is something holy, which should not and cannot be changed.

It is as though drunkards when advised how they could become sober, were to reply that the advice was unsuitable to their alcoholic condition.

The arguments of all the secular writers, Russian and foreign alike, however divergent in tone and method of presentation, amount essentially to one and the same misapprehension—namely, that Christ's teaching, one of the consequences of which is non-resistance to evil, is unsuitable for us because it demands a change in our way of living.

Christ's teaching is unsuitable because, were it carried into practice, life could not go on as at present; in other words, were we to begin to live well, as Christ taught us, we could not continue to live badly as we are doing and are accustomed to do. But the question of non-resistance is not discussed, and the very mention of the fact that the demand for non-resistance to evil enters into Christ's teaching is regarded as sufficient proof of the inapplicability of his whole teaching.

And yet it would seem that it is at least necessary to indicate some solution to the question, for it lies at the root of almost all the affairs that occupy us.

The question amounts to this: how to settle the conflicts between people who now consider a thing evil that others consider good, and vice versa. To say that evil is what I consider evil although my adversary considers it good, is not a solution of the difficulty. There can be but two solutions: either to find an absolute and indubitable criterion of evil, or not to resist evil by violence.

The first course has been tried since the beginning of history, and as we all know has so far led to no satisfactory results.

The second course—not to resist with violence what we consider evil, until we have found some universal criterion—is the solution proposed by Christ.

We may consider Christ's answer unsatisfactory; we may propose another, better answer in place of it, finding a criterion which would indubitably and at once settle what is evil for all men; or we may simply not understand the substance of the question, as is the case with savages. But we cannot pretend (as the learned critics of the Christian teaching do) that no such question exists or that it can be solved by relegating to certain persons or assemblies of persons (especially if they are ourselves) the right to determine what is evil and to resist it by violence. For we all know that such a relegation does not solve the question at all, since there are always people who do not recognize that this right belongs to the authorized persons or assemblies of persons.

But this assumption that what to us appears evil is evil, shows a complete misunderstanding of the question, and lies at the root of the arguments of the lay critics of the Christian teaching. So that the discussions about my book, both by the ecclesiastics and the lay critics, showed me that the majority of men simply do not understand either Christ's teaching itself or even the questions to which it serves as an answer.

III

Lack of understanding of Christianity by believers.

THUS the information I received after my book appeared convinced me that the Christian teaching in its direct and simple sense has always been and still is understood by a minority of men, but the clerical and lay criticisms, denying the possibility of any such direct understanding, showed that for the majority of men its meaning has been more and more obscured, until it has now reached such a degree of obscurity that people do not understand the very plainest precepts expressed in the Gospels in the clearest words.

The non-comprehension of Christ's teaching in its true, plain, and direct meaning—in our day when its light has already penetrated the darkest corners of human consciousness, when, as Christ expressed it, what he whispered into the ear is now proclaimed from the housetops, when his teaching is influencing every branch of human life—domestic, economic, civil, political, and international—this failure to understand would be incomprehensible were there not causes to account for it.

One such cause is that believers and unbelievers alike are firmly convinced that they have long understood Christ's teaching so fully, indubitably, and finally, that it can have no other significance than that which they attribute to it; and the consequent misunderstanding is due to the false, traditional understanding that has so long been current. Even the strongest current of water cannot add a drop to a vessel that is already full.

Quite difficult matters can be explained even to a slow-witted man, if only he has not already adopted a wrong opinion about them; but the simplest things cannot be made clear even to a very intelligent man if he is firmly persuaded that he already knows, and knows indubitably, the truth of the matter under consideration.

The Christian teaching seems to men of our world to be just such a doctrine, long and indubitably known by everybody in its minutest details, and which cannot be otherwise understood than as it has been.

By those who profess the Church doctrine, Christianity is now understood as a supernatural, miraculous revelation concerning all that is mentioned in the Creeds. By unbelievers it is regarded as an indication of man's desire to believe in the supernatural which has now been outgrown, and as an historical phenomenon fully expressed in Catholicism, Greek Orthodoxy, and Protestantism, but that is no longer of any vital significance for us. For believers the meaning of Christianity is hidden by the Church; for non-believers by science.

I will first speak of the former category.

Eighteen hundred years ago a strange new teaching, unlike any previous religion, appeared in the heathen Roman world, and this was attributed to a man named Jesus.

This new teaching was quite new both in form and substance; new to the Hebrew world whence it sprang, and still more so to the Roman world where it was preached and where it spread.

Amid the elaborate religious precepts of Judaism in which, as Isaiah said, there was rule upon rule, and in the midst of the highly developed and perfected legislation of Rome, this new teaching appeared, denying not merely all the divinities and all fear of them and all auguries and belief in them, but also all human institutions and the necessity for them.

Instead of all the rules of previous religions, this teaching set up the ideal of inward perfection, truth, and love in the person of Christ, and the result of that inward perfection attainable by man in an outward perfection foretold by the prophets—the Kingdom of God, when all men, taught by God and united by love, shall cease to be at enmity and the lion shall lie down with the lamb.

Instead of threats of punishment for non-fulfilment (as was the case with former laws, both religious and secular) and enticements of reward for fulfilment, this teaching called men to itself by the fact that it was true. 'If any man will do his will, he shall know of the doctrine whether it be of God.' (John vii. 17.) 'If I say the truth, why do ye not believe me? But now ye seek to kill a man that hath told you the truth.' 'And the truth shall make you free.' 'God must be worshipped in spirit and in truth.' 'Keep my sayings and ye shall know whether they be true.' 'The spirit of truth will guide you unto all truth.' (John viii and xvi.)

No proofs of the teaching were offered except its correspondence with the truth. The whole teaching consisted in apprehension of the truth and following after it; in a more and more perfect comprehension of it and a closer and closer realization of it in the affairs of life.

According to this teaching no action can justify a man and make him righteous; there is only the model of truth, in the person of Jesus, which attracts all hearts towards inward perfection, and towards outward perfection in the realization of the Kingdom of God.

The fulfilment of the teaching consists in progress along the appointed path towards inward perfection by an imitation of Christ, and towards outward perfection by the establishment of the Kingdom of God. Man's greater or lesser blessedness, according to this teaching, depends not on the degree of perfection he has attained but on the progress he is making.

According to this teaching the progress towards perfection of Zaccheus the publican, of the adulteress, or of the thief on the cross, is a greater state of blessedness than the stationary righteousness of the Pharisee. The lost sheep is more precious than the ninety-nine that are in the fold, the prodigal son, and the coin that was lost and

found again, are more precious to God than those
that were never lost.

Every condition, according to this teaching, is
merely a stage on the path towards unattainable
inward and outward perfection and is therefore
of no significance in itself. Blessedness lies only
in progress towards perfection, and a halt at any
stage is a cessation of this blessedness.

'Let not thy left hand know what thy right
hand doeth.' 'No man having put his hand to
the plough, and looking back, is fit for the Kingdom of God.' 'Rejoice not that the spirits are
subject unto you; but rather rejoice because your
names are written in heaven.' 'Be ye perfect, as
your Father in heaven is perfect.' 'Seek the
Kingdom of God and His righteousness.'

The fulfilment of the teaching lies only in unceasing progress towards the attainment of ever
higher and higher truth, and in an ever greater
realization of this, in oneself by means of ever
increasing love, and outside oneself by the more
and more complete establishment of the Kingdom of God.

Appearing as it did in the midst of the Jewish
and heathen world, this teaching evidently could
not have been accepted by the majority of men
who lived a life totally different from that which
it demanded. Even those who accepted it could
not understand its full significance, since it was
diametrically opposed to their previous ideas.

Only through a series of misconceptions,
errors, and one-sided explanations corrected and
supplemented by successive generations, has the
meaning of the Christian teaching become

clearer and clearer. The Christian conception of life reacted on the Jewish and heathen conceptions, and the Jewish and heathen conceptions reacted on the Christian. And the Christian, being the more vital, penetrated the decaying Jewish and heathen conceptions more and more and stood out more and more clearly, freeing itself from false admixtures that had been imposed upon it. Men grasped its meaning better and better and realized it in life more and more.

The longer humanity endured the more clearly did it understand the meaning of the Christian teaching, as indeed must be the case with every teaching dealing with practical life. Succeeding generations corrected mistakes made by their predecessors and approached nearer and nearer to an understanding of its true meaning.

So it was from the very earliest Christian times. And from the very beginning, also, there appeared men who asserted that the only true meaning of the teaching was the one they attributed to it, and that proof of this was furnished by supernatural occurrences confirming the correctness of their interpretation.

This was actually the chief cause, first of a failure to understand the teaching and secondly of its complete perversion.

It was assumed that Christ's teaching was not transmitted to men like all other truth, but in a special and supernatural manner. Thus the truth of an interpretation of the teaching was proved not by its correspondence with the demands of reason and of man's whole nature, but by the miraculous manner of its transmission

which was advanced as irrefutable evidence of
the correctness of the interpretation. This arose
from a misunderstanding of the teaching, and its
result was to render a proper understanding of
it impossible.

It originated at the very beginning, when the
teaching was very incompletely and often wrongly understood, as is seen in the Gospels and the
Acts of the Apostles. The less men understood
the teaching and the more obscure it appeared,
the more they wanted external proofs of it. The
proposition that we should not do to others what
we do not wish them to do to us, needed no
miraculous proof nor any exercise of faith, for it
is in itself convincing and accords with man's
reason and nature. But the proposition that
Jesus was God had to be proved by quite incomprehensible miracles.

The more obscure the understanding of
Christ's teaching and the more the miraculous
was introduced into it, the more the doctrine was
deflected from its true meaning; and the more
confused its meaning became and the more it was
deflected from its original meaning, the more
necessary did it become for certain men to assert
their own infallibility, and the less intelligible did
the teaching become.

One can see in the Gospels, the Acts, and the
Epistles, how, from the beginning, failure to
understand the teaching involved a need of miraculous and incomprehensible proofs.

According to the Acts of the Apostles this
began at an assembly of the disciples in Jerusalem
to settle questions that had arisen as to baptizing,

or not baptizing, the uncircumcized and those
who ate meat offered to idols.

The very formulation of the question showed
that those who discussed it did not understand
Christ's teaching, which rejected all outward rites
—ablutions, purifications, fasts, and sabbaths. It
plainly said: 'Not that which goeth into the
mouth defileth a man; but that which cometh
out of the heart.' And so the question about the
baptism of the uncircumcised could only have
arisen among men who, though loving their
Master and dimly feeling the grandeur of his
teaching, still only obscurely understood the
teaching itself. And so it was.

In proportion to the failure of the members of
the assembly to understand the teaching, was
their need of some external confirmation of their
inadequate conceptions of it. And so—to settle
a question the very formulation of which indicated a failure to understand the teaching—as is
described in the Acts of the Apostles, those dreadful words which were to produce so much evil
were uttered for the first time: 'It seemed good
to the Holy Ghost and to us.' (Acts xv. 28.) That
is, it was asserted that the correctness of their
decisions was attested by the miraculous participation of the Holy Ghost, i.e. of God, in those
decisions. But the assertion that the Holy Ghost,
that is, God himself, spoke through the Apostles,
needed proof in its turn. And so it became necessary to assert that at Pentecost the Holy Ghost
descended in the shape of tongues of fire upon
those who made this assertion. (In the account
of it the descent of the Holy Ghost precedes the

assembly, but the Acts of the Apostles were written down much later than either.) But the descent of the Holy Ghost, too, had to be proved for those who had not seen the tongues of fire (though it is incomprehensible why a tongue of fire burning above a man's head should prove that what that man says is infallibly true), and so yet other miracles and healings, resurrections, and puttings to death were needed, and all those equivocal miracles of which the Acts are full, and which, far from convincing men of the truth of the Christian teaching, can only repel them. The consequence of such a method of confirming the truth was that the more these confirmations of the truth by stories of miracles were piled upon one another, the more was the teaching itself turned aside from its original meaning and the more incomprehensible did it become.

Thus it was from the earliest period, and so it went on, continually increasing, till in our time it has reached its logical climax in the dogmas of transubstantiation and the infallibility of the Pope, or of the Bishops, or of the Scriptures, that is, in something absolutely incomprehensible and utterly absurd; and in a demand for blind belief, not in God or in Christ, or even in the teaching, but in a person (as in Catholicism), or in several persons (as in the Orthodox Greek faith), or in a book (as in Protestantism). The more widely Christianity became diffused and the more it embraced people unprepared for it, the less was it understood, the more absolutely was the infallibility of the interpretation of it insisted on, and the less possible did it become to understand the

true meaning of the teaching. By the time of
Constantine the whole interpretation of the
teaching was a *résumé* sanctioned by the temporal
power—a compendium of the disputes that took
place in the Church Councils: the Creeds in
which it says that: I believe in so-and-so and so-
and-so, and finally in the one, holy, Catholic and
Apostolic Church—that is, in the infallibility of
those persons who call themselves the Church.
So that it all comes to this: that a man no longer
believes in God or in Christ as they have been
revealed to him, but in what the Church commands him to believe in.

But the Church is holy. The Church was
founded by Christ. God could not leave men to
interpret His teaching arbitrarily and so He
founded the Church. All these assertions are so
utterly unjust and unfounded that one feels
ashamed to refute them. Nowhere, nor in anything but in the Church's assertion, is it shown
that God or Christ founded anything at all resembling what churchmen understand by the
Church. In the Gospels there is a warning
against the Church as an external authority, and
this most clearly and self-evidently in the passage
where Christ's followers are told to call no man
master or father. But nowhere is anything said
of the foundation of what churchmen call the
Church.

In the Gospels the word 'church' is used twice.
Once in the sense of an assembly of men to settle
a dispute, and again in connexion with the obscure utterance about the rock, Peter, and the
gates of hell. From these two mentions of the

word 'church' (meaning merely an assembly)
what is now meant by the word 'Church' has
been deduced.

But Christ could certainly not have established
the Church, that is, the institution we now call
by that name, for nothing resembling our present
conception of the Church—with its sacraments,
its hierarchy, and especially its claim to infallibility—is to be found either in Christ's words or
in the conceptions of the men of his time.

The fact that people called an institution
established later, by a name Christ had used to
designate something quite different, in no way
gives them the right to assert that Jesus founded
'the one true Church'.

Besides, had Christ really founded such an institution as the Church for the basis of our entire
faith and doctrine, he would probably have announced this institution clearly and definitely,
and—besides such stories of miracles as have
been current in all mythologies—would have
given this one true Church unmistakable tokens
of its genuineness. But we find nothing of the sort
and there have been and still are various institutions each calling itself the one true Church.

The Roman Catholic Catechism says: *L'église
est la société de fidèles établie par notre Seigneur Jésus-
Christ, répandue sur toute la terre et soumise à l'autorité
des pasteurs légitimes, principalement notre Saint Père,
le Pape*[1]—meaning by 'pasteurs légitimes' a

---

[1] The Church is the Society of the Faithful, established by
our Lord Jesus Christ, spread over the whole earth, and subject
to the authority of its lawful pastors, and principally of our
Holy Father, the Pope.

human institution under the supremacy of the
Pope and consisting of certain persons bound
together in a special organization.

The Orthodox Greek Catechism says: 'The
Church is a society founded on earth by Jesus
Christ, and it is united in one whole by the divine
teaching and by the sacraments, under the guidance and government of a hierarchy established
by God'—meaning by the last words, the Orthodox Greek hierarchy, consisting exclusively of
certain individuals occupying such and such
positions.

The Lutheran Catechism says: 'The Church is
holy Christianity, or the assembly of all believers
under Christ, their head, in which the Holy
Ghost through the Gospels and the sacraments,
offers, imparts, and administers, divine salvation'
—meaning that the Roman Catholic Church has
erred and gone astray and that the true tradition
is preserved in Lutheranism.

For the Roman Catholics the divine Church
is the Romish hierarchy and the Pope. For the
Greek Orthodox the divine Church is the establishment and priesthood of Russia.[1]

---

[1] Khomyakóv's definition of the Church, which has had
some vogue among Russians, does not improve matters, if we
recognize with Khomyakóv that the Orthodox is the one true
Church. He asserts that the Church is an assembly of people
(both clergy and congregation) united by love, and that only
to people united in love is the truth revealed ('Let us love one
another in unity', &c.) and that such a Church is the one that
in the first place acknowledges the Nicene Creed, and in the
second place has not since the separation of the Churches
recognized the Pope or the new dogmas. But with such a
definition of the Church it is still more difficult to identify, as
Khomyakóv wishes us to do, the Church which is united in
love, with the Church which acknowledges the Nicene Creed

For a Lutheran the divine Church is identical with a society of men who acknowledge the Bible and Luther's Catechism.

Usually when speaking of the origin of Christianity people belonging to one of the existing Churches use the word 'Church' in the singular, as though there were and had been only one Church. But this is incorrect. The Church as an institution declaring itself to be in possession of infallible truth, only appeared when there was no longer one, but at least two, Churches.

As long as the believers were in accord among themselves and there was only one society, it had no need to call itself the Church. Only when the believers split into opposing parties which denied one another, did the need arise for each to affirm its correctness by claiming infallibility.

The conception of one holy Church only arose from the quarrels and strife of two parties, each of which, denouncing the other as a heresy, claimed to be the one infallible Church.

If we know that there was a Church which in A.D. 51 decided to admit the uncircumcised, that Church arose only because there was another

and the doctrine of Photius. Thus Khomyakóv's assertion that this Church which is united by love and is therefore holy, is the same Church that the Russian priesthood professes faith in, is even more arbitrary than the similar assertions made by the Roman Catholics or the Russian Old Believers.

If we admit the idea of a Church in Khomyakóv's sense—that is, as an assembly of people united in love and truth—then all that any man can say of this assembly is that it is very desirable to be a member of it if it exists, that is, to dwell in love and in truth; but that there are no external signs by which one could account oneself or anyone else, a member of, or excluded from, this holy assembly, since no external institution can correspond to that conception.—L.T.

Church—of the Judaisers—which had decided not to admit the uncircumcised.

If there is now a Catholic Church which affirms its infallibility, it does so only because there are other Churches: Russo-Greek, Old Orthodox, and Lutheran—each of which asserts its own infallibility, thus rejecting all the other Churches. So the idea of the one Church is only a fantastic conception which lacks any sign of reality.

As a real historical fact many congregations of men have existed and still exist each of which asserts that it is the one and only true Church established by Christ and that all the others calling themselves Churches are heresies and schisms.

The catechisms of the most widespread Churches—Catholic, Orthodox, and Lutheran —plainly say so.

The Catholic Catechism says: *Quels sont ceux, qui sont hors de l'église?—Les infidèles, les hérétiques, les schismatiques.*[1] The Orthodox Russo-Greeks are regarded as schismatics and the Lutherans as heretics, so that according to the Catholic Catechism the Church consists of Catholics only.

The so-called Greek Orthodox Catechism says: 'By the one Church of Christ is understood the Orthodox Church, which remains fully in accord with the Oecumenical Church. As for the Roman Church and other sects [the Lutherans and others are not even denominated Churches] they cannot be accounted as belonging to the one true Church since they have separated them-

---

[1] Who are those who are outside the Church? The infidels, the heretics, and the schismatics.

selves from it.' According to this definition, the
Catholics and Lutherans are outside the Church
and only the Orthodox are within it.

But the Lutheran catechism says: *Die wahre
Kirche wird darin erkannt, dass in ihr das Wort Gottes
lauter und rein ohne Menschenzusätze gelehrt und die
Sakramente treu nach Christi Einsetzung gewahret wer-
den.*[1]

According to this definition, all who have
added anything to the teaching of Christ and
the Apostles—as the Catholic and the Greek
Churches have done—are outside the Church,
which consists only of Protestants.

The Catholics assert that the Holy Ghost has
uninterruptedly operated in their hierarchy; the
Orthodox Greeks assert that the same Holy
Ghost has uninterruptedly operated in their hierarchy; the Arians asserted that the Holy Ghost
operated in their hierarchy, and did so with as
much right as the existing Churches. All kinds
of Protestants—Lutherans, Reformers, Presby-
terians, Methodists, Swedenborgians, and Mor-
mons—assert that the Holy Ghost operates only
in their assemblies.

If the Catholics assert that at the time of the
division of the Church into Arian and Greek
the Holy Ghost left the apostatizing Churches
and remained in the one true Church, then the
Protestants of every denomination can with just
the same right assert that at the time of the
separation of their Church from the Catholic, the

[1] The true Church is known by this: that in it the word of
God is given clearly and purely without human admixtures,
and the Sacraments are administered truly as Christ ordained.

Ghost left the Catholic Church and came to the one they recognize. And this they do.

Every Church derives its profession through an uninterrupted tradition from Christ and the Apostles. And in fact every Christian faith, having proceeded from Christ, must inevitably have reached the present generation through a certain tradition. But this does not prove that any one of these traditions is indubitably the correct one, excluding all others.

Every twig on a tree comes in unbroken connexion from the root, but that does not prove that each twig is the only one. And just so with the Churches. Each Church presents the same proofs of succession, and even the same miracles, in support of its own authenticity. So that there is only one strict and precise definition of what a Church is (not as something fantastic that we should like it to be, but what it is and has been in reality)—a Church is a body of men who assert that they, and they alone, are in complete and exclusive possession of the truth.

And these very assemblies having subsequently become powerful institutions by the help of the temporal powers, have been the chief obstacles to the diffusion of a true understanding of Christ's teaching.

Nor could it be otherwise: the chief characteristic of Christ's teaching, which distinguishes it from all previous teachings, is that those who accepted it tried to understand and fulfil the teaching ever more and more, whereas the Church doctrine asserts its own final and complete comprehension and realization of it.

Strange as it may seem to us brought up in the false conception of the Church as a Christian institution and in contempt of heresy, it was only in what we call heresy that there was real movement—that is, true Christianity—and it only ceased to be such when its progress in these heresies ceased, and it too was moulded into the immobile form of a Church.

What indeed is heresy? Read all the theological works dealing with heresies—which first require an exact definition, for every theology speaks of the true doctrine as surrounded by false ones—that is, heresies; and nowhere will you find even the semblance of a definition of heresy.

An example of this total absence of any kind of definition of what the word 'heresy' means, may be found in the discussion of this subject by the learned historian of Christianity, E. de Pressensé, in his *Histoire du Dogme*, the epigraph of which is, *Ubi Christus, ibi ecclesia*. (Paris 1869.) This is what he says in his introduction (page 3): *Je sais que l'on nous conteste le droit de qualifier ainsi* (that is, to call them 'heresies') *les tendances qui furent si vivement combattues par les premiers Pères. La désignation même d'hérésie semble une atteinte, portée à la liberté de conscience et de pensée. Nous ne pouvons partager ces scrupules, car ils n'iraient à rien moins qu'à enlever au christianisme tout caractère distinctif.*[1]

---

[1] I know that our right thus to qualify [as heresies] the tendencies that were so actively opposed by the early Fathers is contested. Even the use of the word heresy seems like an attack on liberty of conscience and of thought. We cannot share these scruples, for they amount to nothing less than depriving Christianity of all distinctive character.

And having mentioned that after Constantine the Church really did abuse its power to condemn as heretics and persecute those who did not agree with it, he says, discussing the first ages of the Church: *L'église est une libre association: il y a tout profit à se séparer d'elle. La polémique contre l'erreur n'a d'autres ressources que la pensée et le sentiment. Un type doctrinal uniforme n'a pas encore été élaboré; les divergences secondaires se produisent en Orient et en Occident avec une entière liberté, la théologie n'est point liée à d'invariables formules. Si au sein de cette diversité apparaît un fond commun de croyances, n'est-on pas en droit d'y voir non pas un système formulé et composé par les représentants d'une autorité d'école, mais la foi elle-même, dans son instinct le plus sûr et sa manifestation la plus spontanée? Si cette même unanimité qui se révèle dans les croyances essentielles, se retrouve pour repousser telles ou telles tendances, ne serons-nous pas en droit de conclure que ces tendances étaient en désaccord flagrant avec les principes fondamentaux du christianisme? Cette présomption ne se transformera-t-elle pas en certitude si nous reconnaissons dans la doctrine universellement repoussée par l'église, les traits caractéristiques de l'une des religions du passé? Pour dire que le gnosticisme ou l'ébionitisme sont les formes légitimes de la pensée chrétienne, il faut dire hardiment qu'il n'y a pas de pensée chrétienne ni de caractère spécifique qui la fasse reconnaître. Sous prétexte de l'élargir on la dissent. Personne, au temps de Platon, n'eût osé couvrir de son nom une doctrine qui n'eût pas fait place à la théorie des idées, et l'on eût excité les justes moqueries de la Grèce, en voulant faire d'Épicure ou de Zénon un disciple de l'Académie. Reconnaissons donc que s'il existe une religion ou une doctrine, qui s'appelle le christianisme elle peut avoir ses hé[r]ésies.*[1]

The author's whole argument comes to this: that every opinion which does not agree with the dogmatic code professed by us at a given time is a heresy. But people do profess something or other at any given time and place, and that profession of something, somewhere, at some particular time, cannot serve as the criterion of truth.

It all amounts to this, that *ubi Christus, ibi ecclesia.* And Christus is there where we are!

Every so-called heresy accounting what it professes as truth, can in just the same way find in

---

[1] The Church is a free association, to separate oneself from which offers many advantages. In its conflict with error its only resources are thought and feeling. No uniformity of doctrine has yet been elaborated, and minor divergences develop in the East and in the West quite freely; theology is not in the least bound by invariable formulas. If amid this diversity a common ground of belief appeared, has not one the right to recognize in it, not a system fixed and formulated by the representatives of academic authority, but the faith itself in its surest instinct and most spontaneous manifestation? If that same unanimity which showed itself in the essential beliefs is again shown in repelling certain tendencies, shall we not be right in concluding that those tendencies were in flagrant disaccord with the fundamental principles of Christianity? Does not this presumption become a certainty if we recognize in the doctrine that is universally repelled by the Church, the characteristic features of one of the religions of the past? To say that Gnosticism or Ebionism are legitimate forms of Christian thought, would be to assert boldly that there is no Christian thought or specific character which renders it recognizable. Under pretext of enlarging it one denies it. No one in Plato's day would have dared to shelter under his name a doctrine that did not find place for the theory of ideas, and one would have rightly aroused the mockery of Greece had one wished to represent Epicurus or Zeno as a disciple of the Academy. Let us then recognize that if a religion or a doctrine exists that calls itself Christianity, it may have its heresies.

the history of the Church a coherent explanation
of what it professes, and can employ all Pressensé's arguments for its own purpose and assert
that it alone is true Christianity—as all the
heresies have done.

The only definition of heresy (the word αἵρεσις
means a *part*) is that it is the name given by a
body of men to any opinion which refutes a part
of the creed professed by them. A more special
meaning—generally attributed to the word
heresy—is that it is an opinion which rejects a
doctrine of the Church established and supported
by the temporal power.

There is a remarkable and voluminous work,
though very little known, *Unparteiische Kirchen-
und Ketzer-Historia* (1729), by Gottfried Arnold,
which deals with just this subject and points out
how wrong, arbitrary, senseless, and cruel is the
use of the word 'heresy' in the sense of rejection.
That book is an attempt to write the history of
Christianity in the form of a history of the
heresies.

In his introduction the author propounds a
series of questions: (1) Regarding the makers of
heresy themselves (*von denen Ketzermachern selbst*),
(2) Regarding those whom they cause to become
heretics, (3) Regarding the subjects of heresy,
(4) Regarding the way in which heretics are
made, and (5) Regarding the purpose of making
heretics.

On each of these points he puts dozens of questions to which he afterwards supplies answers
from the works of well-known theologians, but
for the most part leaves the reader to draw his

own conclusions from the exposition given in the
whole book. As examples of these questions
which partly contain their own answers, I will
cite the following: On the fourth head, how
heretics are made, he says in one of his questions
(the seventh): Does not all history show that the
chief makers of heretics and masters of that craft
were just those wise men from whom the Father
hid his secrets—that is, the hypocrites, the Pharisees, and lawyers: men utterly godless and perverted? (Questions 20–21.) And in the most
corrupt times of Christianity were not just these
very men, who were specially endowed by God
with great gifts and in the days of pure Christianity would have been highly esteemed, rejected by these hypocrites and envious men?
And on the contrary would not these men, who
during the debasement of Christianity elevated
themselves above all others and acclaimed themselves as teachers of the purest Christianity,
would not they, in the times of the apostles and
disciples of Christ, have been regarded as the
most shameless heretics and anti-Christians?

In these questions he expounds, among other
things, the thought that any verbal expression of
the essence of belief, such as was demanded by
the Church and a departure from which was regarded as heresy, could never completely cover
the believer's life-conception, and that therefore
the demand for an expression of faith in certain
words was itself productive of heresy, and he says
in Question 21:

'If the divine actions and thoughts present
themselves to a man as being so great and

profound that he does not find words suitable to
express them, ought he to be accounted a heretic
because he cannot precisely express his conception?'

And in Question 33: 'Was it not for this reason
that there were no heresies in the early days,
because Christians judged one another not by
their words but by their hearts and actions, with
freedom of expression for their thoughts and
without fear of being accounted heretics?' Was
it not the easiest and most ordinary ecclesiastical
practice (says he in Question 31) for clerics, if
they wanted to get rid of or ruin anyone, to cast
suspicion on his teaching and throw a cloak of
heresy upon him—thereby condemning and getting rid of him?

'Though it is true that there were sins and
errors among the so-called heretics,' says he later,
'it is none the less true and evident from the innumerable examples here cited (i.e. in the history
of the Church and of the heresies) that there is
not and has not been a single sincere and conscientious man of any importance whom Churchmen, out of envy or for other causes, would not
have ruined.'

So the real meaning of heresy was already
understood nearly two hundred years ago, and
yet the habitual conception of it continues to
exist till now. It is bound to exist as long as the
present conception of the Church exists. Heresy
is the obverse side of the Church. Wherever the
Church exists there must be the conception of
heresy. A Church is a body of men who assert
that they are the possessers of infallible truth.

Heresy is the opinion of people who do not admit the indubitability of the Church's truth.

Heresy is a manifestation of movement in the Church, an attempt to destroy the numbness of its affirmations and reach a living understanding of the teaching. Every step of progress towards an understanding and fulfilment of the teaching has been made by heretics: Tertullian, Origen, Augustine, Luther, Huss, Savonarola, Chelčický, and the rest. It could not be otherwise.

A follower of Christ, whose service consists in an ever-growing comprehension of the teaching and an ever-growing fulfilment of it in a movement towards perfection, cannot, for that very reason, assert—for himself or anyone else—that he understands Christ's teaching and fully fulfils it. Still less can he assert this of any body of men.

Whatever stage of comprehension and perfection a follower of Christ may reach, he always feels the inadequacy of his conception and of his fulfilment of the teaching and always strives towards an increase of both. Therefore a claim by any individual or society to be in possession of a perfect understanding and a complete fulfilment of Christ's teaching, is to renounce the spirit of the teaching.

Strange as it may seem, the Churches as Churches have always been and cannot fail to be institutions not only alien to, but directly hostile towards, Christ's teaching. Not for nothing did Voltaire call the Church *l'infâme*, nor is it for nothing that all or nearly all the so-called sects of Christians have accounted, and do account, the Church to be the Scarlet Woman foretold in the Apocalypse; and it is with good reason that the history of the Church is the history of the greatest cruelties and horrors.

Many people suppose the Churches, as Churches, to be institutions that have a Christian principle for their basis though they have deviated somewhat from the straight path, but this is not so. The Churches, as Churches—as institutions affirming their own infallibility—are anti-Christian institutions. Between the Churches as such and Christianity, not only is there nothing in common except the name, but they are two quite opposite and opposing principles. The one represents pride, violence, self-assertion, immobility and death: the other humility, penitence, meekness, progress, and life.

It is impossible to serve both these masters at the same time; one or the other has to be chosen.

The servants of the Churches of all denominations, especially of late, try to appear to favour progress in Christianity. They make concessions, wish to correct abuses that have crept into the Church, and say that one should not on account of those abuses deny the principle of the Christian Church which alone can unite all men and be the mediator between men and God. But that is not true. Not only have the Churches never united, they have always been one of the chief causes of disunion among men, of hatred of one another, wars, massacres, Inquisitions, Eves of Saint Bartholomew, and the like. And the Churches never serve as mediators between man and God. Such mediation is unnecessary, and distinctly forbidden by Christ, who revealed his doctrine directly and immediately to each individual. The Churches set up dead forms in place of God, and far from revealing Him they conceal Him from men's sight. The Churches, which arose from a failure to understand Christ's teaching, and maintain this misconception by their immobility, cannot but persecute and drive out every true conception of the teaching of Jesus. They try to conceal this, but it is impossible to do so, for every step forward along the path indicated by Christ is a step towards their own destruction.

To hear and read the articles and sermons in which modern Churchmen of various kinds speak of Christian truths and virtues; to hear and read these skilful arguments, exhortations, confessions—sometimes apparently sincere—is to be ready to doubt whether the Church can be antagonistic to Christianity. 'It is impossible that these people can be hostile to Christianity, when they can point to such men as Chrysostom,[1] Fénelon, Butler, and other preachers,' one thinks, and is tempted to say: 'The Churches may have deviated from Christianity, they may be in error, but they cannot be hostile to it.' But to judge of the tree we must look at the fruit, as Christ taught. And we see that their fruits are evil, that the results of their activity is the perversion of Christianity, and we cannot but admit that

[1] St. John Chrysostom (A.D. 345–407), the most famous of Greek Fathers of the Church. He retired to the desert (370) for ten years, became Bishop of Constantinople in 398, denounced the palace extravagances, and was deposed by a Council of the Church in 404.—A.M.

however good these men were, the work of the
Church in which they took part was not Christian. The goodness and worth of all these men
who served the Church, was the goodness and
worth of the men themselves and not of the institution they served. All those good men—Francis
of Assisi and Francis of Sales, our Russian Tíkhon
Zodónsky, Thomas à Kempis, and others—were
good men *in spite of* the fact that they served a
cause hostile to Christianity. They would have
been still better and worthier had they not been
under the influence of the error which they
served.

But why speak of the past and judge of the
past, which is but little known to us and may
have been wrongly represented? The Church
with its foundations and its activity is not a thing
of the past. The Churches are before us now,
and we can judge of them directly by their
activity and their influence on men.

In what does the activity of the Churches now
consist? How do they act upon men? What do
the Churches do among us, among the Catholics
and Protestants of every denomination? What
is their practical work, and what are its results?

The activity of our Russian, so-called Orthodox, Church is plainly before our eyes. It is a
vast fact which cannot be concealed and about
which there can be no dispute.

In what does the activity of this Russian
Church consist—that immense institution which
operates so strenuously, consists of an army of
half a million men, and costs the people tens of
millions of rubles?

The activity of this Church consists in instilling by all possible means into the minds of the hundred million Russian people those antiquated and obsolete beliefs devoid now of any justification, which were once upon a time professed by a people alien to us, and in which hardly anyone any longer believes—often not even those whose office imposes on them the duty of propagating these false beliefs.

To instil into our people those formulas of Byzantine ecclesiastics, which have no meaning for men of our day—about the Trinity, the Mother of God, the Sacraments, Grace, and so forth—forms part of the activity of the Russian Church. Another part consists in maintaining idolatry in the most literal sense of the word —worshipping holy relics and icóns, offering sacrifices to them and expecting from them the fulfilment of the worshippers' wishes. I will not speak of what is said and written by the clergy with a shade of learning and liberalism in their ecclesiastical periodicals, but of what is actually done by the clergy throughout the whole of Russia among a population of a hundred million people. What do they assiduously, persistently, energetically, and without intermission teach the people? What is required of them in the name of the so-called Christian faith?

I will begin at the beginning—with the birth of a child. At its birth the clergy teach that a prayer must be pronounced over the mother and child in order to purify them, since without this prayer the mother who has given birth to a child is polluted. For this purpose the priest holds the

child in his arms in front of depictions of some
saint (which the people simply call Gods), and
pronounces words of exorcism, thus purifying
the mother.

It is also demanded of them that the child
must be baptized, under the threat of punishment for non-fulfilment—that is, that it must
be dipped three times in water[1] by the priest,
while certain words are read that nobody understands, and certain still more incomprehensible
actions are performed: a smearing of various
parts of the body with oil, and a shearing of the
hair, while the godparents blow and spit on an
imaginary devil. All this is to purify the child
and make him a Christian. Then it is impressed
on the parents that the child must receive the
eucharist[2]—that is, a part of Christ's body in the
guise of bread and wine must be given him to
eat, as a result of which he will receive the grace
of Christ, and so forth. Then it is impressed on
them that the child as he grows up must be taught
to pray. To pray means that he should place
himself directly in front of the wooden boards on
which are painted the face of Christ, the Mother
of God, or some Saint; bow his head and whole
body, and with the right hand (its fingers
folded in the prescribed form) touch his fore-
head, stomach and shoulders, and utter Church-
Slavonic words, of which the most usual taught
to all children, are: 'Mother of God, rejoice!'
and so on. Then as the child is brought up, it is

[1] The child is completely immersed three times by the
priest.—A.M.

[2] In the Russo-Greek Church the eucharist is administered
to infants.—A.M.

instilled into him that at the sight of any church or icón he must repeat this action—that is, must cross himself. Then he is instructed that on holidays (holidays are the day on which Christ was born—though nobody knows when that was —the day on which he was circumcised, that on which the Mother of God died, that on which the cross is carried in procession, that on which the parish icón was set up, that on which an idiot saw a vision, and so on)—on holidays he must put on his best clothes and go to church, and buy candles and place them in front of the pictures of the Saints, and hand in little notes with the names of the dead to be prayed for, and little loaves out of which the priest cuts small triangular pieces. Then he must pray many times for the health and prosperity of the Tsar and the bishops, and for himself and his own affairs, and finally kiss the cross and the priest's hand.

Besides these observances he is taught that at least once every year he must prepare to receive communion. This preparation means going to the church and telling his sins to the priest, on the supposition that informing another man of one's sins quite cleanses one of them, and after that he must swallow a bit of bread and some wine out of a little spoon, which purifies him still more. Then it is instilled into him that if a man and a woman wish their physical intercourse to be sacred, they must go to church, put on metallic crowns, drink a certain potion, and walk three times round a table to the sound of singing. Their physical intercourse will then be sacred and quite different from other unions.

The necessity of following rules in life is also impressed on him—not to eat meat or drink milk on certain days, and on other specified days to have prayers and memorial services performed for the dead, to entertain the priest on holidays and give him money, and several times a year to take the boards depicting saints, or Christ, or his mother (icóns), sling them on linen bands, and carry them through the fields and his house. It is inculcated on him that before death a man absolutely must eat bread and wine out of a little spoon, and that it will be still better, if time allows, for him to be smeared with oil. That will ensure his welfare in the future life. After his death it is instilled into his relatives that for the salvation of the dead man's soul it is desirable to place in his hands a printed paper with a prayer on it; it is also desirable that a certain prayer should be read aloud over his body, and that at a certain time the dead man's name should be read out in church.

In this the faith obligatory on everyone is considered to consist.

But if anyone wishes to take care of his soul more particularly, this faith teaches that the greatest assurance of welfare for the soul in the next world is attained by giving money to the churches and monasteries, thereby engaging holy men to pray for him. Also, according to this faith, it conduces to the salvation of the soul to make pilgrimages to monasteries and kiss miracle-working icóns and relics.

According to this faith, miracle-working icóns and relics concentrate in themselves particular holiness, strength, and grace; and proximity to these objects, touching them, kissing them, placing tapers before them, and crawling under them when they are being carried in procession, contributes much to salvation, as do masses ordered to be performed before these objects of veneration.

And it is just this faith called the Orthodox, and no other, that is the true faith, which under the guise of Christianity has been instilled into the people for many centuries, and is instilled with particular energy at the present time.

And let it not be said that Orthodox teachers place the essence of their teaching in something else, and that these are only ancient forms which it is not considered necessary to destroy. That is not true. This and nothing but this, is the faith taught throughout Russia by the whole Russian priesthood and latterly with particular intensity. There is nothing else. Other things are spoken of and written about in the capitals, but among the hundred million Russian people this and only this is done and taught. Churchmen may *talk* of something else, but this is what they teach by all possible means.

All this, with the adoration of persons and icóns, is included in theologies and the catechisms. The masses are assiduously taught it, both theoretically and practically, by every method of solemnity, pomp, authority, and hypnotic influence. They are obliged to believe in these things, and any attempt to free them from these savage superstitions is zealously guarded against.

Before my eyes, as I said in reference to my book *What I believe*, Christ's teaching and his own words about non-resistance were made the subject of ridicule and jests for many years, and the Churchmen not only raised no opposition, they even encouraged that scoffing at sacred things. But try to say a disrespectful word about that monstrous idol called the Iberian Mother of God[1], which is sacriligiously carried about in Moscow by drunken men—and a howl of indignation is raised by those same Orthodox Churchmen. What is taught is simply an idolatrous external cult. And let it not be said that the one thing does not interfere with the other, that 'these ought ye to have done and not to leave the other undone', that 'all things whatsoever they bid you, these do and observe; but do not ye after their works; for they say, and do not.' (Matt. xxiii. 3.) That was said of the Pharisees who fulfilled all the external injunctions of the law, and so the words: 'Whatsoever they bid you, do and observe', refer to works of mercy and goodness, but the words 'do not ye after their works; for they say, and do not', refer to the performance of ceremonies and to the neglect of good works, and have just the opposite meaning from that which Churchmen wish to attribute to the passage, explaining it as an injunction to observe ceremonies. An

---

[1] This wonder-working icón of the Virgin was an exact copy of an icón that came miraculously across the sea to Mount Athos in A.D. 929 and was kept there in the Íversky monastery. The copy stood in a chapel of its own near one of the gates of the Kremlin, and by being taken about in a carriage to visit and cure the sick proved a source of considerable revenue to the Church. It was usual for the Tsars when they visited Moscow to go to worship before the Íversky.—A.M.

external cult and the service of truth and goodness are hardly compatible, the one generally excludes the other. So it was with the Pharisees,
and so it is now with Church-Christians.

If a man can be saved by the redemption, by
sacraments and prayers, then he does not need
good works.

The Sermon on the Mount, or the Creeds. It
is impossible to believe them both. And the
Churchmen have chosen the latter: the creeds
are taught and read as prayers in the churches,
but the Sermon on the Mount is excluded even
from the reading of the Gospels in churches, so
that the congregation never hears it in church
except on days when the whole of the Gospel is
read. Nor could it be otherwise. People who believe in an angry and unreasonable God who
cursed the human race and devoted his son to be
sacrificed, and a part of mankind to eternal torment—cannot believe in the God of Love. The
man who believes in a God-Christ returning
again in glory to judge and punish the living and
the dead, cannot believe in the Christ who bade
us turn the other cheek to an assailant, not to
judge, to forgive, and to love our enemies. The
man who believes in the divine inspiration of the
Old Testament and the holiness of David, who
on his death-bed left instructions for the murder
of an old man who had offended him and whom
he could not himself kill, because he was bound
by an oath to him (I Kings, ii. 8.), and similar
abominations of which the Old Testament is full,
cannot believe in Christ's moral law. And a man
who believes in the teaching and sermons of the

Church about the compatibility of executions and wars with Christianity, cannot believe in the brotherhood of all men.

Above all, a man who believes in salvation through faith in the redemption or the sacraments, cannot employ all his strength in applying Christ's moral teaching in his life.

A man who has been taught by the Church the blasphemous doctrine that he cannot be saved by his own efforts but that there is another means, will inevitably have recourse to that means rather than to his own efforts, on which he is assured it is a sin to depend. The teaching of any Church with its redemption and its sacraments, excludes Christ's teaching, and the Orthodox doctrine with its idolatry does so most of all.

'But the masses have always believed this and believe it now!' people say. 'All Russian history proves it. It is not right to deprive the people of their traditions.' And just in this lies the deception! The masses did at one time believe something resembling what the Church believes in now, though it was far from being the same. The masses, besides the superstition of icóns, hobgoblins, relics, and the seventh Thursday after Easter with its wreaths and birch-twigs, had also a deep moral and vital understanding of Christianity which has never existed in the Church as a whole but is only met with in its best representatives. The masses, despite all obstacles placed in their way by the Government and the Church, have in their best representatives long outgrown that crude stage of comprehension, as is shown by the spontaneous birth everywhere of rationalist sects, with which Russia teems at the present time and with which the churchmen struggle so ineffectually. The masses are advancing in their consciousness of the moral and vital side of Christianity. And now comes the Church, not to support them but to intensify the inculcation of its obsolete paganism in its legalized form, striving to thrust the masses back into the darkness from which with such effort they are emerging.

'We do not teach the people anything new, only what they already believe, but in a completer form,' say the Churchmen. That is as if a man were to bind up a growing chick and thrust it back into the shell from which it had emerged.

I have often been struck by something that would be comic were its results not so terrible—namely the way in which people are interlocked in a circle, deceive one another, and cannot get out of that enchanted circle.

The first question—the first doubt of a Russian who begins to think—is the question of the miraculous icóns, and even more of the miraculous relics. Is it true that they are incorruptible, and that miracles are worked by them? Hundreds and thousands of people set themselves these questions and find it difficult to answer them—chiefly because the bishops, metropolitans, and all the dignitaries, kiss the relics and wonder-working icóns. Ask the bishops and the dignitaries why they do so, and they will say that they do it for the sake of the people; but the people kiss the icóns and relics because the bishops and men in authority do so.

Despite all the external veneer of modernity,

learning, and spirituality, which its members are nowadays beginning to assume in their books and in the articles in their clerical periodicals and sermons, the practical work of the Russian Church consists not merely in keeping the masses in their present condition of rude and savage idolatry, but even in intensifying and disseminating superstition and religious ignorance by suppressing that vital understanding of Christianity which has existed among them side by side with the idolatry.

I remember being present at the Monastery bookstall of the Óptin Hermitage when an old peasant was choosing some books for his grandson, who could read. The monk was pressing upon him accounts of relics, Church festivals, miracle-working icóns, Psalters, and the like. I asked the old man whether he had the Gospels. 'No.' 'Give him the Gospels in Russian,' I said to the monk. 'That won't do for him,' he replied. And that in brief is the activity of the Church.

'But that is so only in barbarous Russia,' a European or American reader will say. And such an observation is correct, but only in so far as it refers to the Government which aids the Church in its stultifying and depraving activity in Russia.

It is true that nowhere in Europe is there such a despotic Government or one so closely allied with the ruling Church. And therefore the share the temporal power has in the corruption of the people is greatest in Russia. But it is not true that the Russian Church differs from any other Church in its influence on the people.

The Churches are alike everywhere, and if the Roman Catholic, the Anglican, and the Lutheran Churches, have not at hand a government as compliant as the Russian, that is not due to the absence of a desire to make use of such a government.

The Church, as a Church, whatever it may be—Catholic, Anglican, Lutheran, or Presbyterian—every Church, in so far as it is a Church, cannot but aim at what the Russian Church aims at: namely, at hiding the real meaning of Christ's teaching and substituting its own doctrine which puts men under no obligation, excludes the possibility of understanding the true and vital teaching of Jesus, and above all, justifies the existence of priests who are fed by other people.

Has Roman Catholicism ever done, or does it now do, anything else by its prohibition to read the Gospel and its demand for unreasoning submission to ecclesiastical directors and the infallible Pope? Does Catholicism preach anything different from the Russian Church? There is the same external cult, similar relics and miracles and statues, wonder-working Madonnas, and processions; the same loftily foggy pronouncements on Christianity in books and sermons, but when it comes to facts—the same maintenance of gross idolatry.

And is not the same thing done by Anglicanism, Lutheranism, and every denomination of Protestantism that has formed itself into a Church? There is the same demand on the flock to believe in dogmas formulated in the fourth century, which have lost all meaning for men of our time, and the same demand for idolatrous worship, if not of relics and icóns then of the Sabbath Day and of the letter of the Bible. There is the same activity directed to concealing the real demands of Christianity and substituting externals which impose no duties, and the same 'cant', as the English admirably express the thing they are particularly addicted to. In Protestantism this tendency is particularly noticeable, since it has not even the excuse of antiquity. And does not the same thing take place in modern Revivalism—that modernized Calvinism and Evangelicalism which has given birth to the Salvation Army?

And just as the position of all the Church doctrines is the same in reference to Christ's teaching, so also is their method.

Their position is such that they have to make special efforts to conceal the teaching of Christ whose name they use.

The incompatibility of all the Church confessions and creeds with Christ's teaching is such that most strenuous efforts are needed to hide this incompatibility from men. Imagine the position of any adult, not even educated but quite a common man, who has picked up certain ideas that are now in the air concerning physics, chemistry, cosmology, and history, when for the first time he consciously considers the beliefs instilled into him in childhood and maintained by the Churches: that God created the world in six days, that there was light before the creation of the sun, that Noah packed all the animals into his ark, and the rest; that Jesus is also God the

Son, who created everything before time began, that this God came down to the earth on account of Adam's sin, that he rose from the dead, ascended into heaven, and sits at the right hand of his Father, and will come on the clouds to judge the world, and so forth.

All these propositions were formulated by men of the fourth century and had some significance at the time, but they have none for men of our day. Men of our generation may repeat these phrases with their lips, but they cannot believe them, because for us it does not make sense to say that God lives in heaven, and that the heaven opened and a voice from there said something, that Jesus rose from the dead and flew up somewhere into the sky and will come again from somewhere on clouds, and so forth.

A man who regarded the sky as a limited and solid vault might believe or disbelieve that God created it, that it opened, and that Jesus flew up into it; but for us all these words have no meaning at all. Men of our time can only believe that they ought to believe all that—which they do. But they cannot really believe in what for them has no sense.

If all these phrases should be understood allegorically and as metaphors, we know in the first place that not all Churchmen agree to this, but that on the contrary the majority of them insist on the literal interpretation of the Scriptures, and in the second place, that these metaphorical interpretations are very varied and lack evidence to support them.

Even if a man wishes to make himself believe

in the doctrine of the Church just as it is taught, the general diffusion of knowledge and of the Gospels, as well as intercourse between people of different creeds, presents an even more insuperable obstacle to his doing so.

A man of our day only need buy a copy of the Gospel for a penny and read Christ's words to the woman of Samaria—plain words it is impossible to misconstrue—that God desires worshippers not in Jerusalem, not in this or that mountain, but in spirit and in truth; or the saying that a Christian should pray not as the heathen do, publicly and in temples, but in secret, that is, in his own room; or that Christ's followers should call no man master or father. He need only read these words to be convinced that no spiritual pastors, calling themselves teachers in opposition to Christ's precept and disputing among themselves, can constitute any authority, and that what the Churchmen teach us is not Christianity. But more than that: even if a man of our time continued to believe in miracles and did not read the Gospels, his mere association with men of other creeds and faiths—which has become so easy in our day—would oblige him to doubt the truth of his own creed. It was easy for a man who never met people of other beliefs than his own to suppose that his was the only true religion, but a thinking man need only come in contact (as now constantly occurs) with equally good and bad men of various denominations mutually critical of one another's doctrines, to lose faith in the validity of the creed he himself professes. Nowadays only a quite ignorant man or one totally indifferent to the vital questions with which religion deals, can remain in the Church faith.

What endless and cunning exertions the Churches have to employ to be able—despite these conditions so destructive of their faith—to continue to build churches, to perform services, to preach, to teach, to convert, and above all to obtain for this activity the enormous emoluments required for all these priests, pastors, incumbents, superintendents, abbots, archdeacons, bishops, and archbishops.

Special superhuman efforts are required, and such efforts, ever more and more strenuous, the Church has recourse to. With us in Russia besides the other methods, simple brutal violence is employed by the secular power which is at the Church's command. Men who deviate from the external profession of the faith and openly express their non-conformity are either directly punished or are deprived of their rights, while those who strictly observe the external forms of worship are rewarded and receive privileges.

Such are the tactics of the Orthodox Church, but all Churches without exception employ any means for the same purpose—the most important of which is what is now termed hypnotism.

All the arts from architecture to poetry are employed to affect men's souls and stupify them, and this influence is incessantly at work. This use of hypnotic influence to bring people to a state of stupefaction is especially displayed in the activity of the Salvation Army, which resorts to new and unfamiliar methods: trumpets, drums, songs, banners, uniforms, marches, dances, tambourines, tears, and dramatic gestures.

But this only seems strange to us because the methods are novel. Is not the practice of the older Churches essentially the same, with their peculiar lighting, their gold and glitter, their candles, choirs, organs, bells, vestments, lachrymose sermons, and so on?

But powerful as this hypnotic influence may be, it is not the chief or most harmful activity of the Churches. Their chief and most pernicious activity is that directed to the deception of the children—those very children of whom Christ said: Woe unto him that shall cause one of these little ones to stumble.

From the very first awakening of a child's consciousness it is deceived, and solemnly taught what his teachers themselves do not believe in, and it is instilled into him until it has become engrafted into his very nature. He is diligently deceived in the most important matter of life, and when the deception is so rooted in his being that it is hard to tear it out, the whole world of knowledge and reality is opened to him—a world which can in no way be harmonized with the beliefs that have been instilled into him—and he is left to extricate himself as best he can from amid these contradictions.

Indeed if we set ourselves the task of entangling a man so that he could not, while retaining a sound mind, escape from the perplexity of the two contradictory world-conceptions that have been instilled into him from childhood—no more efficient plan could be devised than that which s being carried out with all young men brought up in our so-called Christian society.

What the Church does to men is terrible, but if we consider the condition of those who form the Church institutions we see that they cannot act otherwise. The Churches are in a dilemma: the Sermon on the Mount or the Nicene Creed? The one excludes the other. If a man sincerely believes in the Sermon on the Mount, the Nicene Creed, and with it the Church and its representatives, inevitably loses its meaning and significance for him. But if a man believes in the Nicene Creed, that is, in the Church or, in other words, those who call themselves its representatives—then for him the Sermon on the Mount becomes superfluous. And therefore the Churches cannot but use all possible means to obscure the meaning of the Sermon on the Mount and draw people to themselves. Only thanks to the strenuous activity of the Churches in this direction has their influence been maintained till now. Were the Church even for a short time to cease to influence the masses by hypnotism and by deceiving the children, men would understand Christ's teaching. But that understanding would destroy the Churches and their significance.

And so the Churches do not for a moment relax their strenuous activity, their hypnotism of adults and deception of children. And it is this activity of the Churches in imbuing men with a false conception of Christ's teaching, that serves as the obstacle to its being understood by the majority of so-called believers.

IV

Misconception of Christianity by Men of Science

I WILL now deal with another false conception of Christianity which hinders a true understanding of it, namely the scientific conception.

The Churchmen substitute for Christianity a conception they have themselves formed, and regard this as the only indubitably true interpretation.

Scientists regard Christianity as merely what the different Churches have been professing and, assuming that these creeds exhaust its whole meaning, regard it as a teaching that has outlived its time.

To see clearly how impossible it is to understand the Christian teaching while holding such an opinion, we must form an idea of the place religions in general and Christianity in particular really have held and do hold in the life of mankind, and contrast this with the significance attributed to them by science.

Just as an individual cannot live without some conception of the meaning of his life, and his conduct is always, though often unconsciously, influenced by the notion he has formed, so aggregates of men living in similar conditions—nations—cannot but have a conception of the meaning of their collective life and an activity resulting therefrom. And as an individual on reaching a fresh period of life inevitably changes his life-conception, so that a grown man sees its meaning differently from a child, so also nations—aggregates of men—in conformity with their develop-

ment inevitably change their life-conception and
the activities resulting therefrom.

The difference between an individual and
humanity as a whole, is this: the individual when
forming his view of life and of the conduct that
results from it, may be helped by indications
received from men who have already passed
through the stage of growth on which he is about
to enter; but humanity cannot find such aid, for
it is always moving along an untrodden track and
has no one to consult as to how to understand
life and how to act in the new conditions it is
encountering and which no one has ever yet
experienced.

And yet, just as a man with wife and children
cannot continue to see life as he understood it
when he was a child, so, too, in the face of the
various changes that have occurred—the greater
density of population, the increased intercourse
between the nations, a greater mastery of nature,
and the accumulation of knowledge—humanity
cannot continue to understand life as formerly,
but must establish a new life-conception from
which should also flow an activity adapted to the
new conditions it has entered, or is entering, upon.

This need is met by a special capacity mankind
possesses of segregating certain men who supply
a new meaning to the whole of human life—a
meaning from which a whole new activity results
differing from the former one. And the formation of this new life-conception, appropriate to
man in the new conditions on which he is entering, and the activity which results from it, is what
is called religion.

And therefore, in the first place, religion is not, as scientists suppose, a phenomenon that once corresponded to the development of humanity but afterwards became obsolete: it is a phenomenon always inherent in the life of humanity, and in our time is as inevitably inherent in humanity as at any other period. In the second place, religion is always a definition of the activity of the future and not of the past, and so an investigation of past phenomena obviously fails to cover the essence of religion.

The essence of every religious teaching does not, as men of science imagine, lie in a desire to give symbolic expression to the forces of nature, nor does it lie in fear of those forces, or in a craving for the miraculous, or in the external forms in which it is manifested. The essence of religion lies in man's faculty of foreseeing prophetically, and pointing out, the path of life along which humanity must progress, and in a new definition of the meaning of life—differing from its previous one—from which the whole future activity of humanity will result.

This capacity to foresee the path humanity must follow is in a greater or lesser degree common to all men; but there have always been some in whom it has shown itself with particular force, and these men have clearly and definitely expressed what was vaguely felt by all men, and have established for hundreds and thousands of years a new comprehension of life from which an activity resulted differing from what had gone before.

We know three such conceptions of life: two

that humanity has already outlived, and the third now extant—which is Christianity. There are three and only three such conceptions, not because we have arbitrarily brought together all the theories of life under these three heads, but because the actions of men always have as their base one of these three life-conceptions—for we can only understand life in these three ways.

The three views of life are these: first, the personal or animal; secondly, the social or pagan; and thirdly, the universal or divine.

In the first, man's life consists solely in his personality, the aim of his life is in the gratification of his individual will. In the second, man's life is not contained in his personality alone, but exists in an aggregate and succession of personalities—in the family, tribe, race, or nation—and the aim of life consists in gratifying the will of this aggregate of persons.

In the third, man's life is comprised neither in his own personality nor in an aggregate and succession of persons, but in the source and origin of life—in God.

These three life-conceptions constitute the foundation of all past and present religions.

The savage sees the meaning of life only in himself, in his own personal desires. The good of his life is centred in himself alone. The greatest good for him is the completest satisfaction of his desires. The motive of his life is personal enjoyment. His religion consists in propitiating the deity in his own favour, and in the worship of the gods, whom he imagines as persons living only for their personal aims.

A pagan of a social group, recognizing life not in himself alone but in an aggregate of persons—in the tribe, the family, the race, or the state—is ready to sacrifice his personal good for them. The motive of his life is glory. His religion consists in the glorification of the heads of his group—his ancestors, his forefathers, his rulers—and in the worship of gods—the special protectors of his family, his race, his people, or his state.[1]

A man who holds the divine understanding of life recognizes life not in his own personality, and not in associations of personalities—the family, the clan, the nation, the fatherland, or the government—but in the source of eternal, immortal life; in God. And to do the will of God he sacrifices his personality and domestic and social welfare. The motive of his life is love. And his religion is the worship in deed and truth of the source of all things—God.

The whole historic life of humanity is nothing but a consecutive transition from the personal, animal, conception of life, to the social; and from the social to the divine. The whole history of the ancient nations, lasting for thousands of years and ending with the history of Rome, is the history of the transition from the animal and personal understanding of life to the social and

[1] The identity of this life-conception is not infringed by the fact that so many different forms of life, as the tribal, the family, the racial, the national, and even the life of humanity, as theoretically imagined by the Positivists, are founded on this social or pagan view of life. All these various forms of life are founded on the same conception, that a personal life is an insufficient aim and that the meaning of life can only be found in an aggregate of personalities.—L.T.

political life-conception. The whole history since the time of imperial Rome and the appearance of Christianity, has been the history of the transition, through which we are still passing, from a political understanding of life to the divine understanding of it.

And it is just this latter understanding of life and the Christian teaching founded upon it, which governs our whole life and lies at the root of our whole activity both practical and theoretical, that the pseudo-scientists, who judge it only by its outward symptoms, regard as something obsolete and of no significance for us.

According to the scientists Christianity consists only of dogmatic doctrines—concerning the Trinity, the Redemption, miracles, Churches, sacraments, and so forth—and is only one of a vast number of religions which have arisen among mankind and now, having played its part in history, has outlived its time and is melting away before the light of science and true enlightenment.

We have here an instance of what in the majority of cases is the source of the grossest human errors. Men on a lower level of understanding when they encounter phenomena of a higher order, instead of making efforts to understand them and rise to the point of view from which they ought to regard the matter, judge these phenomena from their own lower standpoint. And the less they understand what they are talking about, the more boldly and confidently do they pass judgement upon it.

For the majority of learned men, who view

Christ's vital moral teaching from the lower standpoint of the social conception of life, this teaching is only a very indefinite and incongruous combination of Hindu asceticism, Stoic and Neoplatonic philosophy, and Utopian antisocial reveries having no serious significance for our time. For them its whole meaning is centred in its external manifestations—in Catholicism, Protestantism, its dogmas, and its conflict with the secular powers. Estimating the significance of Christianity by these phenomena they are like deaf men who would judge the meaning and worth of music by watching the movements of the musicians.

The result of this is that all these men, beginning with Comte, Strauss, Spencer, and Renan —not understanding the meaning of Christ's words and not understanding what they refer to or why they were uttered, not even understanding the questions to which they serve as answer— do not take the trouble to grasp their meaning, and if they are inimically inclined, simply deny the rationality of the teaching or, if they deign to be condescending, correct it from the height of their superior understanding, assuming that Christ wished to say just what they have in mind but that he was not able to say it.

They deal with his teaching much as self-confident men often correct the words of an interlocutor they consider much their inferior, saying: 'Yes, what you mean to say is so-and-so.' This correction is always made in order to reduce the higher, divine, life-conception to the level of the lower, social conception.

People usually say that the moral teaching of Christianity is good but exaggerated—that in order to make it satisfactory we must reject what is superfluous and unsuitable to our way of life. 'For a doctrine which demands too much, and requires what cannot be performed, is worse than one which demands of men only what is possible and in conformity with their strength', these learned commentators on Christianity think and affirm, repeating what was said long ago and is and could not but be said by those who not having understood the Teacher crucified him—the Jews.

It appears that in the judgement of the learned men of our time, the Hebrew law of an eye for an eye and a tooth for a tooth—the law of just retaliation known to mankind five thousand years ago—is better than the law of love preached eighteen hundred years ago by Christ in place of that very law of justice.

It turns out that all that has been done by those who understood Christ's teaching directly and lived in accord with such an understanding of it, all that has been said and done by all the true Christians, by all the Christian saints, everything that now transforms the world under the guise of socialism and communism—is simply an exaggeration not worth talking about.

Men educated in Christianity for eighteen centuries have convinced themselves in the persons of their foremost men, the scholars, that the Christian religion is one of dogmas, that its vital teaching is a misconception—an exaggeration which infringes the true and legitimate demands of morality that correspond to the nature of man, that the doctrine of retribution which Christ rejected and in the place of which he put his teaching, is much more advantageous for us.

To these learned men the doctrine of not resisting evil by force seems exaggerated and even irrational. It will be much better to reject it, think they, not noticing that they are not talking of the teaching of Jesus at all, but of something that seems to them to be his teaching.

They do not realize that to say that the law of non-resistance in Christ's teaching is an exaggeration, is like saying when considering the properties of circles, that it is an exaggeration to state that all the radii of a circle are equal. And those who speak thus, act just like a man who, having no idea of what a circle is, should declare that it is exaggerated to demand that every point of its circumference should be an equal distance from the centre. To advise the rejection or modification of the statement concerning the equality of the radii of a circle indicates a failure to understand what a circle is. To advise a rejection or modification of Christ's vital teaching of the law of not resisting by violence him that is evil, indicates a failure to understand the teaching.

And those who do so have in fact quite failed to understand it. They do not understand that this teaching is the institution of a new conception of life corresponding to the new conditions on which men entered eighteen hundred years ago, and is a statement of the new conduct of life which flows from it. They do not believe that Christ wished to say what he did say, or he

seems to them to have uttered what he said in
the Sermon on the Mount and elsewhere, from
infatuation, irrationality, or lack of development.[1]

Matt. vi. 25–34

'Therefore I say unto you, Take no thought
for your life, what ye shall eat, or what ye shall
drink, nor yet for your body, what ye shall put
on. Is not the life more than meat, and the body
than raiment? Behold the fowls of the air, for
they sow not, neither do they reap, nor gather
into barns, yet your heavenly Father feedeth
them. Are ye not much better than they? Which
of you by taking thought can add one cubit to his
stature? And why take ye thought for raiment?

[1] This, for instance, is a characteristic argument of that kind
from the American periodical, *The Arena*, of October 1890, in
an article entitled 'A New Basis of Church Life'. Discussing
the significance of the Sermon on the Mount and of non-
resistance in particular, the author, being under no such
obligation to conceal its significance as Churchmen are, says:
'Devout common sense must gradually come to look upon
Christ as a philanthropic teacher who, like every enthusiast
who ever taught, went to an utopian extreme in his own
philosophy. Every great agitation for the betterment of the
world has been led by men who beheld their own mission with
such absorbing intensity that they could see little else. It is
no reproach to Christ to say that he had the typical reformer's
temperament; that his precepts cannot be literally accepted
as a complete philosophy of life; and that men are to analyse
them reverently, but at the same time in the spirit of ordinary
truth-seeking criticism', &c.

'Christ did in fact preach absolute communism and anarchy,
but'—and so forth.

Christ wanted to say the right thing, but did not know how
to express himself so precisely and clearly as we do, in the
spirit of criticism, and so we will correct him. All his talk
about humility, sacrifice, poverty, not taking thought for the
morrow—he said accidentally, owing to his inability to express
himself scientifically.—L.T.

Consider the lilies of the field, how they grow; they toil not, neither do they spin; and yet I say unto you that even Solomon in all his glory was not arrayed like one of these. Wherefore, if God so clothe the grass of the field, which to-day is, and to-morrow is cast into the oven, shall He not much more clothe you, O ye of little faith? Therefore take no thought, saying, What shall we eat? or What shall we drink? or Wherewithal shall we be clothed? For after all these things do the Gentiles seek, for your heavenly Father knoweth that ye have need of all these things. But seek ye first the kingdom of God and his righteousness, and all these things shall be added unto you. Take therefore no thought for the morrow, for the morrow shall take thought for the things of itself. Sufficient unto the day is the evil thereof.'

Luke xii. 33–34

'Sell that ye have, and give alms; make for yourselves purses which wax not old, a treasure in the heavens that faileth not, where no thief draweth near, neither moth destroyeth. For where your treasure is there will your heart be also.'

Sell what thou hast and follow me, and he who will not leave father, or mother, or children, or brethren, or fields, or house, cannot be my disciple. Deny thyself, take up thy cross each day and follow me. My meat is to do the will of Him that sent me, and to perform His works. Not my will but Thine be done, not what I will, but what Thou wilt, and not as I will, but as Thou wilt.

Life is to do not one's own will, but the will of God.

To men who hold the lower life-conception, all these propositions seem to be the expression of some ecstatic exaltation which has no direct application to life. Yet they follow from the Christian conception of life, just as surely as the propositions that a man should work for the common good and sacrifice his life for the defence of his country follow from the social conception of life.

Just as a man of the social life-conception might say to a savage: 'Come to your senses, think what you are doing! Your personal life cannot be true life, for it is wretched and transient. Only the life of an aggregate and sequence of personalities—a family, clan, race, or nation—endures, and so a man must sacrifice his own person for the life of the family and the nation.' So a man of the Christian perception says to a man of the social and communal conception of life: 'Repent ye, μετανοεῖτε, that is, bethink yourself or you will perish. Understand that this corporeal personal life which is here to-day and is destroyed to-morrow, can have no permanence, that no external measures, no arrangement of it, can give it firmness or make it rational. Bethink yourselves, and understand that the life you are living is not true life; the life of the family, of society, of the state, will not save you from destruction. A true, rational life is possible for man only in the measure to which he can participate, not in the family or the state but in the source of life, the Father; to the extent to which he can merge his life with that of the Father.' Such is indubitably the Christian conception of life shown in every utterance of the Gospel.

It is possible not to share this view of life, it is possible to reject it or show its inaccuracy or error, but it is impossible to judge of the teaching without having understood the life-conception from which it proceeds. It is still more impossible to judge of a subject of a higher order from a lower point of view—to judge of a spire by looking at a crypt. But this is just what the learned men of our time are doing. They do so because they share an erroneous idea—resembling that held by the Churchmen—that they possess an infallible means of investigating the subject. They fancy that if only they apply their so-called scientific methods of criticism, there can be no doubt of the correctness of their understanding of the subject under consideration.

It is just this supposed possession of an infallible instrument of cognition that is the chief hindrance to an understanding of the Christian teaching by so-called scientific unbelievers, whose opinion influences the vast majority of unbelievers among so-called educated people. From such pseudo-understandings result all the misapprehensions of scientific men about the Christian teaching and especially two strange misconceptions which, more than anything else, impede a true understanding of it.

One of these misconceptions is that the vital Christian teaching is impracticable and so is either not at all obligatory, that is, should not be accepted as a guide, or should be altered and adapted to the limits within which its fulfilment is possible in our society. The other misconception is that the Christian teaching of love of God, and therefore of His service, is a vague and mystical demand which presents no definite object of love and should therefore be replaced by a more precise and comprehensible teaching about loving men and serving humanity.

The first misconception about the impracticability of the teaching consists in this, that men of the social comprehension of life, not understanding the method by which the Christian teaching guides men and taking the Christian indications of perfection to be rules which determine life, think and say that to follow Christ's teaching is impossible because a complete fulfilment of its demands destroys life.

'If one man only were to carry out what was preached by Christ,' they say, 'he would destroy his own life, but if all men carried it out the human race would come to an end.'

'If we take no thought for the morrow, of what we shall eat and drink and in what we shall be clothed; if we do not defend our lives, do not resist by force him that is evil; if we lay down our lives for our friends and observe perfect chastity —the human race cannot exist,' they think and say.

And they are quite correct if one takes the indications of perfection as given by Christ for rules every man is obliged to fulfil, just as in the social doctrine he is obliged to pay his taxes and take part in courts of law.

The misunderstanding consists in this, that

E

Christ's teaching guides men differently from the teachings based on a lower understanding of life. The precepts of the social conception of life guide men by demanding a precise performance of rules and laws. Christ's teaching guides men by indicating to them that infinite perfection of the heavenly Father towards which it is natural for each man, at whatever stage of imperfection he may be, voluntarily to strive.

The mistake made by people who judge of the Christian teaching as they would of social problems, is this: assuming that the perfection indicated by Christ can be fully attained, they ask themselves (as they would ask concerning social laws) what will be the result if this is all carried out? The assumption is false, because the perfection pointed out to Christians is infinite and can never be attained; and Christ delivers his teaching with the fact in view that complete perfection will never be attained, but that striving towards full and infinite perfection will constantly increase the good of men, and so that good can be endlessly increased.

Christ is teaching not angels but men living an animal life and actuated by it. And to this animal motive force Christ applies, as it were, a new and different force—the consciousness of divine perfection—and thereby directs the movement of life along the resultant of these two forces.

To suppose that human life will move in the direction indicated by Christ is like supposing that a boatman crossing a rapid river and directing his boat almost against the current, will progress in that direction.

Christ recognizes the existence of both sides of the parallelogram of the two eternal indestructible forces of which man's life is compounded: the force of his animal nature and the force of the consciousness of his sonship to God. Without saying anything of the animal force, which asserts itself, remains always the same, and is beyond man's power, Christ speaks only of the divine force, calling man to the fullest recognition of it, and the fullest emancipation of it from all retarding influences, and bringing it to the highest degree of intensity.

In this liberation and intensification of that force does man's true life consist, according to Christ's teaching. In the old doctrine true life consisted in the fulfilment of the rules of the law; according to Christ's teaching it consists in the greatest approach to the divine perfection indicated to man and of which he is conscious within himself, and in an ever greater approach towards a blending of his own will with God's—a blending towards which man strives, and which would lead to the destruction of the life we now know.

Human life is an asymptote of divine perfection towards which it always tends and approaches, but which can only be reached by it in infinity.

The Christian teaching seems to make life impossible only when people mistake the indication of an ideal for the laying down of a rule. Only then do the principles presented by Christ's teaching appear to make life impossible. In reality those principles alone make true life possible and without them it cannot exist.

'Too much should not be demanded,' people usually say when discussing the requirements of the Christian teaching. 'It is an impossible demand that we should not take any care for the future, as is said in the Gospel—though one should not be too careful about it. It won't do to give away everything to the poor, but one should give a certain definite part. It is not necessary to strive after chastity, but one should avoid debauchery. One need not leave wife and children, but should not have too great a partiality for them'—and so on.

But to speak like that is the same as to tell a man who is swimming a rapid river and directing his course against the current, that it is impossible to cross a river directing one's course against the stream, but that to cross it one must swim in the direction of the spot one wishes to reach.

Christ's teaching differs from former teachings in that it guides men not by external rules but by an inward consciousness of the possibility of reaching divine perfection. And in man's soul we find not moderate rules of justice and philanthropy, but the ideal of complete, infinite, divine perfection. Only a striving towards that perfection deflects the direction of man's life from its animal condition towards the divine, in so far as that is possible in this life.

In order to reach the place to which he wishes to go, it is necessary for him to direct his course towards a point far higher up.

To lower the demands of the ideal, means not only to diminish the possibility of perfection but

o make an end of the ideal itself. The ideal that
acts on men is not an invented ideal, but one that
every man carries in his soul. Only this ideal of
complete, infinite perfection acts on men and
moves them to action. Moderate perfection has
no power to influence men's souls.

Christ's teaching then has power only when it
demands absolute perfection, that is, the fusion
of the divine nature that exists in each man's soul,
with the will of God—a union of the son with the
Father. It is only in this freeing of the son of God
existing in each man from the animal, and its
approach to the Father, that life consists according to Christ's teaching.

The existence in man of the animal—merely
the animal—is not human life. Life solely in the
will of God is also not human life. Human life is
a compound of the animal and the divine. And
the more that compound approaches to the
divine the more is life increased.

Life, according to the Christian teaching, is
progress towards divine perfection. No one condition can, according to that teaching, be higher
or lower than another. Each condition, according to that teaching, is merely a particular stage,
indifferent in itself, on the road towards unattainable perfection, and therefore it does not
in itself constitute either a lower or a higher stage
of life. According to this teaching, increase of life
consists only in quickening the movement towards perfection. And therefore the movement
towards perfection of the publican Zaccheus, of
the woman who was a sinner, or of the thief on the
cross, is a higher degree of life than the stagnant

righteousness of the Pharisee. And therefore according to this teaching, no obligatory rule can exist. A man on a lower level but moving towards perfection, lives a more moral and better life and is fulfilling the teaching more than one who, though on a much higher level of morality, is not advancing towards perfection.

In that sense the lost sheep is more precious to the Father than those that have not strayed the prodigal son, and the coin lost and found again, are more precious than those that were never lost.

The fulfilment of the teaching is in the progress from ourselves towards God. In this fulfilment there can evidently be no definite laws or rules. All degrees of perfection and imperfection are equal before this teaching; no fulfilment of the rules constitutes a fulfilment of the doctrine, and therefore for this teaching there are and can be no obligatory laws or rules.

From this radical difference between Christ' teaching and all previous ones founded on the social conception of life, a corresponding difference arises between the social and Christian commandments. Social commandments are for the most part positive, prescribing certain actions justifying men and making them righteous. But the Christian precepts (the law of love is not strictly a precept, but the expression of the very essence of the teaching)—the five commandments of the Sermon on the Mount—are all negative, and show only what, at a certain stage of human development, men should not do. These commandments are, as it were, sign-posts on the infinite road to perfection towards which mankind is moving—they mark the degree of perfection possible at a certain period of development.

In the Sermon on the Mount Christ expressed both the eternal ideal towards which it is natural for men to aspire, and that degree of its attainment which mankind can even now reach.

The ideal is to have no ill-will towards anyone, not to provoke ill-will, but to love all men; but the commandment indicating the level below which it is quite possible for men not to descend at their present stage of progress towards that ideal, is not to offend anyone by a word. And that is the first commandment.

The ideal is perfect chastity, even in thought. The commandment indicating the level below which it is quite possible not to descend in man's progress towards this ideal, is that of a pure married life, refraining from adultery. And that is the second commandment.

The ideal is not to be concerned for the future, and to live in the present. The commandment which indicates the level below which it is quite possible not to descend, is not to take an oath, not to promise anything for the future. And that is the third commandment.

The ideal is never for any purpose to employ violence. The commandment showing the level below which it is quite possible not to descend, is not to return evil for evil, but to endure wrongs, to give up one's shirt. That is the fourth commandment.

The ideal is to love our enemies and those that

hate us. The precept showing the level below which it is quite possible not to descend, is to do no evil to our enemies, to speak well of them, and not to make distinctions between them and our compatriots. That is the fifth commandment.

All these precepts are indications of what we are quite capable of not doing and what we should now labour to attain, what we should by degrees transfer into the domain of instinctive and unconscious habit. But these precepts far from constituting the whole of the teaching, are only some of the innumerable stages on the path towards perfection.

Beyond these precepts others more and more lofty must and will follow on the road to perfection pointed out by the teaching.

And so it is natural for Christianity to set forth higher requirements than those expressed in these commandments, and certainly not to lower the demands either of the ideal itself or of these precepts, as is done by those who judge the Christian teaching from the standpoint of the social conception of life.

Such is one misunderstanding of the men of science as to the meaning and significance of Christ's teaching; another, arising from the same source, consists in substituting the love and service of humanity for the love and service of God that is required by Christianity.

The Christian teaching that we must love and serve God, and that love and service of our neighbour follows only as resulting from this, seems obscure, mystical, and arbitrary, to the men of science: and they completely discard the requirement of love and service to God, supposing that the teaching of love of men, of humanity, is much more intelligible and firm and better grounded.

Scientific men teach in theory that the only reasonable and good life is one of service to the whole of humanity, and this for them is the import of the Christian teaching. To this doctrine they reduce Christ's teaching, and they look for confirmation of this teaching of theirs in Christ's words, assuming that their teaching and the Christian are one and the same.

That opinion is quite mistaken. The Christian teaching has nothing in common with that of the Positivists, the Communists, or any of the preachers of a universal brotherhood of man based on the advantageousness of such a brotherhood. They differ from one another especially in that the Christian teaching has a firm and clear basis in the human soul, while love of humanity is only a theoretical deduction from analogy.

The doctrine of love of humanity alone is based on the social conception of life.

The essence of the social conception of life consists in a transference of the meaning of one's personal life to the life of a society of individuals: family, clan, race, or State. That transference has been and is easily accomplished in its first forms—in the transference of the meaning of life from one's own personality to that of family or clan. A transference to the race or nation is already more difficult and requires special training. And a transference of the sentiment to the State is the furthest limit of such transference.

To love oneself is natural to everyone, and each man loves himself without being incited to do so. To love one's clan who support and protect one; to love one's wife, the joy and help of one's existence; one's children, the hope and consolation of one's life; one's parents who gave one life and brought one up—is natural. And such love though not nearly so strong as love of oneself, is met with quite often.

A love of tribe or nation for one's own sake, for personal pride, can still be met with, though it is already not so natural. Love of one's own people who are of the same blood, the same tongue, and the same religion as oneself, is still possible, though far from being as strong as love of self or even love of family or kin. But love for a State, such as Turkey, Germany, the British Empire, Austria, or Russia, is already almost an impossible thing, and though it is zealously inculcated it does not actually exist, but is only supposed to do so. And with that aggregate man's capacity of transferring his affection ceases, and he cannot experience any direct sentiment to such fictitious entities. The Positivists however and all the preachers of scientific fraternity, not considering the weakening of the feeling that accompanies the widening of its object, argue further in that direction. 'Since it was advantageous for the individual to transfer his interest to the family, the tribe, and subsequently to the nation and the State,' they say, 'it will be still more advantageous to transfer his interest to humanity as a whole.'

Theoretically that would certainly be more

advantageous. Having transferred our love and interest from our personality to our family, and from our family to our tribe or nation or State, it would be quite logical, in order to free ourselves from the struggles and calamities that result from the division of humanity into nations, to transfer our love and interest to the whole of humanity and to live for humanity collectively, as men do for their family and State.

That would seem to be quite logical, but it is merely a theory advanced by people who do not notice that love is a sentiment that may be felt but cannot be taught; that love moreover has an object, and that humanity is not a real object but a fictitious one.

The family, the tribe, and even the State, were not invented by men but were formed spontaneously like swarms of bees or anthills, and have an actual existence. A man who loves his family for his own animal personality, knows whom he loves: Anna, Mary, John, Peter, and so on. A man who loves his kindred and is proud of them, knows that he loves all the Guelphs or all the Ghibellines; a man who loves his nation knows that he loves France bounded by the Rhine and the Pyrenees, especially its principal city Paris, and its history, and so on. But what does a man love who loves humanity? There is such a thing as a State and a nation, and there is an abstract conception of humanity, but there is not and cannot be any concrete perception of humanity.

Humanity? Where are its limits? Where does it end, and where does it begin? Does humanity exclude the savage, the idiot, the dipsomaniac, or the insane person? If we draw a line excluding from humanity its lowest representatives, where are we to draw that line? Shall we exclude negroes as the Americans do, or Hindus as some Englishmen do, or Jews as some others do? Or if we include all men without exception, are we going to include only men and not the higher animals many of whom are superior to the lowest specimens of the human race?

We do not know humanity as the highest object, we do not know its limits. Humanity is a fiction and it is impossible to love it. It would indeed be very advantageous if men could love humanity just as they love the family. It would be very advantageous to replace a competitive organization of human activity, of groups and individuals, by a universal organization of each for all and all for each as the Communists talk of doing. Only there are no motives for it. The Positivists, the Communists, and all the apostles of fraternity on scientific principles, advocate an extension to the whole of humanity of the love men feel for themselves, their families, and their country. They forget that the love they are discussing is a personal love, that can extend in a rarified form to the family and in a still more rarified form to a man's native country, but which disappears as it extends to an artificial State (such as Austria, the British Empire, or Turkey), and which we cannot even conceive of in relation to the whole of humanity, which is an absolutely mystical conception.

'A man loves himself (his animal personality),

he loves his family and even his native country.
Why should he not also love the human race?
It would be so good if he did! And incidentally
that very thing is inculcated by Christianity.' So
think the Positivist, Communist, and Socialist
advocates of fraternity. It would indeed be very
good, but it is quite impossible because the love
based on the personal or social conception of life
cannot go beyond the love of country. The mistake these people make is to overlook the fact
that the social understanding of life on which the
love of family and of nation is based, rests on love
of self, and that this love grows weaker and
weaker as it is extended from personality to
family, tribe, nationality, and State, till in the
State it reaches the extreme limit beyond which
it cannot go.

The necessity of extending the sphere of love
is unquestionable. But that very necessity of
extending its object indefinitely, destroys its possibility, and proves the insufficiency of personal
human love.

And here the advocates of Positivist, Communist, and Socialist fraternity propose to draw
upon Christian love to support this human love
which has proved unreliable—but they want the
fruit without the root. They propose love of
humanity alone without a love of God.

But such love cannot exist. There is no motive
for it. Christian love results only from a Christian understanding of life, in which the meaning
of life consists in the love and service of God.

By a natural transition from the love of self,
to family, tribe, nation, and State, the social

conception of life has led men to consciousness of
the necessity of a love for humanity, a conception having no definite limits and merging into
all that exists. Why has this conception, which
evokes no feeling in man, led to a contradiction
the social understanding of life cannot solve?

Only the Christian teaching in its full significance solves it, by giving a new meaning to life.
Christianity recognizes love of self, of family, of
the nation, and of humanity, and not of humanity only but of all that lives and exists. It recognizes the necessity of an endless extension of the
sphere of love. But it finds the object of this love
not outside itself in aggregates of individuals—
the family, the race, the State, humanity, or the
whole external world—but in itself, in a divine
personality the essence of which is that very love
which the animal personality, through consciousness of its own perishable nature, is brought to
feel the need of widening.

The difference between the Christian teaching
and those which preceded it, is this: The social
doctrine said: 'Live contrary to your nature
(meaning only the animal nature), subduing it
to the external law of the family, the society, and
the State.' Christianity says: 'Live in accord
with your nature (meaning your divine nature);
do not subject it to anything—either to your
own or to another's animal nature—and you
will attain just what you are striving to attain by
subjecting your external nature to external laws.'

The Christian teaching brings man back to the
elementary consciousness of himself: not of himself as an animal but of himself as God—the

divine spark of himself, a son of God of the same nature as the Father but confined in an animal husk. And the consciousness of himself as such a son of God, whose chief quality is love, also satisfies all those demands for an extension of the sphere of love to which the man of a social conception of life has been brought. There, with an ever widening and widening of the sphere of love for the salvation of the personality, love was a necessity and adapted itself to certain objects—self, family, society, and humanity. With the Christian outlook on life, love is not a necessity to be adapted to anything but is the essential nature of man's soul. Man does not love because it is advantageous for him to love this man or those men, but because love is the essence of his soul—because he cannot help loving.

The Christian teaching consists in indicating to man that the essence of his soul is love, that his happiness comes not because he loves this or that man but because he loves the source of all, God, whom he recognizes in himself through love, and so this love will extend to all men and all things.

In that lies the fundamental difference between the Christian teaching and that of the Positivists and all the non-Christian theorists of universal fraternity.

Such are the two chief conceptions concerning the Christian teaching which lead to most of the false opinions about it. One is that Christ's teaching, like previous teachings, inculcates rules men are obliged to follow, and that these rules are impracticable. The other is that the whole purport of Christianity is to teach men to live advantageously together as one family, for which, without reference to the love of God, it is only necessary to follow the rule of love of humanity.

The false opinion of scientific men, that the doctrine of the supernatural forms the essence of the Christian teaching and that its vital teaching is impracticable, together with the misconceptions following from that false opinion, are another cause of the misunderstanding of Christianity by people of our time.

V

The contradiction between our life and our Christian consciousness.

THERE are many reasons why Christ's teaching is not understood. One is that people imagine they have understood it when they have decided (as the Churchmen do) that it was transmitted to us in a supernatural manner, or when (as the scientists do) they have studied some of the external forms in which it has been expressed. Another is a misconception as to its impracticability, and a feeling that it should be replaced by a teaching of love for humanity. But the chief reason for all the misunderstandings is that Christ's teaching is considered to be one that can be accepted without changing our life.

People accustomed to the existing order of things, liking it, and fearing to change it, try to understand the doctrine as a collection of revelations and rules that can be accepted without altering their lives; whereas Christ's teaching is not a mere setting forth of rules for man to follow, but the elucidation of a new meaning of life, and it defines a whole human activity, entirely new, quite different from all that has preceded it, and appropriate to the period on which mankind is now entering.

The life of humanity, like that of individuals, progresses and moves through different periods, and each period has its corresponding life-conception which people inevitably absorb. Those who do not consciously absorb the life-conception proper to the period, are brought to it unconsciously. What occurs with the change of outlook of individuals takes place also with the change of outlook in the life of nations and humanity generally. If the father of a family continued to be guided in his activity by a childish conception of life, things would become so difficult for him that he would involuntarily seek another outlook on life, and readily accept one appropriate to his age.

That is just what is happening with humanity during the stage through which we are now passing: that of transition from a pagan conception of life to a Christian conception. The socialized man of our time is being brought by life itself to the necessity of abandoning the pagan conception which is unnatural for humanity's present stage, and of submitting to the demands of Christian teaching, the truths of which are known to him however perverted and misrepresented they may have been, and which alone furnish a solution of the contradictions amid which he is entangled.

If the requirements of Christianity seem strange and even alarming to a man of the social life-conception, the demands of the social doctrine seemed no less strange, incomprehensible, and alarming to the savage of ancient times when he did not yet fully understand them and could not foresee their results.

'It is absurd,' said the savage, 'to sacrifice my own tranquillity, or even my life, in order to defend something incomprehensible, intangible, and conditional—the family, the tribe, or the country—and above all it is dangerous to put myself in the hands of a strange authority.'

But a time came when the savage on the one hand realized, if but dimly, the value of social life and the significance of its chief stimulus, glory, and public approval or censure, and when on the other hand the sufferings of his personal life became so great that he could no longer believe in the validity of his former conception of life. And then he accepted the social and political doctrine and submitted to it.

The same thing is now taking place with social and political man.

'It is irrational,' says the socialized man, 'to sacrifice my welfare and that of my family and country for the fulfilment of some sort of higher law which demands the renunciation of my most natural and praiseworthy feelings: love of self, of family, and of country; and above all it is dangerous to part with the security of life afforded by the state organization.'

But the time comes when, on the one hand, a dim consciousness in his soul of the higher law of love towards God and his neighbour, and on the other hand the sufferings that result from the contradictions of life, force him to abandon the social life-conception and assimilate the new Christian conception of life that is offered him and that solves all the contradictions and removes the sufferings of his life. And that time has now come.

To us, who thousands of years ago passed through the transition from the personal, animal view of life to the socialized view, it seems that that transition was natural and inevitable; but this one through which we have been passing for these last eighteen hundred years seems arbitrary, unnatural, and alarming. But that seems so only because the other transition has already been accomplished and its activity has already become subconscious, while the present transition is not yet completed and we still have to complete it consciously.

It took hundreds and thousands of years for the social conception of life to permeate man's consciousness. It passed through various forms, and now, having entered the sphere of the subconscious transmitted to us by heredity, education, and habit, seems to us natural. But five thousand years ago it seemed just as unnatural and alarming as the Christian doctrine in its true sense now appears to us.

It seems to us now that the Christian doctrine of universal brotherhood, elimination of national distinctions, abolition of private property, and

the strange injunction not to resist evil by violence, are impossible demands. But so—thousands of years ago in more primitive times—
seemed the demands not only of the State but of
the family, such as that parents should support
their children, that the young should maintain
the old, and that husbands and wives should be
true to one another. Still more strange and even
insensate appeared the State-demands: that the
citizen should submit to an appointed authority,
should pay taxes, go to war for the defence of his
country, and so on. It appears to us that all those
demands were simple, understandable, natural,
and have nothing mystical or even strange about
them; but three or five thousand years ago such
demands seemed to require what was impossible.

That is why the social life-conception served as
the basis of religion—because, at the time it was
presented to men, it seemed to them incomprehensible, mystical, and supernatural. Now that
we have outlived that phase of life we see the
rational grounds for the union of men in families,
communities, and States. But in ancient times
the requirement for such unions was presented
in the name of a supernatural authority and was
confirmed by it.

Patriarchal religions deified the family, race,
and nation. State religions deified kings and
empires. Even now, most ignorant people—such
as our peasants who look upon the Tsar as an
earthly God—submit to the state laws not because they recognize their necessity or because
they understand the meaning of the State, but
from a religious sentiment.

In just the same way the Christian teaching now seems a supernatural religion to men of the social or pagan life-conception though in reality there is nothing secret, mystic, or supernatural, about it. It is simply a teaching of life corresponding to the age and the stage of material development humanity has now reached, and which it must therefore inevitably accept.

A time will come, and is already coming, when the Christian principles of equality (the brotherhood of man, the community of property, and non-resistance to evil by violence) will appear just as natural and simple as the principles of family, social, or national life do now.

Neither an individual man nor humanity in general can go backwards in its development. The social, family, and State conception of life has been outlived, and it is necessary to go forward and assimilate the next and higher conception of life. And that is what is occurring now.

This movement is being accomplished in two ways: consciously by spiritual causes and unconsciously by material causes.

As it very rarely occurs that an individual changes his way of life solely at the promptings of reason, but for the most part continues his former way of life in spite of the new understanding and new aims indicated by reason, and changes it only when it has become quite opposed to his conscience and therefore intolerable to him; so, too, humanity, having learnt through its religious leaders a new meaning of life and discerned new aims towards which it must strive, continues for a long time (in the person of most of its representatives) to live on as before, and is brought to an acceptance of the new understanding of life only by finding it impossible to continue living the old life.

Despite the necessity for a change of life, recognized and expressed by religious leaders and admitted by the wisest men, the majority of men, despite their reverent attitude to those leaders—that is, despite their faith in their teaching—continue in their perplexed existence to be guided by the former view of life. It is as if the father of a family, knowing how he ought to live at his time of life, should through habit and frivolity continue his former childish amusements.

That is just what is taking place in the transition from one stage to another through which humanity is now passing. Humanity has outgrown its social and governmental stage and has entered upon a new one. It knows the doctrine that should be made the basis of life in this new period, but through inertia continues to keep to the old forms of life. From this discord between the new understanding of life and its practice, a series of contradictions and sufferings results which poisons our life and demands its alteration.

It is only necessary to compare the practice of life with its theory, to be horrified at the glaring antagonism between the conditions of our life and our consciousness.

Our whole life is in flagrant contradiction with all that we know and believe to be necessary and right. This contradiction prevails in everything: in all our economic, political, and international dealings. We seem to have forgotten what we know and to have put aside for the present what we believe in (and cannot but believe in for it is the sole basis of our life), and to do the very opposite of what our conscience and common sense require.

We are guided in economic, political, and international questions by principles that were suitable for men three or five thousand years ago but are directly opposed to our present consciousness and conditions of life.

It was well enough for a man of antiquity to live amid a division of mankind into masters and slaves when he believed that this distinction was from God and could not be otherwise. But is such a division possible in our day?

A man of the ancient world could believe he had a right to avail himself of the good things of this world at the expense of other people, causing them to suffer from generation to generation, for he believed that men were of different breeds, base and noble, of Japhetic or Hamitic race. Not only did the greatest sages of the world and teachers of humanity, Plato and Aristotle, justify the existence of slavery and demonstrate its lawfulness, but even three centuries ago when describing Utopia—an imaginary society of the future—men could not imagine it without slaves.

Men of ancient times and even of the Middle Ages firmly believed that men are not equal, that only the Persians, only the Greeks, only the Romans, or only the Franks, were real men. But we cannot believe that now. And those who now champion aristocracy and patriotism do not and cannot believe in what they say.

Even if we have never heard or read it clearly expressed and have never expressed it ourselves, we all—having imbibed this consciousness from the very air of Christianity—know and cannot help knowing with our whole heart this fundamental truth of the Christian teaching: that we are all sons of one Father no matter where we live or what language we speak; are all brothers, and are subject only to the law of love which the common Father has implanted in our hearts.

Whatever may be a man's way of thought and degree of education—be he an educated liberal of whatever shade, a philosopher of whatever camp, or a scientist or economist of whatever school; be he an uneducated or even a religious man of this or that creed—every man of our time knows that all men have the same right to life and to the benefits of this world, and that no one set of people is better or worse than another, but that all are equal. Everybody knows this beyond doubt with his whole being. Yet at the same time he sees around him a division of men into two castes: one labouring, oppressed, needy, and suffering; the other idle, oppressing, and living in luxury and pleasure. Not only does he see this, but he involuntarily takes part in one way or other in this division of men which his reason condemns, and he cannot but suffer from the consciousness of this contradiction and from his own participation in it.

Be he master or slave, a man of our time cannot but experience a constant and painful contradiction between his consciousness and the facts of life and the sufferings that result from it

The toiling masses, the immense majority of mankind, suffering from incessant, senseless, unrelieved toil and privation absorbing their whole life, suffer most of all from the consciousness of the glaring contradiction between what exists, and what ought to be according to everything professed by them and by those who have placed them in such a position and keep them there.

They know that they are in slavery and are perishing in want and darkness to serve the desires of the minority who keep them there. They know this and say it plainly. And this consciousness not only increases their sufferings but forms the essence of them.

A slave of antiquity believed himself to be a slave by nature, but our labourer while feeling himself to be a slave, knows that he ought not to be so and therefore experiences the torments of Tantalus, for ever desiring but not able to obtain what might and should be his. And the sufferings of the labouring classes which result from the contradiction between what is and what ought to be are increased tenfold by the envy and hatred engendered by that consciousness.

A labourer of our day, even though his work may be much lighter than that of a slave of ancient times, and even if he obtains an eight-hour working day and a wage of three dollars a day, will not cease to suffer, because—making things which he will not enjoy and working not for himself of his own will but by compulsion, at the will of luxury-loving and idle people in general and for the profit of a single rich man (the owner of the factory or workshop) in particular—

he knows that all this is going on in a world in which not only is it scientifically stated that work alone is wealth and that to exploit the labour of others is unjust, dishonest, and punishable by law, but in a world professing the teaching of Christ that we are all brothers, and that true dignity and merit lies only in serving one's neighbour and not in exploiting him.

He knows all this and cannot but suffer keenly from the crying contradiction between what is and what should be. 'According to all principles and by everything all men profess,' says a workman to himself, 'I ought to be free, equal to everyone else, and beloved. But I am a slave, humiliated and hated!' And he, too, is filled with hatred, and seeks a means of escape from his position, and to shake off the foe who is pressing him down and sit on him in turn.

People say: 'The workers are blameworthy for wanting to put themselves in the capitalists' place and to let the poor supplant the rich.' That is a mistake. The workers and the poor would be wrong if they wished to do so in a world in which it was admitted that slaves and masters, rich and poor, are appointed by God; but they are living in a world professing faith in the Gospel teaching, the first principle of which is that all alike are sons of God and therefore brothers and equals. And however men may try, it is impossible to conceal the fact that one of the first conditions of Christian life is love not in words but in deeds.

A man of the so-called educated classes lives in yet greater inconsistency and suffering. Every such man, if he believes in anything, believes if not in the brotherhood of man then in humanity, if not in humanity then in justice, or if not in justice then in science; and all the while he knows that his whole life rests on conditions directly contrary to all that—contrary to all the principles of Christianity, humanity, justice, and science alike.

He knows that all the habits in which he has been brought up and which he could not forgo without suffering, can only be gratified by the tormenting and often ruinous toil of oppressed workmen—that is, by the most flagrant and barefaced infringement of those principles of Christianity, humanity, justice, and even of science (I refer to the demands of political economy), which he professes. He professes the principles of brotherhood, humanity, justice, and science, and yet his daily life necessitates that oppression of the workers which he disapproves of, and his whole life is based on the fruits of this oppression, and not only does he live so, but his activities are directed to the maintenance of this state of things, directly contrary to everything he believes in.

We are all brothers, yet every morning a brother or a sister must empty my po. We are all brothers, but every morning I must use a looking-glass, smoke a cigar, consume sugar, &c. —all articles the production of which ruins the health of my brothers and sisters, who are my equals. Yet I require these articles and even demand them.[1] We are all brothers, but I live

[1] When Tolstoy wrote these lines in Russia in 1893, the tobacco factories, sugar refineries, and the coating of

by working in a Bank, or a house of business, or a shop, trying to get a higher price for the things my brothers need. We are all brothers, but I live by receiving a salary for arraigning, judging, and condemning the thief or prostitute whose existence my easy way of life tends to produce and whom I know ought not to be punished but reformed. We are all brothers, but I live on a salary for collecting taxes from needy workmen to be employed in buying luxuries for the idle and rich. We are all brothers, but I draw a stipend for preaching a pseudo-Christian faith in which I do not myself believe and which hinders men from understanding the truth. I take a stipend as a clergyman, or a bishop, for deceiving men about what is most important. We are all brothers, but I only give my educational, medical, or literary works to the poor for money. We are all brothers, but I receive a salary for preparing myself to commit murder. I learn to kill, or

---

looking-glasses with mercury, were carried on under conditions which ruined the health of many workers.

The business in cigars and hand-filled cigarettes was a very large one, partly a sweated home-industry, the workers in which suffered from lung trouble due to inhaling the fine tobacco dust, which also affected the workers in the large and crowded tobacco factories.

In the manufacture of looking-glasses mercury was then used and the workers suffered from its poisonous effects.

In the large and hot sugar refineries, the smell of decaying blood taken from abattoirs and used for refining the sugar, had the effect of making the workers sick, and disease was common among them.

In all these cases modern methods of manufacture are much better, and the three industries mentioned are not now necessarily unhealthy, but other industrial diseases, such as silicosis and asbestosis, are still a reproach to the social system of to-day.—A.M.

manufacture weapons and explosives, or build fortresses.

The whole life of our upper classes is a constant inconsistency, which is the more tormenting the more sensitive is a man's moral consciousness.

A man with a sensitive conscience cannot but suffer if he lives this life. The only way for him to avoid this suffering is to stifle his conscience, but even if such men succeed in stifling their conscience they cannot stifle fear. The insensitive people of the upper and dominating classes who have stifled their conscience, suffer from fear and hatred instead. And they cannot but suffer. They know of the hatred that exists towards them in the working classes and must inevitably exist. They know that the workers realize that they are deceived and exploited, and that they are beginning to organize themselves to throw off the oppression and revenge themselves on their oppressors. The upper classes see workers' unions, strikes, and May-day celebrations, and scent the trouble that threatens them, and the fear they experience poisons their lives and passes eventually into a feeling of self-defence and hatred. They know that if they weaken for a moment in the struggle with their oppressed slaves they will perish, because the slaves are exasperated and their exasperation increases every day that the oppression lasts. The oppressors cannot cease to oppress even if they wish to do so. They know that they will themselves perish directly they cease, or even weaken, in their oppression. So they act accordingly in spite of their seeming concern for the workers' welfare, for an eight-hour day, for regulation of the labour of women and children, for pensions and wages. All that is a deception, or a care that the slave should have strength to do his work. But the slave remains a slave, and the master, unable to live without him, is less than ever prepared to set him free.

In relation to the workers the ruling classes are in the position of a man who has felled his adversary, and is holding him down less because he does not wish to let him go than because he knows that if he did so even for a moment he would himself be struck down, for his adversary is enraged and has a knife in his hand. And so whether their conscience is sensitive or not, our wealthy classes (unlike the ancients who believed in their right to do so) cannot enjoy the good things they have filched from the poor. Their whole life and all their enjoyments are embittered by the stings of conscience or by fear.

Such is the economic contradiction. Still more striking is the political contradiction.

All men are brought up in the habit of obedience to the State laws first of all. The whole life of men of our time is defined by the State laws. A man is married and divorced, educates his children, and even (in many countries) professes his religion, in accordance with the law. What is this law which defines men's whole life? Do they believe in it? Do they regard it as good? Not at all!

In the majority of cases men of our time do not believe in the justice of that law; they despise it but yet they obey it. It was well for men of the

ncient world to fulfil their law. They believed,
eally believed, that their law (which was for the
nost part religious) was the one true law every-
ne ought to obey. But we? We know and can-
ot help knowing that our State law is not the
ne eternal law but is only one of many laws
nade by different governments—equally imper-
ect and frequently palpably false and unjust,
nd criticized from all sides in the press. It was
vell for a Jew to submit to his laws when he did
ot doubt that they were written by the finger
f God; or for a Roman when he thought they
vere inspired by the nymph Egeria; men might
ven observe the laws when they believed that
ne kings who made them were the anointed of
jod, or that the legislative assemblies wished to
ormulate the best laws and were able to do so.
ut we know how our laws are made. We have
ll been behind the scenes, we know that they
re the product of cupidity, trickery, and party
trife, and that there is not and cannot be real
istice in them. And so men of our time cannot
elieve that obedience to civil or State laws can
itisfy the demands of reason or of human nature.
Ien have long known that it is unreasonable to
bey a law the justice of which is doubtful, and
> they cannot but suffer in submitting to a law
hich they do not recognize as reasonable and
inding.

A man cannot but suffer when his whole life
defined beforehand by laws which he must
bey under threat of punishment, and in the
asonableness and justice of which he not only
pes not believe, but the injustice, cruelty, and

artificiality of which are often plainly apparen
to him. We recognize the uselessness of custom
and import duties, but have to pay them. W
recognize the uselessness of expenditure on th
maintenance of the Court and many grades o
the service; we acknowledge the evil influenc
of Church teachings, but we have to take par
in the maintenance of these institutions. We re
gard as cruel and shameful the punishments in
flicted by law, but have to participate in them
We regard as unjust and pernicious the presen
distribution of landed property, but we have to
submit to it. We do not acknowledge the necessity for armies or wars, but have to bear terrible
burdens to maintain them both.

But even this contradiction is nothing compared with what confronts us in international
relations and, under menaces threatening the
destruction of the sanity and even the existence
of the human race, now demands a solution.
That is the contradiction between Christian consciousness and war.

We are all Christian nations living the same
spiritual life, so that every good and fruitful
thought arising at one end of the world is at once
communicated to the whole of Christian humanity and evokes everywhere the same feelings of
joy and pride independently of nationality. We
love not only the thinkers, benefactors, poets, and
learned men of other nations, and are proud of
the heroism of Father Damien as if it were our
own, but we love ordinary men of other nationalities: French, German, American, English. We
not only respect their qualities but are simply

glad to meet them, and greet them with a happy smile; and not only cannot we regard war with them as an achievement, we cannot even think without horror that any disagreement could arise between them and us which would have to be decided by mutual murder. Yet we are all called on to take part in those murders, which must inevitably occur to-morrow if not to-day.

It was well for a Jew, a Greek, or a Roman, not only to defend the independence of his people by slaughter, but to subdue other nations by slaughter also, when he firmly believed that his people were the only true, good, fine people beloved of God, and all the rest were Philistines and barbarians. Men of the Middle Ages and at the end of the last and the beginning of the present [nineteenth] century could still believe these things. But now, however provoked we may be, we can no longer believe them, and this contradiction has become so intolerable in our time that we feel it impossible to go on living without solving it.

'We live in a time full of contradictions,' writes Count Komaróvsky, professor of International Law, in his learned treatise. 'The press of all countries expresses a general desire for peace and a general sense of its necessity for all countries. Representatives of the governments, private persons, and official organs, say the same thing, which is repeated in parliamentary speeches, diplomatic exchanges of opinion, and even in international treaties. Yet every year the governments increase their military strength, impose fresh taxes, raise loans, and leave as a legacy to future generations the obligation to pay for the senseless policy of the present. What a flagrant inconsistency between word and deed!

'Of course the governments justify these measures by pointing out the strictly defensive character of all these expenses and armaments, but it remains puzzling to every impartial spectator where an attack is to be expected from, since all the Great Powers unanimously pursue a purely defensive policy.

'In reality it looks as if each of these Powers was every moment expecting to be attacked by the others, and the consequence is universal distrust and superhuman efforts by each government to surpass the strength of the others. Such a rivalry itself increases the danger of war. The nations cannot for long endure the constant increase of armaments and sooner or later will prefer war to all the disadvantages of the present position and to the constant menace. Thus an insignificant cause may suffice to kindle the fire of a general war throughout Europe. It is an error to suppose that a crisis of this sort can heal the political and economic troubles that crush us. The experience of recent wars teaches us that every war only exasperates the enmity of nations, makes their military burdens more insupportable, and renders the political and economic condition of Europe more grievous and confused than ever.'

'Contemporary Europe keeps an active army of nine million men under arms,' says Enrico Ferri, 'and besides that fifteen million of reserves, expending on them four milliards of francs per year. Arming itself more and more it paralyses the sources of social and individual welfare and is like a man who condemns himself to waste away for lack of nutrition in order to provide himself with a gun—thus losing the strength to use the gun he is procuring and under the burden of which he will finally collapse.'

In a speech delivered in London before the Association for the Reform and Codification of the Law of Nations, on July 26th, 1887, Charles Booth said the same thing. After quoting the same figures of over nine millions on active service and fifteen millions in reserve, and the enormous expenditure by governments for the support of these armies and equipments, he goes on to say: 'But this forms only a small part of the actual cost, for besides the figures set down in the military budgets of the nations we must take into consideration the enormous loss to society resulting from the withdrawal of so many able-bodied men from productive industry, together with loss of interest on the prodigious capital invested in warlike preparations and appliances which are absolutely unproductive. One necessary result of this expenditure on war and preparations for war is the steady increase of national debts. The aggregate national debts of Europe, by far the larger proportion of which has been contracted for war purposes, amount to a total of £4,680,000,000, and these debts are increasing year by year.'

Komaróvsky says elsewhere: 'We are living in hard times. Everywhere we hear complaints of the slackness of business and industry and in general of the bad economic conditions: people point out the hard conditions of life of the labouring classes and the universal impoverishment of the masses. But in spite of this the governments in their endeavour to maintain their independence, reach the utmost limits of madness. Everywhere they invent new taxes and imposts, and the financial oppression of the nations knows no limits. If we look at the budgets of the European states for the last hundred years we shall first of all be struck by their progressive and rapid growth. How can we explain this extraordinary phenomenon which threatens us sooner or later with inevitable bankruptcy?

'It is incontestably due to the expenditure on the maintenance of an army which swallows one third and even one-half of the budgets of the European states. What is most lamentable in this connexion is that no end can be foreseen to such increase of the budgets and impoverishment of the masses. What is Socialism, if not a protest against this abnormal condition in which the greater part of the population of our part of the world finds itself?'

'We are ruining ourselves,' says Frédéric Passy (in a note read at the last Congress of Universal Peace in London in 1890) 'in preparing the means for taking part in the mad butcheries of the future, or to pay the interest of debt bequeathed to us by the mad and culpable butcheries of the past. We die of starvation in order to be able to kill one another.'

Speaking later of how the matter is regarded in France, he says: 'We believe that a hundred years after the Declaration of the Rights of Man and of the citizen, the time has come to recognize the rights of nations and to renounce at once and for ever all those undertakings based on force and fraud, which under the name of conquests are veritable crimes against humanity and which, whatever the vanity of monarchs and the pride of nations may think, weaken even those who seem to profit by them.'

'I am always very much surprised,' said Sir Wilfrid Lawson at the same Congress, 'at the way religion is carried on in this country. You send a boy to Sunday School, and you tell him: "Dear boy, you must love your enemies. If another boy strikes you, don't hit back but try to reform him by loving him." Well, the boy stays in the Sunday School till he is fourteen or fifteen and then his friends say: "Put him in the army." What will he do in the army? He certainly will not love his enemy; on the contrary, if he can only get at him he will run his bayonet through him. That is the nature of all religious teaching in this country, and I do not think it is a very good way of carrying out the precepts of religion. I think that if it is a good thing for the boy to love his enemy, it is good for the grown-up man to love his enemy, too.'

And further: 'There are in Europe twenty-eight million men under arms, to settle disputes by murdering one another, instead of by talking things over. That is the accepted way of settling disputes among Christian nations. This method is at the same time expensive, for according to statistics I have seen, the nations of Europe have since the year 1872 spent the almost incredible sum of £1,500,000,000 sterling on preparing to settle their disputes by killing one another. Now it seems to me that with that state of things one of two positions must be admitted: either that Christianity is a failure, or that those who profess to expound it have failed to do so properly.'

'Until our ironclads are withdrawn and our army disbanded, we are not entitled to call ourselves a Christian nation,' says Mr. F. Jowett-Wilson.

In a conversation that arose on the subject of the duty of Christian ministers to preach against war, G. D. Bartlett said among other things: 'If I at all understand the Scriptures, I say that men are only playing at Christianity as long as they ignore this question' (that is, say nothing about war). 'Yet in the course of a longish life I have heard our ministers preach on universal peace hardly half a dozen times. Some twenty years ago in a drawing-room, where there were forty or fifty people, I dared to moot the proposition that war is incompatible with Christianity. They looked upon me as an arrant fanatic. The idea that we could get on without war was regarded as unmitigated weakness and folly.'

The Roman Catholic Abbé Defourny expressed himself in the same spirit: 'One of the first precepts of the eternal law inscribed on the consciences of men is that which forbids taking the life of one's fellow-creature and the shedding of human blood without just cause and without being constrained by necessity. It is one of those laws which are most indelibly graven on the human heart. . . . But if it is a question of war, that is, of the shedding of human blood in torrents, men of the present day do not trouble themselves about a just cause. Those who take part in it do not think of asking themselves whether these innumerable murders are justified or not, that is, if the wars or what go by that name are just or iniquitous, legal or illegal, permissible or criminal, whether or not they violate the primordial law which prohibits homicide and murder without just cause. Their conscience is mute in this matter. For them war has ceased to be an act which has anything to do with morality. They have no other joy in the fatigues and perils of the camp than that of being victorious, and no other sadness than that of being vanquished. Do not tell me that "they serve their country". A long time ago a great genius uttered these words which have become proverbial: "Reject justice, and what are the empires but great societies of brigands?" And are not bands of brigands little empires? Brigands themselves have laws or conventions by which they are ruled. They, too, fight for the conquest of booty and for the honour of the band. . . .

'The principle of the institution'—he is speaking of the establishment of an International Tribunal—'is that the nations of Europe may cease to be nations of brigands and their armies bands of robbers—and one must add, not only robbers but slaves. Yes, the armies are simply gangs of slaves at the disposal of one or two commanders or ministers, who exercise a despotic control over them without any real responsibility as we very well know.

'What characterizes a slave is that he is a mere tool in the hands of his master, a chattel and not a man. That is just what soldiers, officers, and generals are, going to murder and be murdered at the arbitrary will of a ruler or rulers. . . . Thus military slavery is an actual fact, and it is the worst form of slavery, especially now when by means of compulsory service it lays its fetters on the necks of all the strong and capable men of a nation, making them instruments of murder, killers by profession, butchers of human flesh— for that is all they are taken and trained for.

'Two or three rulers meeting in their cabinets concert secretly without protocols or publicity, and therefore without responsibility, and send men to slaughter.'

'Protests against armaments burdensome to the people began before our time,' says Señor E. J. Moneta. 'Listen to what Montesquieu wrote in his day: "France" (now we may substitute "Europe") "will perish by her soldiers. A new malady is spreading in Europe, it has affected our princes and forced them to maintain an incredible number of troops. This malady is eruptive and therefore infectious so that as soon as one State increases its army all the others immediately do the same. So that nothing is gained by it but the common ruin.

'"Each Government maintains as many troops as it could possibly maintain were the nation threatened with destruction, and this state of tension of each against all is called 'peace'. And therefore Europe is so ruined that if private individuals were in the same condition as the

Governments of this part of the world the richest of them would have nothing to live on. We are poor though we possess the wealth and commerce of the whole world."

'That was written nearly a hundred and fifty years ago, yet it seems like a picture drawn from the world of to-day. The one thing changed is the form of government. In Montesquieu's time it was said that the cause of the maintenance of great armies lay in the despotic power of kings who waged war in the hope of augmenting their private property and gaining glory by conquest.

'It was then said: "Ah, if only nations could choose men who would have the right to refuse soldiers and money to their governments there would be an end of military policy." But yet now that there are representative governments almost throughout Europe, military expenditure and preparations for war have increased in frightful proportions.

'Evidently the folly of princes has passed on to the ruling classes. Now, war is no longer made because one king has been impolite to another king's mistress, as in Louis XIV's time, but exaggerating the natural and honourable feelings of patriotism and dignity and exciting the public opinion of one nation against another it comes at last to this, that it suffices to say (even if the news be not true) that the ambassador of one state was not received by the head of another state, to kindle the most awful and destructive war that has ever been known. Europe now keeps more soldiers under arms than in the time of the great Napoleonic wars. All citizens on our continent, with few exceptions, are obliged to spend some years in the barracks. Fortresses, arsenals, and ships are built, arms are constantly manufactured which in a very short time are replaced by fresh ones—because, sad to say, science, which should be directed to human welfare, contributes to the work of destruction, constantly devising fresh methods of killing the greatest possible number of men in the shortest possible time.

'And to maintain so great a number of soldiers and make such enormous preparations for murder, hundreds of millions are spent every year, sums that would suffice to educate the people and to carry out the most enormous works of public utility and make possible a peaceful solution of the social question.

'Europe then in this respect is still, in spite of all our scientific triumphs, in the same position as in the worst times of the barbarous Middle Ages. Everyone deplores this state of things which is neither peace nor war, and all would be glad to escape from it. The heads of the governments all declare that they desire peace and vie with one another in making most solemn protestations of peace. But the same day, or the next, they present to the legislative assembly a proposal for an increase of armaments and say that they take this precaution in order to make peace secure.

'But that is not the kind of peace we want. And the nations are not deceived by it. True peace is based on mutual confidence, while these enormous armaments show an evident and utter lack of such confidence if not a concealed hostility between the states. What should we say of a man who, wishing to show his friendly feelings for a neighbour, invited him to discuss some question with him and held a loaded revolver in his hand at the discussion?

'And it is this flagrant contradiction between the pacific professions of the governments and their warlike policy, which all good citizens desire to put an end to at any cost.'

People are astonished that sixty thousand suicides are committed in Europe every year, reckoning only the recognized and recorded cases and excluding Russia and Turkey; but they ought rather to be surprised that there are so few. Every man of our time, if we go deep enough into the contradiction between his conscience and his life, is in a most terrible condition. To say nothing of all the other contradictions between life and conscience which fill the life of a man of our day, the contrast between the permanently armed condition of Europe and its profession of Christianity is alone enough to drive any man to despair, to doubt the sanity of mankind, and to induce him to end his life in this irrational and brutal world. This contradiction—which is a quintessence of all the other contradictions—is so terrible that to live participating in it is only possible if one does not think of it and is able to forget it.

What! We are all Christians not merely professing love of one another but actually living one common life; our social existence beats with one common pulse; we aid one another, learn from one another, the bond of love draws us closer and closer together, producing mutual happiness, and this sympathy gives meaning to our life. Yet to-morrow some crazy ruler will utter some stupidity, another will answer in the same spirit, and then I, exposing myself to be murdered, must go to kill other people who have done me no harm and whom besides that I love. And this is not a remote contingency, it is the very thing we are all preparing for and which is not merely probable but unavoidable.

To recognize this clearly is enough to drive a man out of his senses or make him shoot himself. And that is just what occurs, and with especial frequency among military men. A man need only come to himself for a moment to be impelled to such a conclusion. And this is the only explanation of the terrible intensity with which people of our time strive to stupify themselves with wine, tobacco, opium, cards, newspaper-reading, travelling, and all kinds of spectacles and amusements. These things are done as serious and important occupations. They are indeed important affairs. If there were no external means of stupefaction half mankind would promptly shoot themselves, for to live in contradiction to one's reason is the most intolerable condition. And in that condition are all men of our day. All men of the modern world exist in a continual and flagrant antagonism between their consciences and their way of life, an antagonism which is expressed in economic as well as in political relations. But most striking of all is the contradiction between the Christian law of the brotherhood of man, which exists in men's consciousness, and the necessity (under which the general law of compulsory military service places everyone) of each of them being ready for enmity and murder—each of them being at one and the same time a Christian and a gladiator.

VI

The attitude of people of our world towards War.

THE contradiction between our life and our consciousness may be solved in two ways—by changing our life or by changing our consciousness. And no doubt seems possible as to the choice between the two.

A man may cease doing what he thinks wrong, but cannot cease to regard wrong as being wrong.

In the same way humanity in general may cease doing what it considers wrong but it cannot alter, or even check for any length of time, the progressive elucidation and expansion of the recognition of what is evil and therefore ought not to exist. And therefore it would seem that the choice between a change of life and a change of consciousness ought to be clear and beyond all doubt.

It would seem to be inevitable for the Christian humanity of our time to abandon the pagan forms of life which it condemns, and to reconstruct its social existence on the Christian principles it recognizes.

And that would be so were there no law of inertia, as invariable in the life of individuals and nations as in inanimate bodies, and which in man takes the form of the psychological principle so accurately expressed by the Gospel saying that men 'loved darkness rather than light, because their deeds were evil'. That principle shows itself in this, that the majority of men do not think in order to understand the truth but in order to persuade themselves that they already have the truth, and to assure themselves that the life they are living and that is pleasant and habitual to them, coincides with it.

Slavery was contrary to all the moral principles advocated by Plato and Aristotle, yet neither of them saw this, because to renounce slavery would have meant the collapse of the life they were living. And the same thing is now happening in our modern world.

The division of men into two castes, as well as the use of violence in politics and war, conflicts with all the moral principles by which our world lives, and yet the most advanced and educated men of to-day do not seem to see it.

The majority, if not all, of the cultured men of our day unconsciously try to maintain the old social conception of life which justifies their position, and to hide from themselves and others its insolvency, and above all the necessity of assimilating the Christian conception of life which involves the destruction of the whole structure of our present-day life. They try to maintain an order based on the social conception of life, but they do not believe in it themselves, for it has outlived its time and can no longer be believed.

All the literature of our time, philosophic, political, and artistic, is remarkable in this respect. What a wealth of ideas, form, and colour, what erudition and elegance, and what an absence of serious matter and dread of any definiteness of thought or its accurate expression! Equivocations, ambiguities, allegories, witticisms, and the widest abstract reasonings, but nothing simple, clear, and to the point—that is, dealing with the problem of life.

Not only do they write and talk about graceful frivolities, they write and talk about what is simply nasty and savage, and produce most refined dissertations turning men back to primitive savagery, to the principles not merely of pagan but even of animal life, already outlived five thousand years ago.

Nor could it be otherwise. Shying away from the Christian conception of life which destroys the system which for some people is merely habitual, and for others both habitual and advantageous, men cannot but revert to the pagan life-conception and the doctrines based upon it. Not only are patriotism and aristocratism preached to-day as they were two thousand years ago, but also the coarsest epicureanism and animalism. There is only this difference, that the men who preached it two thousand years ago believed what they preached, while now the preachers themselves do not believe in what they say. Nor can they believe, because what they preach no longer has any meaning. It is impossible to remain in the same place when the ground is moving; if you do not advance you must go back. And strange and terrible to say, the cultured people of our time, the leaders of thought, are in reality drawing society back by their subtle arguments not only to paganism but even to a state of primitive savagery.

This tendency on the part of the leading men of our time is nowhere so clearly seen as in their attitude to the phenomenon which expresses in concentrated form the utter insolvency of our social conception of life—their attitude towards war, universal armaments, and general compulsory service.

The indefiniteness if not the insincerity of the relation of educated people of our time to this phenomenon is astonishing. The relation of our educated society to it is threefold: some people regard it as an accidental occurrence that has arisen owing to Europe's peculiar political condition, and think it can be remedied by international diplomatic methods without alteration of the whole structure of life. Others regard it as something terrible and cruel, but inevitable and fatal like disease and death. Others again regard war with cool indifference as an inevitable phenomenon beneficent in its effects and therefore desirable.

These people look at the subject differently, but all alike speak of war as though it were something quite independent of the will of those who take part in it, and therefore do not even admit the natural question which presents itself to every plain man: 'How about me—must I take part in it?' In their view questions of this kind do not even exist, and everyone no matter how he regards war must slavishly submit to the demands of the governments.

The attitude of the first section of thinkers—those who see a means of escape from wars in international diplomatic measures, is very well expressed in the report of the last Peace Congress in London and in the articles and letters about war by prominent writers that appeared in No. 8 of the *Revue des Revues* for 1891. Here are the results: having collected letters and opinions from learned men all over the world, the Congress (which began with a service in a cathedral and finished up with a dinner and speeches) listened for five days to many discourses and arrived at the following resolutions:

'1. The Congress affirms its belief that the brotherhood of men involves as a necessary consequence a brotherhood of nations in which the interests of all are acknowledged to be identical.

'2. The Congress recognises the important influence that Christianity exercises on the moral and political progress of mankind, and earnestly urges upon ministers of the Gospel and other religious teachers the duty of setting forth the principles of Peace and Goodwill, and recommends that the third Sunday in December each year be set apart for that purpose.

'3. This Congress expresses its opinion that all teachers of history should call the attention of the young to the grave evils inflicted on mankind in all ages by war, and to the fact that such wars have been waged, as a rule, for most inadequate causes.

'4. The Congress protests against the use of military drill in connection with physical exercises at school, and suggests the formation of life-saving brigades rather than any of a quasi-military character; and it urges the desirability of impressing on the Board of Examiners who formulate the questions for examinations, the propriety of guiding the minds of children to the principles of Peace.

'5. The Congress holds that the doctrine of the universal rights of man requires that aboriginal and weaker races shall be guarded from injustice and fraud when brought into contact with civilised peoples, alike as to their territories, their liberties, and their property, and that they shall be shielded from the vices which are so prevalent among the so-called advanced races of men. It further expresses its conviction that there should be concerted action among the nations for the accomplishment of these ends. The Congress desires to express its hearty appreciation of the conclusions arrived at by the Anti-Slavery Conference recently held in Brussels for the amelioration of the condition of the peoples of Africa.

'6. The Congress believes that warlike prejudices and traditions which are still fostered in the various nationalities, and misrepresentations by leaders of public opinion in legislative assemblies or through the press, are often indirect causes of war, and that these evils should be counteracted by the publication of accurate statements and information that would tend to the removal of misunderstanding among nations, and it recommends the importance of considering the question of commencing an international newspaper with such a purpose.

'7. The Congress proposes to the Inter-Parliamentary Conference that the utmost support should be given to every project for the unification of weights and measures, coinage, tariff, postal and telegraphic arrangements, &c., which would assist in constituting a commercial, industrial, and scientific union of the peoples.

'8. The Congress, in view of the vast moral and social influence of woman, urges upon every woman to support the things that make for peace, as otherwise she incurs grave responsibility for the continuance of the systems of war and militarism.

'9. This Congress expresses the hope that the Financial Reform Association and other similar societies in Europe and America will unite in considering means of establishing equitable commercial relations between States by the reduction of import duties. The Congress feels that it can affirm that the whole of Europe desires Peace and awaits with impatience the suppression of armaments, which under the plea of defence become in their turn a danger by keeping alive mutual distrust, and are at the same time the cause of the general economic disturbance which stands in the way of satisfactorily settling the problems of labour and poverty, which ought to take precedence of all others.

'10. The Congress, recognising that general disarmament would be the best guarantee of Peace, and would lead to the solution of the questions that now divide States, expresses the wish that a Congress of representatives of all the States of Europe may be assembled as soon as possible to consider the means of effecting a gradual general disarmament.

'11. The Congress, in consideration of the fact that the timidity of a single Power might indefinitely delay the convocation of the above mentioned Congress, is of opinion that the government which should first dismiss any considerable number of soldiers would confer a signal benefit on Europe and mankind, because by public opinion it would oblige other governments to follow its example, and by the moral force of this accomplished fact would have increased rather than diminished the conditions of its national defence.

'12. This Congress, considering that the question of disarmament as of peace in general depends on public opinion, recommends the Peace Societies, as well as all friends of peace, to carry on an active propaganda among the people especially at the time of Parliamentary elections in order that the electors should give their votes to those candidates who are pledged to support Peace, Disarmament, and Arbitration.

'13. The Congress congratulates the friends of Peace on the resolution adopted by the International American Conference held at Washington in April last, which recommended that arbitration should be obligatory in all controversies whatever their origin, except only those which may imperil the independence of one of the nations involved.

'14. The Congress recommends this resolution to the attention of the statesmen of Europe and expresses the ardent desire that similar treaties may speedily be entered into between the other nations of the world.

'15. The Congress expresses its satisfaction at the adoption by the Spanish Senate, on June 16th last, of a project of law authorizing the government to negotiate general or special treaties of arbitration for the settlement of all disputes except those relating to the independence and internal government of the States affected: also at the adoption this month of resolutions to a like effect by the Norwegian Storthing and the Italian Chamber.

'16. The Congress resolves that a Committee be appointed to address communications to the principal political, religious, commercial, and labour and peace organizations in civilised countries, requesting them to send petitions to the governmental authorities praying that measures be taken for the formation of suitable tribunals for the adjudication of any international questions so as to avoid resort to war.

'17. Seeing (a) that the object pursued by all Peace Societies is the establishment of juridical order between nations, and (b) that neutralisation by international treaties constitutes a step towards this juridical state, and lessens the number of districts in which war can be carried on: the Congress recommends a larger extension of the rule of neutralisation and expresses the wish: (1) that all treaties which at present assure to a certain State the benefit of neutrality remain in force, or if necessary be amended in a manner extending neutralisation to the whole of the State, or by ordering the demolition of fortresses which constitute rather a peril than a guarantee for neutrality; (2) that new treaties, in harmony with the wishes of the population concerned, be concluded for the establishment of the neutralisation of other States.

'18. The Sub-Committee of the Congress recommends:

(1) That the next Peace Congress be held immediately before or immediately after the next meeting of the Inter-Parliamentary Conference and in the same town.

(2) That the question of an international Peace Emblem be postponed *sine die*.

(3) That the following resolutions be adopted:

(*a*) Resolved that we express our satisfaction at the official overtures of the Presbyterian Church in the United States of America, addressed to the highest representatives of each Church organisation in Christendom, inviting the same to unite in a general conference to promote the substitution of international arbitration for war.

(*b*) That this Congress, assembled in London from July 14th to 19th, desires to express its profound reverence for the memory of Aurelio Saffi, the great Italian jurist, a member of the Committee of the International League of Peace and Liberty.

(4) That the Memorial to the various Heads of Civilized States, adopted by this Congress and signed by the President, should as far as practicable be presented to each Government by an influential deputation.

(5) That the Organising Committee be em-

powered to make the needful verbal emendations in the papers and resolutions presented.

(6) That the following resolutions be adopted:

(*a*) A resolution of thanks to the Presidents of the various sittings of the Congress.

(*b*) A resolution of thanks to the chairmen, secretaries, and members of the Bureau of the Congress.

(*c*) A resolution of thanks to the conveners and members of the sectional Committees.

(*d*) A resolution of thanks to the Rev. Canon Scott Holland, Doctors Reuen and Thomas, and the Rev. J. Morgan Gibbon for their pulpit addresses before the Congress, and also to the Authorities of St. Paul's Cathedral, the City Temple, and Stamford Hill Congregational Church for the use of those buildings for public services.

(*e*) A letter of thanks to Her Majesty for permission to visit Windsor Castle.

(*f*) And also a resolution of thanks to the Lord Mayor and Lady Mayoress, to Mr. Passmore Edwards, and other friends, who have extended their hospitality to the members of the Congress.

'19. This Congress places on record a heartfelt expression of gratitude to Almighty God for the remarkable harmony and concord which has characterised the meetings of the Assembly, in which so many men and women of various nations, creeds, tongues, and races have gathered in closest co-operation, and for the conclusion of the labours of the Congress; and expresses its firm and unshaken belief in the ultimate triumph of the cause of Peace and of the principles advocated at these meetings.'

The fundamental idea of the Congress is the necessity, in the first place, of diffusing by all means among all people the conviction that war is very unprofitable and that peace is a great blessing, and secondly of rousing governments to a sense of the superiority of international arbitration over war and the consequent advantage and necessity of disarmament. To attain the first aim the Congress has recourse to the teachers of history, to women, and to the clergy, and advises the latter to preach on the evil of war and the blessing of peace every third Sunday in December. To attain the second aim the Congress addresses itself to the governments, proposing that they should disband their armies and substitute arbitration for war.

To preach to men the evil of war and the blessing of peace! But the evil of war and the blessing of peace has been so well known to men that from the beginning of history the best of greetings has been, 'Peace be with you'—so why preach about it?

The evil of war and the blessing of peace was recognized thousands of years ago not only by Christians but also by Pagans. So that the advice to the ministers of the Gospel to preach on the evil of war and the blessing of peace every third Sunday in December is quite superfluous.

A Christian cannot but preach that always, every day of his life. And if Christians and the preachers of Christianity do not do so there must be reasons for it. And until these are removed no advice will be effective. Still less effective will be advice to the governments to disband their armies and substitute international tribunals and boards of arbitration. Governments, too, know very well the difficulty and burdensomeness of raising and maintaining armies, and if in spite of this they continue to collect and maintain armies with terrible strain and effort they evidently cannot do otherwise and the advice of the Congress cannot change it at all. But the learned gentlemen do not want to see this, and always hope to find some political combination by which the governments that make the wars shall be induced to shackle themselves.

'Is it possible to get rid of war?' asks a learned man in the *Revue des Revues*. 'All agree that if it breaks out in Europe its consequences will resemble the great incursions of the barbarians. The existence of whole nations will be at stake, and so the war will be bloody, desperate, and cruel.

'This consideration, together with the terrible implements of destruction at the disposal of modern science, postpones the declaration of war and is maintaining the present temporary order of things which might continue for an indefinite time were it not for the terrible expense that burdens the European nations and threatens to bring on them calamities as great as those of war itself.

'Struck by that reflection men of the various countries have sought means of preventing or at least mitigating the consequences of the terrible slaughter that menaces us.

'Such are the questions presented by the Congress shortly to be held in Rome and the publication of a pamphlet on disarmament.

'Unfortunately it is beyond doubt that with the present organisation of the majority of European states, isolated from one another and guided by conflicting interests, the complete suppression of war is a dream with which it would be dangerous to console ourselves. Still, the adoption by all countries of some more reasonable laws and regulations concerning these international duels might considerably diminish the horrors of war.

'Equally Utopian is it to reckon on disarmament, which is rendered almost impossible by considerations of a national character intelligible to our readers.' (This no doubt means that France cannot disarm till it has had its revenge.) 'Public opinion is not prepared to adopt proposals of disarmament, and international relations moreover are not such as to make their acceptance possible. Disarmament demanded by one nation of another would be equivalent to a declaration of war.

'It must however be admitted that an exchange of views between the nations interested would, to a certain extent, help towards an international understanding and render possible a considerable reduction of the military expenditure which is crushing the European nations to the hindrance of a solution of social problems, and the necessity of this is felt by every nation individually, threatened as they are by civil war as a result of their efforts to safeguard themselves against foreign war.

'We may at least propose the reduction of the enormous expenditure maintained for the purpose of enabling us to seize an opponent's territory in twenty-four hours and fight a decisive battle within a week of the declaration of war!

'We ought to act so that States could not fall on one another, and in twenty-four hours seize the possessions of others.'

This practical idea was expressed by Maxime du Camp, and the conclusion of his article expresses the same idea.

M. du Camp's propositions are these:

'1. A diplomatic congress should meet every year.

'2. No war should be declared in less than two months after the incident provoking it. (The difficulty here would be to determine just which incident provoked the war, as whenever war is declared there are many such incidents, and it would be necessary to decide from which of them the two months were to be reckoned.)

'3. War must not be declared before it has been submitted to a plebiscite of the nations preparing for it.

'4. Hostilities must not begin till a month after the declaration of war.'

'War must not be declared . . . Hostilities must not begin', &c. Who will see to it that war must not be declared? Who will see to it that people must do this and that? Who will force the Powers to await the appointed time? All the others! But all the others are just such Powers whom it is necessary to restrain to keep within their bounds and to compel. Who

will compel? And how? Public opinion! But
if there is a public opinion able to oblige a Power
to wait for a given time, that same public opinion
can oblige the Power not to begin the war at all

But in reply to this it is said that there may be
such a balance of power, *pondération des forces*, that
the Powers will restrain one another. This has
been tried and is being tried even now. Such
was the Holy Alliance, and such is the League
of Peace, &c.

But it is said, what if they all agree? If all
agree there will be no war, and there will be no
need for supreme tribunals or Courts of Arbitra
tion.

'Arbitration will replace war. Disputes will be
decided by a Court of Arbitration. The Ala
bama claims were decided by a Court of Arbitra
tion, and it was proposed that the question of
the Caroline Islands should be submitted to the
Pope's arbitration. Switzerland, Belgium, Den
mark, and Holland, have all submitted an
nouncements that they prefer decisions by a
Court of Arbitration to war.'

Probably Monaco has also announced the
same desire. The pity is that Germany, Russia,
Austria, and France, do not as yet make such
declarations.

It is wonderful how men can deceive them
selves when they want to!

Governments decide their disagreements by
arbitration and disband their armies! The dif
ferences between Russia and Poland, England
and Ireland, Austria and the Czechs, Turkey and
the Slav States, and the differences between

France and Germany to be settled by voluntary agreement!

This is the same as to suggest to merchants and bankers that they should sell nothing for more than they gave for it and should undertake the distribution of wealth without profit, and should therefore abolish money as it would then become unnecessary.

But since commerce and banking business consists entirely of selling dearer than buying, this proposal would be equivalent to an invitation to suppress themselves. And it is the same with governments. To suggest to governments not to have recourse to violence but to decide their differences in accord with equity, is a proposal to abolish themselves as governments, and no government can agree to that.

Learned men form societies (there are many such—more than a hundred of them) and gather at Congresses (such as those recently held in Paris and London and shortly to be held in Rome), deliver addresses, dine, make speeches, publish journals devoted to that cause, and continually prove that the tension of the nations compelled to maintain millions of troops has reached its utmost limits, that this armament contradicts the nature, the aims, and the wishes of all the peoples, but that if many papers are written and many words are spoken, all men can be induced to agree and there will then be no conflicting interests and consequently no war.

When I was a little boy they told me that to catch a bird I must sprinkle salt on its tail. I took some salt and went to the birds, but soon convinced myself that if I could put salt on their tails I could also catch them, and realized that I had been made fun of.

And that is what those who read books and articles on arbitration and disarmament should understand.

If one can put salt on a bird's tail it means that it does not fly and there is no need to catch it. But if a bird has wings and does not wish to be caught it will not let you put salt on its tail, for it is the nature of a bird to fly. And just in the same way it is the nature of a government not to submit to others but to exact submission from them, and a government is a government only in so far as it is able to exact submission and not itself to submit, and so it always strives to that end and will never voluntarily abandon its power. An army gives power to a government, and so governments will never give up the army and its use in war.

The mistake is this: learned jurists, deceiving themselves and others, assert in their books that government is not (what it is) a set of men who do violence to others, but that it is (as science makes it out to be) the representative of the aggregate of citizens. The learned jurists have so long assured others of this that they have come to believe it themselves, and often seriously suppose that governments can be bound by considerations of justice. But history—from Caesar to Napoleon (the First and the Third) as well as Bismarck—shows that government has always in its essence been a force that infringes justice. It cannot be otherwise. Justice can have no binding force for a man, or for men, who keep deluded men trained to do violence (soldiers) and by means of them rule others. And so the governments cannot agree to diminish the number of these trained men who constitute their whole power and significance.

Such is the attitude of some learned men to the contradiction which burdens our world, and such are their methods of solving it. Tell these learned men that the question is solely one of the personal relation of each man to the moral and religious question now facing us all—the question of the rightness or wrongness of taking part in military service—and they will merely shrug their shoulders and will not deign to answer or pay any attention to you. For them the solution of the question consists in reading addresses, writing books, choosing presidents, vice-presidents, and secretaries, and meeting and talking first in one city and then in another. This speechifying and writing will in their opinion cause the governments to cease to draft soldiers (on whom their whole existence depends) and they will listen to the speeches and disband their soldiers, leaving themselves defenceless not only against neighbouring States but against their own subjects—as if brigands, having tied up some unarmed men in order to plunder them, should immediately set them free on hearing speeches about the pain occasioned by the cords.

But there are people who believe in this, busy themselves with peace-congresses, deliver addresses, and write pamphlets. The governments of course express their sympathy and make a show of encouraging them, just as they pretend to support temperance societies while they are living to a great extent on the intemperance of the people; and just as they pretend to promote education though their strength is based on ignorance; and just as they pretend to support constitutional liberty whereas their strength rests only on the absence of freedom; and just as they pretend to be concerned about the betterment of the condition of the workers whereas their existence depends on the oppression of the labouring classes; and just as they pretend to support Christianity though the Christian teaching would destroy all governments.

To be able to do this they have long ago worked out temperance schemes that cannot check drunkenness, made provision for education whereby ignorance is not infringed but even increased, evolved methods of aiding freedom and constitutionalism which are no hindrance to despotism, and methods of protecting the workers which do not free them from slavery; they have elaborated a Christianity, too, which does not destroy governments but maintains them.

To all this they have now added their concern for peace. The sovereigns who travel about with their ministers, deciding of their own accord the question whether to begin the slaughter of millions this year or next—these sovereigns know very well that all these talks about peace will not prevent their sending millions to the slaughter when it occurs to them to do so. They even listen with satisfaction to these peace talks, encourage them, and take part in them.

All this, far from being detrimental, is even of service to the governments, in that it diverts people's attention from the essential question—whether each man should or should not go to military service when called upon to do so.

'Peace will soon be arranged thanks to the leagues, congresses, and booklets and pamphlets. Meanwhile go, put on your uniform and prepare to oppress and torment yourselves for our benefit!' say the governments. And the learned organizers of the congresses and writers of the articles fully agree with this.

That is one relation to the question—a very advantageous one for the governments and therefore one encouraged by the wisest of them.

Another relation to war is the tragic one of those who assert that the contradiction between man's desire for and love of peace and the inevitability of war is terrible, but that such is the fate of man. These people, for the most part sensitive and gifted men, see and realize the whole horror and irrationality and cruelty of war, but through some strange twist of mind do not see, and do not seek, any way out of this position, but as it were chafe their wound by feasting their eyes on the desperate situation of humanity.

Here is a noteworthy example of this attitude towards war provided by the remarkable French writer, Guy de Maupassant. Watching from his yacht some French soldiers drilling and firing, the following reflections occurred to him:

'War! When I but think of this word a sense of horror and bewilderment overcomes me, as though I were being told of sorcery, of the

Inquisition, of something remote, long past, repulsive, horrible and unnatural.

'When cannibalism is spoken of we smile disdainfully, feeling our superiority to those savages. But who are the savages—the real savages? Those who kill in order to eat the vanquished or those who kill for the sake of killing—merely to kill?

'Those chasseurs riding and shooting in that field at the word of command are all foredoomed like a flock of sheep which the butcher drives along the road. They will fall on some plain with their heads cloven or their breasts pierced by a bullet. And they are all young men who might work, produce, and be useful.

'Their old fathers and poor mothers—who for twenty years have loved and adored them as only mothers can adore—will learn in six months or a year that their son, their fine boy reared with so much labour, so much expense, and so much love, has been torn to pieces by a shell, or trampled down and crushed by a charge of cavalry, and has been thrown into a hole like some dead dog. And the mother will ask why they have killed her dear boy—her hope, her pride, and her life. No one knows. But why?

'War! Fighting! Slaughter! Killing men! Yes in our time, with our enlightenment, our science, and our philosophy, there exist special establishments—schools—in which people are taught to kill, to kill from a distance, to kill perfectly, to kill many people at once, to kill poor pitiable men who are guilty of nothing and have

amilies to support, and to kill them without any
pretence of law.

'And what is most astonishing is that
he people do not rise against their governments, either in the monarchies or the
republics. The most astonishing thing
s that society as a whole is not revolted
by the very word "war".

'Yes, apparently we shall always live according
o the old odious customs, the criminal supersti-
ion and bloodthirsty ideas of our forefathers.
Evidently as we were beasts, beasts we shall remain, guided merely by our instincts.

'No one but Victor Hugo could with impunity
have raised his cry for deliverance and the truth!

'To-day force is called "violence", and men
condemn it. They bring war to trial. Civilization
at the plea of the human race arraigns warfare
and presents an act of accusation against all conquerors and leaders of armies.

'Men begin to understand that the magnitude
of a crime cannot be its extenuation; that if
murder is a crime, the murder of many cannot
be a justification; that if robbery is shameful, the
seizure of a nation's territory cannot be glorious.

'Let us proclaim this indubitable truth—let us
dishonour war!

'Vain is the wrath and the poet's indignation,'
continues Maupassant. 'War is more honoured
and respected than ever.

'A skilled proficient in this business, that murderer of genius, von Moltke, once replied to some
peace delegates in the following terrible words:

'"War is sacred, it is instituted by God, it is

one of the divine laws of the world, it upholds i men all the great and noble sentiments—honou. self-sacrifice, virtue and courage. It is War alon that saves men from falling into the grosses materialism."

'To assemble four hundred thousand men i herds, to march night and day without rest, wit no time to think, read, or study, without bein of the least use to anybody, wallowing in filth sleeping in the mud, living like animals in con tinual stupefaction, sacking towns, burning vil lages, ruining the whole population, and ther meeting similar masses of human flesh and fallin upon them, shedding rivers of blood, strewin the fields with mangled bodies mixed with muc and blood; losing arms and legs and havin brains blown out for no benefit to anyone anc dying somewhere on a field while your ol parents and your wife and children are perishin of hunger—that is called saving men from fallin into the grossest materialism!

'Soldiers are the greatest scourge in the world We struggle with nature and ignorance to bette our wretched existence if but a little. Learnec men devote their whole lives to seeking means o aiding and alleviating the lot of their fellows Working arduously and adding one discovery tc another they open new fields to human intel ligence, extend the realm of science, add new knowledge every day, and day by day increase the welfare, comfort, and strength of the people.

'Then comes war. In six months the generals destroy all that labour, patience, and genius has accomplished in twenty years. And that is called being saved from falling into the grossest materialism!

'We have seen war! We have seen how men again become beasts, how like maniacs they kill for pleasure, from fear, from bravado, and for praise. We have seen how, freed from the restraint of law and right, they have shot innocent men overtaken on the high road and who seemed suspicious only because they were frightened. We have seen how they killed dogs chained to their masters' doors, just to try out their new revolvers. We have seen how they shot cows lying in a field, without any reason, just for the fun of shooting. And that is called saving men from falling into the grossest materialism!

'To invade a country, to cut to pieces a man who defends his own home, because he wears a blouse and has no military cap on his head, to burn the houses of the poor who have nothing to eat, to smash and steal the furniture, to drink the wine found in the cellars, to violate women in the streets, to burn millions of francs' worth of gunpowder, and leave ruin and disease in one's track—that is called not falling into the grossest materialism!

'What have they done—these military men? What are their great deeds? None. What have they invented? Cannon and guns. That is all.

'What has Greece left us? Her literature and her marbles. Was she great because she conquered, or because she created? Was it the Persian invasion that hindered Greece from sinking into gross materialism? Did the invasion of the barbarians save and regenerate Rome? Did

Napoleon I carry forward the great intellectual movement begun by the philosophers at the end of the eighteenth century?

'No! If governments assume the right to send populations to death, can it be strange if the people sometimes assume the right to send governments to death?

'They defend themselves and they are right. No one has the right to rule over others. That ought to be done only for the benefit of those who are governed. And it is as much the duty of any one who governs to avoid war as it is the duty of the captain of a vessel to avoid shipwreck.

'When a captain is responsible for the wreck of his vessel he is tried, and if he is found guilty of negligence or even of incapacity he is condemned and punished.

'Why should the governments not be put on trial after every declaration of war? If only the people understood that, if they judged the rulers who lead them to the slaughter, if they refused to be needlessly slaughtered, if they turned their arms against those who gave them—if that were ever to happen, war would die.

'But this will never be!' (*Sur l'eau.*)

The author sees all the horror of war. He sees that it is caused by governments deceiving people and obliging them to go to kill and be killed without receiving any advantage. He sees, too, that the men who compose the armies could turn their arms against the governments and call them to account. But he thinks that that will never happen, and that there is therefore no escape from the present position. He thinks war is terrible but inevitable, that the government's demand that men should go as soldiers is as inevitable as death, and that since governments will always make that demand war will always exist.

So writes this gifted and sincere author, who is endowed with the power of penetration to the inmost core of a subject, which is the essential endowment of an artist. He brings before us all the cruelty of the contradiction between man's moral sense and his actions, and, without solving the contradiction, seems to acknowledge that this contradiction must continue and that in it lies the poetic tragedy of life.

Another no less gifted writer (Edouard Rod) describes the cruelty and insanity of the present state of things yet more vividly, to the same end of admitting its tragedy without suggesting or foreseeing any issue from it.

'What is the good of undertaking or doing anything?' he says. 'And how are we to love people in these troublous times when the morrow is a continual menace? . . . All that we have begun, all our ripening thoughts, all the things we proposed to do, all the little good we might accomplish—will it not all be swept away by the storm that is brewing? . . .

'Everywhere the earth trembles under our feet, and the gathering storm-clouds will not spare us.

'If it were only the revolution that we have to fear! As I cannot imagine a society more abominably arranged than ours, I do not fear that which will replace it. If the change were worse for me, I should be consoled by the reflection that the executioners of to-day were the victims of yesterday, and should endure the worse while awaiting something better. But it is not that remote peril which frightens me. I see another danger nearer at hand and more cruel because it has no justification and because it can lead to no good. Every day we weigh the chances of war for the morrow. And every day that eventuality becomes more unavoidable.

'Imagination refuses to believe in the possibility of the catastrophe which is coming at the end of our century as the result of all the progress of our era, and yet we must become accustomed to facing it.

'For twenty years past all the resources of science have been exhausted in the invention of engines of destruction, and soon a few cannon shots will suffice to destroy a whole army.[1] It is not as formerly when a few thousands of poor fellows were armed for whose blood money had to be paid; now whole nations are armed to the last man, preparing to cut one another's throats.

'They are first robbed of their time (by conscripting them as soldiers) that they may more surely be robbed of their lives later. To prepare them for the butchery their hatred is inflamed by assuring them that they are hated. And kindly men of good will are caught by that trap, and then in obedience to a senseless command crowds

[1] This book was published a year ago, in 1893, and this year, 1894, dozens of fresh instruments of destruction have been devised, as well as a new kind of smokeless powder.—L.T.

But nothing like the poison-gas and bacteriological bombs now available in 1935 were then even thought of.—A.M.

of peaceful citizens fling themselves on one another with the ferocity of wild beasts. And all
his because of God knows what ridiculous
frontier incident or Colonial trade interest.

'And they will go like sheep to the slaughter
not knowing where they are going, but knowing
only that they are leaving their wives and that
their children will go hungry. They will go full
of misgivings, yet intoxicated with loud-sounding
words trumpeted into their ears. And they
will go unprotestingly, submissively and
resignedly, not knowing and not understanding that the strength is theirs, and
that the power would be in their hands if
only they wished it so—that if only they
knew how to agree, and could agree, they
might establish sound sense and brotherhood instead of the barbarous trickery
of the diplomatists.

'But they will go so deluded that they will
believe slaughter and murder to be a duty and
will ask the benediction of God on their bloodthirsty desires. And they will go trampling down
the fields they themselves have sown, burning
towns they themselves have built—will go gladly
with festive music and cries of jubilation. And
their sons will erect statues to those who best
knew how to send their fathers to the slaughter.

'The destiny of a whole generation depends on
the hour at which some ill-fated politician gives
the signal at which they will fling themselves on
one another.

'We know that the best of us will be mown
down, and our works destroyed in the germ.

'We know this, and tremble with rage, but we can do nothing. We are caught in the toils of officialdom and papers with official headings which it is too difficult to tear up.

'We are enslaved by the laws we have made for our own protection and which now oppress us.

'We have ceased to be men and have become the tools of that autocratic abstraction we call the State, which enslaves each of us in the name of the will of all who taken individually would desire the very opposite of what they are forced to do. . . .

'And it would be well if the matter concerned only one generation. But it is much more than that. All these mercenary shouters, these ambitious statesmen availing themselves of the evil passions of the populace, all these imbeciles who are deluded by high-sounding phrases, have so inflamed national hatred that on to-morrow's war the fate of the whole race will be staked. The vanquished will have to disappear, and a new Europe will be formed on bases so unjust, so brutal, so bloody and dishonoured by such crimes, that it cannot but be worse than that of to-day—more iniquitous, barbarous, and more violent.

'One feels that a terrible hopelessness hangs over each of us. We rush about in a blind alley with guns pointing at us from all sides. We work like sailors on a sinking ship. Our pleasures are those of a man condemned to death who is allowed to choose his favourite dish a quarter of an hour before his execution. Terror paralyses our thoughts and the highest exercise of our intelligence is to calculate, by studying the obscure speeches of ministers and the words of monarchs, and by ruminating on the utterances of diplomatists with which the newspapers are filled, when we shall be killed—this year or next.

'A time can hardly be found in history when life was more insecure and more crushed by oppressive horror.' (*Le sens de la vie.*)

Here it is pointed out that the force is in the hands of those who themselves destroy one another, in the hands of the individuals who make up the masses, it is pointed out that the source of the evil is the State. It would seem evident that the contradiction between our consciousness and our life has reached a limit beyond which it cannot go, and beyond which a solution must be found.

But the author does not think so. He sees in this the tragedy of human life and having shown all the horror of the position, concludes that man must spend his life in this horror.

Such is the second relation of men to war, acknowledging it as something fateful and tragic.

A third relation is that of those who have lost all conscience, and therefore all common sense and human feeling.

To that category belongs von Moltke, whose opinion was quoted by Maupassant, and the majority of military men who have been educated in this cruel superstition, who live by it, and are therefore often naïvely convinced that war is not only unavoidable, but necessary and even beneficial. And that view is shared by some civilians, so-called educated and cultivated people.

This, for instance, is what the celebrated academician Camille Doucet writes in that same number of the *Revue des Revues* in reply to the editor's inquiry as to his views on war:

'Dear Sir,

'When you ask the least belligerent of Academicians whether he is a partisan of war, his reply is given in advance. Alas, sir, you yourself speak of the pacific ideal inspiring our generous compatriots at the present time, as a dream.

'Ever since I was born I have heard a great many good people protest against this frightful custom of international butchery which all admit and deplore. But how is it to be remedied? Many efforts have been made to abolish duelling, and that would seem to be so easy! But not at all! All that has been done towards that noble object amounts to nothing, nor will it ever amount to more.

'Whatever may be said at the various Peace Congresses against war and against duelling will be in vain. Above all arbitrations, all arrangements, and all legislations, there will always be man's honour, which has always demanded the duel, and the interests of nations which will always demand war.

'I wish none the less, from the depths of my heart, that the Congress of International Peace may succeed at last in its very honourable and difficult enterprise.

'Accept the assurance, &c.
'Camille Doucet.'

The upshot of this is that personal honour demands that men should fight, and the interests of nations require them to ruin and exterminate each other. As for efforts to abolish war, they call for nothing but a smile.

The opinion of another famous man, Jules Claretie, is of a similar kind. He writes:

'Dear Sir,

'For a man of sense there can be but one opinion about peace and war.

'Humanity is created to live, to live free to perfect and ameliorate its fate by peaceful labour. The general harmony which the International Peace Congress seeks and preaches is but a dream perhaps, but at least it is the fairest of all dreams. Man is always looking towards the Promised Land where the harvest will ripen without danger of being torn up by shells or crushed by cannon wheels. . . . But. . . . Ah! But—

'Since the world is not ruled by philosophers and philanthropists it is well for our soldiers to guard our frontiers and homes, and their arms, skilfully used, are perhaps the surest guarantee of the peace we all love so warmly.

'Peace is a gift only granted to the strong and resolute.

'Accept the assurance, &c.

'J. Claretie.'

Which means that there is no harm in talking of what no one intends to do, and what ought on no account to be done; but when it comes to practice we must fight.

And now here is the view lately expressed

about war by the most popular novelist in
Europe—Émile Zola:

'I regard war as a fatal necessity, which appears inevitable from its close connexion with
human nature and the whole constitution of the
world. I should wish that war might be put off
for as long as possible. Nevertheless the moment
will come when we shall be forced to fight. I am
considering it for the moment from the broad
standpoint of humanity and make no reference
to our disagreement with Germany, which is but
an insignificant incident in the history of mankind. I say that war is necessary and beneficial
since it is one of the conditions of existence for
humanity. War confronts us everywhere, not
only between different peoples but also in family
and private life. It appears as one of the principal elements of progress and every step forward
that humanity has yet made has been attended
by bloodshed.

'People have talked, and still talk, about disarmament, but disarmament is impossible, and
even if it were possible we ought to reject it. Only
an armed nation is powerful and great. I am
convinced that a general disarmament throughout the world would involve something like a
moral decadence which would show itself in
general debility and would hinder the progress
of humanity. The warlike nations have always
been strong and flourishing. The art of war has
led to the development of all the other arts.
History bears witness to it. So in Athens and in
Rome, commerce, industry, and literature never
attained such a development as when those cities

were masters of the then known world by force of arms. To take an example from more recent times, we may recall the age of Louis XIV. The wars of the Grand Monarque not only did not hinder the progress of the arts and sciences, but on the contrary even seem to have promoted and favoured their development.'

So war is useful!

But best of all in that direction is the opinion of the most gifted of the writers of that tendency, the Academician de Vogüé. This is what he writes in an article on the Military Section of the Paris Exhibition of 1889:

'On the Esplanade des Invalides amid the exotic and colonial buildings a structure of more severe style stands out in the picturesque bazaar. All these representatives of the inhabitants of the earth group themselves round the Palace of War. What a splendid occasion for humanitarian rhetoric which does not miss the opportunity to bewail this juxtaposition, affirming that "this will kill that" (*ceci tuera cela*),[1] and that a union of the nations through science and work will overcome the warlike instincts. Let us leave them to cherish the chimera of a golden age which, could it be realized, would soon become an age of mud. All history teaches us that "this" was made by "that", that blood is needed to promote and to cement the union of nations. Natural science has in our day confirmed the mysterious law revealed to Joseph de Maistre by the intuition of his genius and the consideration of primitive dogmas, that

[1] Words from Victor Hugo's *Notre Dame de Paris* with reference to the art of printing that was to kill architecture.—L.T.

the world redeems its hereditary fall by sacrifice.
Science shows us how the world advances to perfection by struggle and violent selection. Both
are statements of one and the same law expressed
in different forms. The statement is no doubt
unpleasant, but the laws of the world are not
made for our pleasure, they are made for our
progress. Let us then enter this necessary and
inevitable Palace of War. We shall there be able
to observe how the most tenacious of our instincts, without losing any of its vigour, is transformed and adapted to the varying exigencies of
historic epochs.'

This idea—that the proof of the necessity of
war is, in his opinion, to be found expressed in
different ways by two great thinkers (de Maistre
and Darwin)—pleases de Vogüé so much that he
repeats it. He writes to the editor of the *Revue
des Revues*:

'Dear Sir,

'You ask my opinion as to the success of the
International Peace Congress. Like Darwin I
believe that violent struggle is a law of nature
which governs all creatures. Like Joseph de
Maistre I hold that this is a divine law: two
different ways of describing one and the same
thing. If, contrary to expectation, some portion
of human society—say even the whole of the
civilized Western world—were to succeed in sus-
pending the operation of that law, other more
primitive nations would apply it against us. In
those nations nature would prevail over human
reason. And they would be successful, because

the full assurance of peace—I do not say "peace" itself, but "full assurance of peace"—would produce a corruption and decadence more destructive for mankind than the worst of wars. I believe that with war—the criminal law of humanity—we must do as with all our criminal laws, that is, mitigate it, apply it as seldom as possible, and use every effort to make it unnecessary. But all history teaches us that we must not abolish those laws so long as two men are left on earth with bread, money, and a woman, between them.

'I should be very glad if the Congress proved me to be in error. But I doubt if it can prove history, the law of nature, and God, to be in error also.

'Accept the assurance, &c.

'E. M. de Vogüé.'

This means that history, the nature of man, and God show us that as long as there are two men, bread, money, and a woman, there will be war. That is to say that no progress will lead men to rise above a savage conception of life which regards no sharing of bread, money (money is particularly good in this context), and a woman, without fighting. It is strange that people should assemble at Congresses and make speeches about how to catch birds by putting salt on their tails—though they must know that that cannot be done. It is astonishing that men like Maupassant, Rod, and many others, see clearly all the horror of war, all the inconsistency that results from the fact that men do not do what is necessary and advantageous for them and ought to be done, and bewail the tragedy of life without seeing that the whole tragedy would cease immediately if only men would cease needless discussions and begin to refrain from doing painful, unpleasant, and repulsive things. Those people are amazing, but these who—like de Vogüé and others professing the doctrine of evolution—declare war to be not merely inevitable but beneficial and therefore desirable—these people are terrible and horrible in their moral perversion. The others at least profess to love good and hate evil, but these men simply declare that good and evil do not exist.

All talk of the possibility of establishing peace instead of everlasting war, is pernicious sentimentality and chatter. There is a law of evolution by which it appears that I must live and act badly. What is to be done? I am an educated man and know the law of evolution, and therefore I will act badly. *Entrons au palais de la guerre* (Let us enter the palace of war.) There is a law of evolution, and so there is nothing good or bad and we must live solely for our personal life leaving the rest to the law of evolution. This is the last word of refined civilization, and of that obscuration of consciousness with which the cultured classes of our time are occupied.

The desire of the educated classes to retain somehow their cherished ideas and the life founded upon them, has now reached its utmost limit. They lie and delude themselves and other in most refined ways to obscure and deaden their conscience.

Instead of changing their way of life to

correspond with consciousness, they try by all means to stifle and deaden consciousness. But the light shineth even in the darkness, and so it is beginning to shine at the present time.

VII

The Meaning of Compulsory Military Service.

EDUCATED people of the upper classes try to stifle the consciousness—which is becoming clearer and clearer all the time—of the necessity of changing the existing social system. But life continues to move in the same direction, becoming more and more complex, increasing the contradictions and sufferings, and bringing men to the extreme limits beyond which matters cannot go. And universal military conscription is such a final limit of inconsistency.

People generally think that military conscription and the ever-increasing arming connected with it, as well as the consequent increase among all nations of taxation and national debts, is an accidental phenomenon due to some particular political condition of Europe which may be removed by certain political considerations without changing the inner structure of our lives.

That is quite erroneous. General military service is the final limit and the exposure, at a certain stage of material development, of the inner contradiction that has crept into the social conception of life.

As we have seen, the social understanding of life consists in the transfer of the aim of life from the individual to groups and their continuance: to the tribe, family, race, or State.

According to the social conception of life it is understood that since the meaning of life is contained in a group of individuals, the individuals themselves voluntarily sacrifice their interests for those of the group. So it has been and still is in certain groups: in the family, tribe, race, or even in a patriarchal State. As a result of habit transmitted by education and confirmed by religious suggestion, individuals of their own free will mingle their interests with those of the group and sacrifice themselves for the general welfare.

But the more complex these groups became and the larger they grew, and (especially) the more often people became amalgamated into a State by conquest, the more frequently did individuals try to attain their own aims to the public detriment, and the more frequently did the government have to employ its power—that is, to use violence—to check these insubordinate individuals.

Defenders of the social understanding of life usually try to confuse the conception of power (violence) with the idea of moral influence, but the two are quite incongruous.

The effect of moral influence on a man is to change his desires and make them correspond with what is demanded of him. A man controlled by moral influence acts in accord with his wishes. But power—as that word is generally understood—is a means of forcing a man to act contrary to his desires. A man who submits to power does not do as he chooses, but as he is compelled to do by that power. To compel a man to act contrary to his desires instead of as he wishes to, can only be done by physical force or by the threat of it—that is, by depriving him of freedom, by blows, mutilation, or by easily executed threats of such punishments. This has always been, and still is, the nature of power.

In spite of the unceasing efforts of those in power to conceal this and to attribute some other significance to it, power has always meant for man the chain with which he can be bound and dragged along, or the whip with which he can be flogged, or the knife or axe with which his hand, foot, nose, ears, or head can be cut off—and the use of these means or at least the threat of them. So it was under Nero and Genghis Khan, and so it is now under the most liberal governments in the American and French republics. If men submit to power it is only because they fear that those measures will be applied to them in case of non-submission. All governmental demands for tax-payments, all performance of state business, all submission to punishment (banishments, fines, and the like) to which people seem to submit voluntarily, have physical violence or the threats of it always at their base.

The basis of power is physical violence. And the possibility of inflicting physical violence on people is afforded chiefly by an organization of armed men trained to act in unison in submission to one will. Such bands of armed men submissive to a single will are what constitute an army. An army has always been and still is the basis of power. Power always lies in the hands of those who control the army, and every ruler—from the Roman Caesar to the Russian and German Emperors—is concerned first of all about the army and courts popularity in the army, knowing that if the army is with him, power is in his hands.

And this very formation and augmentation of the army essential for the maintenance of power, has brought into the social understanding of life the principle that is decomposing it.

The object of power and its justification lies in the restraint of those who would wish to attain their own interests to the detriment of society. But however the power has been obtained— whether by the formation of a new army, by inheritance, or by election—those who possess power by means of an army differ in no way from other men, and are therefore no more disposed than others to subordinate their own interests to the interests of society. On the contrary, having in their hands the power to do so, they are more disposed than others to subordinate public interests to their own. Whatever men have devised to deprive those in power of the possibility of subjecting the general interest to their own, or for entrusting power only to infallible people, no means of attaining these objects has yet been discovered.

All the methods employed: Divine consecration, selection, succession, voting and elections, assemblies, parliaments and senates — have proved and still prove ineffective. Everybody knows that not one of these methods has succeeded either in preventing the misuse of power or in entrusting it only to immaculate men. Everybody knows on the contrary that men possessed of power—be they emperors, ministers, chiefs of police, or policemen—are for that very reason more apt to become demoralized (that is, to subordinate the public interest to their own) than men who do not possess power, nor can it be otherwise.

The social conception of life could justify itself only as long as men voluntarily sacrificed their own interests to the interests of the community. But as soon as there were individuals who did not voluntarily do so and power was needed to restrain them, there crept into the social life-conception and the structure of life founded on it the disintegrating principle of violence, that is, coercion exerted by some people against others.

For power (of some men over others) to attain its object of restraining those who for personal aims strive to override the public interest, it ought to be placed only in the hands of the impeccable, as it is supposed to be among the Chinese and as it was supposed to be in the Middle Ages and is even now supposed to be by those who believe in the beneficent effect of consecration. Only under that condition would the social structure be justified.

But as that is not so, but on the contrary those who possess power are for that very reason never holy, a social organization based on power has no justification.

If there ever was a time when, owing to a low standard of morality and the general tendency of individuals to violence, the existence of a government which restrained such violence was advantageous (that is, governmental violence was less than the violence inflicted by individuals on one another), this advantage could evidently not be permanent. As the tendency of individuals towards violence decreased and manners became less harsh, while those in authority became more demoralized owing to the lack of restraint upon them, the advantages of government diminished more and more. The whole history of the last two thousand years consists of this alteration of relations between the moral development of the masses and the demoralization of governments.

In its simplest form this is what happened. Men lived in families, tribes, and races, at enmity with one another—doing violence, plundering, and killing one another. Such violence occurred on a large and on a small scale—individual fighting with individual, tribe with tribe, family with family, race with race, and nation with nation. Larger and more powerful communities conquered the weaker, and the larger and stronger they became the less internal violence there was within the group, and the more secure did the continuence of the group appear to be.

Members of a family or tribe uniting into one community were less hostile among themselves, and families and tribes do not die like individuals, but continue their existence. Between the members of one State subject to one authority, strife appeared still weaker and the life of the State still more secure.

These unions into larger and larger aggregates

were not the result of a conscious recognition that such unions were more advantageous (as is told in the legend of the invitation to the Varángians to rule over the Russian land) but were produced on the one hand by natural growth and on the other by struggle and conquest.

When the conquest was accomplished the power of the conqueror really put an end to civil wars, and so the social conception of life received a justification. But that justification was only temporary. Internal dissensions disappeared only to the extent of the pressure exerted by the authorities over those formerly in conflict. The violence of the internal feud suppressed by the authority, reappeared within that authority itself. The men constituting that authority—not being different from other men and having power in their hands—were often ready to sacrifice the general welfare for the sake of their own personal advantage, but with this difference—that their violence was not moderated by any opposition from the oppressed, and they were consequently exposed to all the demoralizing influence of power. Thus the evil of violence, passing into the hands of a government, always tends to increase and become greater than that which it is supposed to destroy, while it becomes less and less necessary as the tendency to use violence among the individual members of society progressively diminishes.

Governmental power, even if it suppresses private violence, always introduces fresh forms of violence into the lives of men and does this increasingly as it continues and grows stronger.

So that though governmental violence (being expressed not in strife but in submission) is less noticeable than individual violence committed by members of a society against one another, it nevertheless exists and generally to a greater degree than in former times.

And it could not be otherwise, since apart from the fact that the possession of power corrupts men, the interest or even the unconscious tendency of those employing force will always be to reduce those subject to violence to the greatest degree of weakness, for the weaker the oppressed the less effort is needed to keep them in subjection.

And so the oppression always grows to the farthest limit to which it can go without killing the goose that lays the golden eggs. If that goose does not lay, as in the case of the American Indians, the Fijians,[1] and the Negroes, it is killed despite the sincere protests of philanthropists.

The best confirmation of this is supplied by the condition of the working classes of our epoch who are in reality in the position of a conquered people.

Despite all the pretended efforts of the upper classes to ameliorate the position of the workers the working classes of the present day are held down by an inflexible iron law by which they ge

---

[1] Readers may have noticed that in Chapter XVIII of *What Then Must We Do?* Tolstóy accepts as reliable an account Professor Yánzhul had given of the annexation of the Fiji Islands and the subsequent fate of its inhabitants. That account constitutes an indictment of our Colonial method which, I imagine, would hardly be accepted as reliable by those more fully acquainted with the historical facts.—A.M.

only what is barely necessary, so that, while retaining strength to work, they are constantly
impelled to labour for their employers—that is,
for their conquerors.

So it has always been. In proportion to the
duration and strengthening of authority its advantages for those under subjection have always
decreased and its disadvantages increased.

So it has been and is, independently of the
forms of government under which nations have
lived. The difference is only this, that under a
despotic form of government the power is concentrated in the hands of a small number of
oppressors and the violence is cruder, while
in constitutional monarchies, and republics like
France and America, the power is divided among
a larger number of oppressors and is expressed
less crudely. But the fact of violence, under
which the advantages of a government are exceeded by its disadvantages, and the process by
which it reduces the oppressed to the farthest
limits of enfeeblement to which they can be reduced with advantage to the oppressors, remains
the same everywhere.

Such has been and still is the condition of all
who are subject to violence, but hitherto they
have not recognized the fact. In most cases they
have naïvely believed that governments exist for
their benefit, that without the State they would
perish, that the very idea of people living without
governments is sacrilegious and must not even be
expressed—that it is the doctrine of anarchism,
with which for some reason is associated the conception of all sorts of horrors.

People have believed, as though it were something fully proven and therefore needing no proof, that since up to the present all nations have developed in a governmental form, that form must always be a necessary condition of humanity's development.

So it has gone on for hundreds and thousands of years, and governments—that is men in power —have tried, and now try still harder, to maintain that mistake in people's minds.

So it was under the Roman emperors, and so it is now. Despite the fact that the sense of the uselessness and even the harmfulness of governmental violence penetrates men's consciousness more and more, things might have gone on so for ever, had it not been necessary for governments to increase their armies in order to maintain their power.

It is generally supposed that governments increase their armies only to defend the state from other governments—oblivious of the fact that armies are needed by governments first of all for their own defence against their oppressed and enslaved subjects.

This was always necessary, and became increasingly necessary with the diffusion of education among the masses and with the increase of intercourse between nationalities, and it has become particularly necessary now in face of communism, socialism, anarchism, and the labour movement generally. And governments feel this to be so, and increase their chief strength—the disciplined armies.[1]

[1] The fact that abuses of power exist in America despite the

Recently in the German Reichstag in reply to a question as to why money was needed for an increase of the salary of non-commissioned officers, the German Chancellor frankly declared that reliable non-commissioned officers were necessary for the struggle against socialism. Caprivi only said aloud what everybody knows, though it is usually carefully hidden from the people. What he said explains just why Swiss and Scottish guards were hired by the French kings and by the Popes, and why in Russia recruits are carefully distributed so that regiments stationed in the central districts are made up of men from the border provinces, while the regiments in those provinces are made up of recruits from central Russia. The meaning of Caprivi's speech, put into plain language, is that funds were needed not for defence against foreign foes but to bribe non-commissioned officers to be ready to act against the oppressed labouring classes.

Caprivi accidentally uttered what everyone well knows or feels if he does not know, namely, that the existing order of life is what it is not because it is natural or because people wish it, but because it is maintained by governmental

small size of its army, not only does not refute but confirms this proposition. In America there is a smaller army than in other countries, and that is why there is nowhere less oppression of the working classes and nowhere does the abolition of the abuses of the government, and of government itself, seem so near. But of late, as the solidarity of the workers gains in strength, demands for an increase of the army are heard more and more frequently, though no attack from abroad threatens America. The upper, ruling, classes, knowing that fifty thousand troops will soon be insufficient, and no longer relying on Pinkerton's army, feel that only an increase of the army can safeguard their position.—L.T.

violence—by the armies with their bought non-commissioned officers, officers, and generals.

If a labouring man has no land and cannot avail himself of the natural right of every man to obtain subsistence for himself and his family from the land, that is not because the people wish it to be so, but because some people (the land-owners) have been given the right of allowing or refusing admission to the land. And this un-natural state of things is maintained by the army. If the immense wealth produced by the workers is regarded as belonging not to them but to some exceptional people, if the power to collect taxes from toil and to use that money as they think fit is left to certain people, if workmen's strikes are repressed while coalitions of capitalists are en-couraged, if it is left to certain people to decide the form of civil and religious instruction and the education of children, and if certain people have the right to formulate the laws which all must obey, and to dispose of the lives and property of human beings—all this occurs not because the people wish it and because it naturally should be so, but because the governments and the ruling classes desire it for their own benefit and establish it by means of physical violence.

Every man who does not already know this will find it out at his first attempt to disobey or alter the existing order of things. And so all the governments and ruling classes need armies chiefly to maintain this order, which has not grown from the needs of the people but is often plainly detrimental to them and advantageous only to the government and the ruling classes.

Armies are needed by all governments first of all to keep their subjects in submission and to exploit their labour. But a government is not alone; besides it there is another government exploiting its subjects by violence in the same way and always ready to rob its neighbour of the toil of its already enslaved subjects. And so every government needs an army not only for use at home but also to protect its booty from neighbouring brigands. Every government is thus involuntarily led to increase its army in rivalry with others, and the increase of armies is infectious as Montesquieu already remarked a hundred and fifty years ago.

Every increase of the army in a State, though directed mainly against its own subjects, is dangerous to its neighbours also and evokes an increase in their forces.

The armies have reached their present millions not merely because the governments were threatened by their neighbours, but chiefly from the necessity of subduing any attempt at revolt on the part of their own subjects. The increase of armies arises simultaneously from two causes, each of which reciprocally evokes the other: armies are needed both against enemies at home and to maintain the position of a State against its neighbours. The one conditions the other. The despotism of a government at home increases in proportion to the increase and strengthening of its army and its external successes; and the aggressiveness of governments grows in proportion to the increase of their internal despotism.

As a result of this the European governments,

constantly increasing their armies against one
another, arrived at the unavoidable necessity of
universal military service, since that was the way
to get the greatest number of soldiers in time of
war with the least expense. Germany was the
first to hit on this plan, and as soon as one State
had adopted it the others had to do the same.
And as soon as this happened all citizens were
under arms to maintain all the injustices inflicted
on them, and all the citizens became their own
oppressors.

Universal military service was an inevitable
logical necessity, but at the same time it is the
final expression of the contradiction inherent in
the social conception of life which began when
violence became necessary for its maintenance.
With universal military service this contradiction
becomes obvious. Indeed the significance of the
social conception of life consists in this, that man
recognizing the cruelty of the struggle between
individuals and the transitoriness of personal life
transfers the aim of his life to an aggregate of
human beings.

But the result of general military conscription
is that men, after making every sacrifice to release
themselves from the cruelty of strife and the
transitoriness of their personal lives, are again
called on to bear all the dangers from which they
thought they had freed themselves, and besides
that the State itself—for whose sake they had
renounced their personal interests—is again sub
jected to the same risk of destruction which in
previous times threatened the individual himself

Governments were to free men from the cruelty

of individual strife, to give them security in the permanence of a group life. But instead of that they subject men to the same necessity of strife, merely substituting strife with other States for strife with individual neighbours, and the danger of destruction both for the individual and for the State they leave just as it was.

The establishment of general military service resembles what happens when a man wants to prop up a rotten house. The walls bend inwards and he inserts supports, the roof sags down and other supports are put up, boards give way between the supports and still more supports are erected. And it comes to this, that though the supports hold the house up they render it impossible to live in it.

It is the same with universal military service. It destroys all the benefits of the social order of life which it was employed to maintain.

The advantages of the social form of life consist in the security given to property and labour, and in associated action for the general welfare, but general military service destroys all this.

The taxes collected from the people for war preparations consume most of the production of labour that the army was intended to protect.

The tearing away of all men from their customary course of life infringes the possibility of labour itself.

The threat of war, ready to break out at any moment, renders all reforms of social life vain and useless.

In former times if a man were told that if he did not acknowledge the authority of the State he would be exposed to the attacks of evil men—domestic and foreign enemies—and would have to fight them himself and be liable to be murdered, and that therefore it was to his advantage to put up with some hardships to secure himself from such evils, he might well believe it, since the sacrifices he made for the State were only private sacrifices and afforded him the hope of a tranquil existence in a permanent State. But now when the sacrifices have been increased tenfold, and not only this, but the promised advantages have disappeared, it is natural for anyone to conclude that submission to authority is quite useless.

But the fatal significance of universal military service as a manifestation of the contradiction inherent in the social conception of life is not seen in that alone. The chief manifestation of this contradiction is contained in the fact that under universal military service every citizen, on being made a soldier, becomes a prop of the governmental organization and a participant in all the things the government does—the rightness of which he does not admit.

Governments assert that armies are chiefly needed for external defence, but that is not true. They are needed first of all against their own subjects, and every man who performs military service involuntarily becomes an accomplice in all the acts of violence the government inflicts on its subjects.

To convince oneself of this one need only remember what things are done in every State in the name of order and public welfare and the execution of which always falls on the army. All he civil outbreaks arising from dynastic or party reasons, all the executions following such disturbances, all the repressions of insurrection, and the employment of military forces to disperse meetings and suppress strikes, all forcible collection of taxes, all unjust distribution of land, all the restrictions on labour—are either carried out directly by the army or by the police supported by the army. Anyone performing military service shares responsibility for all these things, about which he is in some cases dubious and which in many cases are directly opposed to his conscience. People are unwilling to be ejected from land they have cultivated for generations, or are unwilling to disperse when ordered to do so by the authorities, or they are unwilling to pay taxes demanded of them, or to acknowledge laws as binding on them when they have had no hand in making them, or to be deprived of their nationality—and I, fulfilling my military service, have to go and beat these men. Having to take part in these things how can I avoid asking myself whether they are right, and whether I ought to assist in carrying them out?

Universal military service is the last stage of violence that governments need for the maintenance of the whole structure, and it is the extreme limit to which submission on the part of their subjects can go. It is the keystone of the arch holding up the edifice, and its removal would bring down the whole building.

The time has come when the ever-increasing misuse of their power by governments, and their mutual strife, has led to their demanding such sacrifices (not only material but also moral) from their subjects, that every man has to reflect and ask himself: Can I make these sacrifices? And for whose sake must I make them? The sacrifices are demanded of me for the sake of the State. For its sake I am required to renounce all that can be precious to man: tranquillity, family, security, and human dignity. What is this State for whose sake such terrible sacrifices are demanded? And why is it so absolutely necessary?

'The State', they tell us, 'is absolutely necessary, first because without it we should have no protection from violence and the attack of evil men; secondly because except for the State we should be savages and have no religious, educational, commercial, or cultural institutions, or other public establishments, or roads of communication, and thirdly because without a State we should be subject to enslavement by neighbouring States.'

'Without a State', we are told, 'we should also be subject to violence and attacks from evil men in our own country.'

But who are these evil men in our midst from whose attacks and violence we are preserved by the State and its army? If three or four centuries ago, when men boasted of their warlike prowess and weapons and when it was considered heroic to kill people, such evil men really did exist; there are none now, for nobody to-day carries arms and all profess humane principles and sympathy for their neighbours, and wish—as we all do— for the possibility of a quiet and peaceful life. So that these special users of violence from whom the State must defend us are no longer there. And if by people from whom the State saves us we are to understand those who commit crimes, we know that they are not different creatures— like beasts of prey among sheep—but are just such people as ourselves and no more naturally inclined to commit crimes than are those against whom they commit them.

We know that threats and violence cannot decrease the number of such people, but that that can only be done by a change of surroundings and by moral influence. So that the justification of State violence on the ground of the defence it affords from those who do violence, if it had any foundation three or four centuries ago, has none now. At present the contrary may rather be said: namely, that the action of the governments with their cruel methods of punishment so far behind the general level of morality, with prisons, exiles, penal servitude, and guillotines, tends to brutalize the people rather than to humanize them, and consequently to increase rather than diminish the number of those who have resort to violence.

'Except for the State', we are also told, 'we should have no religion, education, culture, or means of communication, and so on. Without the State people would be unable to organize the social institutions we all need.' But that argument could only have had a basis some centuries ago.

If there was a time when people were so disunited and the means of association and interchange of ideas were so little developed that they could not co-operate and agree together in any common affair, commercial, economic, or educational, without the State as a centre, such isolation no longer exists. The widely developed means of intercourse and interchange of ideas have made men quite able to form societies, associations, corporations, and learned, economic and political institutions; and for men of our time in most cases the State hinders rather than helps the attainment of these objects.

Since the end of the eighteenth century almost every step in advance made by humanity has been hindered rather than encouraged by governments. Such was the case with the abolition of corporal punishment, of torture, and of slavery, as well as the attainment of liberty of the press and the right of public meeting. In our day the governments, far from being an assistance, are actually a hindrance to the activities by which men work out for themselves new forms of life. The solution of the problems relating to labour and land, as well as political and religious questions, are not merely not helped but are directly hindered by the governmental authorities.

'Without governments nations would be enslaved by their neighbours.'

It is scarcely necessary to refute that last argument. It contains its own refutation.

The government with its army, we are told, is necessary to defend us from neighbouring states. But that is what all governments say of one another, and yet everyone knows that all the European nations profess the same principles of liberty and brotherhood and so are in no need of defence against themselves. And if they mean defence against barbarians, then a one-thousandth part of the troops now under arms would suffice. So it turns out that what actually happens is quite contrary to what is asserted. The power of the State, far from saving us from attacks by our neighbours, is on the contrary itself the cause of the danger of such attacks.

So that every man whose compulsory service forces him to reflect on the meaning of the State, for whose sake the sacrifice of his peace, his security, and sometimes his very life, is demanded, must see that there is now no justification for such a sacrifice.

But apart from the theoretical point of view, every man must see that the sacrifices demanded by the State have no justification even from a practical standpoint. No man, weighing all the burdens laid on him by the State, can help seeing that compliance with its demands and acceptance of military service is in most cases less advantageous for him personally than refusal.

If most men choose to submit rather than refuse, that is not the result of a sober balancing of advantages and disadvantages, but because they are induced to submit by the hypnotization to which they are subjected. When submitting they simply yield to the demands of the State without having to reflect or make any effort of will. Resistance calls for independent thought, and an effort of will of which not everyone is capable. But apart from the moral significance of compliance or non-compliance, and considering it merely from the standpoint of personal advantage, refusal will generally be more advantageous for a man than submission.

Whoever I may be, whether I belong to the well-to-do dominating class or to the oppressed labouring class, the disadvantages of non-submission are less and its advantages greater than those of submission.

If I belong to the dominating minority, the disadvantages of non-submission to the government's demands will consist in my being tried for refusing to comply and at best I shall be discharged, or (as is done with the Mennonites in Russia) I shall be obliged to serve my time at some non-military work. At worst I shall be condemned to exile or imprisonment for two or three years (I speak from examples that have occurred in Russia), or possibly for an even longer term, or to death—though the probability of such a penalty is very small.

These are the disadvantages of non-submission. But the disadvantages of submission are these: at best I shall escape being sent to kill people and shall escape being myself exposed to great danger of being maimed or killed, and shall merely be enrolled into military slavery. I shall be dressed up like a clown and domineered over by every man above me in rank from a corporal to a field-marshal. I shall be forced to contort my body as they please, and after being kept from one to five years I shall for another ten years have to hold myself in readiness to be called up at any moment to go through all these things again. In the worst case I shall, in addition to all these conditions of slavery, be sent to war, where

I shall be compelled to kill men of other nations who have done me no harm, and where I may be maimed or killed or (as happened in Sevastopol and as happens in every war) sent to certain death, or (most terrible of all) be sent against my own countrymen and compelled to kill my brothers for dynastic or other reasons quite alien to me.

Such are the comparative disadvantages.

The comparative advantages of submission and non-submission are these:

For a man who submits, the advantages are that after enduring all the humiliations and performing all the cruelties demanded of him, he may if he is not killed receive a gaudy red or gold decoration for his clown's dress, and may even, if he is very fortunate, obtain command of hundreds of thousands of men as brutalized as himself, and be called field-marshal and receive a lot of money.

The advantages of a man who refuses are the reservation of his human dignity, the respect of good men, and above all the certainty that he is doing God's work and so is indubitably doing good to his fellow-man.

Such are the advantages and disadvantages on both sides for a man of the oppressing, wealthy classes. For a man of the poor working class the advantages and disadvantages are the same, but with an important addition to the disadvantages. The disadvantages for a man of the labouring classes who has not refused military service comprise also this, that by entering the military service he by his participation and apparent approval, confirms the oppression to which he himself is subject.

But the question of the necessity of the State or its abolition will not be decided by reflection as to how necessary or unnecessary to men is the government they are called on to support by their participation in military service, still less will it be decided by consideration of the advantages and disadvantages to each man of his submission or rejection of State demands. That question will be decided irrevocably and beyond appeal by the religious consciousness or conscience of every man who in connexion with universal military service has involuntarily to face the question of whether the State is to continue to exist or not.

VIII

Inevitability of acceptance by men of our world of the Christian doctrine of not resisting by violence him that is evil.

PEOPLE often say that if Christianity were true it should have been accepted by everybody as soon as it appeared, and ought then to have changed men's lives for the better. But this is like saying that if a seed is fertile it ought to sprout, flower, and yield fruit immediately.

The Christian teaching is not a legal system which being forcibly introduced can immediately change men's lives. Christianity is a new and higher conception of life. And a new life-conception cannot be imposed, it can only be freely assimilated by men.

And the free assimilation of a conception of life can only come about in two ways: in a spiritual (internal) or an experimental (external) way.

Some people—a small minority—immediately divine the truth of a teaching by some prophetic instinct, abandon themselves to it, and fulfil its precepts. The majority are only brought to a recognition of the truth and the necessity of its assimilation, by a long course of error, experience, and suffering.

And by that external, experimental method the mass of Christian humanity has now reached the necessity of accepting the teaching.

We sometimes wonder what need there was for that perversion of Christianity which is now the greatest obstacle to the acceptance of its true meaning. Yet this very perversion, which has brought men to their present state, was a necessary condition of rendering the majority of men able to receive it in its true significance.

If Christianity had been presented to men in its true, unperverted form, it would not have been accepted by the majority, to whom it would have remained as alien as it now is to the nations of Asia. But having accepted it in a perverted form the nations came under its slow but certain influence, and by a long experimental path of error and consequent suffering have been brought to the necessity of accepting it in its true meaning.

The perversion of Christianity, and its acceptance in its perverted form by the majority of men, was as necessary as it is that a seed should remain in the earth for a time after it has been sown.

Christianity is a teaching of the truth and at the same time a prophecy.

Eighteen hundred years ago Christianity revealed to men how they ought to live, and at the same time foretold what human life would become if they refused to live by it and continued to live by their previous principles, and what it would become if they accepted the Christian teaching and lived in accord with it.

Laying down in the Sermon on the Mount the principles that should guide men's lives, Christ said: 'Every one therefore which heareth these words of mine, and doeth them, shall be likened unto a wise man, which built his house upon the rock: and the rain descended, and the floods came, and the winds blew, and beat upon that house; and it fell not: for it was founded upon the rock. And every one that heareth these words of mine, and doeth them not, shall be likened unto a foolish man, which built his house upon the sand: and the rain descended, and the floods came, and the winds blew, and smote upon that house; and it fell: and great was the fall thereof.' (Matt. vii. 24–27.)

And now after eighteen centuries the prophecy is being fulfilled. Not having followed Christ's teaching in general and its application to social life in non-resistance to evil, men have involuntarily come to that inevitability of destruction foretold by Christ for those who fail to follow his teaching.

Men often think that the question of resistance or non-resistance to evil by violence is an invented question which can be avoided.

But it is a question life presents to all men, and it demands an answer from every thinking man. From the time the Christian doctrine was preached, that question has stood for men in their social life as the question stands for a traveller when he reaches a fork in the road he has been following. He must go on. But he cannot say: 'I will not think about it but will go on just as I did before.' There was only one road formerly, now there are two, and it is impossible to go on as before. He must choose one or the other.

In just the same way, since Christ's teaching has become known to men it is impossible to say: 'I will live as I did before, without deciding the question of resistance or non-resistance to evil by violence.' With every new struggle that arises it is inevitably necessary to decide whether or no to resist by violence what I regard as evil.

The question of resistance or non-resistance by violence to him that is evil, arose when the first fight occurred between men; for every fight is nothing but a resistance by violence to what each of the combatants considers to be evil. But before Christ men did not see that resistance by violence to what each considers evil (simply because he considers evil what the other considers good) is only one way of deciding the struggle, and that another way consists in not resisting evil by violence at all.

Before Christ's teaching it seemed to men that the only way of deciding the struggle was by violent resistance to evil, and they acted accordingly, each trying meanwhile to convince himself and others that what he considered evil was actually and absolutely evil.

And from the earliest times men have tried for this purpose to devise definitions of evil which should be obligatory for everyone. And these definitions of evil were expressed sometimes in laws supposed to have been supernaturally revealed, and sometimes in decisions of men or of assemblies of men, who attributed infallibility to themselves. Men employed violence against others and assured themselves and others that they were employing this against what everyone admitted to be evil.

That method has been employed since remote antiquity especially by those who have usurped power, and men for a long time did not see its irrationality.

But the longer humanity lived and the more complex men's relations became, the more obvious did it become that it was irrational to oppose by violence whatever seemed evil to any of them; that strife was not lessened by so doing, and that no human definition could make everyone believe evil to be what one set of men considered it to be.

Even at the time of the appearance of Christianity and in the place where it appeared, in the Roman Empire, it was clear to many men that what Nero and Caligula considered evil and what they resisted by violence, could not be considered evil by other people. Even then men had begun to understand that human laws which were announced as divine had been written by men, that men could not be infallible no matter with what grandeur they were invested, and that erring men do not become infallible by assembling together and calling themselves a Senate or by any other name. Even then this was felt and understood by many. And it was then that Christ preached his doctrine, which not only set forth that evil should not be resisted by violence, but also gave a new comprehension of life. And the application of this new comprehension to social life taught how to put an end to strife among all men, not by making it the duty of one section of mankind to submit without a struggle to what certain others in authority prescribe, but by making it the duty of all—and consequently also of those (and chiefly of those) who rule—not to employ violence against anyone in any circumstances.

This teaching was accepted at the time by only a very small number of disciples. The majority of men, especially those who ruled over others, continued to maintain the principle of violently resisting what they considered to be evil, even after nominally accepting Christianity. So it was under the Roman and Byzantine emperors, and so it continued later.

The invalidity of this principle (that evil could be defined by some external authority and should be resisted by violence) became still more obvious with the breaking up of the Roman empire into independent States with mutual hostilities and internal feuds.

But men were not ready to accept the solution given by Christ, and the former method of defining evils that should be resisted, by setting up laws obligatory on everyone and so enforced, continued to be applied. The authority that decided what should be considered evil and suppressed by force was at one time the Pope, at another the Emperor, then a king, and then an assembly of elected persons, or a whole nation. But both within the State and outside it there were always men who did not accept as obligatory on themselves either the laws issued as the commands of the Deity, or the decrees made by men clothed in sanctity, or by the institution supposed to represent the will of the people; and there were men who thought good what the authorities considered evil, and who struggled against the authorities with violence such as was employed against themselves.

The men clothed in sanctity considered as evil what the men and institutions invested with secular power considered good, and vice versa; and the struggle grew more and more cruel.

And the longer men kept to that way of deciding conflicts the more obvious it became that that method will not do, for there is not and cannot be any such definition of evil by an external authority as will be accepted by everybody.

So matters went on for eighteen centuries and reached the present stage, when it is completely evident that there is and can be no external definition of evil obligatory upon all. It has come to this, that people have not merely ceased to believe in the possibility of finding and establishing a general definition, but have ceased even to believe in the necessity of producing such a definition. People holding power have ceased to produce evidence that what they consider evil is evil, and have simply taken to saying that they consider evil whatever displeases them. And people who submit to the authorities, now submit not because they believe that the definition of evil presented to them by the authorities is just, but simply because they cannot help themselves. Nice is annexed by France, Lorraine by Germany, Bohemia by Austria, Poland is divided up, Ireland and India are subjected to British rule, the Chinese are attacked, Africans are slaughtered, America expels its Chinese immigrants, Russia oppresses the Jews, landlords possess land they do not cultivate, and capitalists take wealth produced by others—not because these things are good, necessary, or useful for people, or because the contrary would be evil, but merely because those in power wish it to be so.

It has come to this, that some people now do violence without even a pretext of resisting evil, but simply for their own profit or caprice, and others submit to that violence not because they suppose (as was the case in former times) that this violence is practised upon them to secure them from evil, but simply because they cannot avoid it.

If a Roman, a man of the Middle Ages, or a Russian of half a century ago as I remember him, was fully convinced that the violence done by the powers that be was necessary to preserve him from evil—that taxes, requisitions, serfdom, prisons, scourgings, the knout, penal servitude, executions, army service, and wars, really ought to exist—it is difficult now to find a man who believes that all this violence frees anyone from any evil, or who fails to see clearly that most of the violence to which he is exposed, and in which he has some share, is itself a great and useless evil.

There is hardly a man to-day who fails to see both the uselessness and the stupidity of collecting taxes from labouring men for the enrichment of idle officials, or the senselessness of inflicting punishments on weak and demoralized men by banishing them from one place to another or confining them in prisons where, provided for and living in indolence, they merely become weaker and more depraved; who fails to see not only the uselessness and stupidity but the positive insanity and cruelty of military preparations and wars that ruin and destroy the people and lack any explanation or justification. Yet such acts of violence continue, and are even supported by the very people who see their uselessness, stupidity, and cruelty, and suffer from them.

If fifty years ago both a rich and idle man and a poor and illiterate one were alike convinced that their respective states (of continual holiday for the one and continual toil for the other) were ordained by God Himself, now (in Russia as well as in the rest of Europe owing to mutual intercourse and to the spread of education and reading) there is hardly a man, rich or poor, who does not from one cause or another doubt the justice of this state of things. Not only are the wealthy conscious of being to blame by the very fact that they are rich, and try to expiate their guilt by donations to science or art (as they formerly atoned for their sins by contributing to Churches) but the greater part of the working people openly regard the existing order as a false one, bound to be changed or destroyed. Some religious people, of whom there are millions of so-called sectarians among us in Russia, consider the existing order unjust and ripe for abolition on the basis of the Gospel teaching as taken in its true meaning; others consider it unjust on the basis of socialistic, communistic, or anarchistic theories, which have now already penetrated to the lowest strata of the working people.

Violence now rests not on any belief in its necessity, but merely on the fact that it has existed a long time and is so organized by those to whom it is profitable—that is, by the governments and ruling classes—that those who are in their power cannot extricate themselves from it.

Governments in our time—all of them, the most despotic and the liberal alike—have become what Herzen aptly termed 'Genghis-Khans with telegraphs'; that is, organizations of violence based on nothing but the grossest tyranny, and yet having at their disposal all the means science has devised for the peaceful, collective, social activity of free and equal men—which they, however, employ for the enslavement and oppression of the people.

The governments and ruling classes now base themselves not on right, or even on any semblance of justice, but on an organization so cunningly devised by the aid of scientific inventions that men are caught in a circle of violence from which it is impossible to extricate themselves.

That circle is now made up of four methods joined together and supporting one another like the links of a chain-ring.

The first and oldest method is intimidation. It consists of presenting the existing State organization (whatever it may be—free republic, or the most savage despotism) as something sacred and immutable, and in punishing most barbarously any attempts to alter it. This method is still employed as of old wherever a government exists: in Russia against the so-called Nihilists, in America against the Anarchists, and in France against the Imperialists, Legitimists, Communards, and Anarchists.

Railways, telegraphs, telephones, photography, and the perfected method of disposing of men permanently without killing them, by condemning them for life to solitary confinement in which, hidden from the world, they perish and are forgotten; and many other modern devices favoured by governments, give them such strength that when once power has come into certain hands and the secret and public police and the administration with all kinds of prosecutors, gaolers, and executioners, are zealously at work, there is no possibility of overthrowing the government however senseless and cruel it may be.

The second method is corruption. It consists in taking wealth from the working population by means of taxes and distributing it among officials who for this remuneration have to maintain and strengthen the enslavement of the people.

These bought officials—from the highest mini

sters to the poorest clerks—make up an unbroken network of men united by the same interest, that of living at the expense of the people. The more submissively they carry out the will of the government always, everywhere, sticking at nothing, and supporting by word and deed in all departments the violence on which their own welfare rests, the more money they get.

The third means is what I can only describe as the hypnotization of the people. This consists in retarding the spiritual development of men, and by various suggestions keeping them back in a conception of life that humanity has outgrown but on which the power of the government rests. This hypnotization is now organized in a most complex manner, beginning in childhood and continuing to act on people till death. This hypnotization begins at a very early age in the compulsory attendance at schools specially set up for that purpose, and in which a conception of the world is instilled into them which was natural to their ancestors but is in direct conflict with the consciousness of the modern world. In countries where there is a State religion, children are taught the senseless blasphemies of the Church catechism together with the duty of obedience to the powers that be. In republican countries they are taught the savage superstition of patriotism, and the same pseudo-obligation to obey the State. In later years this hypnotization is continued by the encouragement of religious and patriotic superstitions. Religious superstition is encouraged by the erection of temples with money collected from the people, by processions, monuments and festivals, with the aid of sculpture, architecture, music, and incense, to stupefy the people, and chiefly by maintaining the so-called priesthood, whose duty it is to befog the people's minds and keep them in a permanent state of stupefaction by their performances, the pathos of their services and sermons, and their interference in private life—at births, marriages, and deaths. The patriotic superstition is encouraged by governments and the ruling classes with money collected from the people, by national solemnities, festivals, monuments, and pageants, which encourage men to believe in the exclusive importance of their own country and the greatness of their ruler and his government, and to feel ill will or even hatred of other nations. Despotic governments simply forbid the printing and dissemination of books and the utterance of speeches which enlighten people, and deport or incarcerate all who are likely to rouse the people from their torpor. Besides this all governments without exception conceal from the masses everything that might further their emancipation, and encourage all that corrupts and demoralizes them, such as writings that maintain them in the barbarism of their religious and patriotic superstitions, all sorts of sensual amusements, shows, circuses, theatres, and even physical means of stupefaction such as tobacco and alcohol, the taxes on which constitute one of the chief revenues of the State. Even prostitution is encouraged, and not only recognized but even regulated by most governments. Such is the third method.

The fourth method consists in selecting a certain number from among men enchained and stupefied by the methods mentioned above, and subjecting them to special and intensive methods of stupefaction and brutalization and so making of them submissive instruments for carrying out all the cruelties and brutalities needed by the government. This result is attained by taking them at an age before they have had time to form any clear conception of morality, and removing them from all natural human conditions of life: home, family, birthplace, and reasonable labour. They are shut up together in barracks, dressed in special clothes, and under the influence of shouts, drums, music, and glittering objects, made to go through certain daily exercises devised for this purpose, and in this way are brought to an hypnotic condition in which they cease to be men and become senseless machines submissive to the will of those who have hypnotized them.

And it is these physically strong young men (in these days of universal military service, all young men), hypnotized and furnished with murderous weapons, always submissive to the governing authorities and ready at their command to commit any act of violence, that constitute the fourth and chief means of enslaving men.

By this means the circle of violence is completed.

Intimidation, corruption, and hypnotization bring people to a condition in which they go as soldiers; the soldiers give the power of plundering people and executing them (and buying officials with the spoils), and hypnotizing and enlisting them into the very army that gives the government the power to do all this.

The circle is complete, and there is no possibility of breaking out of it by force.

If some people say that freedom from violence or at least a diminution of it, can be gained by the oppressed forcibly overthrowing the oppressing government and replacing it by a new one which will have no need to employ such violence and such enslavement, and if some people try to do this, they only deceive themselves and others and make the position no better but rather worse. Such people's activity only increases the despotism of the governments. Their attempts at emancipation only afford a convenient pretext for the governments to intensify their power.

Even if we admit that under circumstances specially disadvantageous for the government, as in France in 1870, a government may be forcibly overthrown and the power transferred into other hands, the new authority would be no less oppressive than the former: on the contrary—defending itself from all its dispossessed and exasperated enemies—it would be more despotic and cruel, as has been the case in all revolutions.

If the socialists and communists consider an individualist capitalist organization of society an evil, the anarchists regard government itself as an evil, and there are monarchists, conservatives, and capitalists who consider any socialist or communist organization or anarchy an evil, and all these parties have no means other than violence for bringing people to agreement. Whichever of these parties might triumph it would have to employ not only all the existing methods of violence but also to devise new ones in order to bring its schemes into operation and maintain its power. Other men would be enslaved and forced to do other things, but the violence and oppression would be the same or even more cruel, since hatred of one another would be increased by the struggle, and intensified forms of oppression would have to be devised.

This has been the case after all revolutions, all attempts at revolution, all conspiracies and all forcible changes of government. Every conflict merely strengthens the means of oppression in the hands of those who for the time being are in power.

The position of our Christian society and especially its popular and widely spread ideals, prove this most convincingly.

There now remains only one sphere of human life not encroached on by governmental power—the domestic, economic sphere—the sphere of private life and labour. And now even this—thanks to the efforts of communists and socialists—is being gradually encroached on, so that labour and recreation, housing, dress, and food, will all (if the hopes of the reformers are fulfilled) gradually be prescribed and allotted by the governments

The whole course of life of the Christian nations for the last eighteen hundred years has inevitably led them back to the necessity of deciding the question they have evaded—that of accepting or rejecting Christ's teaching—and the question arising from it in social life, of resisting or not resisting evil by violence. But there is this difference, that formerly men were free to accept or refuse the solution given by Christianity, whereas now that solution has become imperative because it alone delivers men from the condition of slavery in which they have entangled themselves as in a snare.

But it is not only the misery of their position that brings men to this necessity.

Side by side with the negative evidence of the falsity of the pagan organization of life, the positive evidence of the truth of Christian teaching has become plainer.

Not in vain did the noblest men in all Christendom, having apprehended the truth of the teaching by an internal spiritual intuition, bear witness to it before all men during eighteen centuries in spite of threats, privations, sufferings, and torture. These men by their martyrdom sealed the truth of the teaching and transmitted it to mankind.

Christianity penetrated into human consciousness not only by the negative demonstration of the impossibility of continuing in the pagan life, but also by its simplification, its elucidation, its liberation from the superstitions intermingled with it, and its diffusion among all classes of the people.

Eighteen centuries of Christianity have not passed without effect on people who accepted it even if but externally. Those eighteen centuries have had this effect: that men, continuing to live a pagan life no longer consistent with the stage humanity has reached, now already not merely see clearly all the wretchedness of their condition, but in the depths of their souls believe (and are really alive only because they believe) that salvation from this condition is to be found only in the fulfilment of the Christian teaching in its true significance. As to how and when this salvation will be accomplished people think differently according to their mental development and the prejudices current in their particular circle. But every man of our world recognizes that our salvation lies in the fulfilment of the law of Christ. Some believers in the supernatural character of Christian teaching consider that salvation will come when all men are brought to believe in Christ and that the second advent approaches. Others, also believing in the divinity of Christ's teaching, consider that that salvation will come through the Church, which subjecting all men to itself will imbue them with Christian virtues which will transform their lives. Others again, who do not regard Christ as God, consider that salvation will come by a slow and gradual progress through which the principles of pagan life will be replaced by the principles of freedom, equality, and fraternity—that is, by the Christian principles. A fourth section, who believe in a social revolution, consider that salvation will come when through a violent revolution men are compelled to adopt community of possessions, absence of governments, and collective instead of individual industry—that is, by the materialization of one side of the Christian teaching.

Thus in one way or other all men of our day

in their inner consciousness not only condemn the existing antiquated pagan order of life, but also admit (often without themselves being aware of it and while regarding themselves as hostile to Christianity) that our salvation lies only in the application to life of the Christian teaching, or of a part of it, in its true significance.

As its teacher said, Christianity could not be realized immediately by the majority of men but had to grow like an immense tree from a tiny seed. And so it grew and has spread, if not in actual life at least in the consciousness of men of our time.

Now, not only the minority who have always comprehended Christianity by an inner path acknowledge it in its true significance, but also the immense majority of people who by their social life seem quite estranged from it. Look at individual men in their private life. Listen to their appraisals of conduct when judging one another. Hear not only their public sermons and speeches but the advice given by parents and teachers to those they are educating, and you will see that however far their social life, involved in governmental violence, may be from the fulfilment of the Christian truths, yet in private life only the Christian virtues are considered indisputably good, by all and for all without exception, while the anti-Christian vices are unquestionably and without exception considered bad by all and for all.

Those are regarded as the best people who unselfishly devote their lives to the service of humanity and sacrifice themselves for others; the selfish who take advantage of their neighbours' misfortunes are regarded as the worst of men.

If the non-Christian ideals, such as strength, wealth, and courage, are still acclaimed by some people as yet untouched by Christianity, those ideals are antiquated and are not shared and followed by everybody and certainly not by those recognized as the best men. The only ideals accepted by all and regarded as binding on all are the Christian.

The position of our Christian humanity, if you look at it from outside with its cruelty and its degradation of men, is terrible indeed. But looking at it from within, in its inner consciousness, it presents quite a different spectacle.

All the evil of our life seems to exist only because things have been like that for so long, and those who do it do not wish to do it, but have not yet learnt to stop doing it.

All that evil exists for some other reason which seems to be independent of men's consciousness.

Strange and contradictory as it appears, all the men of our time hate the very order of things they are themselves supporting.

I think it is Max Müller who tells of the amazement of an Indian converted to Christianity, when, having absorbed the essence of the Christian teaching, he came to Europe and saw how Christians live. He could not overcome his astonishment at a sight so completely contrary to what he had expected to find.

If we are astonished at the contradiction between our beliefs and convictions and our conduct, that is only because we, too, are affected by the influences that conceal that contradiction from others. We need only look at our life from the standpoint of that Indian, who understood Christianity in its true significance without any concessions or adaptations, and at the savage brutalities of which our life is full, to be horrified at the contradictions amid which we live often without noticing them.

We need only think of the preparations for war, the mitrailleuses, the nickel-plated bullets, torpedoes—and the Red Cross; the arrangements for solitary confinement, the experiments in electrocution—and the care for prisoners' welfare; the philanthropic expenditure of the rich, and their lives which produce the poor to whom they are benefactors. And these contradictions do not arise, as we might suppose, because people pretend to be Christians while they are pagans, but because of something lacking in men, or some force hindering them from being what in their inner consciousness they feel themselves to be and really wish to be. Men of our time do not merely pretend to hate oppression, inequality, class distinctions, and all kinds of cruelty not only to men but to animals—they really do hate all this, but do not know how to abolish it or cannot make up their minds to part with the system that supports it all but seems to them indispensable.

Indeed, ask any man separately whether he considers it laudable or worthy for a man of this age to occupy himself (for a salary disproportionate to his work) with collecting from people —often in poverty—taxes to be spent on cannon, torpedoes, and other engines for murdering people with whom we wish to be at peace and who wish to live at peace with us; or to receive a salary for devoting his life to constructing murderous weapons or to preparing himself and other people to murder. And ask him whether it is laudable and worthy and suitable for a Christian to be employed, again for money, in catching wretched, erring, often illiterate and drunken people for appropriating someone else's property (on a much smaller scale than we do), or for killing people (not in the manner we approve of), and putting them in prison, ill-treating them, and killing them for so doing. And whether it is laudable and worthy for a man and a Christian—again for money—to preach to people obviously absurd and harmful superstitions under the name of Christianity. And whether it is laudable and worthy for a man to take from his neighbour for his own gratification what is necessary to satisfy that neighbour's primary needs, as is done by large landlords. Or to increase his wealth by forcing his neighbour to work beyond his strength and ruin his health, as is done by factory owners and manufacturers. Or to take advantage of people's needs to increase his own wealth, as merchants do. And each man separately, especially if he is speaking of someone else, will answer: 'No!' Yet at the same time the very man who sees all the baseness of these actions, will of his own free will and sometimes even without the pecuniary inducement of a salary, but simply out of childish vanity, for the sake of being allowed to wear a porcelain decoration, a ribbon, or a bit of lace, enter military service, or act as an examining magistrate, a justice of the peace, a minister, a village policeman, an archdeacon, a prelate, or a deacon: positions in which he will be obliged to do things the shame and baseness of which he cannot but be aware of.

I know that many of these people will argue with assurance that they consider their position not merely legitimate but essential, and will say in their defence that the powers that be are ordained of God, and that the functions of the State are essential for the welfare of humanity, that riches are not contrary to Christianity, that the rich young man was told to give away his property only if he wished to be perfect, that the existing distribution of wealth and our commercial system should be what they are, and that they are advantageous to everybody, and so on. But however they may try to deceive themselves and others, they all know that what they are doing is opposed to everything they believe in and live for. And in the depths of their souls when they are alone with their conscience they feel ashamed and it hurts them to remember what they are doing, especially if the baseness of their activity has been pointed out to them. A man of our time, whether he believes in the divinity of Christ or not, cannot help knowing that to take part—in the capacity of Tsar, minister, governor, or policeman—in taking its last cow from a poor family for a tax to be spent on cannon, or on the pay and pensions of idle, luxurious, and harmful officials; or to take part in imprisoning the supporter of a family because we have demoralized him, and to let his family go begging; or to participate in murdering and plundering in war; or in inculcating idolatrous superstitions in place of the law of Christ; or to impound a cow which belongs to a man who has no land, and that has strayed on to someone else's land; or to charge a landless man, or a factory workman, for an article he has accidentally spoilt; or to exact from a poor man double its value for an article merely because he is in extreme need—a man of our time cannot help knowing that all these things are horrible and shameful and should not be done. All men know this: they know that what they are doing is wrong, and would on no account do it were they able to withstand the forces that close their eyes to the criminality of their actions and impel them to commit them.

In nothing is the degree of contradiction in man's life to-day so strikingly seen as in universal conscription—that last resource and final expression of violence.

It is only because this state of universal armament and compulsory service has come about step by step unnoticed, and because governments have employed every resource of intimidation, corruption, stupefaction, and violence to support it, that we fail to see its flagrant inconsistency with those Christian sentiments and ideas with which all men of our time are permeated.

That contradiction has become so customary to us that we do not even see all the hideous folly and immorality of the conduct not only of those who of their own free will choose the profession

I

of murder as though it were an honourable one,
but also of those unfortunate men who under
compulsion agree to perform military service, or
even of those who in countries where compulsory
service has not been introduced voluntarily give
their services to hiring soldiers and preparations
for murder. Yet all these people are either Christians or men who profess humane and liberal
principles, and know that by doing these things
they become participants, and in case of personal
military service executants, of most senseless, pur-
poseless and cruel murders. And yet they do it.

More than that. In Germany, where general
compulsory military service began, Caprivi has
stated what was formerly carefully concealed—
that the men the soldiers will have to kill are not
foreigners alone but their own countrymen—
those same working men from among whom most
of themselves are taken. And even this admission
has not opened people's eyes or horrified them!
They still continue as before to go like sheep to
the recruiting office and submit to all that is
required of them.

And more yet. The German Emperor has
recently shown the meaning and purpose of war
still more definitely by distinguishing, thanking,
and rewarding, a soldier for having killed a defenceless prisoner who tried to escape. By thanking and rewarding a man for an action always
regarded as base and mean, even by those on the
lowest level of morality, Wilhelm showed that a
soldier's chief duty, and the one most highly
appreciated by the authorities, is to be an executioner—and not an executioner like a profes-

sional who kills only condemned criminals, but an executioner who kills all the innocent men the authorities order him to kill.

Even that is not all. In 1891 that same Wilhelm, the *enfant terrible* of State rule, saying in plain words what others only think, when addressing some soldiers, publicly pronounced the following words which next day were printed in thousands of newspapers:

'Recruits!' said he. 'You have sworn fidelity to *me* before the altar and a minister of God. You are still too young to understand the full importance of what has been said here; but take care above all to obey the orders and instructions given you. You have sworn fidelity to *me*, lads of my Guard: that means that you are now *my* soldiers, that you have *given yourselves to me, body and soul*. For you there is now but one enemy— *my* enemy. In these days of socialistic sedition *it may come to pass that I command you to fire on your own kindred, your brothers, even your own fathers and mothers—which God forbid—and even then it will be your duty to obey my orders without hesitation.*'

That man expressed what all sensible rulers think but carefully conceal. He says openly that men serving in the army serve *him* and his advantage, and must be ready for *his* advantage to kill their own brothers and fathers.

In most brutal words he plainly exposes the whole horror and criminality for which men prepare by entering the army and the abyss of ignominy to which they descend by promising obedience. Like a bold hypnotist he tests the degree of insensibility of the hypnotized subject.

He touches his skin with red-hot iron, the flesh sizzles and smokes but the sleeper does not awake.

This miserable deranged man, crazed by power, by those words outrages everything that can be sacred to a man of our time. And Christian men, liberals, educated people, are not only not indignant at that outrage but do not even notice it. The last, most extreme, test is put to men in its coarsest and crudest form; and they do not even notice that it is a test and that a choice stands before them. They seem to think that there is no choice and no path but that of slavish submission. It would seem that those insane words, which outrage everything a man of the present day holds sacred, must arouse indignation, but nothing of the sort happens.

All the young men throughout Europe are exposed year after year to that test, and with very few exceptions they all renounce everything a man can hold sacred, and express their readiness to kill their brothers and even their fathers at the order of the first misguided man dressed up in a livery with red and gold trimmings, and only wait to be told whom and when they are to kill. And they are ready!

Every savage has something he holds sacred, for which he is ready to suffer but will not yield up. But what is sacred to a man of our time? He is told: 'Come and be my slave, come into such slavery that you may have to kill your own father,' and he, often an educated man having studied science at the university, submissively puts his neck into the collar. He is dressed up in a fool's attire, ordered to jump, to contort himself, to salute, and to kill—and he does it all submissively. And when they let him go he returns to his former life like a man possessed, and continues to hold forth on man's dignity, liberty, equality, and fraternity.

'Yes, but what is one to do?' people often ask in genuine perplexity. 'If everyone refused it would be well, but by myself I should suffer without doing good to anyone or anything.'

And it is true that a man of the social conception of life cannot refuse service. The aim of his life is his personal welfare. For his personality it seems better to submit, and he does so.

Whatever they may do to him, however they may torture or humiliate him, he will submit, for alone he can do nothing; he has no principle for the sake of which he alone could resist violence. And those in authority will never allow him to unite with others.

It is often said that the invention of terrible instruments of destruction will put an end to war: war will destroy itself. That is not true. As it is possible to increase the means of slaughter, so is it also possible to increase the means of bringing men of the social life-conception to submission. Let them be slaughtered and torn to pieces by thousands and by millions, they will still go to the slaughter like senseless cattle because they are driven by the lash; others will go because they may be allowed to wear scraps of ribbon or gold lace, and they will even be proud of it.

And with such people, so stupefied that they promise to kill their own parents, men active in public affairs—conservatives, liberals, socialists, and anarchists—propose to construct a reasonable and moral society! What reasonable and moral society can be built up with such men? As you cannot build a house with rotten and twisted beams however you may arrange them, so there is no constructing a reasonable and moral society out of such people. They can only go forward like a herd of cattle directed by the shouts and lashes of the drovers. And so it is!

Here on one side are people, nominally Christian, professing liberty, equality, and fraternity and yet ready in the name of liberty to accept the most slavish and humiliating degradation in the name of equality are ready to accept the crudest and most senseless division of men (merely by externals) into upper and lower classes, allies and enemies; and in the name of fraternity are ready to murder their brothers.[1]

The contradiction in men's consciousness, and the wretchedness resulting from it, has reached the final stage beyond which it cannot go. Life built on the principles of violence, has reached the negation of the very purpose for which it was organized. The organization of society on principles of violence for the purpose of securing personal, family, and social welfare, has brought men to an absolute negation and destruction of that welfare.

[1] That some nations (England and America) have not yet adopted conscription (though voices in favour of it are raised among them), but recruit and hire soldiers, does not alter the position as regards the servility of the citizens to the governments. Here each man has himself to go to kill or be killed. There everyone has to give of the fruits of his toil for the hire and preparation of murderers.—L.T.

The first part of the prophecy has been fulfilled upon the men and generations who did not accept Christ's teaching, and their descendants are now brought up against the necessity of testing the truth of its second part.

IX

An acceptance of the Christian conception of life frees men from the wretchedness of our pagan way of life.

THE condition of Christian peoples to-day remains as cruel as it was in pagan times. In many respects, especially as to the oppression of men, it has become even more cruel than it was then.

But between the condition of men then and now, there is the same difference as between the last days of autumn and the first days of spring for plant life. In autumn the external lifelessness of Nature corresponds to its internal condition, but in spring it is in the sharpest contradiction to the inward condition of vitality and of its transition to a new form of life. The same is true of the external resemblance between ancient pagan life and the life of to-day. The resemblance is only external. The inward condition of men now is quite different from what it was in the days of paganism.

In pagan times the external condition of cruelty and slavery corresponded to men's inner consciousness, and every forward movement increased this conformity. But now the external condition of cruelty and slavery is in complete contradiction to men's Christian consciousness, and every step forward only increases the contradiction.

Sufferings are being endured that are, as it were, unnecessary and useless. What goes on resembles the pangs of childbirth. All is ready for the new life, but that new life still does not appear.

There seems to be no way out of the position. And there would be none if a man (and therefore all men) had not the possibility of reaching another, higher, understanding of life which at once frees him from the bonds by which he seemed permanently fettered.

And such an understanding is the Christian view of life revealed to mankind eighteen hundred years ago.

A man need only make that understanding of life his own, and the fetters which seemed to bind him so securely will drop off of themselves and he will feel himself perfectly free, as a bird feels itself free when it spreads its wings and flies over the fence by which it was surrounded.

People talk about emancipating the Christian Church from the State, about granting or not granting freedom to Christians. In all such thoughts and expressions there is some strange misconception. Freedom cannot be granted to or taken away from Christians. Freedom is their inalienable possession.

If we talk of giving freedom to Christians or withholding it from them, we are evidently not talking of real Christians but of people who are such only in name. A Christian cannot but be free, because the attainment of the aim he sets before himself cannot be prevented or even hindered by anyone or anything.

A man has only to understand his life as Christianity teaches him to understand it—that is, he need only understand that his life does not belong to himself or his family or the State but to Him who sent him into the world, and that he must therefore fulfil not the law of his personality or family or State but the infinite law of Him from Whom he has come—and he will feel himself absolutely free from all human authorities and will even cease to regard them as able to trammel anyone.

Let a man but realize that the purpose of his life is to fulfil the law of God, and that law will dominate him and supplant all other laws, and by its supreme dominion will in his eyes deprive all human laws of their right to command or restrict him.

A Christian is free from every human authority by the fact that he regards the divine law of love implanted in the soul of every man, and of which Christ has made us conscious, as the sole guide of his life and of the lives of others.

A Christian may suffer external violence, he may be deprived of bodily freedom, may not be free from his passions (he that sins is the slave of sin), but he cannot be in bondage in the sense of being forced by any threat of external harm to commit an action which is contrary to his conscience.

He cannot be forced in this way because the deprivations and sufferings inflicted by violence, which form a powerful instrument against men

of the State conception of life, have for him no
compulsory force. Deprivations and sufferings
which take from men of the social life-conception
the welfare for which they live cannot infringe
the happiness of a Christian, which consists in
consciousness of fulfilling the will of God, but
when they are endured for the sake of fulfilling
that will can only increase it.

And therefore a Christian is bound only by the
inner and divine law and can neither obey the
requirements of external laws when they are incompatible with the divine law of love of which
he is conscious (as occurs with regard to governmental exactions) nor acknowledge an obligation to submit to any individual or institution or
the duty of what is called allegiance. For a
Christian the oath of allegiance to any government whatever—the very act that is considered
the basis of political life—is the direct negation
of Christianity. For the man who promises in
advance unconditional obedience to all the laws
which have been and will be enacted by certain
men, by that very promise absolutely renounces
Christianity which consists in exclusive and unconditional obedience to the divine law of love
man is conscious of within himself.

It was possible under the pagan conception
of life to promise obedience to the temporal
authorities without infringing the will of God,
which was supposed to consist in circumcision,
keeping the Sabbath, fixed times for prayer,
abstinence from certain kinds of food, and so on.
The one law did not contradict the other. But
that is just the difference between Christianity

and paganism—that Christianity does not require certain external negative actions but sets man in a different relation to his fellows from which most various actions may result which cannot be defined in advance. And so a Christian cannot promise to do another person's will without knowing what will be required of him, nor can he submit to transitory human laws or promise to do or abstain from doing any specified thing at any given time, for he cannot know what may be required of him at any time by that Christian law of love, obedience to which constitutes the purpose of his life. A Christian by promising unconditional obedience to the laws of men in advance, would indicate by that promise that the inner law of God does not constitute the sole law of his life.

For a Christian to promise obedience to men or to laws made by men is as though a workman, having hired himself out to one master, should at the same time promise to carry out any order given him by someone else. Man cannot serve two masters.

A Christian is independent of human authority because he only acknowledges the authority of God, whose law revealed by Christ he recognizes in himself and voluntarily obeys.

And this liberation is gained not by means of struggle, not by the destruction of existing forms, but only by a change in the understanding of life. A Christian recognizes the law of love revealed to him by his teacher, as perfectly sufficient for all human relations, and therefore regards all use of violence as unnecessary and wrong. He also, with his different conception of life, regards those deprivations, sufferings, or threats of deprivation and suffering, by which a man of the social conception of life is reduced to the necessity of obedience, merely as inevitable conditions of existence (like sickness, hunger, and all sorts of calamities), which he patiently endures without forcible resistance, but not as anything that can serve as a guide for his actions. The only guide for a Christian's actions is to be found in the divine principle that dwells within him, which cannot be checked or governed by anything else.

A Christian acts according to the prophetic words that were applied to his teacher: 'He shall not strive nor cry; neither shall any man hear his voice in the streets. A bruised reed shall he not break, and smoking flax shall he not quench, *till he send forth judgment unto victory.*' (Matt. xii. 19, 20.)

A Christian will not quarrel with anyone or attack anyone or use violence against anyone. On the contrary he will endure violence. And by that very attitude towards violence he not only frees himself from all external power, but the world also.

'Ye shall know the truth, and the truth shall make you free.' (John viii. 32.) If there were any doubt of Christianity being the truth, that perfect liberty which a man experiences as soon as he has assimilated the Christian understanding of life and which nothing can curtail, would be an indubitable proof of it.

Men in their present condition are like a swarm

of bees hanging from a branch in a cluster. The position of the bees on that branch is temporary and must inevitably be changed. They must bestir themselves and find a new dwelling. Each of the bees knows this and wishes to change its position and that of the others, but no one of them is willing to move till the rest do so. And the whole swarm cannot move at once because one bee hangs on to another and hinders it from separating from the swarm, and so they all continue to hang there. It would seem that there was no way out of this state for the bees, just as there seems no escape for worldly men who are entangled in the toils of the social conception of life. And there would be no escape for the bees if each of them were not a separate living creature possessing a pair of wings. Nor would there be any deliverance for men if each individual were not a separate living being endowed with capacity to assimilate the Christian life-conception. If each bee who could fly would not do so, the others too would not stir and the whole swarm would remain as it was. And if every man who has assimilated a Christian understanding of life waited for other people before beginning to live in accordance with that understanding, the condition of mankind would never be altered. Yet as it is enough for one bee to spread her wings, rise up and fly away, and a second, a third, a tenth, and a hundredth, will do the same and the cluster that hung inertly becomes a freely-flying swarm of bees; so let but one man understand life as Christianity teaches us to understand it, and begin to live accordingly, and a second, a third, and a hundredth will do the same, till the enchanted circle of social life from which there seemed to be no escape will be destroyed.

But people think that the deliverance of mankind by this means is too slow, and that they must discover and employ some other method by which to set all men free at once. It is as if the bees, wishing to start to fly away, should consider it too long a process to wait till the whole swarm started one by one, and that some method must be devised by which the whole swarm could fly where it wanted to go without its being necessary for each bee to spread its own wings separately and fly. But that is impossible. Until the first, second, third, and hundredth bee spreads its wings and flies away of its own accord, the swarm cannot fly off and find a new life. Until each individual man makes the Christian understanding of life his own and begins to live in accord with it, the contradiction in human life will not be solved nor will a new form of life be established.

One of the most astonishing phenomena of our time is the propaganda of slavery carried on among the masses, not only by governments who profit by it, but by men who advocate socialistic theories and regard themselves as champions of freedom.

These men affirm that the amelioration of life and the adjustment of the facts of life to our sense of what ought to be, will come about not by the personal efforts of individuals, but spontaneously by a violent reconstruction of society by somebody. They say that people need not go on their own feet to where they wish to go and ought to go, but that some kind of a floor will be placed under them which will carry them where they ought to go without their having to use their own feet. Accordingly all their efforts should be directed not to proceeding as far as their strength will allow towards the spot they wish to reach, but towards arranging this imaginary floor, without moving from the spot where they are standing.

In regard to economics a theory is preached which amounts to saying that 'the worse the better'. The greater the accumulation of capital and consequent oppression of the workers, the nearer their deliverance, and therefore any personal effort made by an individual to free himself from the oppression of capital is useless. Politically it is maintained that the greater the power of the State—which according to this theory should control the hitherto independent domain of private life—the better, and that therefore the interference of the government in private life should be invoked. In political and international affairs it is maintained that an increase in the means of destruction and an increase of armies will lead to the necessity of disarmament by means of congresses, arbitration, and so on. And marvellous to say, the inertia of humanity is so great that people believe these theories despite the fact that the whole course of life and every step forward exposes their falseness.

Men suffer from oppression, and to free them from this oppression they are advised to devise general measures for the improvement of their condition, which measures are to be applied by the State authorities to whom they must continue to submit. And obviously the results will only be an increase in the power of the authorities, and consequently greater oppression.

Of all human errors this is the one that most hinders men from attaining the aim towards which they strive. Men do all sorts of very different things to reach their aim, except the one simple and direct thing that is within the reach of everyone. They devise most cunning means of changing the conditions that burden them, except the very simple one that each man should refrain from doing things that produce those conditions.

I have been told a story of a gallant police officer who came to a village where the peasants had been riotous, and to which troops had been summoned. He decided to suppress the disturbance by his own personal influence, like Nicholas I. He sent for some cart-loads of switches, and collecting all the peasants together in a barn he went in with them and fastened the door. At first he so frightened the peasants by his shouts that they obeyed him and began to flog one another, until one simpleton was found who did not submit and shouted to his fellows not to flog one another. Only then did the flogging cease, and the police-officer had to make his escape. But the advice given by that simpleton is not taken by men of the social conception of life among us, for they unceasingly flog one another and teach people that such self-castigation is the last word of human wisdom.

Indeed, can one imagine a more striking

example of the way people flog themselves than the submissiveness with which men of our time perform the very obligations imposed on them to keep them in servitude—especially military service? We see men enslaving themselves, suffering from this slavery, and believing that so it should be, that it does not matter, and will not hinder the emancipation of men which is being prepared somewhere and somehow in spite of the ever-increasing slavery.

Take a man of our time—be he who he may—(I do not speak of a true Christian, but of an ordinary man of our time) educated or un-educated, a believer or an unbeliever, rich or poor, married or single: such a man lives, work-ing at his work, amusing himself with his amuse-ments, and spending the fruits of his own or other people's toil on himself and on those near to him, and hating every kind of oppression, deprivation, dissension, and suffering, like everybody else. Such a man is living quietly when suddenly people come to him and say: 'First you must promise and swear to us that you will slavishly obey us in everything we prescribe to you, and obey and unquestionably accept as absolute truth everything we devise, decide on, and call law. Secondly you must hand over to us part of the fruits of your labour (we shall use the money to keep you in slavery and to prevent your forcibly resisting our arrangements). Thirdly you must elect others, or be yourself elected, to take a pretended part in the government, know-ing all the while that the administration will pro-ceed quite independently of the foolish speeches you and others like you may utter, and that things will proceed according to our will—the will of those in whose hands is the army. Fourthly you must at the appointed time come to the lawcourts and take part in the senseless cruelties we perpetrate on erring people whom we have perverted—in the shape of imprisonments, banishments, solitary confinements, and executions. And fifthly and finally, besides all this, although you may be on the friendliest terms with men of other nations, you must be ready, as soon as we order it, to consider as your enemies those whom we shall point out to you, and co-operate, personally or by hiring others, in the destruction, plunder, and murder of their men, women, children, and aged alike—perhaps also of your own fellow countrymen or even your parents, should we require that.'

What, one would think, can any man of our day who is not stupefied reply to such demands? It would seem that every mentally healthy man would say: 'But why should I do all this? Why should I promise to obey everything that is ordered by Salisbury to-day or by Gladstone to-morrow, by Boulanger[1] one day and by a chamber of similar Boulangers the next, by Peter III[2] to-day, by Catherine to-morrow, and

---

[1] In 1889 General Boulanger had been returned to the Chamber of Deputies for the city of Paris by an overwhelming majority, and had seemed near effecting a *coup d'état* and becoming master of France. He committed suicide in 1891, but was still remembered in 1893 when *The Kingdom of God is Within You* was written.—A.M.

[2] Peter III, who was little better than a moron, was strangled in 1762 with the connivance of his wife, Catherine the Great.—A.M.

Pugachëv[1] the day after to-morrow, one day by a mad Bavarian king[2] and the next by Wilhelm? Why should I promise to obey them, knowing them to be bad or worthless people or not knowing them at all?

'Why should I give them the fruits of my toil in the form of taxes, knowing that the money will be spent to buy officials, prisons, churches, armies, and on evil deeds and my own enslavement? Why should I flog myself? Why should I waste my time and hoodwink myself and give an appearance of legality to these users of violence by taking part in elections and pretending that I am sharing in the government when I know very well that the real control of the State is in the hands of those who have got hold of the army? Why should I go to the law-courts to take part in tormenting and punishing people because they have gone astray—knowing, if I am a Christian, that the law of revenge has been replaced by the law of love, and if I am an educated man, that punishments do not reform but deprave those subjected to them? And why should I consider as my enemies people of a neighbouring country with whom I have till now lived, and desire to live, in love and harmony, and why

[1] Pugachëv was a Cossack ensign who raised a serious rebellion in 1773, overran the Volga and Ural districts, and was for a while a serious menace to the rule of Catherine the Great. He was, however, captured in 1774, taken to Moscow in an iron cage, and executed in 1775.—A.M.

[2] Ludwig I of Bavaria got into trouble by his reckless expenditure on buildings and works of art, came under the control first of the Jesuits and then of an Irish adventuress, Lola Montez, and abdicated during the revolutionary disturbances of 1848.—A.M.

should I hire soldiers, or go myself, to kill and ruin them and expose myself to their attacks, merely that the keys of a church in Jerusalem should go to one bishop rather than to another,[1] or that one German rather than another should reign in Bulgaria,[2] or that English merchants should catch seals rather than American[3]?

'And why, above all, should I co-operate, personally or by hiring military forces, in the enslavement and murder of my brothers and father? I do not want to do all this and it is all hurtful to me and in every way immoral, base, and nasty. So why should I do it? If you say that unless I do someone will make it worse for me, then, in the first place, no one else threatens me with anything as bad as the harm you will cause me if I obey you; and secondly, it is quite clear to me that if we refuse to flog ourselves, no one will flog us. As for the government—the kings, ministers, and officials with pens—they

---

[1] One cause of the Crimean War (in which Tolstóy served as an artillery officer) was a dispute as to whether the key of the Church of Bethlehem should be held by the Orthodox Greek or the Latin Christians.—A.M.

[2] Prince Alexander of Battenburg, who was Russia's candidate, was elected to the Bulgarian throne in 1879, but in 1886 he was seized in his palace, forced to sign his abdication, and deported from the country. In 1887 Prince Ferdinand of Saxe-Coburg-Gotha was elected to succeed him.—A.M.

[3] The United States Government had purchased from Russia her territorial rights in Alaska and the adjacent islands, and in 1886 three British sealing vessels were captured by an American revenue cutter and were condemned on the ground that they had been sealing within the limits of Alaska territory. In 1887 further captures followed. The resultant quarrel between the American and British governments was proceeding when *The Kingdom of God is Within You* was being written, but was fortunately settled by arbitration soon afterwards.—A.M.

(like that police officer) cannot force me to do anything. It is not they who might drag me to the law-courts, to prison, or to execution; it is the very men who are in the same position as we are. But it is as useless and harmful and unpleasant for them to be flogged as it is for me, and so there is every likelihood that, if I open their eyes, they not only will not treat me with violence but will do what I do.

'Thirdly, even if I should have to suffer for it, it would still be better for me to be exiled or imprisoned for upholding what is sensible and right and what must triumph if not to-day or to-morrow at least before long—than to suffer for folly and wrong which will end to-day or to-morrow. And therefore even in that case it is better for me to risk being banished, shut up in prison, or even executed, than of my own free will to spend my whole life in bondage to wicked men, and risk being ruined by an invading enemy and stupidly mutilated or killed by them, fighting for a gun, a bit of land no one needs, or a senseless rag called a standard.

'I do not wish to flog myself and will not do it. There is no reason why I should! Do it yourselves if you want it done, but I won't do it.'

It would seem that, apart from religious and moral feeling, the simplest reflection and consideration would impel any man of the present day to answer thus and act thus. But no. Men of the social life-conception consider that to do so is not necessary but is even prejudicial to the cause of man's emancipation from slavery, and that we should continue to flog one another like

the police-officer's peasants, consoling ourselves
with the reflection that since we chatter in parliaments and at meetings, form trade unions,
parade the streets on the 1st of May, get up conspiracies, and secretly ridicule the government
that is flogging us, we shall very soon be free
though we are enslaving ourselves more and
more.

Nothing impedes the liberation of men so
much as this amazing delusion. Instead of each
man directing his energies to changing his conception of life and freeing himself, people seek for
an external, collective method of emancipation
and continue to rivet their chains more and more
firmly.

It is as if men were to maintain that to make
a charcoal fire warm the house, it was not necessary to kindle the pieces of charcoal but only to
arrange them in a certain pattern.

And yet as time goes on it becomes more and
more evident that the freedom of all men will
actually be brought about only by the liberation
of the individuals separately. The freedom of
separate individuals from State slavery in the
name of a Christian conception of life, which was
formerly an exceptional and unnoticed phenomenon, has of late acquired a threatening significance for the power of the State.[1]

[1] During the last decade of the Nineteenth Century when
The Kingdom of God is Within You was written, some Russian
nonconformist religious bodies, numbering thousands of
members, publicly refused military service and endured persecution for so doing; but that movement seems to have receded
before the onflowing tide of violence of the Great War and the
Bolshevik Revolution.—A.M.

If in Roman times it happened that a Christian confessed his faith and refused to offer sacrifices or to worship the emperors or the gods, or if in the Middle Ages he refused to worship images or acknowledge the authority of the Pope, such cases were in the first place casual. A man might be so placed that he had to confess his faith, but he might also happen to live his whole life without being faced by that necessity. But now all men without exception are exposed to this trial of their faith. Every man of the present day is under the necessity of taking part in the cruelties of pagan life or rejecting them. And secondly, in those days refusals to worship the gods, or the images, or the Pope, were not incidents of essential importance to the State. However many men worshipped or did not worship the gods, or the images, or the Pope, the State remained equally powerful. But now refusals of the unchristian demands of governments undermine the very roots of State authority, because the whole power of the government rests on compliance with those unchristian demands.

The secular powers have been brought by the course of life to this position, that for their maintenance they have to demand from all men actions which cannot be performed by men who cherish true Christianity.

And therefore at the present time every profession of true Christianity by any individual man saps the power of government in what is most essential to it, and inevitably conduces to the emancipation of all men.

What it would seem is there important in such

an incident as the refusal of some dozens of
'crazy' (as they are called) men to take an oath
of allegiance to the government, to pay taxes, or
to take part in trials at law, or in military service?
These people are punished and removed, and
life goes on as before. It would seem that these
incidents were of no importance, but yet it is just
these things more than anything else that undermine the power of the State and prepare the way
for man's emancipation. These are the individual bees who are beginning to detach themselves from the swarm, and hover around it
waiting for what must soon happen—that is, for
the whole swarm to rise and follow them. And
the governments know this, and fear such incidents more than all the socialists, communists,
and anarchists, with their plots and dynamite
bombs.

A new reign is beginning.[1] According to the
general rule and established order all subjects
have to take an oath of allegiance to the government. General orders are issued and all are
bidden to assemble in the Cathedral to take the
oath. Suddenly a man in Perm, another in Túla,
a third in Moscow, and a fourth in Kalúga,
declare that they will not take the oath, and
without having consulted together they all explain their refusal in one and the same way,
namely, that swearing is forbidden by the law of
Christ, and that even if swearing were not forbidden, the spirit of the Christian law would prevent their promising to perform the evil actions

[1] Nicholas II ascended the throne in 1894, shortly after this
book was written.—A.M.

demanded of them by the oath: such as informing against all those opposed to the interests of
the government, defending their government by
armed force, or attacking its enemies. They are
brought before police officers, district police
captains, priests, and governors. They are admonished, urged, threatened, and punished, but
they hold to their resolution and do not take the
oath. And among the millions who swear, there
are some dozens who do not. And they are
questioned:

'How is it you didn't take the oath?'

'I just didn't.'

'And didn't anything happen?'

'Nothing.'

The subjects of the State are all bound to pay
taxes. And they all pay, till one day a man in
Khárkov, another in Tver, and a third in Samára,
refuse to, and again they all say the same thing
as if by agreement. One says he will only pay
when he knows how the money he pays will be
spent. 'If it is for a good purpose,' says he, 'I
will give of my own accord even more than is
demanded of me.' But if for evil purposes he
will give nothing voluntarily because by the law
of Christ, which he obeys, he cannot take part
in evil deeds. The others say the same, though
in different words, and will not voluntarily pay
the taxes.

Those who have anything that can be taken,
have it taken from them by force, while those
who have nothing are left alone.

'Well, didn't you pay the tax?'

'No.'

'And did nothing happen?'

'Nothing.'

Passports are instituted. Everyone who leaves his place of residence has to take one and to pay a tax for it. Suddenly in various places people appear who say that passports should not be taken out, for they are an acknowledgement of dependence on the State which exists by violence. And these people do not take out passports or pay the tax on them. And again there is no way of obliging them to do what is required. They are put in prison and let out again, and continue to live without passports.

All the peasants are bound to perform the police duties of village constable and so on. Suddenly in Khárkov a peasant refuses to perform this duty, explaining his refusal on the ground that by the law of Christ which he obeys he could not bind any man, or imprison him, or drag him from place to place. The same is announced by a peasant in Tver and another in Tambóv. These peasants are abused, beaten and put in prison, but they hold to their resolution and do not do the things that are contrary to their convictions. And they are not chosen to do police duty again, and again nothing happens.

All citizens have to take part as jurymen in the law-courts. Suddenly people of different classes, carriage-builders, professors, tradesmen, peasants, and gentlemen, as though by agreement refuse that duty, and not on grounds recognized by the law but because the law-courts themselves, according to their convictions, are wrong and unchristian and ought not to exist.

These people are fined—those in power trying not to allow them to explain their motives in public—and their places are taken by others.[1] Others who on similar grounds refuse to appear as witnesses, are dealt with in just the same way. And again nothing can be done.

All young men at the age of twenty-one have to draw lots for military service. Suddenly one young man in Moscow, another in Tver, a third in Khárkov, and a fourth in Kiev, appear at the recruiting station and as if by previous agreement declare that they will not take the oath or serve, because they are Christians. Here are details of one of the first of such cases since they recently became more frequent. It is a case well known to me.[2] Almost the same things happened in all the other cases.

At the Moscow Town Hall a young man of average education was refusing military service. No attention was paid to what he said and they demanded that he should pronounce the words of the oath like the others. He refused, pointing to the particular passage in the Gospels where swearing is forbidden. They paid no attention to his reasons and demanded compliance with the order, but he did not comply with it. Then it was assumed that he was a sectarian and there-fore did not understand Christianity properly— that is to say, not as it is understood by priests in

[1] Tolstóy had an experience of that kind himself in the autumn of 1883, when he was summoned to serve as a jury-man at a small town near Yásnaya Polyána, and refused to do so.—A.M.

[2] All the details of this case and of the preceding ones are authentic.—L.T.

the pay of the government. And the young man was sent under escort to the priests to be admonished. The priests began to reason with him, but their efforts to persuade him to renounce Christ in Christ's name evidently did not convince him and he was pronounced incorrigible and sent back to the army. He still did not take the oath and openly refused to perform military duties. Such a case had not been provided for by the laws. Refusal to comply with the orders of the government cannot be allowed, but to treat such a case as a simple breach of discipline is also impossible. After deliberating among themselves the military authorities decided to get rid of this troublesome young man by treating him as a revolutionary, and they sent him under guard to the secret police. The police and gendarmes examined him, but nothing that he said fitted in with the crimes dealt with in their department and there was no way of accusing him of revolutionary acts or conspiracy, as he declared that he did not wish to destroy anything, but on the contrary repudiated all violence, concealed nothing, and sought occasion to say and do everything in the most open manner. And the gendarmes, though they are not restricted by the laws, found no reason to accuse the young man, and like the priests returned him to the army authorities.

Again the commanders consulted together and decided to take the young man, though he had not taken the oath, and enroll him among the soldiers. He was put in uniform, allotted to a company, and sent under guard to army quarters. There the commander of the unit to which he had been assigned again required him to perform military duties. Again the young man refused, and in the presence of the other soldiers gave the reasons for his refusal, saying that as a Christian he could not voluntarily prepare himself to murder, which is forbidden even by the law of Moses.

The affair took place in a provincial town. It aroused interest and sympathy not only among outsiders but even among the officers, and so the commanders decided not to employ the disciplinary measures usual in cases of insubordination. For the sake of appearance however the young man was put in prison, and they wrote to the higher military authorities asking what they were to do with him. From the official point of view a refusal to serve in the army, in which the Tsar himself serves and which is blessed by the Church, presents itself as insanity; and so they wrote from Petersburg that as the young man must be out of his mind they should, without employing severe measures against him, send him to an insane asylum for his mental condition to be inquired into and treated. He was sent to the asylum in the hope that he would remain there, as had happened ten years before in Túla to another young man who refused military service and who was ill-treated in a lunatic asylum till he submitted. But even this measure did not free the military authorities from this inconvenient young man. The doctors examined him, were much interested by him, and as they naturally did not find any indications of mental

derangement, they sent him back to the army.
There his superiors received him and, as if they
had forgotten about his refusal and its motive,
he was again told to go to drill and again refused
in the presence of the other soldiers, and stated
the reasons of his refusal.

The affair attracted increasing attention both
among the soldiers and the inhabitants of the
town. Again they wrote to Petersburg, and from
there received a decision to transfer the young
man to a regiment stationed on the frontier
where the army was on a war footing and he
could be shot for a refusal to obey, and where
moreover such a thing could pass without attracting attention, as in that distant region there
were few Russians and Christians, the local
inhabitants being chiefly natives and Mohammedans. So it was done. The young man, in
company with a party of convicts, was transferred to a division stationed in the Transcaspian
district and commanded by an officer known for
his harshness and severity.

All that time, during all these transportations
from place to place, the young man was treated
roughly, kept in cold, hunger, and dirt, and in
all ways his life was made a torment to him. But
these sufferings did not make him change his
decision. In the Transcaspian Territory, where
he was again ordered to go on guard, he again
declined to obey. He did not refuse to go and
stand beside some haystacks where he was sent,
but refused to carry a weapon, declaring that
in no case would he use violence against anyone.
All this took place in the presence of other

oldiers. To let such a refusal pass unpunished vas impossible, and the young man was put on rial for breach of discipline. The trial took place and he was sentenced to confinement in a military prison for two years. Again he was sent under convoy with a party of convicts to the Caucasus, and there he was put in prison and came under the irresponsible power of the gaoler. He was tormented for a year and a half, but still did not alter his decision not to bear arms, and explained why he would not do this to everyone with whom he came in contact, and towards the end of the second year he was set free before his term was up, those in authority accounting his confinement in prison as military service (contrary to the law) and anxious only to get rid of him as quickly as possible.

In just the same way as if by preconcerted agreement other men in different parts of Russia act in the same way, and in all these cases the government behaves in a similarly timorous, undecided, and secretive manner.

Some of these people are sent to insane asylums, some are enrolled as clerks and transferred to service in Siberia, some are sent to labour in the forests, some are shut up in prison, and some are fined. And at the present time some such men, who have refused, are in prison not for their main offence—that is, denying the legality of the actions of the government—but for non-fulfilment of special demands made by the authorities. Thus not long ago an officer of the reserve who did not report a change of residence, and who declared that he would not serve in the army

again, was fined thirty rubles for non-complianc
with the authorities' order—a fine he also de
clined to pay voluntarily. And similarly som
peasants and soldiers who recently refused to b
drilled and to bear arms were placed unde
arrest for breach of discipline and for answering
their superiors.

And such cases of refusal to comply with Stat
demands that are contrary to Christianity, and
especially of refusals of military service, occu
of late not only in Russia but everywhere.

Thus I happen to know that in Serbia me
of the so-called sect of Nazarenes steadily refus
military service, and the Austrian Governmen
for some years has struggled with them in vain
punishing them with imprisonment.[1] In 188
there were a hundred and thirty such cases. I
Switzerland I know that in the eighteen eightie
there were men incarcerated in the castle o
Chillon for refusal of military service, and thei
resolution had not been shaken by their punish
ment. Similar refusals have occurred in Sweden
and in just the same way the men who refused
obedience were sent to prison and the govern
ment carefully concealed the matter from th
public. There were similar cases also in Prussia
I know of a non-commissioned officer of the
Guards who, in 1891, announced to the authori
ties in Berlin that he, as a Christian, would no
continue to serve, and despite all admonitions

---

[1] Tolstóy's statement is not quite clear; but the facts are
that Serbia though not actually under Austrian rule wa
much under its influence, and there were also many Sla
Nazarenes in Austria.—A.M.

threats, and punishments, he held to his resolution. In the south of France a community has
arisen called the Hinschists (this information I
take from *The Peace Herald* of July 1891) the
members of which refuse military service on the
ground of their Christian principles. At first
they were sent to serve in the hospitals, but now,
as their numbers increase, they undergo punishment for insubordination, but they still do not
take arms.

The socialists, communists, and anarchists,
with their bombs, riots, and revolutions, are not
nearly so much dreaded by governments as these
scattered individuals in various countries all
justifying their refusals on the ground of one and
the same familiar doctrine. Every government
knows how and with what to defend itself against
revolutionaries, and has the means of doing so,
and therefore does not dread these external foes.
But what are governments to do against these
people who show the uselessness, superfluity, and
harmfulness of all governments, and instead of
contending with them merely show that they
do not need them, that they can get along without them and therefore are unwilling to take part
in them?

The revolutionaries say: 'The government
organization is bad in this and that respect. It
must be destroyed and replaced by this and that.'
But a Christian says: 'I know nothing about the
governmental organization or in how far it is
good or bad, and for that reason I do not wish
to overthrow it, but for the same reason I do not
want to support it. And I not only do not want

K

to, but I cannot, because what it demands of me is against my conscience.'

And all the State obligations are against the conscience of a Christian: the oath of allegiance, taxes, law proceedings, and military service. And the whole power of the government rests on these very obligations.

The revolutionary enemies attack the government from outside. But Christianity does not attack it at all, it destroys the foundation of government from within.

Among the Russian people, especially since the time of Peter I, the protest of Christianity against the government has never ceased, and the social organization has been such that people migrate in whole communities to Turkey, to China, and to uninhabited districts, and not only need no government but always regard it as an unnecessary burden only to be endured as an affliction, whether it be Turkish, Russian, or Chinese. Among these Russian people, cases of conscious self-emancipation on Christian grounds from subjection to the State occur of late more and more frequently.

These occurrences have become more and more alarmingly frequent, and are feared by the government now because the refusers are often not members of the so-called lower uneducated classes but are men of fair or higher education, and because they do not explain their refusals by any mystical and exceptional beliefs, as used to be the case, and do not connect them with different superstitions and fanaticisms as is done by the Russian sects of self-immolators and

'Fugitives' (*Beguni*), but present very clear and simple reasons for their refusal, understandable and recognized as true by everybody.

So they refuse voluntary payment of taxes, because taxes are spent on deeds of violence, on the pay of users of violence, on the military, and on building prisons, fortresses, and cannon. As Christians they regard it as sinful and immoral to take part in such affairs. Those who refuse to take the oath of allegiance do so because to promise obedience to the authorities (that is, to men who employ violence) is contrary to the sense of the Christian teaching. Those who refuse to take the oath in the law-courts do so because oaths are plainly forbidden in the Gospels. They refuse to fulfil police duties because those duties require them to use violence against their fellow-men and to ill-treat them—things a Christian cannot do. They refuse to take part in trials at law because they consider all prosecutions a fulfilment of the law of vengeance and incompatible with the Christian law of forgiveness and love. They refuse to take any part in preparations for war or in the army, because they do not wish to be, and cannot be, executioners, and are unwilling to prepare themselves to be such.

The motives in all these cases are such that however despotic governments may be they cannot openly inflict punishments for them. To punish such refusals it would be necessary for the governments themselves finally to renounce reason and goodness—in whose name they assure people they rule.

What are governments to do against such people?

They can of course crush, execute, or keep in perpetual imprisonment or in convict settlements all enemies who wish to overthrow them by violence, can bribe and lavish gold on the people they need, and can keep in subjection to themselves millions of armed men prepared to destroy all their enemies. But what can they do against men who, not wishing to destroy anything, simply wish for their part, for their own life, to do nothing contrary to the law of Christ and therefore refuse to perform the most ordinary (and therefore for the governments the most indispensable) duties?

If these men were revolutionaries, advocating and practising violence and murder, it would be easy to resist them: some of them could be bought over, some duped, and some terrorized, while those who could neither be bought, duped, nor terrorized, could be exposed as evil-doers and enemies of society and forthwith imprisoned or executed—and people would approve the action of the government. If they were fanatics preaching some peculiar doctrine, it might be possible, while refuting the superstitious errors mixed up in their teaching, to discredit also the truth they professed. But what is to be done with men who neither advocate revolution nor preach any peculiar religious dogmas, but simply because they do not wish to harm any man refuse to take oaths, pay taxes, take part in legal proceedings, or serve in the army—obligations on which the whole fabric of the State rests? What is to be done with such men? They cannot be bought over, the risks to which they voluntarily expose themselves prove their disinterestedness. To dupe them into believing that these things are required by God is also impossible, for their refusal is based on the clear and indubitable law of God, professed even by those who try to compel men to act contrary to that law. To terrify them by threats is still more impossible because the privations and sufferings they will be subjected to for their belief only strengthens their desire to proclaim it, and in their law it is plainly said that man should obey God rather than men and should fear not those who can kill the body but Him who can destroy both the body and the soul. To kill these people or keep them in perpetual confinement is also impossible. They have a past and they have friends, and their way of thinking and acting is well known. Everybody knows them to be gentle, good, peaceable people, and it is impossible to pronounce them evil-doers who must be removed for the safety of society. And to execute men everybody knows to be good causes others to take their part and to explain their refusal. And it is only necessary to explain the reasons why these Christians refuse to fulfil the governments' requirements, to make it plain to everyone that those reasons apply equally to all men, and that they all ought long ago to have done the same.

Faced by the refusals of Christians, the ruling powers find themselves in a desperate position. They see that the prophecy of Christianity is coming to pass—that it is breaking the bonds

of the captives and setting free those who are in
bondage, and they realize that this deliverance
must inevitably be the end of those who hold
mankind in bondage. The ruling authorities see
this and know that their hours are numbered,
but cannot help themselves. All they can do for
their safety is to postpone the hour of their ruin.
And this they do, but still their position is
desperate.

The position of the governments is like that
of a conqueror who wishes to preserve a city set
on fire by its own inhabitants.[1] As soon as he
extinguishes the fire in one place it is alight
again in two others; as soon as he separates the
burning portion of a building from the rest of
the edifice, the same building starts burning from
both ends. These separate fires may as yet be
few, but they burn with a flame which, starting
from small sparks, will not be extinguished till
everything has been consumed.

And now, when the governments, faced by
people who profess Christianity, find themselves
in such a defenceless position, and but little is
needed for all this apparently majestic power
built up through so many centuries to crumble
away—social reformers are busy teaching that
it is not only unnecessary but even harmful and
immoral for each man separately to free himself
from this slavery!

It is as if one set of men, wishing to free a
dammed-up river, had worked hard and dug a
canal, and all that remained was to open the

[1] Tolstóy evidently had in mind the fate of Moscow when
captured by Napoleon in 1812.—A.M.

flood-gates and let the water do the rest, when another set of people came along and began advising them that instead of releasing the water it would be much better to construct a machine with buckets, which would bale the water out on one side and pour it into the same river again on the other.

But things have already gone too far. The governments already feel their weakness and defencelessness and men of Christian conciousness are awakening from their apathy and already begin to feel their strength.

'I am come to send fire on the earth,' said Christ, 'and how I am straitened till it is kindled.'[1]

And this fire is beginning to burn.

X

The uselessness of State violence for the destruction of evil. The moral progress of humanity is accomplished not only by a recognition of truth, but also by the establishment of a public opinion.

CHRISTIANITY in its true sense puts an end to the State. It was so understood from its very beginning, and for that Christ was crucified. It has always been so understood by people who were not under the necessity of justifying a Christian State. Only since rulers adopted a nominal external Christianity have men begun to devise all

[1] The allusion is evidently to Luke xii. 49–50, but the Russian translation, as often happens, is not identical with our Authorized Version.—A.M.

those impossible, cunningly spun theories which
pretend to make Christianity compatible with
the State. But to every serious and sincere man
of our time the incompatibility of true Christianity (the doctrine of humility, forgiveness, and
love) with the State and its pomp, violence, executions, and wars, is quite obvious. The profession of true Christianity not only excludes the
possibility of recognizing the State, but even
destroys its foundations.

But if so, and if it is true that Christianity is
incompatible with the State, then the question
naturally arises: 'Which is more necessary for
the good of humanity, which better secures men's
welfare: the political form of life, or its downfall
and replacement by Christianity?'

Some men say that the State is more necessary
for humanity, and that the destruction of the
political form of life would involve the destruction of all that humanity has gained; that the
State has been, and still is, the only form for the
development of humanity, and that all the evils
we see among the nations who live under a political form of life arise not from that type of
society but from abuses which can be corrected,
and that humanity can develop and reach a high
degree of well-being without infringing the political form.

And in confirmation of their opinion the men
who think this adduce philosophic, historical,
and even religious arguments which seem to
them incontrovertible. But there are men who
hold the opposite opinion, namely, that as there
were times when humanity lived without a poli-

tical form, that form is temporary and a time must inevitably come when men will need a new form, and that that time has now arrived. And the men who think so also adduce philosophic, historical, and religious arguments which seem to them incontrovertible in support of their opinion.

Volumes may be written in defence of the former opinion (they have indeed been written long ago and are still being written), but much can also be written against it, though it is only recently that this has been done—and very ably done.

It cannot be proved, as the champions of the State affirm, that the abolition of the State would involve social chaos, mutual robberies and murders, the destruction of all social institutions and a return of mankind to savagery. Nor can it be proved, as opponents of government maintain, that men have already become so reasonable and good that they do not wish to rob and murder one another, but prefer peaceful intercourse to enmity, and will themselves arrange all that they need unaided by the State, and that therefore the State, far from being an aid, exercises a harmful and embittering influence under pretence of protecting people. It is not possible by abstract reasoning to prove either of these contentions. Still less is it possible to prove them by experiment, since the question is whether we should or should not make the experiment. The question whether the time has or has not come for the abolition of the State would be insoluble were there not another, vital, method of deciding it.

Quite independently of any man's opinion as to whether chicks are mature enough for him to drive the mother-hen away from the nest and let them come out of their shells, the question will be indisputably settled by the birds themselves when, unable any longer to find room enough in the shells, they begin to peck with their beaks and come out of their own accord.

It is the same in regard to whether the time has or has not come to do away with governmental authority and substitute a new type of society. If, through the growth of a higher consciousness, men can no longer comply with the demands of the State, if they no longer find sufficient room in it and at the same time no longer need its protection, then the question whether they have matured sufficiently to discard the State form of life is decided from quite a different side—just as in the case of chicks that break out of their shells into which no power on earth can make them return—by the men themselves who have outgrown the State and whom no power on earth can replace in it.

'Very likely the State was needed and is still needed for all those purposes which you attribute to it,' says a man who has made the Christian understanding of life his own. 'But I know that on the one hand I no longer need the State, and on the other I can no longer perform the actions that are necessary for its existence. Arrange what you need for your own lives. I cannot prove either the need or the harmfulness of government in general. I only know what I myself need and do not need, what I can do and what I cannot.

I know for my own part that I do not need to divide myself from other nations, and so I cannot acknowledge my exclusive adherence to any nation or State nor subjection to any government. I know in my own case that I do not need all these governmental institutions that are produced by violence and arranged within the State, and I cannot deprive others who need my labour, in order to give it in the form of taxes to institutions I do not need and which as far as I know are harmful. I know that I need neither the government nor tribunals founded on violence, and therefore I cannot take part in either the one or the other. I know that I do not want either to attack other nations and slaughter them or to defend myself from them with arms, and so I cannot take part in wars or preparations for war. Very likely there are people who cannot help considering all this to be necessary and indispensable. I cannot dispute with them. All I know, know indubitably, is that as far as I am concerned I cannot do these things. And I cannot do them, not because such is my own personal will, but because such is the will of Him who sent me into life and gave me an indubitable law for my guidance.'

Whatever arguments may be advanced to show that the abolition of governmental power would be harmful and would cause calamities, men who have once outgrown the State form of life can no longer find room in it. And however many and varied arguments as to its necessity may be put to a man who has outgrown it, he cannot return to it and cannot take part in its affairs which are rejected by his consciousness, any more than a fully grown bird can return to its former shell.

'But even so,' say defenders of the existing order of things, 'still the abolition of governmental violence can only be possible and desirable when all men have become Christian. So long as among people nominally Christians there are some unchristian wicked men ready to do harm to others to gratify their own personal desires, the abolition of governmental authority far from being a benefit to the rest of the people would only increase their miseries. And the abolition of the State form of life is not only undesirable while just a few people are true Christians, it would be undesirable even if all the people of a nation were Christians if among them or around them there were unchristian men of other nations. For these non-Christians will rob, violate, and kill the Christians with impunity and will make their lives a torment. Bad men will oppress and outrage the good with impunity. And therefore governmental violence should not be abolished until all the bad and rapacious people have been swept away. And as that can never happen, or not for a long time, State authority ought to be maintained for the majority in spite of the efforts of individual Christians to be free from it.' So say the defenders of the State. 'Without the State evil men will do violence to the good and will oppress them. But the power of government makes it possible for the good to restrain the bad.'

But when saying this the defenders of the existing order take for granted the validity of the very proposition they want to prove. When they say that without the government the bad would oppress the good, they take it for granted that the good are just those who are now in power and the bad are those who are in subjection. But that is just what has to be proved. It would be true if what is supposed to happen in China (though it does not really happen) went on in our world, namely, that the good always rule, and that as soon as those at the head of the government cease to be better than those over whom they rule, the citizens are bound to remove them. That is supposed to be so in China, but in reality it does not and cannot happen. For to overthrow a government which employs force, it is not right alone that is needed but also the power to do it. So that this Chinese custom is only an imaginary one.

But in our Christian world no one even imagines that such a custom exists, and there are no grounds for supposing that the kinder or better people rule, and not people who have seized power and hold on to it for their own benefit and that of their descendants. For the better people cannot possibly seize and retain power.

To seize power and retain it, it is necessary to love power. But love of power goes not with goodness but with the opposite qualities—pride, cunning, and cruelty.

Without self-aggrandizement and the abasement of others, without hypocrisy, deceit, prisons, fortresses, executions and murders, no power can arise or maintain itself.

'If the power of the State is abolished, evil men

will oppress the less bad,' say the defenders of State rule. But if the Egyptians subjugated the Hebrews, the Persians the Egyptians, the Macedonians the Persians, the Romans the Greeks, and the Barbarians the Romans, does this mean that the conquerors were always better and kindlier than the conquered?

And it is the same with the transference of power within a country from one set of men to another. Has the power always passed into the hands of those who were better? When Louis XVI was executed and Robespierre and afterwards Napoleon ruled, did better or worse men prevail? And when were better men in power: when the men of Versailles possessed it in 1871 or the Communards? When Cromwell was at the head of the government or Charles I? When Peter III was Tsar or when, after his murder, Catherine ruled one part of Russia and Pugachëv another? Which of these was the good and which the wicked?

All men in power assert that their authority is necessary to keep bad men from doing violence to the good, thus assuming that they themselves are the good who protect others from the bad.

But ruling means using force, and using force means doing what the man subjected to violence does not wish done, and to which the perpetrator would certainly object if the violence were applied to himself. Therefore to rule means to do to others what we would not have done to ourselves—that is, doing wrong.

To submit means to prefer suffering to violence. And to prefer to suffer rather than to use violence means to be virtuous, or at least less evil than those who do to others what they would not like done to themselves.

And so in all probability, now as in the past, those who are in power are no better than those over whom they rule. There may be bad men among those who submit, but it cannot be that the more virtuous rule over the more wicked.

Such a thing could not be supposed even with the inexact, pagan definition of good and evil, but with the clear and exact Christian definition such a supposition is still less possible. If the more and the less good and the more and the less bad could not easily be distinguished in the pagan world, the Christian conception of good and evil is so clearly defined that confusion between them is no longer possible. According to Christ's teaching the good are those who humble themselves, endure, do not resist evil by violence, forgive injuries, and love their enemies; the evil are those who exalt themselves, seek power, fight, and do violence to others. So according to Christ's teaching there is no doubt as to where the good and where the bad are to be found among rulers or ruled. It even seems ridiculous to speak of Christians ruling.

Non-Christians, that is, those who set the aim of their life in worldly welfare, must always inevitably rule over Christians the aim of whose life is the renunciation of such welfare.

So it has always been and so it has become more and more definitely as the Christian teaching has become more widely diffused and clearly understood.

The more widely true Christianity spread, and the more it entered into men's consciousness, the less possible was it for Christians to be among the rulers, and the easier it grew for non-Christians to rule over Christians.

'The abolition of governmental violence in a society in which not all men are true Christians would only result in the wicked dominating the good and doing violence to them with impunity!' say the defenders of the existing order of things.

'The bad will rule over the good and will do violence to them.'

But nothing else ever has been or can be the case. It has been so since the beginning of the world, and is so now. *The evil always domineer over the good and inflict violence on them.*

Cain did violence to Abel, the cunning Jacob domineered over the confiding Esau and was himself dominated by Laban. Caiaphas and Pilate ruled over Christ, the Roman emperors ruled over Seneca, Epictetus, and the good Romans who were living in their times. Ivan IV[1] with his guards (opríchniks), the syphilitic drunkard Peter[2] with his buffoons, the harlot Catherine[3] with her paramours, ruled over the laborious, religious Russians of that time and did violence to them. Wilhelm rules over the Germans; Stambólov[4] over the Bulgarians; and

[1] Iván (John) the Terrible.—A.M.
[2] Peter the Great.—A.M.
[3] Catherine the Great.—A.M.
[4] Stefán Stambólov, a blood-stained revolutionary who obtained power and secured the election of Prince Ferdinand of Coburg to the Bulgarian throne in 1887, himself becoming prime minister. He still held that office when *The Kingdom of*

Russian officials over the Russian people. The Germans[1] once ruled over Italians, and now rule over Hungarians and Slavs; the Turks have ruled and still rule over Slavs and Greeks; the English rule over the Hindus, and the Mongolians over the Chinese.

So that whether governmental violence is or is not abolished, the position of good people oppressed by evil ones will not be altered thereby.

To frighten people by saying that the bad will domineer over the good is not possible, because what is threatened is just what has always been, is, and must inevitably be.

The history of mankind in Pagan times is nothing but a recital of how evil men seized power over the less evil, and having seized it maintained it by cruelties and cunning, proclaiming themselves to be the guardians of justice and defenders of the good against the bad. All the revolutions in history are merely the seizure of power by evil men and their domination over the good. When the rulers say that but for their power the wicked would do violence to the good, it only means that the violators in power do not wish to cede this power to other violators who would like to snatch it from them. But when saying this the rulers only unmask themselves. They say that their power (that is, violence) is

God is Within You was written. He did not lose office till 1894, and was assassinated and mutilated in the streets of Sofia a year later.—A.M.

[1] Till towards the end of the Great War of 1914–18 Austria, dominated by the German element, ruled over Italian provinces, Hungary, and Slavonic Bohemia.—A.M.

necessary for the defence of men against other violators in the present or the future.[1]

That is where the danger of employing violence lies: all the arguments put forward by those who employ it can with equal or even greater justification be used against them.

They plead the danger of violence—usually future and imaginary violence—but themselves unceasingly practise present and actual violence.

'You say that men in the past robbed and assaulted one another and you fear that they will rob and assault one another now if your power is withdrawn. That may be so or it may not. But the fact that you ruin thousands of men in prisons, penal settlements, fortresses, and exile, and break up millions of families and ruin millions of men physically and morally in the army, is certainly so and is not imaginary but actual violence, which according to your own argument ought again to be resisted by violence. And so you are yourselves the evil men against whom by your own argument violence should certainly be employed' is what the oppressed naturally say to the oppressors.

---

[1] In this respect the naïve assurance of the Russian Government—which does violence to other nationalities: to the Poles, the Baltic Germans, and the Jews—is amazing to the verge of absurdity. The Russian Government has oppressed its subjects for centuries, has not troubled itself about the Ukrainians in Poland, the Letts in the Baltic provinces, or the Russian peasants who are exploited by all sorts of people. And now it suddenly becomes the champion of the oppressed—of those very oppressed whom it itself oppresses!—L.T.

The above refers to steps the Russian Government was then taking on behalf of Russian peasants in the Baltic provinces against their German landowners, the so-called Baltic Barons. —A.M.

And non-Christians always speak, think, and act in that way. If the oppressed are fiercer and more wicked than their oppressors they attack them and try to overthrow them and in favourable circumstances succeed in doing so, or more commonly they rise into the ranks of the oppressors and share in their acts of violence.

So that the very thing the defenders of Stateship frighten people with, pretending that except for the violence exerted by the authorities, evildoers would oppress the good, has always existed and incessantly occurs in human society. And therefore the abolition of State violence cannot in any case occasion increased oppression of the good by the bad.

If State violence were abolished, violence would perhaps be committed by people other than those who previously committed it. But the total amount of violence would not be increased by the passing of power from one set of men to another.

'State violence can only cease when there are no more bad men in society,' say the champions of the existing order of things, meaning that since there will always be bad men, violence can never cease. And that would be correct if what they assume were true, namely, that the oppressors are always the better people and that the only means of delivering men from evil is by violence. Then indeed violence could never cease. But as, on the contrary, it is not the better who do violence to the worse, but the worse who do violence to the better, and as there is another means of putting an end to evil besides violence,

which never puts an end to it, the assertion that
violence can never cease is incorrect. The use
of violence grows less and less and evidently must
eventually disappear, but not (as some champions
of the existing order imagine) by the oppressed
becoming better and better under the influence
of government (on the contrary that influence
only makes them worse) but because as men in
general constantly tend to improve, so even the
worse people who are in power will become less
and less wicked—and at last so good that they
will become incapable of using violence.

The forward movement of humanity does not
proceed because the best elements in society
seize power and employ violence against their
subjects to make them better—as both conservatives and revolutionaries imagine. It proceeds
first and foremost because men in general are
steadily and unceasingly advancing towards a
more and more conscious assimilation of the
Christian conception of life; and secondly because, even apart from any conscious spiritual
activity, men are unconsciously brought to a
more Christian attitude to life and the very process of one set of men seizing power and being
replaced by others has this effect. The worse
elements of society, gaining possession of power,
grow ever less and less cruel under the sobering
influence which always accompanies power, and
therefore become incapable of employing cruel
forms of violence, and as a result of this they give
place to others who are again acted on by the
same process of softening and, so to say, unconscious Christianization.

Something occurs among men which resembles a process of effervescence. The majority of men holding the non-Christian view of life strive for power and struggle to obtain it. In this struggle the cruel, coarse, and least Christian elements of society, doing violence to the more mild, more sensitive, and more Christian people, rise by means of that violence to the higher ranks. And then on them is fulfilled what Christ foretold when he said: 'Woe unto you that are rich! Unto you that are full! Unto you when all men shall speak well of you!' The men who are in power and possess the glory and wealth that result from it, having attained the various aims they had set themselves, realize the vanity of these things and return to the position from which they came. Charles V,[1] John IV,[2] Alexander I,[3] experiencing the vanity and evil of power, renounced it because they already saw the evil and were incapable of continuing to use violence as if it were a good thing, as they had formerly done.

But it is not only a Charles or an Alexander who travels that road and recognizes the vanity and evil of power. That path of unconscious softening is trodden by everyone who obtains the power he has striven for, not only every minister, general, millionaire, or merchant, but every head

[1] Charles V, 1500–58, Emperor of Germany and of the Holy Roman Empire, abdicated in 1555, retired to a monastery and passed the rest of his life in seclusion.—A.M.

[2] John IV, Ivan the Terrible, 1530–84. After killing his son he wished to abdicate, and just before his death joined an order of hermits.—A.M.

[3] See the story of Alexander I, entitled 'Fëdor Kuzmich' [World's Classics No. 432].—A.M.

of a government office who has reached the
position he has coveted for ten years past, and
every prosperous peasant who has laid by a
couple of hundred rubles.

And not only individuals pass through this
process but whole groups of people and whole
nations.

The attractions of power and of all the riches,
honours, and luxurious life it brings, appear a
worthy aim of man's activity only as long as they
are not attained. As soon as a man has obtained
them they reveal their emptiness and gradually
lose their attractive force, like clouds that have
form and beauty from afar but whose splendour
disappears when one ascends into them.

People who possess power and riches, sometimes the very men who have acquired them but
more often their heirs, cease to be so greedy for
power and so cruel in their efforts to obtain it

Having learnt by experience, under the operation of Christian influence, the vanity of all that
is gained by violence, men, sometimes in a single
generation, sometimes after several generations,
lose the vices which arouse a passion for power
and riches, and becoming less cruel cease to
retain their position, are pushed from power
by others less Christian and more wicked, and
return to a stratum of society lower in position but
higher in morality, thereby raising the average
of Christian consciousness in men generally. But
immediately after them, worse, coarser, less
Christian elements of society rise to the top; they
again are subjected to the same process as their
predecessors, and again in one or more genera-

tions, having learnt the vanity of what is gained by violence and having come under the influence of Christianity, go back again amongst those subject to violence and are again replaced by new users of violence less coarse than the former, but coarser than those they oppress. So that although power remains externally the same, yet with each change of those who hold it there is a constant increase in the number of men who have been brought by experience to the necessity of assimilating the Christian conception of life, and with each change (though it is still the coarsest, most cruel, and least Christian men who obtain power) they are less coarse and cruel and more Christian than their predecessors.

The worst elements of society are attracted by and obtain power. Power moulds them, making them better and softening them, and returns them to the community.

That is the process by means of which Christianity takes possession of the minds of men more and more—in spite of the violence exercised by the State which impedes the forward movement of humanity. Christianity penetrates into the consciousness of men not only in spite of the violence used by governments, but even because of it.

And so the assertion of advocates of the existing political structure (that if governmental violence were abolished the wicked would dominate the good) not only fails to show that this is to be dreaded (for it is precisely what happens now) but on the contrary proves that State violence, which enables the wicked to oppress the good, is itself the very evil that ought to be abolished and is actually being gradually abolished by life itself.

'But even if it were true that governmental violence will come to an end when those in power become Christian enough to renounce power of their own accord and no one is found willing to take their place,' say the champions of the existing order; 'and if it were true that this process is already taking place, when will it be fully accomplished? If nineteen hundred years have passed and there are still so many people eager to rule and so few ready to obey, there is no probability of its happening soon—or indeed of its ever happening at all!

'Even if there are, as there always have been, men who prefer to renounce power rather than to use it, the supply of men who prefer ruling to submitting is so great that it is hard to imagine it ever being exhausted.

'For this process of the Christianization of all men to take place, and for all men one after another to pass over from the pagan conception of life to the Christian and voluntarily renounce power and wealth, and for no one to wish to make use of them, it would be necessary that not only all those coarse, semi-savage people who are quite incapable of accepting Christianity and following it and of whom there are always many in every Christian society, should be made Christian, but also that the same conversion should be achieved among all the non-Christian peoples who are still so numerous. And so even if we admit that this Christianizing process will some day be accomplished upon all men, still, judging by the amount of progress it has made in nineteen hundred years, that can happen only after many times nineteen hundred years. It is therefore impossible and useless at present to think of this impossible abolition of power. We ought only to try to see that power should be in the best hands.'

That is what the defenders of the existing order say. And that criticism would be perfectly just if the transition from one understanding of life to another were only accomplished by one process—that of each man separately and successively realizing the vanity of power and reaching the Christian truth by an inner spiritual path.

That process goes on unceasingly and men pass over to Christianity by that road one after another. But there is also another external means by which men reach Christianity where the transition is less gradual.

The transition from one order of life to another is not always accomplished by degrees, like sand running through an hour-glass, grain by grain. It is rather like water pouring into a jug floating on a stream. At first the water enters only from one side, slowly and steadily, but as the jug grows heavier it suddenly sinks rapidly and then takes in all the water it can hold.

That is what happens with societies of men when they pass from one understanding—and so from one organization—of life to another. At first people attain the new truth by the inward method and follow it in life only gradually and slowly, one by one. But after a certain stage of the diffusion of truth it is accepted by people no longer gradually or by the inward method, but suddenly and as it were involuntarily.

And so the argument of the defenders of the existing order (that since only a small part of mankind has come over to Christianity in nineteen hundred years it must be many times nineteen hundred years before all the rest do so) is unsound, for that opinion does not take into account the other way in which people can adopt the new truth and pass from one form of life to another—apart from the inward method of assimilating the truth.

The other method by which people make the newly found truth their own and pass to a new organization of life is this: people adopt the truth not only because they come to know it by a prophetic insight, or by experience of life, but also because when the teaching is sufficiently widely diffused men at a lower stage of development accept it all at once, simply through confidence in those who have adopted it by the inward method and are applying it in life.

Every new truth by which the order of human life is changed and which moves humanity forward is first accepted by only a very small number of men who understand it by inward intuition. The rest of mankind, who accepted on trust the preceding truth on which the existing order was based, always oppose the diffusion of the new truth.

But as, in the first place, humanity is not

stationary but continually advances and grows more and more cognizant of the truth and draws nearer to it, and in the second place all men, in varying degrees according to their age, education, and race, are distributed in a certain gradation, beginning with those most capable of understanding the newly revealed truths by intuition, and ending with those least capable of doing so; the men nearest to those who have assimilated the truth by an inward process pass over to the new truth one by one, at first slowly and then more and more quickly, till the number of men acknowledging the new truth becomes greater and greater and the truth becomes more and more understood.

And the more people assimilate the new truth, and the more comprehensible that truth is, the more confidence is evoked among the remainder who have less capacity to understand it for themselves, and the easier it becomes for them to comprehend it and the more readily do they adopt it. And so the movement grows more and more rapid and becomes larger and larger like a snowball, till a public opinion is formed accordant with the new truth, and then the remaining mass of men, no longer singly but in a body, is carried over to the new truth by its momentum, and a new structure of life is established in accord with that truth.

Men who accept a new truth when it has reached a certain degree of dissemination always do so suddenly and in a mass. They resemble the ballast with which every ship is laden to keep it steady and enable it to sail properly. Were it not for the ballast the vessel would not be sufficiently immersed in the water and its course would be changed by the slightest modification of surrounding conditions. This ballast, though at first it seems superfluous and even a hindrance to the ship's progress, is necessary.

The same is true of the bulk of humanity which suddenly, not one by one but always in a mass, passes from one arrangement of life to another under the influence of a new public opinion.

By its inertia this mass always hinders any frequent and rapid transitions, unverified by human experience, from one social order to another, but it also restrains for a long time every new truth that, tested by long struggle, is entering the consciousness of humanity.

And that is why it is a mistake to say that as only a very small part of mankind has assimilated Christianity in nineteen centuries it must take many many times nineteen hundred years for all humanity to assimilate it, and that as that time is so far off we who are living now should not think of it. It is a mistake because people on the lower levels of development, those very people who are regarded as obstacles to the realization of a Christian order of life, are those who always pass over suddenly in masses to any truth that is accepted by public opinion.

And therefore the transformation of human life (through which those in power will renounce power and there will be none anxious to seize it) will not come about solely by all men consciously and separately assimilating a Christian conception of life, but will come when a Christian public opinion so definite and comprehensible as to reach everybody has arisen and subdued that whole inert mass which is not able to attain the truth by its own intuition and is therefore always swayed by public opinion.

Such public opinion does not need hundreds and thousands of years for its formation and growth, for it possesses an infectious quality of acting on people and attracting collective masses with great rapidity.

'But,' say the defenders of the existing order, 'even if it were true that public opinion, when it has attained a certain degree of definiteness and precision, is capable of subjugating the inert masses of men outside the Christian world—as well as the brutal and depraved men in our midst—what are the signs by which we shall know that this Christian public opinion has been born and is able to replace the violence of the State?

'By rejecting the use of violence which maintains the existing order, and relying on the vague and impalpable influence of public opinion, we shall risk allowing the savages within and outside our society to pillage, kill, and do all kinds of violence to Christians, and that will not do.

'Since even the use of force hardly enables us to suppress the non-Christian elements that are always ready to overflow and destroy all the fruits of Christian civilization, is there any probability that public opinion could replace that power and render us secure? Besides, how are we to find the exact moment at which public opinion becomes powerful enough to replace the authority of the State? To reject the use of force and rely on public opinion alone for our protection would be as mad as to remove all weapons of defence from a menagerie and release all the lions and tigers, relying on the fact that the animals seemed amenable enough when kept in their cages and held in check by red-hot irons.

'It follows that those in power are placed by fate or by God in the position of rulers, and have not the right to risk the destruction of all that civilization has gained, merely because they would like to try an experiment and to see whether public opinion is or is not able to replace the protection afforded by authority. And therefore they must not cease to use violence.'

A French writer, Alphonse Karr, now forgotten, when arguing the impossibility of doing away with capital punishment, said somewhere: '*Que messieurs les assassins commence par nous donner l'exemple!*'[1] and I have often heard that *bon mot* repeated by men who thought it a worthy and convincing argument against the abolition of capital punishment. Yet nothing expresses more clearly than that epigram the error in the argument of those who consider it impossible for governments to abandon the use of violence as long as there still are men ready to employ it.

The advocates of governmental violence say: 'Let the murderers set us the example of abandoning killing, and then we too will give it up'; but the murderers say the same, only with a much

---

[1] Let those gentlemen, the murderers, begin by setting up an example.

better right. They say: 'Let those who have undertaken to teach us and guide us, set us an example by ceasing to kill people and then we will imitate them.' And they say this not in jest but in earnest, for that is actually the state of the case.

'We cannot give up the use of violence because we are surrounded by violent men.'

Nothing in our time hinders the forward movement of humanity and the establishment of an organization suitable to its present consciousness, more than this false reasoning.

Those in power are convinced that violence alone guides and controls mankind, and therefore they confidently employ it to support the existing order. Yet the existing system is really maintained not by violence but by public opinion, whose action is impeded by violence.

So the effect of using violence is to weaken and infringe the very thing it is employed to maintain.

Violence at best, even if it is not used merely for the personal ends of those in power, repudiates and condemns under the inelastic form of law, what for the most part has long before been repudiated and condemned by public opinion. But there is this difference, that whereas public opinion repudiates and condemns every action contrary to the moral law (including therefore in its condemnation most various cases) the law which rests on violence prosecutes and condemns only a certain very narrow range of actions, thereby seeming to justify actions of the same kind that do not come under its scope.

Public opinion since the time of Moses has

regarded covetousness, profligacy, and cruelty as
evil, and has censured them. And it condemns
every manifestation of covetousness, not only the
appropriation of another's property by force or
fraud or cunning, but also any cruel use of it; it
condemns every kind of profligacy, whether
wantonness with a mistress, with a slave, with a
divorced woman, or even with one's own wife;
it condemns all forms of cruelty, whether expressed by blows, ill-treatment, or by killing men
or even animals. But the law resting on violence
prosecutes only certain forms of covetousness,
such as theft or swindling; certain forms of profligacy, such as infringements of matrimonial
rights; and certain forms of cruelty, such as
murder or mutilation. Consequently it would
seem to countenance all those manifestations of
covetousness, profligacy, and cruelty, which do
not come under its narrow and often evaded
definitions.

But not only does violence pervert public
opinion, it also leads people to the pernicious conviction that men progress not by spiritual force,
which moves them to seek the attainment of
truth and its realization in life, and which constitutes the true source of every forward movement of humanity, but by violence—that very
action which far from bringing men to the truth
always removes them from it. That delusion is
harmful, because it causes men to neglect the
fundamental force of their life—spiritual activity
—and transfers their attention and energy to the
superficial, futile, and generally harmful activity
of violence.

Such a delusion is like that of men who try to set a locomotive to work by turning its wheels with their hands, not suspecting that the prime cause of its motion is the expansion of steam and not the movement of the wheels. By turning the wheels with their hands and with levers they produce only a semblance of motion, besides wrenching the wheels and impairing the possibility of the locomotive's proper motion.

Yet that is just what is done by those who wish to move men by external violence.

They say that without violence a Christian mode of life cannot be established, because there are savage races outside the pale of Christian society—in Africa and Asia (some men even represent the Chinese as such a peril to civilization) —and because even in Christian societies there are such savage, depraved, and (according to the modern theory of heredity) congenital criminals, that violence is necessary to restrain them from destroying our civilization.

But those savages (outside and within Christian societies) with whom we frighten ourselves and one another, never have been subjugated by violence and are not subjugated by it now.

Nations have never subjugated other nations by violence alone. When a nation that subjugated another stood on a lower level of development, what always occurred was that the conquering nation never introduced by violence its own structure of life, but on the contrary always adopted the structure of life that existed in the conquered nation. If any of the nations subdued by violence were ever subjugated, or nearly subjugated, it was only by the action of public opinion and certainly not by violence, which on the contrary always tends to provoke a people more and more.

When whole nations have sometimes submitted to a new religious creed, and become Christians or Mohammedans, these conversions have been accomplished not because men wielding power rendered them compulsory by violence (on the contrary, violence has more often acted in the contrary direction) but because public opinion made such a change inevitable. Nations forced by violence to accept the faith of their conquerors have always remained antagonistic to it.

And it is the same with savage elements existing in our society. Neither the increase or decrease of the severity of punishments, nor modifications of the prison system, nor increase of the police, either diminish or increase the quantity of crime. Changes only occur in consequence of changes in the moral standard of society. No severities have eradicated duelling and blood-feuds in certain countries. No matter how many Circassians were executed for robbery, they continued to rob out of bravado because no maiden would marry a young man who had not shown his daring by stealing a horse or at least a sheep. If men cease to fight duels and the Circassians cease to rob, it is not from fear of punishment (indeed that makes the bravado more attractive), but through a change of public opinion. And it is the same with all other crimes. Violence can never destroy what is sanctioned by public opinion. On the contrary, public opinion need only be directly opposed to violence to neutralize its whole effect,[1] as has been shown by all martyrdoms both past and present.

What would happen if we did not use violence against hostile nations and the criminal elements of society we do not know. But that the use of violence has not succeeded in suppressing either the one or the other we know by long experience.

Indeed, how can we subdue by violence nations whose whole education, tradition, and even religious teaching, leads them to see the loftiest virtue in a struggle with their enslavers and in striving for liberty? And how are we by violence to eradicate crimes in our midst when what governments regard as crimes are considered achievements by public opinion?[2] To exterminate such people by violence is possible and indeed is done, but they cannot be forced into submission.

The arbiter who decides everything, the fundamental factor that moves men and nations, has always been and is now the one invisible, intangible power—the resultant of all the spiritual forces of a certain aggregate of men and of

[1] A quarter of a century after Tolstóy wrote the above passage, the 18th Amendment to the Constitution of the United States made possible the experiment of enforcing Prohibition by police action. The result furnished as complete an illustration and confirmation of Tolstóy's thesis as he could have desired.—A.M.

[2] Tolstóy was perhaps referring to the relations of the Government and the public to such revolutionaries as Kropótkin, Stepniák, Vera Zusúlich, and Vera Figner, but other examples could be drawn from Ireland and America.—A.M.

all humanity—which is expressed by public opinion.

Violence only weakens this force, retards it, distorts it, and substitutes another influence which far from being conducive to the progress of mankind is harmful to it.

To bring under the sway of Christianity all the savage peoples outside the pale of Christendom—all the Zulus, Manchurians, and Chinese (whom many consider uncivilized)—as well as the savages found in Christian society, there is only one way: the diffusion among those peoples of a Christian public opinion, which can be established only by a Christian life, Christian actions, and Christian examples. And to win over these peoples who have remained unconverted to Christianity, the men of our time, who have one, and only one, way of attaining such a result, act contrary to that way.

To bring under the sway of Christianity savage nations who do not meddle with us and whom we have no call to oppress, we begin by establishing among them new markets for our commerce, aiming solely at our own profit; then we usurp their land (that is, rob them of it), sell them spirits, tobacco, and opium (that is, deprave them), introduce our systems and customs among them; teach them violence in all its forms (that is, teach them to follow the animal law of strife and that alone, lower than which man cannot descend), and do everything to hide from them all that is Christian in us. All this we do instead of leaving them alone or (if we need come in touch with them or wish to do so) influencing them in a Christian manner by Christian teaching enforced by really Christian deeds of patience, humility, forbearance, purity, and brotherly love. After this, having sent them a couple of dozen missionaries prating some artificial ecclesiastical absurdities, we cite these attempts of ours to convert the heathen to Christianity as incontrovertible proofs of the impossibility of applying the Christian truths to practical life.

So also with the so-called criminals living in our communities. To bring these people under the sway of Christianity there is *only one means*, a Christian public opinion, which can only be set up among them by true Christian teaching supported by true examples of Christian life.

And to preach this Christian truth and confirm it by Christian example we set up among them painful prisons, guillotines, gallows, and preparations for murder—on which we expend our full strength. We teach the common people an idolatrous religious teaching that stupefies them, the Government arranges the sale of stupefying poisons—spirits,[1] tobacco, and opium—we even organize legalized prostitution;[2] we grant land to men who do not need it, make a display of insensate luxury in the midst of poverty, destroy every possibility of anything like a Christian public opinion, and studiously suppress such Christian public opinion as was establishing

[1] The Russian Government monopoly of the sale of spirits brought in a large revenue, as did the tax on tobacco, and in this it differed only in degree from other Governments.—A.M.

[2] This refers to the issue of special passports (yellow tickets) to prostitutes and their compulsory weekly medical examination, as well as to the licensing of brothels.—A.M.

itself.[1] And then we produce these same people—whom we have corrupted by all manner of means and whom we have confined like wild beasts in places from which they cannot escape and where they will become still more brutalized, if we do not kill them—as proof that it is impossible to deal with people except by brutal violence!

It resembles what happens when ignorant and fussy doctors place an already convalescent patient in most insanitary conditions and dose him with deleterious drugs, and then declare that he has been saved from death thanks only to their hygiene and treatment, whereas he would long ago have been quite well had they but left him alone.

Violence, which is held up as a means of supporting a Christian organization of life, not only does not produce that effect but on the contrary is just what prevents the social organization from being what it might and should be. The social order has reached its present level not as a result of violence, but in spite of it.

And therefore the assertion by advocates of the existing order, that since violence hardly suffices to restrain the evil and unchristian element of humanity from attacking us, the abolition of violence and substitution of public opinion would leave mankind unprotected, is false. It is false because violence does not protect mankind but on the contrary deprives it of the only possible

[1] The constant censorship, confiscation, and prosecution relating to Tolstóy's own religious writings was an obvious example of the deliberate suppression of such Christian public opinion as was establishing itself.—A.M.

means of effectually protecting itself—that is, by the establishment and diffusion of a Christian public opinion. Only with the abolition of violence will Christian public opinion cease to be perverted and be able to diffuse itself uninterruptedly, and men cease to direct their efforts towards what they do not need and devote them to the service of the spiritual power which alone can truly actuate them.

'But how are we to discard the evident and palpable protection of the policeman with his pistol and depend on something invisible and impalpable—on public opinion? Does it already exist or not? Moreover we know the order of things in which we live. We know its defects, be it good or bad, and are used to it. We know how to act and what to do under present conditions. But how will it be when we abandon them and rely on something invisible, intangible, and quite unknown?' The uncertainty men encounter when they renounce their habitual way of life seems dreadful to them.

It would be all very well to dread the uncertainty if our customary position were firm and lasting. But not only is our position not secure—we know for certain that we are standing on the verge of destruction.

If we must fear, let us fear what is really terrible and not what we merely imagine to be so.

In fearing to make an effort to break away from conditions that are destroying us, merely because the future is not fully clear, we are like passengers on a sinking ship who are afraid to trust themselves to the boat which would take them to shore and shut themselves up in their cabins and refuse to come out; or like sheep which, afraid of a fire in their yard, crowd into a shed and refuse to go out by the wide-open gate.

Standing as we are on the threshold of the terrible calamity of a revolutionary civil war compared to which, as those who are preparing it tell us, the horrors of 1793 will appear trifling,[1] is it possible for us to talk of danger threatening us from the Zulus, the inhabitants of Dahomey, and the rest, who live at the ends of the earth and are not thinking of attacking us; or from those few thousands of perverted rogues, thieves, and murderers, brutalized and corrupted by us and whose number is not lessened by all our tribunals, prisons, and executions?

Moreover this dread of the abolition of visible protection by a policeman is chiefly felt by townsfolk, that is, by people living in abnormal and artificial conditions. Those who live in natural conditions, not in towns but in the midst of nature and struggling with nature, live without such protection, and know how little violence can protect them from the real dangers by which they are surrounded. There is something morbid in this dread, which arises chiefly from the false conditions in which many of us have grown up and live.

A mental specialist has told how, when he was leaving the asylum one summer's day, some of the patients accompanied him to the street gate. 'Come into the town with me!' said he to them.

---

[1] This was written in 1893, and the Bolshevik Revolution came in 1917.—A.M.

Some of the lunatics agreed and a small group followed the doctor. But the farther they went along the street where healthy people were freely moving about, the more timid they grew, and they pressed against the doctor hindering his progress. At last they all asked to return to the asylum, to their insane but customary way of life, to their keepers, blows, strait-jackets, and solitary cells.

So people to-day crowd together and draw back to their irrational mode of life, to their factories, law-courts, prisons, executions, and wars —when Christianity calls them to liberty and to the free and rational life of the coming age.

People say: 'What protection shall we have when the existing order is abolished? What precisely will be the new organization that will replace the present one? Till we know how our life will be arranged we will not move on or quit this spot.'

These demands are as if an explorer going to an unknown country should ask for a detailed description of the land he is to enter.

If the life of an individual were fully known to him before he passed from one period of it to another, he would have nothing to live for. And so it is with the life of humanity. If it had a programme of the life awaiting it when it entered a new stage, that would be the surest sign that it was not living or advancing, but marking time on one and the same spot.

The conditions of the new order of life cannot be known to us, for we ourselves have to work them out. Life consists in just that; in men learning the unknown and making their activity conform to that new knowledge.

In that lies the life of each individual man and in that too lies the life of human societies and of humanity itself.

XI

A Christian public opinion has already come to life in our society and will inevitably end the present order of life based on violence. When will that be?

THE position of Christian humanity with its prisons and gallows, its factories and accumulations of capital, its taxes, churches, drink-shops and licensed brothels, its ever-increasing armaments and millions of stupefied men ready, like chained dogs, to attack those against whom their master may set them, would be terrible indeed were it the product of violence. But it is chiefly the product of public opinion. And what has been established by public opinion not only can be destroyed by it, but is being destroyed by it.

Hundreds of millions of money and tens of millions of disciplined troops, marvellous efficiency in weapons of destruction, with an organization carried to the utmost point of perfection and with whole bodies of men whose vocation it is to delude and hypnotize the people, and by means of electricity which abolishes distance, all this under the control of men who consider such an organization of society not merely advantageous to themselves, but one without which they would inevitably perish, and who therefore exert all their ingenuity for its maintenance—what an invincible power that would seem to be!

And yet we need only realize what is happening, and what no one can prevent—namely, that a Christian public opinion is replacing the pagan one and is being established with the same strength and universality, and that the majority of men to-day are as much ashamed to take part in and profit by violence as they are of swindling, thieving, begging, or cowardice—and at once, without strife or violence, that complex and seemingly powerful organization of life will be destroyed without a struggle.

And for this to happen it is not necessary that anything new should be brought to people's consciousness. Only let the mist evaporate that hides from men the true meaning of certain deeds of violence, and the Christian public opinion that is growing up will overcome the obsolescent pagan public opinion that permits and justifies deeds of violence.

It is only necessary for people to become as much ashamed of participating in deeds of violence and profiting by them, as they now are of being, or being considered, swindlers, thieves, cowards, or beggars. And that is just what is beginning to occur. We do not notice it, just as people fail to notice their movement when they and all that surrounds them are in motion.

It is true that the order of society in its chief features is still the same violent order that it was a thousand years ago, and in some respects (especially in preparations for war and in war itself) it appears even more cruel. But Christian public opinion—the same that at a certain stage of development must replace the pagan order of our life—already begins to make itself felt. The dead tree stands apparently as firmly as ever—it even seems firmer because it is harder—but it is already rotten at the core and ready to fall. So it is with the present order of society based on violence. The external aspect is as before: some exercise violence and others are subject to it. But neither these nor those any longer have the same view of the significance and dignity of their respective positions.

Those who do violence (that is, those who take part in government) and those who profit by violence (that is, the rich) no longer represent as used to be the case the flower of our society and the ideal of human well-being and grandeur towards which all the violated used formerly to strive. Now very often the oppressed do not strive to gain the position of the oppressors or try to imitate them. On the contrary, users of violence often voluntarily renounce the advantages of their position, choose the condition of the oppressed, and try to resemble them in the simplicity of their life.

Not to speak of the now openly despised duties and occupations—such as those of spies, agents of the secret police, usurers, and publicans—a large number of professions held by users of violence which used to be considered honourable (such as those of police officials, courtiers, officers of the law, administrative functionaries, the clergy, the military, the monopolists and bankers) are not only no longer accounted honourable by everyone, but are even condemned by a certain much respected section of people. There are already people who voluntarily abandon these positions which were once accounted irreproachable, and prefer less advantageous positions not connected with violence.

And apart from men in governmental positions, there are already some rich people who, not through religious sentiment as used to happen, but simply through special sensitiveness to the public opinion that is coming to life, relinquish property they inherit, believing that a man can only justly avail himself of what he has gained by his own labour.

The position of a government official or of a rich man no longer presents itself as used to be the case and is the case even now among the non-Christian peoples, as indubitably honourable, deserving of respect, and blessed by God.

The most morally sensitive people (who for the most part are also the most cultivated) avoid such positions and prefer humbler ones that are not dependent on the use of violence.

At the age when still uncorrupted by life and choosing a career, the best of our young people prefer the callings of doctors, technologists, teachers, artists, writers, or even simple tillers of the soil living by their own labour, rather than legal, administrative, ecclesiastical or military positions in the pay of the government, or even to living on their private incomes.

Nowadays monuments are not usually erected in commemoration of statesmen or generals, still less to rich men; they are erected to the learned, to artists, to inventors, to men who not only have had nothing in common with the government and rulers but have often even been in conflict with them. It is not so much State functionaries and the rich, as learned men and artists, who are represented in sculpture, sung in poetry, and honoured by solemn jubilees.

The best men of our time seek these esteemed positions and the circle from which the governing class and the wealthy come is decreasing both in quantity and in quality, so that in intellect and culture and especially in moral qualities, the rich men and those who now stand at the head of governments no longer constitute the flower of society as in olden times, but on the contrary are below the average.

In Russia and Turkey, as in France and America, in spite of the constant change of government officials, the majority of these are self-seeking and venal men of such a low moral standard that they do not even satisfy the low demand of simple integrity expected of them. Nowadays one may often hear ingenuous regrets expressed by persons in authority, that the best men—by some strange chance as it seems to them—are always to be found in the opposite camp. It is as if one regretted that—by some strange chance—executioners are always chosen from among men neither very refined nor very kind.

In the same way the majority of rich people of to-day no longer as formerly constitute the most refined and educated portion of society, but are either coarse money-grubbers only concerned with enriching themselves (frequently by shady methods) or else the degenerate heirs of such money-grubbers, who far from playing any prominent part in society are for the most part held in general contempt.

But not only is the class of those from whom the servants of governments and the wealthy are drawn growing ever smaller and smaller and lower in calibre, they themselves no longer attribute the same importance to their positions that they once did, but are often ashamed of them, and do not perform the duties their positions demand.[1] Kings and emperors now scarcely govern at all and hardly ever decide upon an internal reform themselves, or any new departure in foreign policy, but generally leave the decision of these questions to governmental institutions or to public opinion. Their whole duty now amounts to representing the unity and power of the State. But they perform even that duty less and less successfully. The majority of them not only do not keep up their former unapproachable majesty, but become more and more democratic and even vulgar themselves, throwing aside the last of their prestige—that is, infringing the very thing they were called on to maintain.

It is the same with the army. Military men of the upper classes, instead of encouraging in their soldiers the harshness and brutality indis-

---

[1] When Tolstóy wrote this, there were many cases of Russian government officials being privately friendly to men in active opposition to the government, and this friendliness influenced their official conduct.—A.M.

pensable to their calling, themselves promote education and inculcate humanity among them, and often even themselves share the socialistic ideas of the masses and condemn war. In the last conspiracies against the Russian Government many of those concerned were military men. And the number of such military conspirators is ever increasing. And it often happens (as was the case the other day) that when called upon to suppress disturbances they refuse to fire. Military bravado is simply condemned by the military themselves and is often held up to ridicule. The judges whose business it is to try and to condemn criminals, conduct proceedings so as to acquit them, so that the Russian Government to secure the conviction of those it wants to punish, never now entrusts them to the ordinary courts but hands them over to a so-called military court, which is only the simulacrum of a court of justice.[1] So too with the public prosecutors, who often refuse to prosecute and even, by an evasion of the law, instead of prosecuting defend those they ought to accuse. Learned jurists whose business it is to justify the government violence are more and more disposed to deny the right of punishment, and substitute theories of irresponsibility and even advise not the correction but the cure of those they call criminals.

Warders and governors of prisons frequently

[1] Almost the last case in which a conspicuous political prisoner in Russia was allowed a public trial by jury before an ordinary criminal court, was that of Véra Zasúlich (in 1878) who shot at Trépov, the Governor of St. Petersburg, who had flogged a prisoner. She was acquitted by the jury, who sympathized with her.—A.M.

become the protectors of those they ought to torture. Gendarmes and spies frequently assist the escape of those they are supposed to ruin. The clergy preach tolerance and sometimes even condemn the use of violence, and the more educated among them try in their sermons to avoid the very deception which furnishes the basis of their position and which it is their business to preach. Executioners refuse to carry out their functions, so that in Russia sentences of death can often not be carried out for want of an executioner, since despite the inducements offered to convicts to persuade them to become executioners, there are ever fewer and fewer willing to take up the duty.

Governors, police-officials, and tax-collectors, pitying the peasants, often try to find pretexts for not collecting the taxes from them. Rich men are reluctant to use their wealth for themselves alone, and disburse it for public purposes. Landowners build hospitals and schools on their land, and some of them even renounce the ownership of land and transfer it to the tillers of the soil or establish communities on it. Mill-owners and manufacturers arrange hospitals, schools, savings-banks and pensions as well as dwellings for their work-people. Some of them form companies in which they share equally with the workers. There are capitalists who devote part of their capital to educational, artistic, philanthropic and other public institutions. Others, unable to bring themselves to part with their wealth during their lifetime, leave it to public institutions after their death.

All these facts might appear accidental did they not all come from one common cause, just as it might seem accidental that in spring the buds begin to swell on some of the trees, if we did not know that this is caused by the coming of spring generally, and that if the buds have begun to swell on some of the trees they will certainly do so on all of them.

It is the same with the manifestation of Christian public opinion in regard to violence and all that is based on it. If this public opinion already influences some sensitive people and causes them each in his own sphere to renounce the advantages that violence affords, then it will continue to act on others and will go on doing so until it transforms all the activity of men, and brings it into accord with the Christian consciousness which is already a driving force among the most advanced people.

And if already now there are rulers who refrain from taking decisions on their own authority and who try as far as possible to be unlike monarchs and as much like plain mortals as they can, and who express readiness to give up their prerogatives and to become simply the first citizens of their republics; and if there are now military men who understand all the evil and wickedness of war and do not want to shoot people, either of their own or of another nation; and if there are judges and public prosecutors who do not like to prosecute and condemn criminals; and if there are clergy who renounce their lies, and tax-gatherers who try to fulfil the duties laid upon them as little as possible; and if there are rich men who give up their wealth, then this will inevitably happen with other rulers, other soldiers, other judges, priests, tax-gatherers, and rich men. And when there are no longer men willing to occupy these positions, there will be none of these positions and no violence.

But this is not the only road by which public opinion leads men to the abolition of the existing order and the substitution of another. As positions based on the rule of violence become less and less attractive and there are fewer and fewer candidates to fill them, their uselessness will become more and more apparent.

In a Christian world there are the same rulers and governments and armies and law-courts and tax-gatherers and clergy and wealthy landowners, manufacturers and capitalists, as before, but humanity has quite another attitude towards them and they themselves have quite another attitude towards their own position.

The rulers still have meetings, interview one another, and go about. There are the same hunts, banquets, balls, and uniforms; the same diplomatists still talk about alliances and wars; there are the same parliaments, in which in the same way they discuss the Eastern question, and Africa, and alliances, and breaches of relations, and Home Rule, and the eight-hour day. And one ministry is replaced by another in the same way, and speeches and incidents go on as before. But to men who see how one newspaper article has more effect on the position of affairs than a dozen imperial interviews or sessions of parliament, it becomes more and more evident that these interviews and meetings and debates in parliament do not guide the affairs of men, but that they are guided by something independent of all these and not centred anywhere.

There are the same generals and officers and soldiers and cannon and fortresses and reviews and manœuvres, but no war for a year, for ten years, for twenty years. Moreover it becomes less and less possible to rely on the military for the suppression of internal risings, and consequently more and more evident that the generals and officers are only puppets for pageantry and processions—the plaything of sovereigns, a sort of enormous and too costly *corps-de-ballet*.[1]

There are the same lawyers and judges and the same assizes, but it becomes more and more evident that since the civil courts decide cases on every consideration except that of justice, and that criminal trials have no sense because punishments do not attain the desired effect (as is admitted even by judges themselves), these institutions have no significance other than to provide a means of livelihood for men who are not fit for anything more useful.

There are the same priests, bishops, churches, and synods, but it becomes clearer and clearer that they themselves have long ceased to believe what they preach, and that therefore they cannot convince anyone else of the necessity of believing it.

[1] It was another twenty-two years before the quite needless Russo-Japanese war occurred, and a further nine before the Great War broke out, and in both cases Russia would have fared better had she not fought, but Tolstóy's hope that war was obsolescent was premature if not mistaken.—A.M.

There are the same tax-gatherers, but they grow less and less capable of taking people's property from them by force, and it becomes more and more evident that people can collect all that is necessary by voluntary subscription, without tax-gatherers.

There are the same rich people, but it becomes ever clearer and clearer that they can be useful only in proportion as they cease to be personal managers of their wealth and give the community all or at least part of it.

When all this becomes quite evident to everybody it will be natural for men to ask themselves: 'Why should we feed and maintain all these kings, emperors, presidents, and members of various chambers and ministries, since nothing comes of their meetings and talks? Would it not be better, as some humorist has said, to make an india-rubber queen?

'And what do we want armies for, with their generals, and bands, and cavalry, and drums? What are they wanted for when there is no war and no one wants to conquer anybody? And even if there were a war, other nations would not let us profit by it, and the army will not fire on its own people.

'And what are the judges and lawyers for, who in civil cases decide nothing according to justice, and in criminal affairs themselves recognize the uselessness of punishments?

'And what are the tax-gatherers for, who exact the taxes reluctantly while what is really needed is easily collected without them?

'And what is the use of the clergy, who have

long since ceased to believe in what they have to preach?

'And what is the use of capital in private hands, if it can be useful only after becoming public property?'

And once they ask themselves these questions, men cannot fail to conclude that they ought not to support all these institutions which have become useless.

But not only will men who support these institutions decide to abolish them; men occupying these positions will themselves at the same time be brought to the necessity of giving them up, if indeed they have not done so sooner.

Public opinion condemns violence more and more, and so men, submitting more and more to public opinion, are less and less anxious to occupy positions depending on the use of violence. And if they do occupy such positions they are less and less willing to use violence, and consequently become more and more useless.

And this superfluity, which is more and more plainly felt both by those who support these positions and by those occupying them, will at last become so pronounced that men will no longer be found willing to support or occupy such positions.

I was once present in Moscow at a discussion about faith which was held, as is the custom, in the first week after Easter near the church in Hunter's Row. A group of some twenty people had collected on the side-walk and a serious discussion about religion was going on. At the same time some concert or other was being held in the Assembly of the Nobility, and a police officer, noticing the group of people collected near the church, sent a mounted gendarme to order them to disperse. There was no need at all for the officer to disperse them, the twenty men who had collected were in nobody's way, but the officer had been standing there all the morning and wanted something to do. The young gendarme, his right arm swaggeringly akimbo, and clattering with his sabre, rode up to us and shouted sternly: 'Move on! What have you collected here for?' Everybody looked round at the gendarme and one of the speakers, a modest man in a peasant's coat, quietly and amiably said: 'We are speaking of serious matters and there is no reason for us to move on. You had better get down and listen to what is being said, young man. It will do you good.' And turning round he continued his discourse. The gendarme silently turned his horse round and rode off.

That is what ought to happen wherever violence is used. The officer feels dull. He has nothing to do. He has been put, poor fellow, in a position in which he has to give orders. He is shut off from all rational human existence. He can only look on and give orders, give orders and look on, though nobody needs either his orders or his attention. All our unfortunate rulers, ministers, members of parliament, governors, generals, officers, archbishops, bishops, priests, and even rich men, already find themselves partly, and soon will find themselves completely, in that position. They can do nothing but give orders, and so they make a fuss and send their subordinates about, as that officer sent the gendarme, to interfere with people. And as the people they interfere with ask them not to interfere, they imagine themselves to be quite indispensable men.

But a time is approaching and draws near when it will become perfectly evident to everyone that these people are of no use at all but are merely a hindrance, and those whom they interfere with will say amiably and quietly, like the man in the peasant's coat: 'Don't interfere with us, please!' And then all these emissaries, and those who send them, will have to follow that good advice, that is, cease to ride about with an arm akimbo hindering people, and get off their horses, doff their uniforms, listen to what is being said, and join with others in real human work.

A time is coming, and will inevitably come, when all institutions based on violence will disappear because it has become obvious to everyone that they are useless, stupid, and even wrong.

A time must come when the men of our modern world who fill offices dependent on violence will find themselves in the position of the Emperor in Andersen's fairy-tale, when the little child who saw him undressed naïvely exclaimed: 'Why, he has no clothes on!' And all the people, who had known it before but had not dared to say so, had to admit it too.

The tale is of a monarch fond of new clothes to whom two tailors came offering to make him some wonderful attire. He engaged them and they set to work, saying that the peculiarity of the garments was that no one who was unfit for the position he held could see them.

The courtiers came to look at the tailors' work, but could see nothing, as the tailors were plying their needles in empty space. But remembering the caution, they all pretended they saw the garments, and expressed admiration of them. It was the same with the Emperor himself. The day came for the procession in which he was to go in his new clothes. He undressed and put them on—that is to say, he remained naked and went naked through the town. But remembering the special property of the clothes, no one ventured to say that he had nothing on till the little child exclaimed: 'Why, he has no clothes on!'

The same thing ought to happen with all those who by inertia continue to fill positions that have long ceased to be useful. The first man not interested in 'washing one hand with the other' as the Russian proverb has it, and who therefore has no interest in concealing the uselessness of these institutions, should point it out and ingenuously exclaim: 'But these people have long ago ceased to be of any use!'

The condition of Christian humanity, with its fortresses, cannon, dynamite, rifles, torpedoes, prisons, gallows, churches, factories, custom-houses, and palaces, is really terrible. But neither the fortresses nor the cannon nor the rifles will attack anyone of themselves, the prisons will not of themselves lock anyone up, the gallows will not of themselves hang anyone, nor will the churches delude anyone or the custom-houses hold anyone back, and the palaces and factories do not build themselves or maintain themselves. All this is done by people. And if they once understand that there is no necessity for all these things, these things will disappear.

And men already begin to understand. If they do not all understand, the leaders among them do—those whom the rest will follow. And what the leaders have once understood they cannot possibly cease to understand. And what the leaders have understood the rest of mankind not only can, but inevitably must, understand too.

So that the prediction that a time will come when men will be taught of God, will cease to learn war any more, and will beat their swords into ploughshares and their spears into pruning-hooks (which translated into our own tongue means that all the prisons, fortresses, barracks, palaces, and churches, will remain empty, and that all the gallows, guns and cannon will remain unused), is no longer a dream but a definite new form of life, to which humanity is approaching with ever-increasing rapidity.

But when will this be realized?

Nineteen hundred years ago Christ replied to this question, that the end of the present age (the end, that is, of the pagan organization of the world) would come when the calamities of mankind had increased to the utmost, and when the good news of the Kingdom of God (that is, the possibility of a new system of life free from violence) had been proclaimed throughout the world. (Matt. xxiv. 3–28.)

'Of that day and hour knoweth no man, but

my Father only' (Matt. xxiv. 36), said Christ then. For it can come at any minute, even when least expected.

To the question when that hour will come, Christ replied that we cannot know that, but for that very reason should always hold ourselves in readiness to meet it, as the goodman must be ready who guards his home, and as the virgins with their lamps must be ready to meet the bridegroom, and that we, too, must work for the coming of that hour with all the powers given us, as the servants worked with the talents entrusted to them. (Matt. xxiv. 43, xxv. 1–30.) In reply to the question when the hour would come, Christ exhorted people to devote all their energies to hasten its coming.

And there can be no other reply. Men cannot possibly know at what day and hour the Kingdom of God will come, for its coming depends only on themselves.

The reply is like that which the sage gave when asked whether it was far to the town: 'Walk on!'

How can we tell whether it is far to the goal to which humanity aspires when we do not know how humanity will advance towards it—whether it will choose to move onwards or to stand still, to slacken its pace or increase it?

All we can know is what we (who constitute humanity) must do and must not do to bring about the Kingdom of God. And we all know that. Each of us has only to begin to do what he ought to do and cease doing the contrary. We need only each of us live according to the light that is in us to bring about the promised Kingdom of God towards which the heart of every man aspires.

XII

CONCLUSION

Repent ye, for the Kingdom of Heaven is at hand.

I

I WAS just finishing this two years' work when on September 9th [1892] I had to go by rail to the district in Túla and Ryazán provinces where the peasants suffered from famine last year and are suffering still more this year. At one of the local stations we encountered a special train conveying troops commanded by the Governor of the province and armed with rifles, ammunition, and rods to flog and kill those starving peasants.

Despite the fact that corporal punishment was abolished by law thirty years ago, the flogging of men with rods in execution of decrees issued by the authorities has of late been practised more and more frequently in Russia.

I had heard of this and had even read in the papers about the terrible floggings of which Baránov, the Governor of Nízhni-Nóvgorod, seemed to boast, and of those that took place in Chernýgov, Tambóv, Sarátov, Astrakhán, and Orël. But I had never before happened to see men engaged on inflicting such punishments.

Now I saw with my own eyes kindly Russians imbued with the Christian spirit, travelling with rifles and rods to kill and torture their starving brothers.

The cause of their going was this:

On one of the estates of a wealthy landowner the peasants had grown (that is, had tended during its growth) a wood on land they held in common with the landowner. They had always made use of it, and therefore considered it theirs or at least as held in common, but the landowner, having appropriated that wood, began to cut down the trees. The peasants lodged a complaint. The judge in the first instance, unjustly (I say 'unjustly' on the word of the public prosecutor and the Governor, who should know) decided the case in favour of the landowner. All the higher courts, including the Senate, though they could see that the matter had been decided wrongly, confirmed this decision, and the wood was awarded to the landowner. He again began cutting down the trees, but the peasants, unable to believe that such an evident injustice could be done them by the higher authorities, did not submit to the decision and drove away the workmen sent to fell the trees, declaring that the wood belonged to them and that they would carry the matter to the Tsar but would not let the trees be cut down.

The matter was reported to Petersburg, and from there the Governor received instructions to carry into effect the decision of the court. He asked for troops. And now the soldiers, armed with rifles and bayonets and ball-cartridges as well as a supply of rods expressly prepared for the purpose and heaped up on one of the trucks, were on their way to carry out this decision of the higher authorities.

Decisions of the higher authorities are enforced by the murder and torture of men, or by threats of one or the other, according to whether resistance is offered or not.

In the first case, if the peasants offer resistance, the following course is pursued in Russia (and everywhere where a State organization and private property exist): the commanding officer makes a speech and demands submission. The excited crowd, usually deluded by their leaders, understanding nothing of what the representative of authority has said in official, bookish language, continue to be turbulent. Then the Governor announces that if they do not submit and disperse, he will be obliged to have recourse to force. And if the crowd does not then submit and disperse he gives orders to load rifles and fire over the people's heads. If they still do not disperse he gives the order to fire into their midst. The soldiers fire, and the killed and wounded people fall in the street. Then the crowd usually runs away, and the soldiers, at the Governor's command, seize those who seem to him to be the ringleaders and lead them away under escort.

After that they gather up the bloodstained, dying, maimed, killed and wounded men, sometimes with women and children also among them. The dead they bury and the maimed are sent to hospital. Those they consider to be ringleaders are taken to town and are there tried by a special military court. And if on their side any violence has been committed they are sentenced to be hanged. And then a gallows is set up and several defenceless people are throttled with cords, as has been done repeatedly in Russia and is and must be done wherever the social order is based on violence. This is what happens in cases of resistance.

In the second case, when the peasants submit, something strange and peculiarly Russian takes place. The Governor, having arrived on the scene of action, makes a speech to the people rebuking them for their lack of obedience, and either quarters troops on the houses of the village (where they sometimes remain for a month, their keep ruining the peasants) or contenting himself with threats graciously pardons the people and departs, or as most frequently happens announces that the ringleaders must be punished, and arbitrarily and without trial selects a certain number of men considered to be ringleaders and has them flogged in his presence.

To give an idea of how these things are done I will describe one that took place in Orël and was approved of by the higher authorities.

What happened in Orël was this. Here, just as in Túla province, a landowner wanted to deprive the peasants of some property, and the peasants opposed him in just the same way. The landowner, without the consent of the peasants, wanted to keep the water in his mill-pond at so high a level that it flooded their meadows. The peasants resisted and the landowner laid a complaint before the district commissary, who illegally (as was recognized later by the Court) decided the case in the landowner's favour and granted him permission to raise the level of the water. The peasants were indignant at this unjust decision and when the landowner sent workmen to dam up the canal through which the water flowed down, they sent their women-folk to prevent its being done. The women went to the dam, overturned the workmen's carts, and drove the men away. The landowner lodged a complaint against the women for thus taking the law into their own hands, and the district commissary issued an order to lock up one woman from every homestead in the village. The order was not one that could well be executed for there were several women in each homestead and it was impossible to know which of them was to be arrested. Consequently the police did not carry it out. The landowner then complained to the Governor of the inactivity of the police, and the Governor without looking into the matter gave the chief of rural police strict orders to carry out the commissary's decision. In obedience to his superior the rural chief of police went to the village, and with a disregard for other people characteristic of Russian officials, ordered his men to seize one woman from each house. But since there was more than one woman in each house and no way of knowing which was to be incarcerated, altercations and resistance arose. In spite of this the rural chief gave orders that some one woman should be seized in each home-stead and put into confinement. The peasants began to defend their wives and mothers and would not give them up, and incidentally beat the rural chief of police and his men. This was a fresh and terrible crime—resistance to authority

—and a report of the new offence was sent to the town. Then the Governor went by special train to the scene of action (just as the Túla Governor was now doing) taking a battalion of soldiers equipped with rifles and rods, utilizing the telegraph and telephones and railways, and taking also a learned doctor whose duty it was to supervise the hygiene of the floggings—fully personifying the Genghis Khan with telegraphs foretold by Herzen.

Near the house of the rural communal adminstration stood the soldiers, a detachment of gendarmes with revolvers slung on red cords, the village functionaries, and the accused. Around stood a crowd of a thousand or more. The Governor, having driven up, alighted from his carriage, made an introductory speech, and called for the culprits and a bench. The latter demand was not at first understood. But a gendarme the Governor always took about with him and whose business it was to attend to the preparation of the torture—which had been enacted in the province more than once before—explained that what was required was a bench for flogging. A bench was brought, the rods were produced, and the executioners were summoned. (They had been previously chosen from among horse-thieves of that village, as the soldiers had refused to perform the duty.)

When all was ready the commander ordered the first of the twelve men whom the landowner pointed out as specially culpable, to come forward. He was the father of a family, a man of forty, who had always stood up manfully for the rights of the community and therefore enjoyed the respect of all the villagers. He was led to the bench, stripped, and ordered to lie down.

The man attempted to beg for mercy, but seeing that this was useless, crossed himself and lay down. Two gendarmes rushed forward to hold him. The learned doctor stood by ready to render scientific medical assistance when necessary. The horse-thieves, having spat on their hands, swung their rods and began to flog. It happened, however, that the bench was too narrow, and it was difficult to keep on it the writhing man they were torturing. Then the Governor ordered them to bring another bench and to lay a plank across the two. And men, raising their hands to their caps and saying: 'Yes, your Excellency!' hastened to execute the order. Meanwhile the tortured man, half-naked, pale, and scowling, stood waiting, his eyes fixed on the ground, his teeth chattering and his naked legs trembling. When another bench had been brought they again laid him down, and the horse-thieves again began to flog him. The back, buttocks, thighs, and even the sides of the victim became more and more covered with weals and bruises, and at every blow came dull sounds he was unable to repress. From the crowd standing around arose the wails of the wives, mothers, children, and families of the tortured man and of all the others who had been picked out for punishment.

The miserable Governor, intoxicated by power, and to whom it appeared that he could not act otherwise, counted the blows, bending his fingers as he did so, and smoked cigarettes incessantly—several officious persons hastening to hand him a lighted match at every opportunity. When more than fifty strokes had been given, the peasant ceased to cry out or writhe, and the doctor—educated in a crown establishment to serve his Tsar and his fatherland by his scientific knowledge—went up to the victim, felt his pulse, listened to his heart, and informed the representative of authority that the man had lost consciousness and that, according to the data of science, it might endanger his life to continue the punishment. But the miserable Governor, now completely intoxicated by the sight of blood, ordered them to continue, and the torture continued up to seventy strokes—the number that for some reason seemed necessary to the Governor. When the seventieth stroke had been given, he said: 'Enough! Next one!' And the mutilated victim with his swollen back was carried away in a swoon and another was led up. The sobs and groans of the crowd grew louder, but the representative of the State continued the torture.

They flogged each of the twelve victims in the same way. Each of them received seventy strokes, and each of them begged for mercy, shrieked, and groaned. The sobs and groans of the crowd of women grew louder and more heart-rending, and the men's faces became more and more gloomy. But they were surrounded by troops, and the torture did not cease till it had reached the full measure decided on by the caprice of the miserable, half-intoxicated, and deluded creature they called the Governor.

The officials, officers, and soldiers were not merely present, but by their presence shared in this State action and prevented its being interfered with by the crowd.

When I asked a certain Governor why such tortures were inflicted on people who had already submitted and when troops were already in the village, he replied, with the imposing air of one familiar with all the subtleties of statecraft, that it was done because experience proves that if the peasants are not subjected to torture they soon resist the orders of the authorities again, but that the torture of a few ensures respect for the authorities' orders for ever.

So now the Governor of Túla accompanied by officials, officers, and soldiers, was going to perpetrate an act of this kind! The decision of the highest authority was to be carried out in just the same way by murder or torture. And this decision decreed that a young landowner who had an income of a hundred thousand rubles a year, was to get three thousand rubles more, for timber he had taken by fraud from a whole commune of peasants who were dying of cold and hunger. He might squander that money in two or three weeks in the saloons of Moscow, Petersburg, or Paris.

That was the business the men I met were engaged on.

After my thoughts had been fixed for two years in one and the same direction, fate seemed to have brought me for the first time in my life expressly in contact with an occurrence which plainly showed in practice what had long been clear to me in theory, namely, that the whole order of our lives rests not on principles of jurisprudence (as people occupying advantageous positions are pleased to imagine) but on the simplest, coarsest violence—on the murder and torture of men.

Those who own large estates and fortunes, or who receive large incomes drawn from working people who go short even of necessities; and those who, like tradesmen, doctors, artists, clerks, scientists, cooks, writers, valets, and lawyers, live by serving those rich people, like to believe that the advantages they enjoy result not from violence, but from an absolutely free and proper exchange of services. They like to believe that their advantages—far from being gained by beatings and murders such as took place in Orël and in many other parts of Russia this summer, and that occur continually all over Europe and America—have no kind of connexion with such violence. They like to believe that their privileges exist of themselves, and result from voluntary agreement among people, and that the violence enacted also exists of itself, and results from some general, higher juridical, political, or economic laws. They try not to see that they enjoy their advantages as a result of the very thing which forces the peasants who have tended the wood and are in great need of the timber to yield it up to a wealthy landowner, who took no part in tending it during its growth and is in no need of it—that is, the knowledge that if they do not give it up they will be flogged or killed.

Yet it is clear that the mill in Orël was able to

yield its owner a larger profit, and that the wood planted by the peasants became the property of the landowner, only in consequence of floggings and murders or the threat of them. And in the same way it should be clear that all the other exceptional rights the rich enjoy, depriving the poor of necessities, rest on the same basis. If peasants who need land to maintain their families may not plough the land around their homes, but that land, to an extent sufficient to feed a thousand families, is at the disposal of a single man—a Russian, English, Austrian or any other great landowner, who never works on it or cultivates it himself, and if a merchant who has bought grain from the workers when they were in need can keep it safely in his barns amid starving people, and sell it at three times its cost to the same cultivators from whom he bought it—then this, too, rests on the same basis. And if no one may buy cheap goods from beyond a certain conventional line called a frontier without paying customs duties to men who had no share in their production, and if people are obliged to give up their last cow for taxes which the Government distributes among its officials and spends on the maintenance of soldiers who may have to kill those very taxpayers—it would seem obvious that this, too, has certainly not come about because of any abstract rights, but because of the thing that happened in Orël and may now happen in the province of Túla, the thing that periodically happens in one form or another the world over, wherever there is a governmental organization and wherever there are rich and poor.

As however torture and murder are not employed in all cases of oppression, those who enjoy
the exceptional advantages of the ruling classes
assure themselves and others that their privileges
are not based on torture and murder but on some
mysterious general causes, abstract rights, and
so on. Yet it would seem clear that if men consider it unjust (as all the working classes now
consider it) to yield the chief part of the produce
of their labour to a capitalist or landowner, or
to pay taxes knowing that a bad use is made of
them, they do these things primarily not from
recognition of some abstract rights of which they
have never heard, but simply because they know
that they will be beaten or killed if they refuse
to do them.

And if there is no need to imprison, beat, or
kill men when the landowners collect rent, or a
man in need of corn pays a triple price to a swindling dealer, or a factory-hand puts up with pay
that is proportionately only half of what his em-
ployer takes, or when a poor man pays his last
ruble in customs-dues and taxes—this is only
because so many men have been beaten and
killed for trying to resist what was demanded of
them, that the others firmly remember it.

A trained tiger in a cage who does not eat the
meat put under his nose and who jumps over a
stick at the word of command, does this not because he wishes to, but because he remembers
the red-hot irons or the hunger from which he
suffered every time he did not obey. And in the
same way men who submit to what is disadvantageous and even ruinous to them and that they

consider unjust, do so because they remember what happened to them when they resisted.

But those who profit by the privileges resulting from previous violence often forget, and are pleased to forget, how those advantages were obtained. Yet we need only think of history—not the history of the triumphs of various dynasties and rulers—but real history, the history of the oppression of the majority by a small minority—to see that the advantages of the rich over the poor have originated from nothing but rods, prisons, convict-settlements, and murder.[1]

One need but consider the unceasing and persistent struggle to increase material prosperity that guides everybody in our times, to be convinced that the advantages of the rich over the poor could not and cannot be maintained by anything but violence.

There may be cases where oppressions, beatings, prisons, and executions, are not inflicted to secure the advantages of the propertied classes (though such cases are rare). But one may confidently say that in our society (where for every well-to-do man living in comfort there are ten who are exhausted by labour, envious, covetous, and whose whole families are often suffering) all the advantages of the rich, all their luxuries and superfluities, all that is beyond what an average workman possesses, is obtained and maintained by tortures, imprisonments, and executions.

---

[1] This indictment could to-day be illustrated by reference to the behaviour of the rulers to the ruled in the U.S.S.R. or in Germany, quite as strikingly as by the references Tolstóy was able to use.—A.M.

2

The special train I met on September 9th, going with soldiers, rifles, ball-cartridges, and rods, to secure to the rich landowner the small wood he did not need, and which he had taken from hungry peasants who needed it very badly, showed in a striking way to what a degree men have developed a capacity to commit deeds contrary to their convictions without seeing that they are doing so.

The special train I encountered consisted of one first-class carriage for the Governor, officials, and officers, and several luggage-vans crowded with soldiers.

The brisk young soldiers in their clean new uniforms were standing about in groups, or sitting with their legs dangling from the wide-open doors of the trucks. Some were smoking, others nudging one another, joking, grinning, and laughing. Others were cracking sunflower seeds, self-confidently spitting out the husks. Some of them ran along the platform to the water-butt for a drink, and when they met an officer, slackened their pace and made their stupid gesture of salute, raising their hands to their foreheads with serious faces as if they were doing something not only reasonable but very important. They kept their eyes on the officer till they had passed him, and then ran on still more merrily, stamping along the planks of the platform, laughing and chattering, as is natural to healthy, good-natured young fellows travelling from one place to another in lively company.

They went to the murder of their hungry fathers and grandfathers just as if they were going to some gay, or at any rate quite ordinary, business.

A similar impression was produced by the smart officials and officers scattered about the platform and in the first-class refreshment-room. At a table set out with bottles sat the Governor, the chief of the whole expedition, in a semi-military uniform, eating something and speaking calmly about the weather with some acquaintance he had met, as though his errand were so simple and ordinary that it could not ruffle his composure or interfere with his interest in the change of the weather.

At a little distance from the table and not eating anything sat a chief of gendarmes whose impenetrable face wore an air of boredom, as though he were weary of the tedious formality that had to be enacted. On all sides officers in their handsome gold-braided uniforms moved about and chatted. One, sitting at the table, was finishing a bottle of beer; another, standing at the buffet, munched a savoury patty, brushing the crumbs from the breast of his uniform and with a self-confident air throwing down a coin; another, dragging his feet, sauntered in front of the carriages of our train, staring at the women.

All these men, on their way to murder or torture the hungry and defenceless creatures who provided them with sustenance, had an air of being firmly convinced that they were doing their duty. They were even rather proud of themselves—'swaggering' about it.

How is this?

All these men are within half-an-hour's journey of the place where—in order to ensure that a rich young man should have three thousand rubles he had taken from a whole commune of famishing peasants—they may be obliged, as in Orël, to commit the most terrible things that can be conceived, to murder or torture innocent beings, their fellow men. And they are quite serene as they approach the place where this is to be done and the time draws near to begin it.

To say that these men—all these officials, officers, and soldiers—do not know what is before them and what they are going for, is impossible, for they have prepared for it. The Governor must have given instructions, and the officials must have purchased those birch switches, bargained for them, and entered the item in their accounts. The officers must have received, issued, and executed, the orders about the ball-cartridges. They all know that they are going to torture, perhaps to kill, their brother men who are exhausted by hunger, and that they must set to work on it perhaps within an hour.

To say, as is usually said and as they themselves repeat, that they do this from conviction of the necessity of maintaining the State system, would be mistaken. For these people have hardly ever even thought about the State system and its necessity, they cannot possibly be convinced that the act they are taking part in will tend to support, and not to destroy, the State, and in practice most if not all of them, far from sacrificing their tranquillity or pleasure to support the State, never miss an opportunity of furthering their own interest at its expense. So they are not moved by belief in the abstract principle of the State.

What then?

You see, I know all these men. If I do not know each of them personally I know their characters pretty well, their past, and their way of thinking. They all have had mothers, and some of them have wives and children. They are for the most part mild, kindly, even tender-hearted men who hate all cruelty. Not to speak of the killing of men, many of them would not even kill or torture an animal. Moreover all of them profess Christianity, and regard the use of violence against defenceless people as an abject and abominable action. Not one of them in ordinary life would be capable, for his own petty personal profit, of doing a one-hundredth part of what the Orël Governor did. Each one of them would be insulted at the suggestion that he was capable of anything of the kind in private life.

And yet here they are within half-an-hour's journey of the place where they may unavoidably be forced to do it.

What does it mean?

How could, not only these men travelling by this train and prepared to murder and torture, but those who began the whole business: the landowner, his steward, the judges, and those in Petersburg who gave the order and are responsible for it—the minister, and the Tsar, who are also good men professing Christianity—how could they devise and prescribe such a plan, knowing the consequences? How could the spectators even who took no part in the affair—men who are indignant at any case of violence in private life—how could they allow such a horrible deed to be perpetrated? How was it they did not rise in indignation and stand across the road crying out: 'No, we won't allow you to kill and flog starving men because they won't let their last possessions be taken from them by fraud!'? But not only did no one do that; on the contrary the majority, even the initiators of the affair (the steward, the landowner, the judges, and those who took part in making the peasants yield and arranged it—the Governor, the minister, and the Emperor) are perfectly tranquil and do not even feel a prick of conscience. And all these men who are travelling by train to perform this crime are apparently equally tranquil.

The spectators it seemed were quite unmoved, and for the most part looked on with sympathy rather than with disapproval at all those who were preparing to do this infamous thing. In the carriage with me was a lumber-dealer of peasant origin, and he plainly and openly expressed sympathy with the treatment that awaited the peasants: 'They must not disobey the authorities,' said he. 'That's what the authorities are for. Wait a bit and they'll have their fleas driven from them! They'll learn not to riot, no fear! They're getting their deserts!'

Why is this?

It is impossible to say that all these people— those who instigated and participated in and tolerated this affair—were such wretches that for a salary, for profit, or from fear of punishment, they did an action contrary to their convictions, knowing all the loathsomeness of what they were doing. All of them in certain circumstances are capable of standing up for their convictions. Not one of those officials would steal a purse, read another man's letter, or put up with an affront without demanding satisfaction. Not one of those officers would allow himself to cheat at cards, omit to pay a card debt, betray a comrade, run away from the field of battle, or abandon his flag. Not one of these soldiers would spit out the holy sacrament, or even eat meat on Good Friday. All these men are ready to face any kind of privation, suffering, and danger, rather than consent to do what they consider wrong. And therefore they have the strength to resist doing what is against their principles.

It is still more impossible to say that all these men are such brutes that it is not painful for them to do such deeds, but natural. One need only talk to them to see that they all—landowner, judges, minister, Emperor, Governor, officers, and soldiers—in the depth of their souls not only disapprove of such things, but suffer from the consciousness of their own participation in them when they are reminded of what they imply.

They only try not to think about it.

One need only talk to any of those who are taking part in the affair—from the landowner to the least of the gendarmes or soldiers—to see that in the depths of their souls they all know that it is a wicked thing it would be better to have nothing to do with, and that they suffer on this account.

A lady of liberal tendencies who was travelling in the same train with us, seeing the Governor and the officers in the first-class refreshment-room and learning the object of the expedition, began to abuse the existing order of things, intentionally raising her voice so that the men who were taking part in this affair should hear her. Everyone felt awkward. No one knew where to look. No one contradicted her, however. They assumed an air of not condescending to answer such empty remarks. But it was evident by their faces and their averted eyes that they all felt ashamed. I noticed that it was the same with the soldiers. They, too, knew that what they were being sent to do was a shameful thing, but they did not want to think about it.

When the timber-merchant (and he it seemed to me insincerely and only to show his culture) began to speak of the necessity of such measures, the soldiers who heard him all turned away scowling and pretended not to hear.

All these men, both those who, like the land-owner, his steward, the minister, and the Emperor, were responsible for this act, as well as those who were now to execute it, and even those who were mere spectators, knew that it was a bad business and were ashamed of their part in it.

Why then did they do it? Why are they still doing it? And why do they allow it to be done?

Ask those who, like the landowner, started the business, and those who, like the judges, gave a decision which though legal in form was evidently unjust, and those who decreed the execution of the decision, and those who, like the soldiers, gendarmes, and peasants, themselves carry it out and flog and kill their brothers—and they who have devised, abetted, executed, or tolerated these crimes will all say essentially one and the same thing.

Those in authority who have initiated and abetted and directed the affair will say that they act as they do because such things are necessary for the maintenance of the existing order and the maintenance of the existing order is necessary for the welfare of the country, for humanity, and for the possibility of social existence and human progress.

Men of the lower orders—the peasants and soldiers who have to execute this violence with their own hands—will say that they do so because it is ordered by the higher authorities and the higher authorities know what they are doing. And it appears to them an indubitable truth that the right people constitute authority, and that they know what they are doing. If they admit the possibility of mistakes or errors they do so only in regard to officials of lower rank. The highest power, on whom everything depends, seems to them unquestionably infallible.

Both those in authority and their subordinates, though they explain the motives of their conduct differently, agree that they act as they do because the existing order is just the order that must and should exist at the present time, and that to support it is therefore each man's sacred duty.

On this acceptance of the necessity and therefore the immutability of the existing order rests also the argument by which those who take part in governmental violence always justify themselves. They say that as the existing order is immutable, the refusal of some one individual to fulfil the duties laid upon him has no real influence on things, but only means that his place will be taken by someone else who may do worse than he; that is, may exercise more cruelty and do more harm to the victims.

It is this conviction that the existing order is a necessary and therefore immutable order, to support which is the sacred duty of every man, that makes it possible for good men, of high principles in private life, to take part with more or less untroubled conscience in affairs such as that committed in Orël, and that which the men in the Túla train were going to perpetrate.

But on what is this conviction based?

It is understandable that a landowner should find it agreeable to believe that the existing order is necessary and immutable, because this existing order secures him the income he receives from his hundreds and thousands of acres, thanks to which he leads his customary idle and luxurious life.

It is also understandable that the judge readily believes in the necessity of that order as a result of which he receives fifty times as much as the most industrious labourer earns. And the same applies to the judges of the higher Court who receive a salary of six thousand rubles or more, and to all the higher officials. Only under the existing order can Governors, public prosecutors, senators, and members of various councils, receive this salary of several thousand rubles a year without which they and their families would immediately perish, since except in those particular posts they could not, with their capacity, industry, and knowledge, get a one-thousandth part of that sum. The minister, the Emperor, and every one of the higher authorities, is in the same position; only with this difference, that the higher and more exceptional their position the more necessary it is for them to believe that the existing order of things is the only possible order. For without it they would not only be unable to get an equally good position but would have to stand much lower than the rest of mankind. A man who voluntarily enters the police force at a wage of ten rubles a month, which he could easily earn in any other position, stands in little need of the preservation of the existing régime, and can therefore get along without believing in its immutability. But a king or an emperor, receiving millions in that office and knowing that around him there are thousands of people who would like to thrust him aside and take his place, knowing also that in no other position would he receive such an income or such honours, knowing even (in the majority of cases of more or less despotic rule) that if he is thrown out he will be tried for all his abuse of power—a king or emperor cannot but believe in the immutability and sanctity of the existing order. The higher the position a man occupies, the more advantageous and therefore the more unstable it is, and the more terrible and dangerous his fall, the more does such a man believe in the immutability of the existing order, and therefore for the maintenance of that order (and not as it were for himself) he is able to perpetrate most cruel and wicked deeds with a tranquil conscience.

This is the case with all those—from the lowest police-officers to the highest authorities—who occupy more advantageous positions than they could hold but for the existence of the present régime. All these people believe more or less in the immutability of the existing order, chiefly because it is advantageous for them.

But what makes the peasants and soldiers (who stand on the lowest rung of the ladder and can have no advantage from the present régime, under which indeed they are in a position of the utmost subjection and humiliation) believe that the existing order is the one that ought to exist and which they ought to support even by doing evil deeds contrary to their conscience?

What makes these men hold the false opinion that the existing order is immutable and that they must therefore support it, when that order is obviously only immutable because they support it?

What causes these men (taken only yesterday from the plough and dressed in these indecorous and unseemly clothes with light blue collars and gilt buttons) to go with guns and sabres to murder their famishing fathers and brothers? They gain no advantage by so doing, nor have they any desirable position to lose, for their present position is worse than that from which they were taken.

People of the higher classes: kings, landowners, merchants, judges, senators, governors, ministers and officers, taking part in such affairs support the existing order because it is advantageous for them. Moreover these (in many cases good and kindly) people are enabled to take part in such affairs by the fact that their participation is limited to instigations, decisions, and the issuing of orders. They do not themselves do what they instigate, decide on, or order to be done. For the most part they do not even see how the terrible deeds they have instigated and authorized are carried out.

But the unfortunate people of the lower orders who gain no advantage from the existing régime, being on the contrary held in the greatest contempt as a result of it, tear people from their families, bind them, confine them in prisons, drive them into exile, keep guard on them, and shoot them with their own hands for the maintenance of that order. Why do they do it?

What forces them to believe that the existing order is immutable and should be maintained?

All actual physical violence rests on these men who beat, bind, imprison, and kill, with their own hands. If it were not for them—these soldiers and policemen and armed men in general, ready to do violence and to kill all whom they are ordered to—not one of those who sign sentences of death, imprisonment, and exile for life, would ever hang, imprison, or torture a one-thousandth part of those whom they now, quietly sitting at their desks, order to be hanged or tortured in all sorts of ways simply because they do not see it and it is done not by them but by servile tools somewhere far off.

All the injustices and cruelties customary in present-day life have become habitual only because there are men always ready to carry out these injustices and cruelties. If it were not for them there would not only be no one to wreak violence on those immense masses of oppressed people, but those who issue the orders would never venture to do so, and would not even dare to dream of the sentences they now confidently pass.

Were it not for these men ready to torture or kill anyone they are commanded to, no one would dare to claim what is confidently claimed by all the non-working landowners, namely that land surrounded by men who are suffering for lack of land, is the property of a man who does not work on it, or that stores of grain collected by trickery ought to be preserved untouched in the midst of a population dying of hunger, because the merchant wants to make a profit. But for the existence of these people, ready at the will of the authorities to torture and kill anyone they are told to, it could never enter the head of a landowner to deprive the peasants of a wood they had grown, or of the officials to consider it proper to receive salaries taken from the famishing people for oppressing them, not to mention executing, imprisoning, or evicting people for exposing falsehood and preaching the truth.[1] In fact all this is demanded and done only because the authorities are all fully convinced that they

---

[1] This last allusion refers to the religious persecutions of nonconformist peasants, which engaged much of Tolstóy's attention at that time and subsequently.—A.M.

have always at hand servile people ready to carry
out all their demands by means of tortures and
killings.

Only because of that are such deeds committed
as are perpetrated by all tyrants, from Napoleon
to the most insignificant of company commanders
who fires on a crowd. The power supplied by
the obedient people standing behind them, ready
to carry out whatever order may be given, stupefies them. All power therefore depends on those
who with their own hands execute the deeds of
violence—that is, on the soldiers and police,
chiefly the soldiers, for the police can only do
their work because they have the army behind
them.

What brings these good people—obliged to do
all these terrible things with their own hands and
reaping no advantage from it—to the amazing
delusion that the existing unprofitable, ruinous
order, tormenting to them as it is, is the very
order that ought to exist?

Who has given them this amazing delusion?

They have not persuaded themselves that they
ought to do what is tormenting, disadvantageous,
and ruinous for them and their whole class (constituting nine-tenths of the population) and is
also contrary to their conscience.

I have often asked different soldiers: 'How can
you kill people when the law of God says "Thou
shalt not kill"?', and my question has always
caused the man uneasiness and confusion by
reminding him of what he would like to forget.
He knew that there is an obligatory law of God:
'Thou shalt not kill', he knew too that there is an

obligatory military service, but he had never considered the contradiction between the two. The drift of the timid replies I received to that question was always approximately this: that to kill in war and to execute criminals on the order of the Government is not included in the general prohibition of murder. When I said that this limitation is not made in the law of God, and reminded them of the teaching of brotherhood, forgiveness of injuries, and love—which cannot be reconciled with killing—they usually agreed, but in their turn set me a question. 'Why is it', they asked, 'that the Government' (which according to their precepts cannot do wrong) 'sends the army to war when necessary, and orders the execution of offenders?' When I replied that the Government does wrong when it acts so, they were thrown into still greater confusion and either broke off the conversation or grew angry with me.

'They must have found such a law, and I expect the bishops know better than we do,' one of them said to me. And by saying this he evidently set his mind at rest and felt fully convinced that his spiritual guides had discovered the law under which his forefathers had to serve the Tsars and the Tsars' heirs and which compelled him and millions of other men to serve. He felt that what I had said to him was a jest—some sort of subtle conundrum or hoax.

Everyone in our Christian world is firmly convinced by tradition, by revelation, and by the irrefutable voice of conscience, that murder is one of the most fearful crimes a man can commit, as the Gospel tells us; and that the sin of murder cannot be limited to certain people—so that it should be a sin for some people to murder but not a sin for others to do so. Everyone knows that if murder is a sin, it is always a sin whoever may be murdered, just as it is with the sins of adultery, robbery, or anything else. Yet at the same time, from their childhood and youth up, people see that murder is not only permitted but even blessed by those whom they are accustomed to regard as their spiritual guides, appointed by God. They see their civil leaders, too, organizing murder with assurance, carrying instruments of murder themselves and being proud of them, and in the name of the law of the country, and even of God, demanding participation in murder from everybody. Men see that there is some contradiction here, but being unable to unravel it involuntarily assume that this contradiction is only the result of their own ignorance. The very grossness and obviousness of the contradiction confirms them in this conviction.

They cannot imagine that the learned men who instruct them could so confidently preach two propositions so obviously contradictory as the law of Christ and murder. An unperverted child or youth cannot imagine that those who stand so high in his estimation, and whom he regards as holy and learned men, could mislead him so shamefully for any purpose whatever. But that is just what has been and is constantly being done. It is done, first, by instilling by example and by direct instruction from childhood to old age into all the working people who have not time to examine moral and religious questions themselves, that torture and murder are compatible with Christianity, and that for certain purposes of State they are not only allowable but even necessary; and, secondly, by instilling into certain people—enlisted, conscripted, or hired—that the perpetration of torture and murder with their own hands is a sacred duty, and even a glorious exploit worthy of praise and reward.

The general deception, diffused among all the people and stated in all the catechisms and the books which nowadays replace them in the compulsory education of children, is this: that violence (that is, torture, imprisonments, and executions, as well as murder in civil or foreign war for the maintenance and defence of the existing government—whatever it may be—an autocracy, a monarchy, a convention, a consulate, an empire of the First or Third Napaleon or of a Boulanger, a constitutional monarchy, a commune, or a republic) is absolutely lawful and does not conflict either with morality or with Christianity.

This is stated in all catechisms and books used in schools. And men are so persuaded of it that they grow up, live, and die in that conviction without ever doubting it.

That is one form of deception, a general deception instilled into everyone. But there is another special deception practised on the soldiers and police (selected by one means or another) who carry out the tortures and murders necessary for the maintenance and defence of the existing order.

The military regulations all contain, in these or other words, what the Russian military code says:

(Article 87) 'To fulfil accurately and unquestioningly the orders of a superior officer. To obey his order precisely, without considering whether it is good or not, or whether it is possible to execute it. The superior officer himself answers for the consequences of the orders he gives.'

(Article 88) 'The subordinate must always obey the orders of his superior officer except when he sees clearly that by executing them he . . .' (one naturally expects the following words to be '. . . when he sees clearly that by executing them he will violate the law of God', but nothing of the kind!) '. . . when he sees clearly that by executing them he would violate his oath of fidelity and allegiance to the Emperor.'

It says that a man who is a soldier can and should obey *all* his superiors' orders without exception. And as for a soldier these consist chiefly of murder, it follows that he should break all laws, human and divine, but not his fidelity and allegiance to whoever happens at the given moment to be in possession of power.

So it is expressed in the Russian military instructions, and in just the same way, though in different words, it is said in all manuals of military instructions. Nor can it be otherwise, for the whole power of the army and the State is based essentially on that deception, which releases men from their duty to God and their conscience and substitutes the duty of obedience to the officer who happens to be in command.

On that is founded the terrible assurance of the lower classes that the existing régime, which is pernicious for them, is the régime which ought to exist and which they therefore should support even by torture and murder.

That conviction is based on a conscious deception practised on them by the higher orders.

Nor can it be otherwise. To compel the lower classes, which are the most numerous, to ill-treat themselves by committing actions opposed to their conscience it was necessary to deceive them. And that is what has been done.

A few days ago I once more saw this shameless deception being openly practised, and once more marvelled at the unopposed and impudent way in which it was done.

Early in November, as I was passing through Túla, I once again saw the familiar sight of a dense crowd of people at the gates of the County Council Office, and heard both drunken shouts and the pitiful wailing of mothers and wives. This was a levy of recruits.

As always happens, I could not pass by that spectacle. It drew me to itself as by some evil spell. I again went among the crowd, stood there, looked about, inquired, and was once again amazed at the way in which this hideous crime is perpetrated unopposed and in broad daylight in the midst of a large town.

As in former years on November 1st the village elders in all the hamlets and villages of the hundred-millions of Russians had called up the young men entered on their lists (often including sons of their own) and had taken them to town.

On the road the recruits had drunk all the time and the elders had not hindered them, feeling that to go on such an insane errand, abandoning their wives and mothers and renouncing all that is sacred only to become senseless instruments of murder, would be too agonizing if they did not stupefy themselves with drink.

And so they had driven along, drinking, swearing, singing, fighting, and maiming themselves. They had spent the night in taverns. In the morning they had had another nip and were now gathered at the County Council Office.

Some of them, in new sheepskin coats, with knitted scarves round their necks and with moist, drunken eyes, kept up wild cries of bravado, while some awaited their turn quietly and despondently, squeezing around the gates among the weeping mothers and wives. (I happened to be there on the day of the actual enrolment—that is, the examination of those taken to the office.) Others meanwhile were crowding into the waiting-room.

In the office itself work is proceeding busily. The door is opened and the guard calls up Peter Sídorov. Peter Sídorov starts, crosses himself, and goes into a small room with a glass door where the conscripts have to undress. A comrade of his, who has just been passed for service and has come out of the examination room naked, is hurriedly dressing with chattering teeth. Peter Sídorov has already heard and sees by his face that his comrade has been taken. He wants to question him, but is hurried on and ordered to undress. He throws off his sheepskin coat, draws the long boot from each leg with the other foot, takes off his waistcoat and draws his shirt over his head, and naked, with protruding ribs, trembling all over and exhaling an odour of spirits, tobacco, and sweat, he goes barefoot into the revision office not knowing what to do with his brawny bare arms.

In the revision office, straight in front of him in a great gold frame hangs a portrait of the Tsar in a uniform with a sash. In the corner is a small picture of Christ in a shirt and crown of thorns. In the middle of the room is a table covered with green cloth on which papers are spread, and there is also a three-cornered ornament surmounted by an eagle, called a 'mirror of justice'. Around the room sit the recruiting officers, looking quite confident and tranquil. One is smoking a cigarette, another turns over the papers. As soon as Sídorov comes in a guard goes up to him and places him under the measuring scale, pushing up his chin and putting his feet straight. The man with a cigarette comes up—this is the doctor —not looking at the recruit's face but somewhere beyond it. He feels Sídorov's body with an air of disgust, measures him, pinches him, and orders the guard to make the man open his mouth. He tells him to breathe and to say something. Someone notes something down. At last, without having once looked him in the face, the doctor says: 'He'll do. Next one!' and with a weary air re-seats himself at the table. Again the soldiers hustle and hurry the young fellow. He somehow hurriedly pulls on his shirt, fumbling for the sleeves, pulls on his breeches, wraps his leg-bands round his legs, puts on his boots, looks for his scarf and cap, and catches up his sheepskin coat under his arm. And they lead him into the main hall, where he is fenced off by a bench. Behind that bench those who have been conscripted are waiting. Another village lad like himself, but from a distant province, who is already a soldier with a rifle and a sharp fixed bayonet, stands guard over him ready to stab him should he attempt to run away.

Meanwhile the crowd of fathers, mothers, and wives, jostled by the police, press together at the doors to learn who has been taken and who rejected. One lad who has been turned down comes out and announces that Petrúka has been taken, and Petrúka's young wife, for whom the word 'taken' means separation for four or five years and the dissolute life of a soldier's wife in service as a cook, screams aloud.

But now along the street drives a man with long hair and in a peculiar dress distinguishing him from everybody else, and he gets down from his dróshky and goes up to the County Council Office. The police clear a path for him through the crowd. The reverend Father has come to administer the oath. And now this 'father', who has been persuaded that he is a special and exceptional servant of Christ, and who in most cases is blind to the deception under which he labours, goes into the hall where the conscripts are waiting. He puts on a garment of gold brocade, releases his long hair from under it, opens the Gospel (in which it is forbidden to swear), takes the cross (the cross on which Christ was crucified because he would not do what this pseudo-servant of his is telling men to do) and places them on a lectern, and all those unhappy, defenceless, and deluded lads repeat after him the falsehood which he from habit pronounces so boldly.

He reads and they repeat: 'I promise and swear by Almighty God, upon His holy Gospel', &c., 'to defend', &c.—that is, to murder all those I am ordered to, and to do everything I am ordered to do by men I know nothing of and to whom I am only necessary that I may commit the evil deeds by which they are kept in their position and that oppress my brothers. All the conscripts senselessly repeat these ferocious words, and then the so-called 'father' drives away with a sense of having done his duty efficiently and conscientiously. And all these deluded lads consider that those nonsensical and to them unintelligible words which they have just uttered have freed them from their duties as men for the whole period of their service and bound them by new and more obligatory duties as soldiers.

And this crime is committed publicly, and no one cries out to the deceivers and the deceived: 'Bethink yourselves, and go away! This is a most odious and cunning lie and destroys not only your bodies but also your souls.'

No one does that. On the contrary, when all the recruits have been enrolled and it is necessary to let them out again, the military commander (as though to mock them) goes into the hall where the deceived and drunken lads are confined, and with a self-confidently majestic manner shouts to them in a bold military voice: 'Your health, lads! I congratulate you on entering the Tsar's service.' And the poor fellows (someone has already instructed them) mutter indistinctly in half-tipsy voices something to the effect that they, too, are glad.

Meanwhile the crowd of fathers, mothers, and wives, stand outside waiting; the women with tearful eyes fixed on the door. And now it opens and the conscripts come out staggering and swaggering, Petrúka and Vanúkha and Makár, trying not to look at their own folk and not to see them. The wailing of mothers and wives is heard. Some embrace each other and weep, others try to look brave, others again comfort one another.

The mothers and wives lament and wail aloud, knowing that for three or four years they will, like orphans, remain without their breadwinners. The fathers say little. They regretfully click their tongues and sigh, knowing that they will see no more the helpers they have reared and trained, who will come back not the quiet hard-working labourers they were before, but for the most part depraved and swaggering soldiers unaccustomed to a simple life.

And now all the crowd get into their sledges and move off down the street to the inns and taverns. And songs, sobbing, drunken shouts, the wailing laments of mothers and wives, sounds of accordions, and words of abuse are heard, interrupting one another and growing louder. They all make their way to the pot-houses and taverns which yield revenue to the government, and are overcome by drunkenness that stifles their sense of the wrong which is being done to them.

For two or three weeks they go on living at home, and for the most part make holiday—that is, drink.

On the appointed day they are assembled, driven like cattle to one place, and begin to drill and learn soldierly ways. This is taught them by men like themselves, but deceived and brutalized two or three years earlier. The methods of instruction are: deception, stupefaction, blows, and vodka. Before a year passes, these good, intelligent, healthy-minded lads will become brutalized beings just like their instructors.

'And suppose your own father were a prisoner and he tried to run away?' I asked a young soldier.

'I should stab him with my bayonet,' he replied in a peculiar, unintelligent, soldierly voice. 'And if he made off I should have to shoot him,' he added, evidently proud of knowing what must be done if his father tried to escape.

And when a kindly young man has been brought to this condition, lower than a brute, he is just what is needed by those who use him as an instrument of violence. He is then ready. The man has been destroyed, and a new instrument of violence has been produced.

And all this is done each year, every autumn, everywhere all over Russia in broad daylight and in large towns where all may see it; and the deception is so artful, so cunning, that though everyone sees it and in the depth of his soul knows

N

all its horror and all its terrible consequences
he cannot free himself from it.

3

When a man's eyes are opened to this awful
deception perpetrated on men, he is astonished
that preachers of the Christian religion and of
morality, instructors of youth, or even the good-
hearted intelligent parents to be found every
where, can teach any kind of morality in a
society in which it is openly admitted by all the
churches and governments that torture and
murder form a necessary condition of the life of
the community and that there must always be
special men prepared to kill their fellows, and that
any one of us may have to become such a man.

How can children, youths, and people in
general, be taught any kind of morality (to say
nothing of enlightening them in the spirit of
Christianity) side by side with the doctrine that
murder is necessary for the public (and consequently our own) welfare, and is therefore
legitimate; and that there are people—of whom
any one of us may have to be one—whose duty it
is to torture and murder their neighbours and
commit all kinds of crime at the will of those who
possess power? If men may and should torture,
kill, and commit every sort of crime at the will
of those in power, there is and can be no moral
law, but only a recognition of the right of the
strong. And so it is. In reality that is the doctrine, theoretically justified for some men by the
theory of the struggle for existence, which prevails in our society.

Indeed what moral teaching can there be under which murder, for any purpose whatever, can be sanctioned? It is as impossible as a theory of mathematics which admits the possibility of 2 being equal to 3.

There may be a semblance of mathematics which admits that 2 equals 3, but there can be no real mathematical knowledge. There may also be a semblance of morality which admits of murder in the form of executions, wars, or self-defence, but there can be no real morality. The recognition of the sanctity of the life of every man is the first and only basis of all morality.

The doctrine of an eye for an eye, a tooth for a tooth, and a life for a life, was abrogated by Christianity because that teaching is a justification of immorality and has no real meaning, but is a mere semblance of equity. Life is a quantity having neither weight nor measure and incommensurable with any other, so that the destruction of one life for another can have no sense. Besides, every social law aims at the amelioration of man's life, and how can the destruction of one man's life ameliorate the life of another? The destruction of life is not an act ameliorating life, but a suicidal act.

To destroy another life for the sake of justice, is as though a man having lost one hand should seek to remedy that misfortune by cutting off the other.

To say nothing of the sin of deluding men into regarding the most terrible crime as their duty, of the terrible sin of employing the name and authority of Christ to sanction what he most condemned (as is done in the administration of the oath of allegiance), or the offence by means of which they destroy not only the bodies but the souls of 'these little ones'—not to speak of all that, how can people who value their own way of life and their progress, tolerate among them, even for the sake of their own personal safety, that terrible, senseless, cruel and ruinous force presented by every organized government that rests on its army? The most cruel and terrible band of robbers is not so much to be dreaded as such a State organization. The authority of a robber chief is to a certain degree limited by members of his band who retain some degree of human liberty and can refuse to commit actions contrary to their conscience. But there are no limits for men who form part of a regularly organized government with an army under such discipline as prevails to-day. There are no crimes so revolting that men forming part of a government will not commit them at the wish of the man (Boulanger, Pugachëv, or Napoleon) who may chance to stand at its head.

Often when I see not only the levies of recruits, the military exercises and the manœuvres, but also the policemen with loaded revolvers and the sentries with rifles and fixed bayonets, when for whole days at a time I hear (as I do in the Khamóvniki where I live) the whistling and rattle of bullets as they hit the target; and when I see in the city (where any attempt at violence in self-defence is suppressed, where the sale of drugs and ammunition is prohibited, and where rapid driving and treatment by an unlicenced doctor is forbidden) thousands of disciplined men trained to murder and subject to one man's will, I ask myself: How can people who value their safety quietly allow and put up with this? Apart from its harmfulness and immorality, nothing can be more dangerous. What are men—I do not speak of Christians, ministers of religion, humanitarians, and moralists, but simply men who value their own lives, safety, and welfare—what are they thinking about? For this organization will act in the same way in whosoever's hands it may be. To-day, let us say, the power is in the hands of a tolerable ruler, but to-morrow it may be seized by a Biron,[1] an Elizabeth,[2] a Catherine,[3] a Pugachëv, a Napoleon I[4] or a Napoleon III. And the man in whose hands the power lies may be tolerable to-day but to-morrow may become a beast, or he may be

---

[1] E. J. de Biron (1690–1772), son of Bühren, a Courland proprietor. Peter the Great's niece, Anna Ivánovna, became his mistress and when she came to the throne of Russia he assumed the name and arms of the French dukes de Biron, and ruled Russia in her name. He had more than a thousand people executed, and when the Empress died assumed the regency. Three weeks later a group of conspirators arrested him and banished him to Siberia.—A.M.

[2] Elizabeth (1709–62) was the pre-nuptial daughter of Peter the Great and Catherine I. She seized the throne by a *coup d'état* in 1741.—A.M.

[3] Catherine (the Great) (1729–96) was concerned in the imprisonment and assassination of her husband Paul III and of the young Prince Iván. In her reign Pugachëv revolted and for a while held several provinces in the Volga district.—A.M.

[4] Tolstóy's opinion of Napoleon I is known to readers of *War and Peace*, and his dislike of Napoleon III, in whose reign he witnessed the guillotining of a man in Paris, was hardly less pronounced.—A.M.

succeeded by a mad or crazy heir—like the King of Bavaria,[1] or our Paul I.[2]

And terrible misdeeds can be committed not only by the highest rulers but by all the little satraps who are scattered about everywhere—the various Baránovs, police masters, or even the village police officers, company commanders, and police officials, before there is time for them to be dismissed. And this constantly occurs.

One involuntarily asks oneself how men can tolerate such things, not from higher political considerations alone, but out of consideration for their own safety.

And the reply to that question is that not everybody does tolerate it. The majority of men are deluded and submissive and have no choice but to tolerate anything. But there are those who can occupy advantageous positions only under such an organization, and they tolerate it because the risk of suffering from an irrational or cruel man being at the head of the government or the army, is for them always less than the disadvantages they would be exposed to by the abolition of the organization itself.

A judge, a policeman, a governor, or an officer, can keep his position just the same under Boulanger, Pugachëv, Catherine, or a republic. But should the existing order which secures him his advantageous position collapse, he would cer-

[1] Louis II of Bavaria (1845–86) came to the throne in 1864. He spent extravagant sums on patronizing Wagner and his music, was subsequently declared insane, and drowned himself and his physician in a lake.—A.M.

[2] Paul I (1754–1801), who was mad, was killed by his own officers, with the connivance of his son, Alexander I.—A.M.

tainly lose that position. And so these people are none of them alarmed as to who will be at the head of the organization of violence—they can adapt themselves to anyone. They only fear the abolition of the organization itself, and that is the reason—though sometimes an unconscious one—why they maintain it.

One often wonders why independent people who are in no way compelled to do so—the so-called flower of society—enter the army in Russia, England, Germany, Austria, and even in France, and seek opportunities to become murderers. Why do parents, even moral parents, send their boys to colleges to prepare them for a military career? Why do mothers buy their children helmets, guns, and swords, as their favourite toys? (Peasant children never play at soldiers.) Why do good men and even women, quite unconnected with military matters, go into raptures over the various exploits of Skóbelev[1] and other generals, and vie with one another in glorifying them? Why do men under no obligation to do so and receiving no salary for it (the Marshals of Nobility in Russia, for instance) assiduously devote whole months to the physically disagreeable and morally distressing work of enrolling conscripts? Why do all the emperors and kings go about in military dress? Why do they hold manœuvres and parades, distribute

[1] General Skóbelev, who had a prominent part in the capture of Khiva in 1873 and took part in storming Pleva in 1878, was exceedingly popular. His death in Moscow under particularly shameful circumstances in 1882 caused a considerable sensation. There is a reference to him on the last page of *Tales of Army Life*.—A.M.

rewards to military men, and erect monuments
to generals and successful commanders? Why
do rich people of independent position consider
it an honour to perform a lackey's duties to
crowned personages, humiliating themselves and
flattering them, and pretend to believe in the
special grandeur of these people? Why do people
who have long ceased to believe in the medieval
Church superstitions and who cannot believe in
them, seriously and consistently pretend to be believers, and support those demoralizing and blasphemous ecclesiastical institutions? Why is the
ignorance of the people safeguarded so zealously
not only by the governments but also by private
members of the higher classes? Why do they so
passionately oppose any attempt to break down
religious superstitions for the true enlightenment
of the people? Why do historians, novelists, and
poets, who can now gain nothing by their flattery,
describe as heroes emperors, kings, and military
leaders, who have long been dead? Why do men
who call themselves learned dedicate their whole
lives to composing theories to prove that violence
inflicted by a government on its people is not
violence at all but some peculiar right?

One often wonders why a society woman or
an artist, who would appear not to be interested
either in social or military questions, should
always condemn a workers' strike and advocate
a war, and should always attack the one and
defend the other so definitely.

But one ceases to wonder at all this as soon as
one realizes that it is only done because people
of the ruling classes feel instinctively what it is

that supports, and what it is that destroys, the organization under which they can enjoy the privileges they possess.

The society lady does not deliberately argue that if there were no capitalists and no army to defend them, her husband would have no money and she consequently would have no *salon* and no wonderful gowns; and the artist does not reflect that capitalists defended by armies are necessary for him in order that there may be buyers for his pictures. But instinct, which in this case takes the place of reason, guides them unerringly.

And it is precisely the same instinct that, with few exceptions, guides the people who support all those political, religious, and economic institutions which are advantageous to them.

But is it possible that people of the upper classes support this order of things only because it is advantageous for them? They cannot but see that this order of things is in itself irrational, no longer corresponds to men's consciousness or even to public opinion, and is full of danger. People of the governing classes—the honest, good, clever people among them—cannot fail to suffer from those inner contradictions and to see the dangers they are exposed to. And is it possible that all the millions of people of the lower orders can with tranquil minds perform all the evidently evil actions—tortures and murders—they are compelled to do, merely because they fear punishment? It cannot be so, and neither the one nor the other could fail to see the unreasonableness of their conduct if the complexity of the state-structure did not conceal from them the irrationality and unnaturalness of what they are doing.

This irrationality is concealed by the fact that when any such action is committed there are so many instigators, accomplices, and abettors, that not one of those concerned in the affair feels himself morally responsible.

Murderers oblige all those who witness a murder to strike at the body of the man who has been killed, so that the responsibility may rest on as large a number of people as possible. That same principle, in a more definitely organized form, is applied to the perpetration of those crimes without the constant commission of which no governmental organization could exist. Rulers always try to draw as many citizens as possible into as much participation as possible in the crimes they commit and that are necessary for them.

Of late this has found very obvious expression in the drafting of citizens into the courts as jurors,[1] into the army as soldiers, and into local government—in the legislative assemblies—as electors and representatives.[2]

As all the ends of a wicker basket are so hidden that it is difficult to find them, so responsibility for the crimes committed in a State organization is so concealed from men that they do not see their own responsibility for the most atrocious acts.

[1] Trial by jury was introduced in Russia as part of the judicial reforms in 1864.—A.M.

[2] The Zémstvos (County Councils on an electoral basis) were also introduced in 1864.—A.M.

In ancient times tyrants were accused when evil deeds were committed, but in our day the most atrocious crimes—crimes inconceivable under Nero—are perpetrated and there is no one who can be blamed.

Some people demand the perpetration of a crime, others decide that it shall be done, a third set confirm that decision, a fourth propose its execution, a fifth report on it, a sixth finally decree it, and a seventh carry out the decree. Women, old men, and innocent people, are killed, hanged, and flogged, as was done recently in Russia at the Yúsov works,[1] and as is done everywhere in Europe and America in the struggle with anarchists and other infringers of the existing order. Hundreds and thousands of people are shot or hanged, or millions of people are massacred as is done in war, or people's souls are ruined by solitary confinement or by the corruption of a soldier's life, as is constantly done—and no one is responsible.

At the bottom of the social ladder soldiers with rifles, revolvers, and swords, torture and murder men and by those means compel them to become soldiers. And these soldiers are fully convinced that the responsibility for their deed is taken from them by the officers who order those actions. At the top of the ladder the Tsars, presidents, and ministers, decree these tortures and murders and conscriptions. And they are fully convinced that since they are either placed in authority by God, or the society they rule over demands

[1] Large ironworks founded by an Englishman, Hughes, in South Russia.—A.M.

such decrees from them, they cannot be held responsible.

Between these two extremes are the intermediate folk who superintend the acts of violence and the murders and the conscriptions of the soldiers. And these, too, are fully convinced that they are relieved of all responsibility, partly because of orders received by them from their superiors, and partly because such orders are expected from them by those on the lower steps of the ladder.

The authority that commands and the authority that executes, at the two extremes of the State organization, are joined like the two ends of a chain-ring—each conditions and supports the other and all intermediate links.

Without the conviction that there is a person or persons on whom the whole responsibility rests, not one soldier would raise his hand to torture or murder. Without the conviction that it is expected of them by the people, not a single emperor, king, president, or parliament, would decree those murders or acts of violence. Without the conviction that there are persons standing below him who have to do such deeds for their welfare, not one of the intermediate people would take part in such deeds.

The State organization is such that on whatever rung of the social ladder a man may be, his lack of responsibility is always the same. The higher his grade the more he is under the influence of demands for instructions from below and the less he is controlled by orders from above, and vice versa.

So it was in the case I had before me. The more each of those taking part in that affair was exposed to demands for directions from below and the less under the influence of orders from above, the higher was his position and vice versa.

But not only do all the men involved in the State organization throw the responsibility for their acts on one another—the soldier on the nobleman or merchant who is his officer, and the officer on the nobleman who occupies the post of Governor, and the Governor on the gentleman or son of an official who holds the post of minister, and the minister on the member of the royal family who occupies the position of Tsar, and the Tsar again on all those officials, nobles, merchants, and peasants—not only do people free themselves in this way from the sense of responsibility for their actions, but they also lose their moral consciousness of responsibility because, being involved in a State organization, they so unceasingly, strenuously, and persistently assure themselves and one another that they are not all equal, but differ among themselves 'as one star differeth from another', that they begin really to believe this. Thus some are persuaded that they are not simple people like other folk but are special beings who ought to be specially honoured. And it is instilled into others by all possible means that they are inferior creatures, and should therefore uncomplainingly submit to what those above them dictate.

This inequality, this exaltation of some and degradation of others, is the chief cause of men's capacity to ignore the irrationality and cruelty and wickedness of the existing order, as well as the deception practised by some and suffered by others.

Those in whom has been instilled the idea that they are invested with a special, supernatural importance and grandeur[1] become so intoxicated with their own imaginary dignity that they cease to see their responsibility for their own actions.

Others on whom it is impressed that they are insignificant creatures bound to submit to their superiors in everything, fall into a strange state of stupefied servility in consequence of this continual humiliation, and so lose consciousness of their responsibility for what they do.

The intermediate people—who on the one hand obey the orders of their superiors and on the other give orders to their inferiors—are intoxicated by both power and servility, and so they, too, lose consciousness of their own responsibility.

One need only attend a review and glance at the commander-in-chief intoxicated with self-importance. He is accompanied by his staff, all on splendidly caparisoned horses and wearing special uniforms and decorations. To the sound of harmonious and triumphant military music the commander-in-chief rides before the ranks of soldiers presenting arms and petrified with servile adoration. One need only see that, to understand that at such moments the commander-in-chief, the soldiers, and all the officers,

---

[1] The eccentricities of Kaiser Wilhelm II were then already endangering the peace of the world and the stability of the three Eastern European empires.—A.M.

are in a state of complete intoxication and capable of committing actions they would never dream of committing under other conditions.

The intoxication produced by such spectacles as parades, imperial receptions, Church solemnities and coronations is, however, an acute and merely temporary condition. But there are other forms of intoxication that are chronic and continual, and these are experienced alike by those who have any power (from that of the Tsar to that of a policeman in the street) and by those in subjection to authority and in a condition of stupefied servility.

To justify that condition such people always attribute the greatest possible importance and dignity to those whom they serve—as has been seen and is still seen in the case of all slaves.

It is principally through this false idea of inequality, and the intoxication of power and servility, that men associated in State organizations are enabled to commit without scruple or remorse actions opposed to their conscience.

Under the influence of such intoxication men imagine themselves and represent themselves to others as being not what they really are, men, but as some special conventional beings: noblemen, merchants, governors, judges, officers, Tsars, ministers, or soldiers, not subject to ordinary human duties but to aristocratic, commercial, governatorial, judicial, military, royal, or ministerial, obligations.

Thus the landowner going to law about the wood acted as he did only because he appeared to himself to be not an ordinary man having merely the same human rights as the peasant-folk living beside him, but a great landowner and a member of the gentry, and under the influence of the intoxication of power he felt his dignity offended by the peasants' claim. Only on that account did he send in a claim to be reinstated in his pretended rights without considering the consequences that might result.

In just the same way the judges who wrongfully awarded the wood to the landowner, did so only because they considered themselves to be not ordinary men like everybody else and therefore bound to be guided in everything by truth alone, but, under the intoxication of power, imagined themselves to be guardians of official justice and incapable of error. And while under the intoxicating influence of servility they imagined themselves to be men bound to execute certain rules written down in a certain book, and called laws. And all the other participants in the affair—from the highest representative of authority who signed the report, the marshal of nobility who presided at the recruiting sessions, and the priest who deluded the conscripts, to the lowest of the soldiers now preparing himself to shoot his fellow-men—under the influence of power or of servility considered themselves to be, and represented themselves to others as being, not what they really are but something quite different. They all did what they did, and prepare to do what they still have to do, only because they seem to themselves and to others to be not what they are in reality—men faced by the question whether they ought or ought not to take part in wicked actions which their conscience condemns—but different, conventional characters: one an anointed Tsar, a special being destined to watch over the welfare of a hundred million people; another the representative of the nobility; another a priest who has received special grace by his ordination; another a soldier bound by his oath unreflectingly to do all that he is commanded to do. All these people could only, and can only, act as they do under the influence of intoxication by power or servility, resulting from their imagined positions.

If they were not all firmly convinced that the calling of a tsar, minister, governor, judge, nobleman, landowner, marshal, officer, or soldier, is something real and very important, not one of them could think without horror and aversion of taking part in the things they now take part in.

The conventional positions established hundreds of years ago, recognized for centuries, and now accepted by all around, distinguished by special names and a special dress and confirmed by all kinds of ceremonies which act on the senses, influence men to such a degree that forgetting the normal conditions of life common to all, they regard themselves and everyone else only from this conventional point of view, and estimate their own and other people's actions solely from that conventional view-point.

Thus a man in full mental health and no longer young, suddenly becomes self-assured, proud, and even happy, merely because he is decked out with some gewgaw, or has keys hanging at his backside, or wears a blue ribbon, suitable only for some little girl in costume, and is told that he is a general, a chamberlain, a Chevalier of St. Andrew, or some such nonsense; and on the contrary he grows sad and unhappy and even falls ill, if he is deprived of the expected trinket or nickname, or fails to obtain it. And what is still more striking, a young man quite sane in other respects, independent and well provided for, will tear an unfortunate widow from her little children and lock her up or have her imprisoned, leaving her children uncared for, all because the unhappy woman has secretly trafficked in vodka and so deprived the Crown of twenty-five rubles' revenue. And he does not feel the least remorse for having done this, because he has called himself and been called by others, a public prosecutor or district chief. Or what is still more extraordinary, a man otherwise reasonable and kindly will begin to fire bullets at people merely because he has been given a badge or a uniform and told that he is an excise or customs officer, and neither he nor those around him consider him guilty of anything wrong, but on the contrary consider that he is to blame if he does not fire. And then there are the judges and jurymen who condemn men to death, and the military who kill thousands without the least remorse, merely because it has been instilled into them that they are not simply men, but jurymen, judges, generals, and soldiers.

This strange and unnatural condition of men in political life is usually expressed by words such as these: 'As a man I am sorry for him, but as a watchman, judge, general, governor, tsar, or

soldier, it is my duty to kill or torture him'—
as if any position given or recognized by men
could set aside the obligations imposed on each
of us by our common humanity.

In the case before us, for instance, men are
going to murder and torture others who are
famishing. They admit that in the quarrel with
the landowner the peasants are in the right (the
superior officers told me so). They know that
the peasants are wretched, poor, and hungry,
and the landowner is rich and evokes no sympathy. Yet all these men are going to punish
the peasants in order to obtain three thousand
rubles for the landowner, just because at this
moment each imagines himself to be not a man,
but either a governor, an official, a chief of gendarmes, an officer, or a soldier, and because they
consider as obligatory on them not the eternal
demands of man's conscience but the casual,
temporary demands of their positions as officers
or soldiers.

Strange as it may sound, the only explanation of this remarkable phenomenon is that
these men are in the same state as hypnotized
people who feel convinced that they are whatever character is suggested to them. When, for
instance, it is suggested to a hypnotized person
that he is lame he begins to limp, when it is suggested that he is blind he ceases to see, and when
it is suggested that he is an animal he begins to
bite. And the men going by this train were in
such a state, and so are not only they, but all who
fulfil their State and social duties in preference
to and to the detriment of their duties as men.

The essence of the hypnotic state is that under the influence of an idea suggested to them, people lose the power of reflecting on their actions and do without thinking whatever is consistent with the suggestion to which they are led by example, precept, or insinuation.

The difference between those hypnotized by artificial means and those under the influence of political suggestion, is this: that in the one case the imaginary condition is suggested suddenly, by one person, in a very brief space of time, and so that hypnotism presents itself to us in a glaring and startling form; while the imaginary position induced by political suggestion takes place by degrees, gradually, imperceptibly, from childhood, sometimes for a period of years or even generations, and is moreover induced not by one person only but by the whole of society.

'But', it will be said, 'in all societies the majority of people—all the children, all the women absorbed in bearing and rearing children, all the immense number of working people under the necessity of intense and incessant physical labour, all those of a naturally weak mind and those whose intellectual capacities have been enfeebled by nicotine, alcohol, opium poisoning, or other intoxicants—are always incapable of independent thought and consequently submit either to those on a higher level of reasonable consciousness, or else to family or State traditions—to what is called public opinion—and in this submission there is nothing unnatural or incongruous.'

And it is true that there is nothing unnatural in it and that it is a usual characteristic of people who think little, to submit to the guidance of those on a higher level of consciousness. It is owing to this that men can live in societies submitting to the same reasonable principles. The minority consciously adopt these reasonable principles because they correspond with their reason, while the majority submit to the same principles unconsciously, merely because those demands have become public opinion.

So long as public opinion is not split in two there is nothing unnatural in this submission to public opinion by people who think but little.

But there are times when a higher consciousness of truth reveals itself, and gradually passing from one to another takes hold of such a number of people that the former public opinion, based on a lower level of consciousness, begins to totter, and the new one is ready to establish itself but has not yet done so. There are times resembling the coming of spring. The old public opinion has not yet been demolished and the new one established, but men already begin to discuss their own and other people's actions on the basis of the new consciousness, though they still by inertia and tradition continue to obey the principles that formed the highest stage of reasonable consciousness at an earlier period but are now already in flagrant contradiction to it. At such times men, feeling the necessity of submitting to the new public opinion and yet unable to break with the former, are in an unnatural and wavering condition. And not only the men in that train, but the majority of men in our time, find themselves in such a condition in their relation to Christian truths.

People of the higher classes holding exceptionally advantageous positions are in that state, as well as people of the lower classes who submit absolutely to the orders given them.

The ruling classes, having no longer any reasonable justification for the advantageous positions they hold, are obliged, in order to keep these positions, to repress their higher rational capacities and love for their fellow-men, and to hypnotize themselves into the belief that their exceptional positions are necessary. And the lower classes, crushed by toil and intentionally stupefied, live in a continual condition of hypnotization, deliberately and incessantly induced by people of the upper classes.

Only in this way can one explain the amazing contradiction that fills our life, and of which a striking example was presented by those kindly and mild acquaintances whom I met on the 9th of September, who with quiet minds were going to commit the most cruel, senseless, and vile crimes. Had conscience not been stifled in some way in those men, not one of them could have done a one-hundredth part of what they were preparing to do, and very likely will do.

It is not that they have no conscience forbidding them to do what they are preparing to do— as those who burnt others at the stake and tortured and mutilated men four hundred, three hundred, two hundred, and even a hundred years ago, had no conscience. Conscience does exist in all these people now, but it has been put to sleep. In the case of those in command and those in exceptionally advantageous positions, it has been put to sleep by what the psychiatrists call auto-suggestion. In the case of the soldiers it has been put to sleep by direct intentional suggestion and hypnotization exerted by the higher classes.

But although conscience has been put to sleep in these men, it still exists and may awaken at any moment. Indeed its voice can already be heard in them penetrating the self-suggestion and hypnotization that possess them.

All these men are in a state similar to that of a hypnotized man who under that influence has been ordered to do something contrary to all that he regards as reasonable and right—such as to kill his mother or child. He feels himself bound to carry out the suggestion and it seems to him that he cannot stop, yet the nearer he gets to the time and place of action the more strongly does his benumbed conscience begin to stir, to resist, to writhe, and to try to awake. And one cannot say in advance whether he will or will not do the deed suggested to him. It is impossible to tell which will prevail: his rational consciousness or the irrational suggestion. It all depends on their relative strength.

That is just what is happening to-day, both with the men in that train and with men of our day in general who commit political acts of violence and profit by them.

There was a time when men who set out to torture and murder and make examples, never returned without having accomplished the business they set out to do, and were never troubled by doubts or remorse, but having flogged men to death, quietly returned to their families, petted their children, jested, laughed, and enjoyed the peaceful pleasures of family life. It did not then enter the heads of those who profited by such acts of violence—landowners and wealthy people—that the advantages they enjoyed had any connexion with those cruelties.

But now it is otherwise. People already know, or almost know, what they are doing and why they do it. They can close their eyes and stifle their conscience, but with open eyes and unstifled conscience both those who commit violence and those who profit by it can no longer fail to see its import. Sometimes people understand the significance of an action only after it has already been done, but sometimes they realize it just before its perpetration. The men who arranged the floggings at Nízhni-Nóvgorod, Sarátov, Orël, and at the Yúzov factory, realized what they had done only afterwards, and are now tormented with shame by public opinion and by their own consciences. I have spoken with soldiers who took part in such affairs and they always tried to turn the conversation from that subject, and when they spoke of it did so with perplexity and horror. But there are cases when men recollect themselves just before the commission of the deed. Thus I know of a sergeant who was beaten by two peasants during the suppression of a riot and who reported accordingly, but next day when he saw the tortures inflicted on other peasants, he begged his company commander to tear up the report and to let off the men who had beaten him. I know a case where the soldiers appointed to shoot some men declined to obey, and I know many cases of officers refusing to take charge of floggings and murders. So that men engaged in arranging or committing violence sometimes recollect themselves long before the performance of the deed, sometimes just before its perpetration, and sometimes only after it.

The men travelling by that train set out to injure and murder their fellow men, but no one knows whether they will or will not carry out their object. However much his responsibility may be concealed from each of them, and however strong may be the suggestion instilled into each of them that they are not men, but governors, police-captains, officers, and soldiers, and as such may violate their human duties, the nearer they approach their destination the stronger will be their doubts as to whether they are going to do what is necessary and right, and this doubt will reach its highest degree at the moment of execution.

In spite of the intoxicating effect of his surroundings the Governor cannot help hesitating when he gives the final decisive command to murder and to torture. He knows that the action of the Governor of Orël evoked indignation from the best members of society, and he himself, under the influence of the opinion of the circles in which he lives, has more than once expressed disapproval of that affair. He knows that the public prosecutor, who was to have come, has simply refused to take part because he considered it a shameful affair; and he knows that to-day or to-morrow there may be changes in the government, and that what procured favour yesterday may incur disfavour to-morrow. And he knows that there is a public press, if not in Russia then abroad, which may report this matter and so disgrace him for life. He already scents a change in public opinion, which now repudiates what was formerly demanded. And he cannot feel absolutely sure that at the last moment the soldiers will obey him. He wavers and it is impossible to tell what he will do.

The same is felt in a greater or lesser degree by all the officials and officers with him. They all in the depth of their hearts know that what they are engaged on is shameful, and that to take part in it degrades and pollutes them in the eyes of some people whose opinion they value. Each of them knows that after murdering and torturing defenceless people he will be ashamed to face his betrothed or the woman he is wooing. And besides, they too, like the Governor, are in doubt as to whether their soldiers will obey them. And contrary as it is to the assured appearance with which they saunter about the station and along the platform, they all in the depth of their souls both suffer and hesitate. They assume that self-assured appearance to conceal the hesitation within. And that feeling increases as they approach the scene of action.

And however little noticeable it may be, and strange as it seems to say so, all these young fellows who seem so submissive are in the same state of mind.

They are not the soldiers of former days who had renounced a natural and laborious life and devoted their whole existence to debauchery, plunder, and murder—like Roman legionaries, or soldiers of the Thirty Years War, or even the soldiers of not so long ago who had to serve for twenty-five years. Now they are for the most part men recently taken from their families and still full of recollections of the good, natural, and reasonable life they have left behind them.

For the most part they are peasant lads, who know the business they are engaged on; know that the landlords always take advantage of their brothers, the peasants, and that it is no doubt the same in this case. Moreover more than half of them can now read books, and not all the books they read extol the business of war—there are some that point out its wrongfulness. Among the soldiers there are often free-thinking volunteers, or among the officers young liberals of a similar way of thinking, and seeds of doubt as to the absolute legitimacy and glory of their occupation have been sown.

It is true that they have all passed through that terrible, artificial system of drill, elaborated through centuries and deadly to all initiative in man, and that they are so trained to mechanical obedience that at the command: 'Ready! Present! Fire!' &c., their rifles will be lifted and the habitual movements mechanically performed. But at this moment the word 'Fire!' does not mean amusing themselves by shooting at a target, it means killing their tormented and ill-treated fathers and brothers, whom they see standing huddled together in a crowd in the street with their women and children waving their arms. There they stand, one man with a thin beard and patched coat and plaited bast shoes, just like the father left behind at home in Kazán or Ryazán province; another with a grey beard and bent back, leaning on a big staff, just like grandfather; a third—a young fellow in high boots and a red shirt—just like himself a year ago: he, the soldier who is now going to shoot him down. And there, too, is a woman in a linen skirt and bast shoes, just like the mother left at home. . . . Are they really going to fire on them?

And it is impossible to say what each soldier will do at the final moment. The least indication that it cannot be done, or above all that it is possible not to do it, would be enough to stop him.

All the men travelling by that train, when it comes to doing the thing for which they are going, will be in the position of a hypnotized man to whom it has been suggested that he should chop a log and who, on coming up to what has been pointed out to him as a log and when already swinging his axe, sees that it is not a log at all but the body of his sleeping brother. He may go through with what he has been told to do, or he may come to himself before doing it. In the same way all these men may or may not come to themselves in time.

If they do not come to themselves a terrible crime will be committed, as at Orël, and then the auto-suggestion and hypnotism under which they act will be strengthened in other people. If they do come to themselves, not only will this crime not be perpetrated but many who hear of the turn things have taken will be freed from the hypnotic influence which has held them spellbound, or will at least be nearer to such emancipation.

If even a few come to themselves and refrain from taking part in this affair and boldly point out to others the wickedness of it, the influence of those few may result in all the rest shaking off the influence of the suggestion that oppresses them, and the intended atrocity will not be committed.

If even just a few people who are not taking part in that affair, but are merely present at the preparations for it or have just heard of such things being done in the past, would boldly and plainly express their detestation of those who participate in such affairs and point out to them all the senselessness, cruelty, and wickedness of such acts, instead of remaining indifferent, even that would not pass without some effect.

So it was in the instance before us. It was enough for some participants and non-participants in the affair boldly to express their indignation at the floggings that had been inflicted elsewhere and their repulsion and contempt for those who had taken part in them—it was enough in the present Túla case for some people to express their unwillingness to take part in it, for a lady passenger and a few bystanders at the station to express to those who formed the expedition, their indignation at what they were doing; it was enough for one of the regimental commanders from whom troops were demanded for the restoration of order, to express his opinion that soldiers cannot be executioners—and thanks to these and some other seemingly insignificant private influences brought to bear on those who were under the hypnotic influence of suggestion, the matter took quite a different turn. The troops when they reached the place did not torture the peasants but only cut down the wood and handed the timber over to the landowner.

Had there not been a few people with a clear perception that they were doing wrong, and had there not been in consequence of this an influence exerted in that sense by some people on others, what happened at Orël would have happened in Túla. Had that consciousness been yet stronger and had the influence exerted been greater than it was, the Governor and troops would very likely not have decided to cut down the wood and give it over to the landowner. Had that consciousness been stronger still and those influences yet more numerous, the Governor would very likely not even have decided to go to the scene of the action; and had it been stronger again and the influences still more numerous, the minister would very likely not have made up his mind to prescribe such a decision, or the Emperor to confirm it.

All depends therefore on the strength of the consciousness of Christian truth in each individual man.

And therefore it would seem that the efforts

of all men of our time who profess a wish to promote the welfare of mankind, should be directed to strengthening and elucidating in themselves and others a consciousness of Christian truth and its requirements.

4

But strange to say in our day it is just those people who talk most about the betterment of human life and are regarded as intellectual leaders of public opinion, who declare all this to be quite unnecessary, and say that there are other more effective means of improving man's condition. These men affirm that the improvement of human life is effected not by the moral efforts of individual men towards the recognition, elucidation, and profession of truth, but by a gradual alteration of the general external conditions of life. They believe that the efforts of each individual should be directed not to that moral advance but to a general modification of external conditions. Any individual profession of truth incompatible with the existing order is not merely useless but harmful, because it provokes governmental restrictions that hinder individuals from continuing an activity useful to society. According to this doctrine all alterations of human life are governed by the same laws as those of animal life.

So that according to that doctrine all the founders of religions, such as Moses and the prophets, Confucius, Lao-tsze, Buddha, Christ, and others, preached their doctrines, and their followers adopted them, not because they loved truth and sought to elucidate and propagate it, but because the political, social, and above all the economic circumstances of the nations among whom those teachings appeared and spread were favourable to their manifestation and development.

And therefore the chief activity of a man who wishes to serve society and improve the condition of mankind should be directed not to the elucidation and profession of truth, but to the amelioration of external political, social, and, above all else, economic conditions. And the modification of those conditions is, they say, effected partly by serving the government and introducing liberal and progressive principles into it, partly by contributing to the development of industry and the dissemination of socialistic ideas, and most of all by the diffusion of scientific education.

It is not important for a man to profess the truth that has revealed itself to him, and so inevitably be compelled to apply it in his life or at least to refrain from committing actions contrary to that truth—such as serving the government or strengthening its authority if he considers that authority harmful, profiting by the capitalist system if he regards it as wrong, showing reverence for ceremonies he regards as degrading superstitions, taking part in judicial proceedings when he considers their organization false, serving as a soldier, taking oaths, and in general telling lies and acting as a scoundrel. But it is important for a man, without altering the existing forms of life but conforming to them contrary to his convictions, to introduce liberalism into existing institutions, to promote industry, to propagate socialism, the triumphs of what is called science, and the diffusion of education.

According to that theory a man can remain a landowner, a trader, a manufacturer, a judge, an official in government pay, a soldier or an officer, and still be not merely humane but even a socialist and a revolutionary.

Hypocrisy, which had formerly only a religious basis in the doctrine of the fall of man, the redemption, and the Church, has to-day secured a new scientific basis, and has consequently caught in its net all those who at the stage of development they had reached could no longer find support in religious hypocrisy. So that while formerly only a man professing the teachings of the Church could take part in the crimes committed by the State, profit by them, and yet consider himself free from any taint of sin so long as he fulfilled the external observances of his religion, nowadays everyone, without believing in Church Christianity, can have an equally firm scientific ground for regarding himself as blameless and even highly moral, despite his participation in the evil done by the State and in the advantages he derives therefrom.

We see landowners not only in Russia but everywhere—in France, England, Germany, and America—who, for allowing people living on their land to draw subsistence from it, extort from these (generally needy) people all they possibly can. The owner's right of property in the land is based on the fact that at every attempt on the part of the oppressed to avail themselves, without his consent, of the land he considers to be his, troops come and subject them to punishment and murder. It would seem evident that a man living in such a way is an evil and egotistic creature who cannot possibly consider himself a Christian or a liberal. It would seem evident that the first thing such a man should do if he wishes even to approximate to Christianity or liberalism, is to cease to rob and ruin people by means of his claim to the land, which the government supports by murder and violence. And it would be evident, were it not for this hypocritical reasoning which says that from a religious point of view the possession or non-possession of land is immaterial for salvation, and that from a scientific point of view the giving up of the ownership of the land would be a useless personal sacrifice because the welfare of humanity is not promoted in that way but by a gradual change in external forms. And so we see that man, in no way abashed and never doubting that people will believe in his sincerity, organizing an agricultural exhibition or a temperance society, or distributing, through his wife and children, underclothing and soup to three or four old women, and boldly discoursing in his own house, in other people's drawing-rooms, in committees, and in the press, on the duty of Christian and humanitarian love of one's neighbour in general and the labouring agricultural folk (whom he is continually exploiting and oppressing) in particular. And others who are in the same position as he, believe him, commend him, and solemnly discuss with him measures for improving the condition of those labouring folk on whose exploitation their whole life is based, and devising every possible means except the one without which no improvement is possible—namely, ceasing to deprive men of the land necessary for their subsistence.

(A most striking example of such hypocrisy was given by the landowners last year in their endeavour to combat the famine which they had produced, and of which they took advantage not only by selling grain at the highest possible price, but even by charging the freezing peasants five rubles a *desyatina* [2¾ acres] for potato bines, before they would allow them to be used as fuel.)

Take a trader whose whole business is, as usual, based on a system of trickery, by means of which, taking advantage of the people's needs and of their ignorance, he buys goods below their value and sells them again above it. It would seem evident that a man whose whole occupation is based on what, were it done under other circumstances, he would himself term swindling, ought to be ashamed of his position, and be quite unable to represent himself as a Christian or a liberal while remaining in it. But there is an hypocritical sophistry that tells him he can be regarded as a virtuous man without abandoning his harmful activity: a religious man need only have faith, and a liberal man need only promote the modification of external conditions—the progress of industry. And so that trader who, besides his nefarious occupation, often commits a series of direct frauds (selling adulterated goods, using false weights and measures, or dealing in things pernicious to health such as spirits and opium) boldly regards himself, and is regarded by others, as a model of probity and conscientiousness so long as he does not defraud his associates in business. And if he spends a thousandth part of his stolen wealth on some public institution—a hospital, museum, or educational establishment—he is even regarded as a benefactor of the people on whose exploitation and corruption his prosperity has been founded. And if he devotes a portion of his ill-gotten gains to a church or to the poor, then he is considered a model Christian.

Or take a manufacturer whose profit comes from fines he imposes on his workmen, and whose whole activity is based on compulsory and unnatural labour that ruins whole generations of men. It would seem obvious that if he professes any Christian or liberal principles he should first of all cease to ruin human lives for his own profit. But according to the existing theory he is promoting industry and ought not to cease his activity. It would even be harmful to society for him to do so. And so this man, the cruel slave-driver of thousands of people, having arranged cottages with five-foot gardens for those broken down by toiling for him, and having founded a savings-bank, a poor-house, and a hospital, proudly continues his activity, fully persuaded that he has more than paid for all the human lives he has ruined physically and morally.

Or take a ruler, or some civil, ecclesiastical,

or military employee serving the State either to
satisfy his vanity or ambition, or as is most often
the case simply to receive a salary collected from
exhausted and toil-worn workers (all taxes,
from whomsoever collected, always originate
from labour, that is, from the working people),
and if (which is very seldom the case) he does
not also steal State money in irregular ways, he
considers himself and is considered by his fellows
a most useful and virtuous member of society.

Or take some judge, public prosecutor, or
ruler, who knows that by his sentences or decisions hundreds and thousands of poor wretches
torn from their families are now lingering in solitary confinement or convict settlements, where
they go out of their minds and kill themselves
either with pieces of broken glass or by starving.
He knows that these thousands of people have
thousands of mothers, wives, and children, suffering from their separation, shamed, not allowed
interviews, vainly petitioning for pardons or
even for an alleviation of their sentences; but he
has become so hardened in his hypocrisy that he
and those like him, and their wives and house-
holds, are fully convinced that in spite of it all
he can be a very good and sensitive man. Does
not hypocritical sophistry show that he is doing
a work of social utility? And this man, having
ruined hundreds and thousands of people who
curse him and are driven to desperation thanks to
his activity, believes in goodness and in God and
goes to mass with a beaming and benevolent smile
on his smooth face, hears the Gospel, utters liberal
speeches, pets his children, inculcates moral

principles in them and grows sentimental over imaginary sufferings.

All these people and those who live on them—their wives, tutors, children, cooks, actors, jockeys, and so forth—live on the blood of the working people which in one way or another they suck like leeches, consuming every day for their pleasure hundreds or thousands of the working days of wretched labourers driven to work by threats of murder. They see the sufferings and privations of these workmen and their children, old men, women, and sick people, and they know of the penalties that infringers of that organized spoliation undergo. Yet they not only do not moderate or conceal their luxury, but they insolently display it before these oppressed workmen (who for the most part hate them) as though on purpose to provoke them with their parks and palaces, theatres, hunts, and races. And at the same time they unceasingly assure themselves and one another that they are much concerned about the welfare of those people whom they are always trampling under foot; and on Sundays, in fine clothes, they drive in fine carriages to houses of God specially built for the mockery of Christianity, and there listen to men specially trained in that mockery, and who preach in all sorts of ways (with vestments and without, and wearing or not wearing white ties) the love of man which their daily lives belie. And doing all this, these people so enter into their parts that they seriously believe they really are what they pretend to be.

In general, hypocrisy having entered into the

flesh and blood of all classes in our time has reached such proportions that nothing of that kind any longer arouses indignation. Not for nothing was 'hypocrisy' derived from 'acting'. And anyone can act, that is, play a part. Such facts as that the representatives of Christ, at divine service, bless ranks of murderers holding loaded rifles in readiness to shoot their fellow men, that ministers of all the Christian sects take part at executions as inevitably as the executioners, by their presence acknowledging murder to be compatible with Christianity (a clergyman officiated in America at the first experiment of murder by electricity), no longer occasion surprise to anyone.

There was recently an international prison exhibition in Petersburg where instruments of torture—shackles and models of solitary cells—were shown, that is, instruments of torture worse than rods or the knout, and sensitive gentlemen and ladies went to amuse themselves by looking at them.

No one is surprised that liberal science, with its recognition of the principles of liberty, equality, and fraternity, should admit the necessity of armies, executions, custom-houses, the censorship, the legal regulation of prostitution, the exclusion of foreign labourers, the prohibition of emigration, and the necessity and justifiability of colonization based on poisoning with spirits and opium, plundering, and exterminating whole races of men called savages, and so on.

People talk of a time when all men will profess what is called Christianity (that is, various hostile creeds), when everybody will be well fed and clothed, when all will be united from one end of the earth to the other by telegraphs and telephones and flying machines; when all the workmen will be imbued with socialist doctrines, and the trades unions will have so many millions of members and so many millions of rubles and everyone will be educated, and they will all read newspapers and learn all the sciences.

But what that is good or useful can come of all these achievements, if people will not speak or act in accordance with what they consider the truth?

The miseries of men are due to their discord. And their discord results from their not following the truth which is one, but falsehood which is legion. The only means by which men can be united is by union in the truth. And therefore the more sincerely men seek the truth the nearer will they approach to union.

But how can men be united in the truth or even approach to it when they do not even proclaim the truth they know, but consider that they ought not to do so and pretend to believe in the truth of what they know is false?

So long as people pretend, that is, conceal the truth from themselves, no improvement of men's condition is possible. That improvement can only take place when they recognize that their welfare lies solely in the union of all men in the truth, and are therefore ready to put above everything else the recognition and profession of that truth which has revealed itself to them.

Let all those external improvements that

religious and scientific people dream of be accomplished; let all men accept Christianity and all the improvements the Bellamys[1] and Richets[2] desire be accomplished with all possible additions and corrections, but if at the same time the hypocrisy remains that now exists, if people do not profess the truth they know but continue to feign belief in what they do not themselves believe and veneration for what they do not respect, the condition of people will not merely remain what it is but will become worse and worse. The better men are materially provided for, the more telegraphs, telephones, books, papers and periodicals they have, the more means will there be of spreading contradictory lies and hypocrisies, and the more disunited and consequently unhappy will men become, as indeed occurs now.

Let all those external alterations be realized and the position of humanity will not be bettered. But let each man according to the strength that is in him profess the truth he knows and practise it in his own life—or at least cease to excuse the falsehood he supports by representing it as truth —and at once, in this very year 1893, such changes would be accomplished towards man's liberation and the establishment of truth on earth, as we dare not hope for in hundreds of years.

Not without reason was Christ's only denunciatory and harsh speech directed against hypocrites and hypocrisy. Falsehood is what corrupts,

---

[1] Edward Bellamy, the author of *Looking Backward*.—A.M.
[2] Perhaps this refers to C. R. Richet, who besides being a physiologist was the editor of the *Revue Scientifique*.—A.M.

embitters, and brutalizes people, and therefore divides them—not theft, robbery, murder, adultery, or forgery, but that special falsehood of hypocrisy which wipes out in men's consciousness the difference between good and evil and thereby debars them from avoiding evil and seeking good, depriving them of the very essence of true human life and therefore blocking the path to all improvement.

Those who do evil through ignorance of the truth arouse sympathy for their victims and aversion to evil; they inflict harm only on their victims. But those who know the truth and conceal the evil they do by hypocrisy, injure both themselves and their victims and thousands and thousands of others who are led astray by the falsehood in which the evil they do is disguised.

Thieves, robbers, murderers and cheats, committing acts that are acknowledged as bad by themselves and by everybody else, serve as an example of what not to do and revolt people. But those who commit similar acts of theft, robbery, murder, and other crimes under cover of religious, scientific, and liberal justifications (as is done by all the landowners, traders, manufacturers, and Government servants of our time) invite others to imitate their conduct and so do evil not only to their direct victims but to thousands and millions of men whose power of distinguishing between good and evil is thus obliterated.

One fortune obtained by exploiting the necessaries of life, or by trading in articles that deprave people, or by speculation on the Stock

Exchange, or by acquiring at a low price land the value of which is increased by public needs, or by organizing factories that ruin the life and health of people, or by civil or military service of the State, or by any business pandering to human vices—one fortune acquired by such means, adorned by ostentatious charity, and having not merely the sanction but the approval of leading men of society, corrupts men incomparably more than millions of thefts, frauds, and robberies committed in violation of the recognized forms of law and subject to criminal prosecution.

A single execution carried out dispassionately by prosperous and educated men with the approval and participation of Christian ministers and presented as something necessary and even just, perverts and brutalizes men more than thousands of murders committed by uneducated working people under the influence of passion. An execution such as Zhukóvsky[1] proposed to arrange, which was to arouse in men a sentiment of religious emotion, would have the most depraving influence imaginable.[2]

Every war, even the briefest, with the expenditure usual to war, the destruction of crops, the plundering, the licensed debauchery and murders, the sophistical excuses as to its necessity and justice, the exaltation and glorification of military exploits, patriotism and devotion to the flag, the feigned solicitude for the wounded,

[1] V. A. Zhukóvsky (1783–1852). Poet and translator of Schiller, Byron, and others; he was Alexander II's tutor.—A.M.

[2] See vol. vi of the Works of Zhukóvsky (Russian edition) —L.T.

and so on, does more to deprave people in a single year than millions of robberies, arsons, and murders committed in hundreds of years by individual men under the influence of passion.

The luxurious life of one opulent, respectable, steady, and so-called honourable family which, however, consumes as many days of labour as would suffice for the maintenance of thousands of people living in privation near by, perverts men's minds more than thousands of outrageous orgies by coarse tradesmen, officers, or workmen, abandoning themselves to debauchery, smashing looking-glasses and crockery for amusement, and so on.

One solemn religious procession or service or lying sermon (in which the preacher does not believe) from the altar-step or pulpit, produces incomparably more evil than thousands of forgeries, adulterations of food, and so forth.

We talk of the hypocrisy of the Pharisees. But the hypocrisy of our society far exceeds the comparatively innocent hypocrisy of the Pharisees. They at least had an external religious law the performance of which hindered their seeing their duty to their neighbour. Moreover those duties were not then nearly so clearly indicated. But now there is no such religious law to exonerate men from their duty to their neighbour and to every man without distinction. (I am not speaking of those coarse and stupid people who still fancy that they can be released from their sins by receiving the sacrament, or by absolution from the Pope.) On the contrary, that Gospel law which we all profess in one form or other has plainly pointed out that duty. And that same duty, which had then only been vaguely expressed by a few prophets, is now so clearly expressed that it has become a truism repeated by schoolboys and journalists. And so it would seem quite impossible for men of to-day to pretend that they do not know that duty.

Men of our time, availing themselves of the order of things maintained by violence, and at the same time protesting that they love their neighbours very much, and who do not notice that they are doing evil to those neighbours all the time, are like a man who, after a life of robbery, when at last caught standing with lifted knife in the act of striking a victim who is frantically crying for help, should declare that he did not know that what he was doing was unpleasant to the man he had robbed and was just about to kill. As that robber and murderer could not deny what was evident to everyone, so it would seem impossible for men of our time, living on the sufferings of the oppressed classes, to persuade themselves and others that they desire the welfare of those whom they unceasingly plunder, and that they do not know how the advantages they enjoy are obtained.

We cannot now assert that we do not know of those hundred thousand men in Russia alone who are always confined in prisons and convict settlements for the security of our tranquillity and property, and that we do not know of those trials in which we ourselves take part, and which at our instigation condemn men who have made attempts on our property or security to prisons, exile, or convict settlements where men, no worse than those who sentence them, perish or become corrupt. Nor can we pretend that we do not know that all that we have has been obtained and is maintained for us by murders and violence. We cannot pretend that we do not see the constable who with a loaded revolver walks in front of our windows defending us while we eat our appetizing dinner or see a new play at the theatre, or that we do not know of those soldiers who set off so promptly with rifles and live cartridges to where our property is in danger of being infringed.

We know that if we are not interrupted at our dinner, at our theatre, at balls, Christmas trees, skating-rinks, races, and hunts, it is only thanks to the bullet in the constable's revolver and the soldier's rifle, which will pierce the hungry stomach of the exploited man round the corner who is licking his lips while he watches our pleasures and is ready to disturb them directly the constable with the revolver goes away or there is no soldier in the barracks ready to come at our first call.

And so, as a man caught in robbery in broad daylight cannot persuade us that he did not raise his hand to take his victim's purse and had no idea of cutting his throat, so we, it would seem, can no longer persuade ourselves or others that the soldiers and armed constables who surround us are not there for our protection but only for defence against foreign foes, to maintain order, and in general for ornament, amusement, and parades. We cannot persuade ourselves that we do not know that men dislike dying of hunger, bereft of the right to gain subsistence from the soil on which they live, and that they do not like labouring underground, in water or in scorching heat, for ten to fourteen hours a day, or at night, in factories and mills, manufacturing articles for our pleasure. It would seem impossible to deny what is so evident. Yet that is just what is denied.

And though among the rich there are some people (whom I am fortunate enough to meet more and more often) who are really alive—especially among the women and young people—who when reminded how and at what cost their pleasures are purchased, do not attempt to hide the truth, but clutch their heads and say: 'Ah, don't speak of that! If it is so, why then it is impossible to live!' But though there are such sincere people, who even though they cannot free themselves from their entanglements recognize their sin, the vast majority of men in our time have so entered into their hypocritical role that they boldly deny the fact that stares everyone in the face.

'What you say is all unjust!' they reply. 'No one forces people to work for the landowners and manufacturers. It is a matter of free agreement. Large properties and capital are necessary in order to organize and provide work for the labouring classes. Work at the mills and factories is not nearly as terrible as you make out. And if there are some abuses in factories, the government and society take measures to abolish them and render the work of the labouring classes still easier and more agreeable. The working classes are accustomed to physical toil and are as yet unfit for anything else. The poverty of the people does not result at all from the landlords or from capitalistic oppression, but from other causes: it is the result of the people's ignorance, brutality, and drunkenness. And we, men in authority, counteract that poverty by wise legislation; we capitalists counteract it by the diffusion of useful inventions, we priests by religious instruction, and we liberals by the organization of trades unions and by diffusing and promoting education. By these means we are increasing the welfare of the people without altering our own position. We do not want everybody to be poor like the poor, we want everybody to be rich like the rich. And it is a sophistry to say that the poor are ill-treated and killed to force them to work for the rich. The troops are called out against the people only when—not understanding their own interests—they riot and disturb the tranquillity necessary for the public welfare. The restraint of malefactors for whom prisons, gallows, and penal settlements, are arranged, is also indispensable at present though we ourselves should like to see those things abolished, and are working in that direction.'

Hypocrisy in our time is supported by two things—pseudo-religion and pseudo-science— and has reached such colossal dimensions that were we not living in the midst of it, it would be impossible to believe that men could reach such a degree of self-deception. They have now reached such a strange condition and their hearts are so hardened that though they have eyes they see not, and having ears they hear not, neither do they understand.

Men have long been living in antagonism with their conscience. If it were not for hypocrisy they could not continue to do so. Their present arrangement of life in opposition to their conscience only exists because it is masked by hypocrisy.

And the more the divergence between reality and men's conscience increases, the more is that hypocrisy extended. But hypocrisy has its limits. And it seems that in our day those limits have been reached.

Every man of our time, with the Christian principles he has involuntarily assimilated, finds himself in a position exactly like that of a sleeper who dreams that he must do something that even in his dream he knows he ought not to do. He knows it in the very depth of his consciousness, and yet feels that he cannot change his position or stop doing what he knows he ought not to do. And as happens in a dream, his position becomes more and more tormenting till at last it reaches such a pitch of intensity that he begins to doubt the reality of what is happening and makes an effort of consciousness to shake off the obsession.

Such is the condition of an average man of our Christian society. He feels that all that is being done by him and around him is absurd, monstrous, impossible, and opposed to his conscience. He feels that this position is becoming more and more unendurable and has already reached a crisis of intensity.

Surely it is impossible that men of our time, with the Christian sense of the dignity of man and the equality of man that has permeated our flesh and blood, and with our need of peaceful intercourse and union among the nations, should really live in such a way that our every joy and every convenience must be purchased by the sufferings and death of our fellow men, and that at the same time we should every instant be within a hair's breadth of flinging ourselves on one another like wild beasts, nation against nation, pitilessly destroying men's lives and labour, merely because some deluded diplomat or ruler says or writes some absurdity to another diplomat or ruler as misguided as himself.

It is impossible! Yet every man of our time sees that this very thing is being done and that he too will be compelled to do it. And the situation becomes more and more tormenting.

And as a man who is dreaming does not believe that what presents itself to him as reality is actually real, and tries to awake to another actual reality, so the average man of our day cannot in the depth of his heart believe that the terrible state in which he finds himself and which is growing ever worse and worse can be true reality, and he tries to wake up to the living reality which already exists in his consciousness.

And as it is only necessary for the dreamer to make an effort of consciousness and ask himself: 'But is not this a dream?' in order instantly to destroy the position that seemed to him so hopeless and to wake up to a peaceful and joyful reality, so also the man of to-day need only make a moral effort to question the reality of what is suggested to him by his own and the surrounding hypocrisy, and ask himself: 'Is not this a deception?' to feel himself instantly transported, like an awakening dreamer, from an imaginary and dreadful world to a true, peaceful, and joyful reality.

And for this a man need not perform any achievement or exploit, he need only make an internal effort of consciousness.

5

Freedom

But can a man make this effort?

According to the existing theory indispensable to hypocrisy, man is not free and cannot change his life.

'A man cannot change his life because he is not free, and he is not free because all his actions are conditioned by preceding causes. And whatever a man may do there are always such and such causes which oblige him to do such and such actions. Therefore man cannot be free and cannot change his life,' say the defenders of the hypocritical theory. And they would be quite right if man were an unconscious being incapable of growth in relation to truth, that is, if having once recognized some truth he always remained at the same stage of cognition. But man is a conscious being capable of recognizing truth in higher and still higher degrees. And therefore, even if a man is not free to do such and such actions because previous causes exist for every action, those very causes themselves (which for a conscious man consist in the recognition of such and such truths as an adequate cause for an action) are within his power.

So that while a man is not free in regard to the performance of certain actions, he is free as regards the source of his future actions—just as an engine-driver cannot control the past movement of his locomotive and has not complete control of its present movement, but is able to control its future movements.

Whatever a conscious man may do, he does it either because he now considers that it conforms with the truth and that he ought to act so, or because at some previous time he has recognized a truth and now does from inertia or habit what he formerly did from conviction.

In any case the cause of his action is not some external fact, but the consciousness that a certain conception is true and the consequent recognition of this or that fact as a sufficient reason for the action.

Whether a man eats or refrains from eating, works or rests, runs from danger or exposes himself to it, he does so (if he acts consciously) only because he now considers it to be right and in accordance with the truth or because he believed so at some former time.

But the recognition or non-recognition of a certain truth depends not on external causes but on some cause within the man himself. So that sometimes a man with external conditions apparently favourable for the recognition of a truth will not recognize it, while another, with all the conditions apparently most unfavourable, will recognize it without any apparent cause. As is said in the Gospel: 'No man can come to me, except the Father ... draw him.' (John vi. 44.) That is to say, the recognition of truth which is the cause of all the manifestations of human life, does not depend on external phenomena but on certain inner qualities of a man not subject to his observation.

And so a man, though not free in his actions, always feels himself free in that which serves as the motive of his actions—the recognition or non-recognition of truth. And he feels himself free not only in relation to occurrences external to himself but even in relation to his own actions.

Thus a man, having under the influence of passion committed an action conflicting with his consciousness of truth, remains none the less free to recognize it or not recognize it. That is, he can refuse to recognize the truth, consider his action necessary, and so justify himself for committing it, or he may recognize the truth, consider his action bad, and so condemn himself for it.

A gambler or a drunkard who, instead of resisting temptation, has yielded to his passion, is still free to acknowledge gambling or drunkenness to be wrong or to regard them as harmless amusements. In the first case, even if he does not immediately free himself from his passion, he ultimately gets free from it in proportion to the sincerity with which he admits the truth. In the second case he strengthens his passion and deprives himself of all possibility of freeing himself from it.

In just the same way a man who has not endured the heat and has escaped from a burning house without saving his friend, remains free to consider his action bad and therefore to condemn himself for it (recognizing it to be true that a man should save the life of another even at the risk of his own), or to regard his action as natural and necessary and justify himself for it (not recognizing that truth). In the first case, if he recognizes the truth despite his departure from it, that recognition will result in his preparing himself for a whole series of acts of self-sacrifice. In the second case he will, on the contrary, prepare for a whole series of selfish actions.

Not that a man can always recognize every truth. There are truths long ago recognized by the man himself or conveyed to him by education and tradition and accepted by him on faith, to follow which has become a habit and a second nature. And there are truths that have only presented themselves to him dimly and from afar. A man lacks freedom alike to reject the former or to confess the latter But there are truths of a third kind which have not as yet become unconscious motives of action but yet have revealed themselves to him so clearly that he cannot pass them by, but must inevitably adopt some attitude towards them—recognizing or refusing to recognize them. And it is in regard to these truths that man's freedom is manifest. In his relation to truth every man in life finds himself in the position of a traveller who walks in the dark by the light of a lantern carried in front of him. He does not see what is not yet lit up by the lantern nor does he see what he has left behind in the darkness, and he is powerless to change his relation to the one or the other. But wherever he may be he sees what is revealed by the lantern, and it is always in his power to choose one side or the other of the road he is travelling.

There are always truths a man has not yet perceived, there are always others he has already outlived, forgotten, or assimilated, and there are again always others freshly illumined by the light of his reason and demanding recognition. And it is in the recognition or rejection of these truths that the consciousness of our freedom manifests itself.

The whole difficulty and apparent insolubility of the question of man's freedom arises from the fact that when deciding that question people regard themselves as fixed in relation to truth.

Man is certainly not free if we regard him as immovable and if we forget that the life of man and humanity in general is nothing but a continual movement from darkness to light, from a lower stage of truth to a higher, from truth greatly intermixed with error to truth more free from it.

Man would not be free if he knew no truth at all, and he would not be free or even have any idea of freedom, if the whole truth that should guide him in life were revealed to him once for all in complete purity with no admixture of error.

But man is not fixed in relation to truth. As he passes through life, each individual man and humanity in general gains knowledge of a greater and greater degree of truth and frees himself more and more from error.

And therefore men are always in a threefold

relation to truth. They have already so assimilated some truths that these have become an unconscious basis for their actions; other truths are only beginning to be perceived by them; and a third group, though not yet assimilated, have revealed themselves with sufficient clearness to compel recognition in one way or other—they must either be acknowledged or rejected.

And it is in the recognition or rejection of such truths that man is free.

His freedom does not consist in being able to act spontaneously, independently of the course of life and of the influence of existing causes, but it means that by recognizing and professing the truth revealed to him he can become a free and joyful participant in the eternal and infinite work performed by God or by the life of the world; or he can, by not recognizing that truth, become its slave and be painfully forced to go where he does not wish to go.

Truth not only points out the path of human life, it also reveals the only path along which it can go. And therefore all men must inevitably follow that path willingly or unwillingly—some voluntarily accomplishing the task life sets before them, others involuntarily submitting to the law of life. Man's freedom lies in having that choice.

Freedom within such narrow limits seems so insignificant to men that they do not notice it. Some people (the determinists) consider that amount of freedom so small that they do not recognize it at all. Others (advocates of complete free will) having an imaginary freedom in view, despise the degree of freedom they really possess, which seems to them insignificant. Freedom confined between the limits of complete ignorance of the truth and recognition of a certain degree of it, seems to some people not to be freedom at all, especially as man is inevitably compelled to carry out in life the truth that reveals itself to him, whether he is willing to recognize it or not.

A horse harnessed with others to a wagon is not free to refrain from moving in front of the wagon. If he does not pull, the wagon will knock against his legs and force him to go in the direction in which it is moving, and he will have to pull it against his will. But the horse is free to pull the wagon willingly or to be pushed by it. And so it is with man.

Whether that freedom be great or small in comparison with the imaginary freedom we should like to have, it is the only freedom that indubitably exists, and in it lies the only welfare accessible to man.

And not only does that freedom give welfare to men, it is the sole means of co-operating in the work that is being accomplished by the life of the world.

According to Christ's teaching the man who sees the significance of life in the domain in which it is not free—in the domain of effect, that is of acts—lacks true life. True life, according to the Christian teaching, is only possessed by a man who has transferred his life to the domain in which he is free—the domain of cause, that is, the domain in which lies the knowledge and recognition of the truth that is revealing itself —and who professes that truth and therefore inevitably ensures its fulfilment, as the wagon follows the horse.

If a man's life lies in corporeal affairs, he busies himself with things always dependent on temporal and spatial causes outside himself. He really does nothing himself. His acts are a mere self-deception. Everything he imagines himself to be doing is really done through him by a superior force. He is not a creator of life but its slave. But if a man acknowledges his life to lie in the recognition and confession of the truths that are revealing themselves to him, he identifies himself with the source of universal life and accomplishes acts not personal and dependent on conditions of time and space, but acts unconditioned by external causes, and that themselves constitute the cause of everything else and have an infinite, unlimited significance.

Men of the Pagan conception of life, disregarding the essential of true life which consists in the recognition and profession of truth, and directing all their efforts to strengthening and improving their personal life by external actions—resemble people on a steamer who in order to reach their destination damp down the boiler that hinders them from placing oarsmen, and in a storm, instead of relying on the screw and on the steam already generated, try to propel the ship by oars which do not reach the water.

The Kingdom of God can only be reached by effort, and only those who make such effort reach it. And it is just by this violent effort to rise above external conditions and reach the acknowledgement and announcement of the truth, that the Kingdom of God is taken. And this effort can and should be made in our time.

Men need only understand this, they need only cease to be troubled about general and external affairs in which they are not free, and devote even a one-hundredth part of the energy they now expend on those material affairs, to the affair in which they are free—that is, to the recognition and realization of the truth that is before them and to liberating themselves and others from the lies and hypocrisy which hide that truth—and without violence and conflict there would at once be an end of the false organization of life which makes men miserable and threatens them with still greater calamities. Then the Kingdom of God—or at least that first stage of it for which men are now ready in their consciousness—would be realized.

Just as a single shake may precipitate into crystals a liquid fully saturated with salt, so now a very small effort may be all that is needed to cause the truth that is already disclosed to men, to take hold of hundreds, thousands, and millions of people, and a public opinion corresponding to our consciousness may establish itself and the whole order of life consequently be transformed. And it is for us to make that effort.

If only each one of us tried to understand and acknowledge that Christian truth which in most diverse forms surrounds us on all sides and seeks to enter our souls; if only we ceased from lying and pretending that we do not see this truth, or that we wish to fulfil it but not in the chief demand it makes on us, if only we acknowledged that truth which is calling to us and boldly professed it—we should immediately find that hundreds, thousands, and millions of people were in the same position as ourselves—that they see the truth, and like us are only waiting for others to acknowledge it.

If only people ceased to be hypocrites they would at once see that the whole of this cruel, social organization—which alone binds them and appears to them to be something ordained by God, solid, indispensable, and sacred—is already tottering and is only maintained by that hypocritical lie by which we and others like us support it.

But if that is so, if it is true that it depends on us to destroy the existing order of life, have we a right to destroy it without knowing clearly what to put in its place? What will happen to the world when the existing order of things is at an end?

'What will there be beyond the walls of the world we leave behind?'

'There will be terror—a void, a vast emptiness, freedom . . . How can we advance not knowing whither? How abandon what we have without seeing what we shall obtain? . . .'[1]

Had Columbus reasoned so, he would never have weighed anchor. It is madness to sail the sea without knowing the way, to sail a sea no one has traversed before, and to make for a land the existence of which is doubtful. But by that madness he discovered a new world. Of course if the nations could simply move as it were from one

[1] Quoted from Herzen, vol. v, p. 55.—L.T.

set of furnished rooms to a better one it would be easier, but the trouble is that there is no one to prepare the new quarters. To sail into the future is even worse than to sail the ocean. There is nothing there. The future will be what men and circumstances make it.

'If you are content with the old world try to preserve it, it is very decrepit and will not last long. But if you cannot endure to live in perpetual discord between your convictions and your life, thinking one thing and doing another, then leave your medieval whitewashed cloisters at your own risk. I know very well that this is not easy. It is no trifle for a man to part with all he has been accustomed to from the day of his birth and with which he has grown up to maturity. Men are ready for terrible sacrifices, but not for those demanded of them by the new life. Are they ready to sacrifice their existing civilizations, their manner of life, religion, and the accepted conventional morality? Are they prepared to forgo all the fruits raised with such effort—the fruit we have been boasting of for three centuries? Are they prepared to forgo all the conveniences and delights of our existence, to prefer the crudities of youth to cultured decrepitude, to break down their hereditary castle just for the pleasure of helping to lay the foundation of a new house which will certainly not be built till long after they are gone?' (Herzen, vol. v, p. 55.)

That was written nearly half a century ago by a Russian writer whose penetrating mind even then clearly saw what is now seen by all thoughtful men—the impossibility of continuing life on its former foundations, and the necessity of establishing new forms of life.

From the very simplest, lowest, and most worldly point of view it is already clear that it is madness to remain in a building which cannot sustain the weight of its roof. It is obvious that we must leave it. Indeed it is difficult to imagine a position more wretched than that in which the Christian world now is, with its nations armed one against another, with the ever-growing taxes for the maintenance of its ever-increasing armaments, with the growing hatred of the working classes for the rich, and with war hanging over us all like the sword of Damocles, threatening to fall at any moment and certain to do so sooner or later.

A revolution could hardly be more disastrous for the great mass of the people than the existing order or rather disorder of our life, with its habitual sacrifices to unnatural toil, poverty, drunkenness, and debauchery, and with all the horrors of impending war, which will devour in a year more victims than all the revolutions of a century.

What will become of us and of the entire human race if each of us fulfils what God, through the conscience implanted in us, demands of us? Will it not be disastrous if being wholly in the power of a master I carry out what he orders me to do in the establishment arranged and ruled by him, strange though it may seem to me who do not know his ultimate purpose?

But it is not even the question as to what will happen, that troubles people when they hesitate

to do the master's will. What distresses them is
the question how they are to live without those
customary conditions of life known as science,
art, civilization, and culture. We ourselves feel
all the burden of our present life, we see that this
organization of life if it continues will inevitably
be our ruin, but at the same time we want the
conditions that have grown out of that life (our
science, art, civilization, and culture) to remain
intact when our life changes.

It is as if a man living in an old house and suffering from cold and other inconveniences in it,
knowing too that it will soon collapse, should
consent to its being rebuilt, but only on condition that he should not have to move out of it—a
condition tantamount to refusing to let it be
rebuilt at all. 'What if I leave the house, depriving myself of all its conveniences, and the new
house does not get built or is built differently,
leaving me without the things I am accustomed
to?'

But the materials and the builders being there
the probability is that the new house will be
built better than the former one. Besides there
is not only the likelihood, but the certainty, that
the old house will collapse and crush those who
remain in it.

Whether the former habitual conditions of life
will continue, or whether they will be abolished
and quite new and better ones arise, it is in any
case inevitably necessary to emerge from the
old conditions which have become impossible
and fatal, and to move forward to meet the
future.

'Civilization and culture, science and art, will disappear!'

But all these are only manifestations of truth, and the coming change is to be made solely for the sake of a closer approximation to the realization of truth. How then can manifestations of truth disappear through our realization of it? The manifestations will be different, better, and higher, but they will certainly not cease to be. What was false in them will be destroyed but what was true in them will blossom out and be strengthened.

6

Bethink yourselves men, or believe the Gospel, the teaching of welfare. If you do not bethink yourselves you will all perish, like those whom Pilate slew, and like those upon whom the tower of Siloam fell, like millions and millions who have perished, slayers and slain, executioners and executed, torturers and tortured, and like that man who having filled his barns thinking to enjoy a long life, perished stupidly the very night he meant to begin living. 'Bethink yourselves and believe in the glad tidings,' said Christ nineteen hundred years ago, and he says so yet more convincingly now, because the wretchedness and irrationality of our life, which he foretold, has now reached its utmost limits.

Nowadays after so many centuries of fruitless efforts to make our life secure by the Pagan organization of violence, it should be evident to everyone that efforts in that direction merely bring fresh dangers both into our personal and our social life instead of rendering it more secure.

By whatever names we dignify ourselves, in whatever apparel we attire ourselves, by whatever and before whatever priests we may be smeared with oil, however many millions we possess, however many special guards are stationed along our route,[1] however many policemen guard our wealth, however many so-called miscreant-revolutionaries and anarchists we may execute, whatever exploits we ourselves may perform, whatever States we may found, whatever fortresses and towers we may erect—from the Tower of Babel to that of Eiffel—we are always all of us confronted by two inevitable conditions of life which destroy its whole meaning. There is first of all death, which may at any moment overtake any of us, and there is the transitoriness of all that we do and that is so quickly destroyed leaving no trace. Whatever we may do—found kingdoms, build palaces and monuments, compose poems and romances—everything is transitory, and soon passes leaving no trace. And therefore, however we may conceal it from ourselves, we cannot help seeing that the meaning of our life can be neither in our personal physical existence, subject to unavoidable sufferings and inevitable death, nor in any worldly institution or organization.

Whoever you may be who read these lines, consider your position and your duties—not the position of landowner, merchant, judge, emperor, president, minister, priest, or soldier, tem-

. [1] These references are evidently to the procedure at the Tsar's coronation.—A.M.

porarily attributed to you by men, nor those imaginary duties imposed on you by that position—but your real position in eternity as a creature who by Someone's will has been called out of unconsciousness after an eternity of non-existence, to which by the same will you may at any moment be recalled. Think of your duties—not your imaginary duties as a landowner to your estate, as a merchant to your capital, as an emperor, minister, or official to the State—but those real duties which follow from your real position as a being called to life and endowed with reason and love.

Are you doing what He demands of you who sent you into the world and to whom you will soon return? Are you doing what He wills? Are you doing His will when as landowner or manufacturer you take the produce of the toil of the poor, arranging your life on that spoliation, or when as ruler or judge you do violence, sentencing men to execution, or when as soldiers you prepare yourselves for war, go to war, plunder and kill?

You say that the world is so made that this is inevitable, that you do this not of your own free-will but because you are compelled. But is it possible that so strong an aversion for human suffering, for ill-treatment, for the killing of men, should have been so deeply implanted in you; that you should be so imbued with the need of loving your fellows and a still stronger need of being loved by them, that you see clearly that only by recognizing the equality of all men and by mutual service one of another can the greatest good that is accessible to man be realized; that the same thing is taught you by your heart, by your reason, by the faith you profess, and the same said by science—is it possible that despite all this you can by some very vague and complicated reasoning be forced to do everything directly opposed to it? Are you really, as landowner or capitalist, obliged to base your whole life on the oppression of the people; as an emperor or president are you really obliged to command armies—that is, to be the head and leader of murders; as a government official are you really forced to take by violence from the poor the money earned by the sweat of their brow, to avail yourself of it or hand it over to rich men; as judge or juryman are you really obliged to sentence erring men to ill-treatment and death because the truth has not been revealed to them; and above all (for on this the whole evil is based) are you—and every young man—really compelled to be a soldier, and renouncing your own will and all human sentiments, compelled to promise to kill all those whom men you do not know may order you to kill?

That cannot be!

If people tell you that all this is necessary for the maintenance of the existing order of life and that this social order, with its destitution, hunger, prisons, executions, armies and wars, is necessary for society, that still more miseries would ensue were that organization infringed; all *that* is said only by those who profit by such an organization. Those who suffer from it—and they are ten times as numerous—all think and say the contrary. And in the depth of your soul you yourself know it is untrue, you know that the existing organization of life has outlived its time and must inevitably be reconstructed on new principles, and that therefore there is no need to sacrifice all human feeling to maintain it.

Even admitting that the existing order is necessary, why do you believe that it is just your business to maintain it at the cost of all your best human feelings? Who has made you a nurse in charge of this sick system? Neither society, nor the State, nor anyone else has ever asked you to support the existing organization by occupying the position (of landowner, trader, emperor, priest, or soldier) that you occupy, and you know very well that you occupy your position not at all with the self-sacrificing aim of maintaining an order of life necessary for the welfare of mankind, but for yourself—for the sake of your covetousness, vanity, ambition, insolence, or cowardice. If you did not want that position you would not have done all that it constantly demands of you in order to retain it. Only try to stop doing those complex, cruel, cunning and contemptible things that you constantly do to retain your position and you will quickly be deprived of it. Only try, as a ruler or an official, to give up lying, acting meanly, and participating in acts of violence and executions; try as a priest to give up deception; try in the army not to kill; as a landlord or manufacturer try to cease protecting your property by violence and by the law-courts; and you will immediately lose the position which you pretend is forced upon you and which you pretend oppresses you.

It is impossible for a man to be placed against his will in a situation repugnant to his conscience.

If you are in such a position it is not because it is necessary for anybody, but because you yourself want it. And therefore knowing that your position is directly opposed to your heart, to your reason, to your religion, and even to science in which you believe, you cannot but reflect on the question as to whether by remaining in that position, and above all by trying to justify it, you are doing right.

It might be possible to risk making a mistake if you had time to see it and to retrieve your error and if you ran the risk for something of any importance. But when you know for certain that you may disappear at any moment without the least possibility of retrieving a mistake either for yourself or for others involved in it, and when you also know that whatever you may do in the external arrangement of the world will soon all disappear as certainly as you yourself and without leaving a trace, it is evident that there is no reason for you to risk making so terrible a mistake.

This would be quite simple and clear if only we did not by hypocrisy befog the truth indubitably revealed to us.

Divide up what you possess with others, do not gather riches, do not exalt yourself, do not steal, do not cause suffering, do not kill anyone, do not do to another what you would not have done to yourself, was said not only nineteen hundred but five thousand years ago. And there can be no doubt of the truth of this law, and but for hypocrisy it would be impossible for men —even if they themselves did not conform to it—to fail to recognize at least its necessity, and that he who does not do these things is doing wrong.

But you say there is a public welfare for the sake of which these rules may and should be infringed: for the public good it is permissible to kill, torture, and rob. You say, as Caiaphas did, that it is better for one man to perish than the whole nation, and you sign the death sentence of a first, a second, and a third man, load your rifle against this man who is to perish for the public welfare, put him in prison, and take his possessions. You say that you do these cruel things because as a member of society and of the State you feel that it is your duty to serve them: as a landowner, judge, emperor, or military man to conform to their laws. But besides belonging to a certain State and having duties arising from that position, you belong also to eternity and to God and have duties arising from that.

And as a man's duty to his family or class is always subordinate to his duty as citizen of a State, so that duty in its turn is of necessity subordinate to his duty in relation to the universal life and to God.

And as it would be irrational to cut down telegraph posts to obtain fuel for a family or a society to increase their welfare, thus infringing the laws which guard the welfare of the country as a whole, so also is it irrational to torture, execute, and kill a man in order to make the State secure and increase its welfare, thus violat-

ing the unquestionable laws which guard the
welfare of the world.

The obligations which result from your citizen-
ship of the State must be subordinate to your
higher eternal obligations to the infinite life of
the world and to God, and cannot contradict
these, as Christ's disciples said nineteen hundred
years ago: 'Whether it be right to hearken unto
you more than unto God, judge ye' (Acts
iv. 19), and 'We ought to obey God rather than
men' (Acts v. 29).

We are told that in order not to infringe the
ever-changing system established yesterday by
a few men in one particular corner of the world,
we must do acts of violence, commit murder, and
oppress men, thus violating the eternal and immutable order of the world established by God
and by reason. Is that possible?

And therefore we cannot but reflect that our
position as landowner, trader, judge, emperor,
president, minister, priest, or soldier, is bound
up with oppression, violence, deceptions, and
murder, and recognize that it is wrong.

I do not say that if you are a landowner you
are bound immediately to give your land to the
poor; if you are a capitalist to give your money
or your factory to the workpeople; if you are a
tsar, minister, official, judge, or general, that
you should at once renounce your advantageous
position; or if you are a soldier (if, that is to say,
you occupy the position on which all violence is
based) that you should immediately refuse military service despite all the danger of doing so.

Were you to do this you would be doing the

very best thing possible, but it may be, as is most
likely, that you have not the strength. You have
ties; a family, dependents, and superiors; you
are under such powerful influences that you are
not strong enough to shake them off. But to
recognize the truth as a truth and avoid lying
about it is a thing you can always do. It is always
in your power to cease asserting that you remain
a landowner, a manufacturer, a merchant, an
artist, or a writer, because that is useful to mankind; that you are a governor, a public prosecutor, or tsar, not because it is agreeable to you
and you are used to it, but for the public good;
that you continue to be a soldier not from fear of
punishment but because you consider the army
necessary for the security of people's lives. It is
always in your power to stop lying like that to
yourself and to others, and you not only can but
should do this, because in this alone—in freeing
yourself from falsehood and confessing the truth
—lies the sole welfare of your life.

You need only free yourself from falsehood
and your situation will inevitably change of itself.

There is one and only one thing in life in which
it is granted man to be free and over which he
has full control—all else being beyond his power.
That one thing is to perceive the truth and profess it.

And yet, just because other wretched, erring
creatures like yourself assure you that you are
a soldier, an emperor, a landowner, a rich man,
a priest, or a general, you do evil deeds obviously
contrary to your reason and your heart: you
torment, plunder, and kill people, base your

existence on their sufferings, and above all instead of fulfilling the one duty of your life—acknowledging and confessing the truth known to you—you carefully pretend not to know it and hide it from yourself and from others, acting thereby in direct opposition to that sole purpose to which you are called.

And in what circumstances do you do that? You who may die at any moment, sign death sentences, declare war, go to war, fleece the labourers, sit in judgement, and punish people; you live in luxury surrounded by the poor, and teach weak men who trust you that these things must be, and that such is the duty of men. And yet it may be that at the very moment you are doing these things a germ or a bullet may come in your direction and you will rattle in your throat and die and forever lose the possibility of repairing the evil you have done to others and above all to yourself. You will have ruined the only life given to you in the whole of eternity, without having accomplished the one thing you unquestionably ought to have done.

However simple and however old it may be and however we may have stupefied ourselves by hypocrisy and the auto-suggestion resulting from it, nothing can destroy the certainty of this clear and simple truth, that no external efforts can safeguard our life which is inevitably attended by unavoidable sufferings and ends in yet more inevitable death, which may come to each of us at any moment, and that consequently our life can have no other meaning than the constant fulfilment of what is demanded of us by that Power that has placed us in this life and given us an indubitable guide—our rational consciousness.

That power cannot want of us what is irrational and impossible—the establishment of our temporary carnal life, the life of society or of the State. It demands of us what alone is certain, rational, and possible—the service of the Kingdom of God, that is, our co-operation in establishing the greatest possible unity among all living beings—a unity possible only in the truth. It therefore demands that we acknowledge and profess the truth revealed to us—the only thing that is always in our power.

'Seek ye first the Kingdom of God and his righteousness, and all these things shall be added unto you.'

The sole meaning of human life lies in serving the world by promoting the establishment of the Kingdom of God. This service can be accomplished only by the recognition and avowal of the truth by each separate individual.

'The Kingdom of God cometh not with outward show; neither shall they say, Lo here! or, lo there! for, behold, the Kingdom of God is within you.'

APPENDIX

(*A Variation of Chapter VIII*)

This was at first intended to be the final chapter of the work. It gradually expanded, however, into several chapters and some parts of it were used in them. What is here given consists chiefly of passages not used elsewhere.

THERE is a proverb: 'If you do not listen to your father and mother you will have to listen to the ass's skin'—that is, to the drum. And that proverb is applicable even in its direct meaning to men of our time who have not accepted Christ's teaching or who have accepted it in a perverted, ecclesiastical form. Men who have not accepted Christ's teaching in its full significance are compelled now to renounce everything human and to obey only the drum. And there is but one way of escape from the drum, and that is the confession of Christ's teaching in its full significance and not shorn of its chief demands.

For a long time now, for more than a century, the European peoples have struggled with the task of setting up new forms of life that have long since been accepted by man's consciousness. But our life is still controlled by the same old coarse despotism, and not only do the new forms of life fail to find application but those of life's phenomena which have long been rejected by man's conscience (such as slavery, the exploitation of some people for the benefit of the idle and luxurious life of others, executions, and wars) become ever more and more cruel. The reason of this is that there is no definition of good and evil on which all men are agreed, and therefore whatever forms of life may be established have to be supported by violence.

Whatever cunning forms professedly securing freedom and equality may be devised by a man of the social understanding of life, he cannot free himself from violence for he is himself a violator.

And therefore however much governments may increase their despotism, and whatever terrible calamities may be inflicted, a man of the social understanding of life will always submit. Such a man will exert himself to justify violence and to show that what is bad is good, or will comfort himself with the idea that before long he will, unknown to the government, devise means of upsetting it, and that when he has accomplished this he will set up a quite different and good government under which all that now seems to him wrong will be abolished. But till a change of existing forms (from which he expects salvation) is accomplished, and whether this comes quickly or slowly, he will slavishly obey the existing rulers, whoever they may be and no matter what they may demand, for though he cannot approve of the power which is employing violence at the moment he not only does not reject violence and its instruments but considers them to be indispensable. On this ground he will always submit to existing governmental violence. A man of the social understanding of life is a believer in violence and is therefore always and inevitably a slave.

The submissiveness with which the people of Europe, especially those who boast so of their liberty, have accepted one of the most despotic and shameful measures ever invented by tyrants (that is, universal military conscription) is a most obvious proof of this. The unopposed acceptance of general conscription not only without indignation but with a sort of peculiar, liberal exaltation and with rivalry in its adoption by all nations, serves as a striking proof of how impossible it is for men of the social understanding of life to free themselves from violence and alter the existing structure of society, no matter what oppression and humiliation may be put upon them.

What could be more insensate and painful than the position in which the European peoples now live, spending a great part of their wealth on preparations to annihilate their neighbours from whom nothing divides them and with whom they live in close spiritual intercourse? What could be more terrible than that which always awaits these European nations, when at any moment in an unlucky hour some madman calling himself a potentate may say something displeasing to another such madman? What could be more terrible than all these newly devised and still to be devised means of destruction: cannon, shells, bombs, rockets with smokeless powder, torpedoes and other instruments of death? Yet everybody acquiesces in this state of affairs. To-morrow a war may begin, and men, driven like cattle to the slaughter, will go where they are sent and perish unprotestingly, and destroy other men without even asking themselves why they do it. And not only will they feel no remorse about it, they will even swagger and be proud of the gewgaws they are allowed to wear for their skill in killing people, and they will exalt those unhappy or wicked men who placed them in such a position, and erect monuments to them.

The people of liberal Europe rejoice that they are allowed to write all sorts of nonsense in booklets and to say what comes into their heads at dinners, meetings, and in parliaments; and it seems to them that they are quite free—as oxen feeding in the market-garden of a slaughter-house imagine they are quite free. Yet despotic power has hardly ever caused such tribulations to people as it is now causing, and hardly ever has it held the people in such contempt as it does now. The effrontery of those who employ violence, and the meanness of those subjected to it, never reached such a degree as it has reached now. . . .

Young men go to the recruiting office, and their fathers and mothers, whom they have to promise to kill, calmly accompany them. There is evidently no longer any humiliation or shame that men of our time will not endure. There is no meanness or wickedness they will not commit if it affords them even a little pleasure and frees them from even a little danger. Never before has either the violence of the rulers or the debasement of the ruled reached such a degree. For all men in possession of their spiritual strength there is and has always been something they consider sacred and would not abandon for anything, and for the sake of which they are ready to endure deprivation, suffering, and even death. Almost every man however low his stage of development has something spiritual in him he would not abandon for any material advantage. Tell a Russian peasant to spit out the sacrament, or defile an icon: he would die rather than do it! He has been deceived and does not consider sacred what is really sacred—that is, the life of man. But he considers an icon a sacred thing, and recognizes something as sacred which he will not abandon. There is a limit to his pliancy. He has a backbone that does not bend. But where is that backbone to be found in a civilized man who becomes a slave to his government?

It is not there! He is all soft and doubles up completely. If there is anything that should be sacred to him (judging by what is uttered with so much hypocritical pathos in his class) it is humanitarianism—that is, respect for man, for his rights, his liberty and his life. And yet what happens? He, a learned, progressive man, educated in the highest establishments where he has become acquainted with all that mankind has produced, and who considers himself superior to the crowd; he who is always talking of liberty, rights, and the inviolability of human life; allows himself to be taken, dressed up in a clown's garb, ordered to straighten himself up at the word of command and to abase himself before all whose uniforms have more braid on them than his own. He is ordered to pose, to bow, to grimace, and to promise to kill his brothers and his parents— and he is ready to do it all and only asks when and how he is to do it. To-morrow he may be discharged, and then like one possessed he will once more preach impressively about liberty, and the inviolability of man.

And the liberals, socialists, anarchists, and people of the social view of life in general, talk of establishing, with people like these—who promise to kill their own parents—a society in which men will be free! What moral or rational society can be formed of such people? Rearrange them as you will, nothing better can be formed of them than a herd of cattle directed by cries and the whip.

A terrible weight of evil hangs over the people of the world and presses them down. And men standing beneath that weight, and more and more oppressed by it, seek means of release.

They know that by their collective strength they could lift that weight and throw it off, but they cannot agree to do so, and each of them bends lower and lower, letting it lie on other shoulders. And the weight presses on people more and more and would long ago have crushed them had there not been some men among them who were guided in their actions not by the consideration of external consequences but by a desire to make them agree with the voice of conscience. There have been and are such people —Christians, for the essence of Christianity lies in substituting an inward aim (to attain which no one else's consent is necessary) in place of external aims (to attain which everyone's agreement is necessary). And therefore salvation from the slavery men are enduring—impossible for men of the social life-perception—has been and is achieved by Christianity—simply by substituting the Christian in place of the social conception of life.

The aim of universal life cannot be fully known to you, says the Christian teaching to each man, and presents itself to you only as a nearer and nearer approach to the infinite welfare of the world—to the establishment of the Kingdom of God. But the aim of the personal life is certainly known to you, and consists in realizing in yourself the infinite perfecting of love, essential for the realization of the Kingdom of God. And that aim is always known to you and always attainable.

The best particular external aims may not be known to you, obstacles may be put to their attainment. But an approach to inward perfection, the increase of love in yourself and in others, cannot be hindered by anyone or anything. It is only necessary for a man to set himself the one true, indubitable, and attainable inward aim of life, in place of the false, external, social aim, and the chains by which he seemed immutably bound will fall asunder and enable him to feel perfectly free.

A Christian frees himself from the dominion of State law by not requiring it either for himself or for others, by accounting human life better secured by the law of love which he professes, than by laws relying on violence for their maintenance.

A Christian who has learnt to know the demands of the law of love, not only cannot regard the demands made by the law of violence as obligatory, but regards those demands as being just the very human errors which should be exposed and abolished.

The essence of Christianity is the fulfilment of the will of God. But to fulfil God's will requires complete external liberty. Freedom is a necessary condition of Christian life. . . .

The profession of Christianity frees men from every external authority. And it not only frees them from external authority, it gives them at the same time a possibility of obtaining the betterment of life they vainly sought to attain by external means.

It seems to men that their position is improved as a result of alterations in the external forms of life; whereas the alteration of external forms is always, in reality, merely the result of an alteration of consciousness, and improves life only to the extent to which it is based on that alteration of consciousness.

The external forms of life not based on an alteration of consciousness not only fail to improve man's condition but for the most part make it worse. It was not governmental decrees that did away with the slaughter of children, with torture, and with slavery, it was the change in men's consciousness that rendered such decrees inevitable. And the improvement of life was only accomplished to the extent to which it was based on a change of consciousness, that is, to the extent to which the law of violence was replaced in men's consciousness by the law of love.

But it seems to men that if it is true that a change of consciousness influences the forms of life, the contrary should also be the case, and as it is easier and pleasanter to direct one's activity to external changes (the results of which are more in evidence) people always prefer to direct their efforts to altering external forms rather than to changing their consciousness, and therefore, for the most part, occupy themselves with appearances rather than with what is essential. The external, fussy useless activity that consists of setting up and applying external forms of life, hides from men the essential inward activity of a change of consciousness, which alone can improve their lives. And it is this very delusion that is the greatest obstacle to a general improvement in men's lives.

A better life is only possible when man's consciousness changes for the better. And therefore all the efforts of those who wish to improve life should be directed towards a change in their own and other people's consciousness. But that is exactly what people do not want to do. On the contrary they direct all their efforts to altering the forms of life, hoping that by means of these alterations consciousness will also be changed.

Christianity and Christianity alone liberates men from the slavery in which they are involved in our day, and Christianity and Christianity alone gives them a possibility of really improving their personal life and that of the society in which they live.

It should one would think be clear that only Christianity offers salvation to each individual, and that it alone affords a possibility of improving the common life of humanity. But men could not receive Christianity before the social life-conception had been thoroughly tested—before the field of errors, cruelties, and sufferings belonging to the social and State forms of life had been explored in all directions.

It is often cited as a most convincing proof of the vagueness, and still more the impracticability, of Christ's teaching, that though it has been known to men for nineteen hundred years it has not been accepted in its full significance, but only in an external form. 'If it has been known for so many years and yet has not become a guide

for people's lives, and if so many martyrs and
professors of Christianity have perished vainly
without altering the existing state of things, then
the teaching must be false and impracticable,'
people say.

To say and think so, is as if one said or thought
that a seed is defective and infertile because it
lies for a time in the earth and disintegrates instead of producing flower and fruit as soon as it
is sown.

It was both necessary and inevitable that the
Christian teaching when it first appeared should
be accepted only in an external and perverted
form and not in its full significance.

A teaching that destroyed the whole previous
outlook on life and set up a new one, could not
be received in its full significance at its first appearance. It could be accepted only in a perverted external form, and its acceptance in that
form and in an external manner only, was necessary that men who were at first unable to accept
it in a spiritual way, should be brought to such
an acceptance of it by life itself.

Can you imagine Romans and Barbarians accepting the teaching of Christ as we now understand it? How could the Romans and Barbarians
believe that violence can never lead to anything
but an increase of violence; that tortures, executions, and wars, clear up nothing and decide
nothing, but only confuse and complicate everything?

The vast majority of men were not in a condition to understand the teaching of Christ by the
spiritual path alone; it was necessary that they

should be brought to an understanding of it by life itself—that having learnt by experience that every deviation from that teaching leads to destruction, they should recognize it to be the truth.

So the teaching was accepted, as could not be otherwise, as an external worship of God replacing paganism, and life continued to progress farther and farther along the path of paganism. But that perverted Christian teaching was inseparably bound up with the Gospels, and the priests of that pseudo-Christianity could not conceal the essence of the teaching from men despite all their efforts. Contrary to their wish the teaching gradually disclosed itself to men and has become a part of man's consciousness. . . .

For nineteen centuries this dual work, positive and negative, has gone on: on the one side an ever greater and greater withdrawal of men to the path of paganism and away from the teaching of Christ that was revealing itself; on the other an ever greater and greater elucidation and simplification of the truths of Christ's teaching. And the further this dual work proceeded the more clearly was it seen what was delusion and what was truth. . . .

People might not bethink themselves, might not confess their faith in the Gospel, till the delusion of violence had reached its utmost limits as it has done in our day, but such faith has now become inevitable. Men can no longer fail to bethink themselves and confess their belief in the Gospel, when each of them is called upon not to pour oblations to pagan gods, as was the case of old, but to take part in most horrible and cruel homicides after a preliminary announcement of the possibility and necessity of patricide. General conscription is the last stone laid on a wall with a crooked base, and will cause the collapse of the whole edifice of social violence which rests on shaky foundations.

And that edifice is collapsing not because the economic weight laid upon it by armaments is too great to be borne; not because the expected wars are too awful; and not because the calamities chanted by Ravachol are so dreadful. It is collapsing because the demand presented to men as the crown of the social structure—military conscription—is so contrary to the Christian teaching which has entered into men's consciousness, that they cannot fail to understand from these demands the whole falsity of the social structure in which they have lived and the full truth of the teaching which for nineteen hundred years has been rejected.

The Christian truth, formerly realized only under the influence of a lofty flow of prophetic feeling, has now become quite accessible to the simplest man, and the challenge to profess it presents itself to every man at every step.

The growth of consciousness proceeds steadily, not by leaps, and it is never possible to draw a line dividing one period of the life of humanity from another. Yet there is such a line, as there is one between childhood and youth, between winter and spring, and so forth, or if there is no definite line there is a transitional period. And European humanity is now passing through such a period. Everything is ready for passing from one condition to another and only a push is needed to complete the change. That push may be given at any moment. Public consciousness already rejects the former arrangements of life and has long been ready to adopt a new one. Everybody knows and feels this. But the inertia of the past and timidity as to the future sometimes delays for a long time the passing into reality of what has been prepared in consciousness. At such a time a single word is sometimes sufficient for consciousness to reach expression, and for public opinion—the chief force in humanity's collective life—to alter the whole present organization instantaneously and completely.

The position of our European humanity, with its officials, taxes, priests, prisons, guillotines, fortresses, cannon, and dynamite, seems really terrible. But it only seems so. All this, all these horrors that are now committed and those that are awaited, are the product of our imagination. Such a state of things is utterly impossible, and according to the present condition of man's consciousness ought not to exist. Power does not lie in prisons, fetters, gallows, cannon and powder, but in the consciousness of those who put others in prison, hang men from the gallows, and stand by the cannon. And these men's consciousness is now in a state of tense and glaring contradiction, being drawn in two contrary directions. Christ said that he had overcome the world and he has really done so. The evil of the world, however terrible, no longer exists since it has ceased to exist in man's consciousness. Only a slight push is needed for it to be destroyed and changed to a new form of life. . . .

Large and heavy towns have been built on the ice, but the ice is already thawing and hardly holds, and the heavier those towns are the sooner will they be submerged by the water and nothing left of them.

In early Christian times a soldier, Theodore, told the authorities that being a Christian he could not bear arms, and when he was executed for this the responsible authorities quite sincerely regarded him as a madman and far from trying to conceal such an occurrence, exposed him and men like him to public scorn at their execution. But now, when in Austria, Prussia, Sweden, Switzerland, Russia, and everywhere in Europe, cases of refusals of military service occur more and more frequently, these cases are no longer regarded by the authorities as madness, but as a very dangerous awakening from madness, and the governments far from holding such cases up to public scorn carefully conceal them, knowing that the salvation of men from humiliation, enslavement, and ignorance, will come about not by revolutions, trades-unions, peace-congresses, and books, but in the simplest way—by each man who is called upon to share in the infliction of violence on his fellow-men and on himself, asking in perplexity: 'But why should I do this?'

No astute, clever arrangements of alliances, arbitration, and so on, will save humanity, but this way of regarding things when it becomes general will do so. And it may and should soon become general. The position of men of our day is exactly like that of a man tormented by an oppressive nightmare. He sees himself in a terrible position and awaits fearful calamities in which he must himself participate. He knows he ought not to do so but cannot help himself, and the calamity draws nearer and nearer. He becomes desperate, feels that these things cannot continue, and asks himself: 'But is it all true?'

And it is only necessary for him to doubt the reality of what presents itself to him and he will wake up, and everything that so oppressed and tormented him will vanish instantly.

It is the same with the present condition of violence, enslavement, and cruelty, and our unavoidable participation in it—this terrible contradiction between a Christian consciousness and the barbarous way of life in which European humanity finds itself. It is only necessary that men should arouse themselves from the state of stupor they are in, and awaken to the higher understanding of life that was revealed to them already nineteen hundred years ago and that beckons them to itself from all sides—and all that is so horrible will vanish instantaneously. And as on awakening from a nightmare a man's soul rejoices that things are what they are, and it even becomes difficult to imagine how he could have dreamt such nonsense, so it is only necessary for us to awaken for a moment from the constant state of stupefaction in which the governments try to keep us, and to regard what we are doing from the standpoint of the moral demands we make to children and even to animals, forbidding them to fight, in order to feel horrified at the obvious contradictions amid which we live. A man need only awaken from the hypnotism of imitation in which he lives, and look soberly at what the State demands of him, in order not merely to refuse obedience, but to feel a fearful astonishment and indignation that men could address such demands to him.

And that awakening may occur at any moment.

1893.

CHRISTIANITY AND PATRIOTISM

Preface

THE Franco-Russian celebrations that took place in France in October of last year (1893) aroused in me, as well probably as in many other people, at first a feeling of amusement, then of perplexity, and at last of indignation, which I wished to express in a short magazine article. But as I considered the chief causes of that strange phenomenon more and more seriously I arrived at the opinions I now present to the reader.

———

Russians and Frenchmen have lived for many centuries knowing one another and sometimes coming into friendly but more often unfortunately into very hostile relations with one another, aroused by their governments. And now suddenly, because a French squadron visited Kronstadt two years ago and its officers came ashore and ate a great deal in various places and drank a quantity of various kinds of wine while listening to and uttering many false and foolish words, and because a similar Russian squadron visited Toulon last year and its officers went to Paris and ate and drank a great deal while hearing and uttering still more false and foolish words, it has come to pass that not only the men who ate, drank, and talked, but all those who were present and even those who were not present but merely heard and read of it in the papers—all these millions of Russian and French people suddenly imagined themselves to be particularly fond of one another, that is, that all the French love all the Russians and all the Russians love all the French.

These feelings were expressed in France during October in most extraordinary ways.

This is how the reception of the Russian sailors is described in *Sélsky Véstnik (Rural News)*, a paper that collects its information from all the other newspapers:

When the Russian and French vessels met, besides firing salvos they greeted one another with ardent and enthusiastic cries of 'Hurrah!' *'Vive la Russie!'* *'Vive la France!'*

There were also bands of music on many private steamers playing the Russian national anthem, 'God Save the Tsar', and the French *Marseillaise*, and the public in private boats waved hats, flags, handkerchiefs, and bouquets of flowers. There were many barges loaded entirely with peasant men and women and their children who all held bouquets of flowers, and even the children waved their bouquets and shouted with all their might, *Vive la Russie*. At the sight of such popular enthusiasm our sailors were unable to restrain their tears. . . .

The French men-of-war at Toulon were all drawn up in the harbour in two lines and our squadron passed between them, led by the admiral's ironclad which was followed by the other vessels. An extraordinarily solemn moment had arrived.

The Russian flagship fired a salute of fifteen guns in honour of the French squadron, and the French flagship replied with a double salute of thirty guns. The strains of the Russian national anthem thundered from the French ship. The French sailors climbed up their masts and rigging and loud cries of welcome poured forth unceasingly from both squadrons and from the surrounding vessels. The sailors' caps and the hats and handkerchiefs of the spectators were all waved rapturously in honour of the precious guests. From all sides, from the water and from the land, thundered the universal acclaim: 'Hail to Russia! Hail to France!'

In accord with naval usage Admiral Avelan with the officers of his staff went ashore to greet the local authorities. At the landing-stage they were met by the French general naval staff and the senior officers of the port of Toulon. A general friendly shaking of hands ensued amid the thunder of guns and the pealing of bells. The naval band played the national anthem, 'God Save the Tsar', which was drowned by loud cries from the public of 'Long live the Tsar! *Vive la Russie!*' And these cries mingled into one mighty roar eclipsing both the music and the firing of the guns.

Witnesses report that at that moment the enthusiasm of the countless mass of people attained its highest pitch, and that no words can convey the feelings that overflowed in the hearts of all those who were present. Admiral Avelan, bare-headed and accompanied by the Russian and French officers, set out for the head-quarters of the naval administration where he was awaited by the French Minister of Marine.

When receiving the Admiral, the Minister said:

'Kronstadt and Toulon are two places that bear testimony to the sympathy existing between the Russian and the French peoples. You will be welcomed everywhere as cordial friends. The Government and the whole of France greet you, and those who accompany you, as the representatives of "a great and noble people".'

The Admiral replied that he was unable to express all the gratitude he felt. 'The Russian squadron and the whole of Russia,' he said, 'will be grateful for the reception you have given us.'

On taking leave of the Minister after a short conversation the Admiral again thanked him for his welcome, and added:

'I do not wish to part from you without pronouncing the words that are impressed on the hearts of all Russians: "Long live France!"'[1]

Such was the reception at Toulon. In Paris the reception and the festivities were even more extraordinary.

This is how the newspapers described the reception in Paris:

All looks are directed to the Boulevard des Italiens, whence the Russian sailors are to appear. At last from a long way off the roar of a whole hurricane of exclamations and applause is heard. The roar grows stronger and clearer. The hurricane is evidently drawing nearer. There is a great crush and pressure in the square. The police rush to clear the route to the *Cercle Militaire*, but this proves to be a far from easy task. There is an indescribable crush and pressure among the crowd. . . . At last the head of the procession appears in the square. At the same moment a deafening cry of *Vive la Russie! Vive la Russie!* rises above it. All heads are bared, the public packed tightly at the windows, on the balconies, and even on the roofs, wave hats, flags, and handkerchiefs, and applaud frantically, throwing down from the windows clouds of small, multi-coloured cockades. A whole sea of handkerchiefs, hats, and flags wave above the heads of the crowd standing in the square. *Vive la Russie!*

[1] *Sélsky Véstnik*, 1893, No. 41.

Vive la Russie! shouts that crowd with its hundred-thousand throats. And they strive hard to get the best possible view of their dear guests, stretching out their hands to them and expressing their sympathy in every possible way.[1]

Another correspondent writes that the enthusiasm of the crowd approached delirium. One Russian journalist then in Paris describes that procession of sailors as follows:

They say truly that it is an event of world-wide importance, amazing, moving us to tears, uplifting the soul and making it quiver with the love which sees men as brothers and hates blood and violent annexation and the tearing of children from a beloved mother. I have been in a kind of delirium for some hours. I felt it strange and overwhelming to stand at the Gare de Lyons among the representatives of the French Government in their gold-embroidered uniforms, among the members of the municipality in dress-coats, and to hear the cries of *Vive la Russie! Vive le Tsar!* and our national anthem played over and over again. Where was I? What had happened? What magic current had blended all this into one feeling, one comprehension? Does one not indeed feel the presence of the God of love and brotherhood, the presence of some higher ideal that descends on men only at exalted moments? One's heart is so full of something beautiful and pure and elevated that the pen is unable to express it. Words are pale beside what I saw and what I felt. This was not rapture—that word is too banal —it was better than rapture, more picturesque, deeper, more joyful and more varied. It is impossible to describe what it was like at the *Cercle Militaire* when Admiral Avelan appeared on the

[1] From the *Nóvoe Vrémya* newspaper.

balcony of the second story. Here words are of no avail. During the service, when the choir were singing in church: 'O Lord, save thy people!'—the triumphal strains of the *Marseillaise* played by a band of wind instruments in the street burst through the open doors. It produced an astonishing impression no words can convey.[1]

II

The Russian sailors who had arrived in France went from one fête to another for a whole fortnight, and during and after each fête they ate, drank, and talked. And the reports of what and where they drank on Wednesday, and what and where they drank on Friday, and of what was then said, was communicated by telegraph to all Russia. As soon as one of the Russian captains drank to the health of France, that fact was immediately announced to the world, and directly the Russian Admiral said: 'I drink to *la belle France!*' those words were at once transmitted all over the world. But more than that, the zeal of the newspapers was such that not only the toasts but even the menus of the dinners were reported, with all the pâtés and hors-d'œuvres consumed at them.

Thus in one newspaper it was stated that the dinner was a work of art:

> Consommé de volailles, petits pâtés.
> Mousse de homard parisienne.
> Noisette de bœuf à la béarnaise.
> Faisans à la Périgord.
> Casseroles de truffes au champagne.
> Chaud-froid de volailles à la Toulouse.

[1] *Nóvoe Vrémya*, October 1893.

Salade russe.
Croûte de fruits toulonaise.
Parfaits à l'ananas.
Desserts.

In the next number of that paper it was said that: 'In its culinary aspect the dinner left nothing to be desired. The menu was as follows:

Potage livonien et St.-Germain.
Zéphyrs Nantua.
Esturgeon braisé moldave.
Selle de daguet grand veneur. . . .'

In the following day's paper a fresh menu was given. With each menu a description was also given of the drinks swallowed by the festive party, some sort of 'vudka',[1] some sort of Bourgogne vieux, Grand Moët, and so on. In an English newspaper all the intoxicating drinks consumed during these fêtes were enumerated, the quantity of it being so enormous that all the drunkards in Russia and in France could hardly have swallowed it in so short a time.

The speeches made were also reported, but the menus were more varied than the speeches, which invariably consisted of the same words in different combinations and permutations. The meaning of these words was always one and the same: we love each other tenderly and are enraptured that we have suddenly learnt to love each other so tenderly. Our aim is not war, nor *revanche*, nor the recovery of lost provinces: our sole aim is *peace*, the blessings of *peace*, the security of *peace*, the tranquillity and *peace* of Europe. Long live the Russian Emperor and Empress!

---

[1] A French misspelling of *vodka*.

We love them and we love *peace*. Long live the President of the Republic and his wife! We love them too and we love *peace*. Long live France and Russia, their fleets and their armies! We love the army, we love peace, and we love the commander of the squadron!

The speeches generally ended as if with a refrain, with the words: 'Toulon-Kronstadt' or 'Kronstadt-Toulon'. And the names of those places where so many different dishes had been eaten and so many different wines had been drunk, were pronounced as words recalling the most noble and heroic actions of the representatives of both nations—words that left nothing more to be said since all was understood. We love one another and we love peace. Kronstadt-Toulon! What more could be added to that?... especially when said to the triumphal music of bands playing two hymns at the same time: the one hymn glorifying the Tsar and imploring God to send him all prosperity, the other cursing all tsars and kings and invoking destruction upon them.[1]

Those who expressed their feeling of love particularly well received orders and rewards, and some people, for similar services or simply from an overflow of love, were presented with very strange and unexpected gifts. Thus the French squadron made the Russian Tsar a present of some sort of golden book in which it seems nothing was written—or at least nothing that anybody needed to know; while the commander of

[1] The text of the *Marseillaise* (with a literal translation) is given at the end of this article.—A.M.

the Russian squadron received an even more surprising object—a peasant plough (a *sokhá*) made of aluminium and covered with flowers— in addition to many other unexpected gifts.

And all these strange actions were accompanied by even stranger religious rites and public prayers to which one supposed the French had long become unaccustomed. So many public prayers as during that brief period had hardly been performed since the time of the Concordat.[1] The French all at once became extraordinarily devout, and carefully hung up in the rooms of the Russian sailors those very images they had so carefully removed from their own schools as pernicious instruments of superstition, and they prayed continually. The Cardinals and Bishops prescribed prayers everywhere and themselves offered up the strangest prayers. Thus a bishop at Toulon at the launching of the ironclad *Jorigiberi* prayed to the God of peace, letting it be felt however that in case of need he could also apply to the God of war. 'What will be its destiny God alone knows,' said he, speaking of the newly launched vessel. 'Whether it will vomit death from its terrible womb is unknown. But if, having appealed to-day to the God of peace, we have hereafter to appeal to the God of war, we are firmly convinced that the *Jorigiberi* will go to meet the foe hand in hand with the mighty vessels whose crews have to-day entered into such close and brotherly union with our own. But may that pass us by and the present celebra-

---

[1] The Concordat of 1801, concluded between Napoleon and Pope Pius VII.—A.M.

tions leave only peaceful memories, like the remembrance of the Grand Duke Constantine,[1] who was present here at the launching of the *Quirinal*, and may the friendship of France and Russia make the two nations the guardians of peace. . . .'

Meanwhile tens of thousands of telegrams were flying from Russia to France and from France to Russia. French women greeted the Russian women. Russian women expressed their gratitude to the French women. A troupe of Russian actors greeted the French actors, and the French actors informed them that they had laid the greeting of the Russian actors deep in their hearts. Russian graduates of law at the District Court of some town or other announced their rapture to the French nation. General So-and-so thanked Madame This-and-that, and Madame This-and-that assured General So-and-so of the ardour of her sentiments for the Russian nation. Russian children wrote greetings in verse to French children, French children replied in verse and in prose. The Russian Minister of Education testified to the French Minister of Education of the sudden feelings of love for the French entertained by all the teachers and writers under his supervision. The Society for the Protection of Animals testified its ardent attachment to the French, and a similar announcement was made by the Municipality of Kazán.

The Canon of Arras assured the Most Reverend Chief Priest of the Russian Court clergy that a

---

[1] Constantine Nikoláevich, second son of Nicholas I. He was a General and Admiral, and visited Toulon in 1857.—A.M.

love of Russia and of his Imperial Majesty
Alexander III and his Imperial Family was
deeply implanted in the hearts of all the Cardinals and Archbishops of France, and that
French and Russian priests alike reverence the
Most Holy Virgin and profess an almost identical faith, to which the Most Reverend Chief
Priest replied that the prayers of the French
clergy for the Imperial Family had echoed joyfully in the hearts of all the Russian people,
lovingly attached to their Tsar, and that as the
Russian people worshipped the Most Holy Virgin
in the same way they confidently relied on France
in life and death. Very similar announcements
were made by all sorts of generals, telegraph
clerks, and grocery-store dealers. They all con-
gratulated somebody on something and thanked
somebody for something.

The excitement was so great that most extraordinary things were done, and no one noticed
their strangeness. On the contrary, everyone was
approving and delighted, and made haste to do
something of the same sort as quickly as possible
in order not to be left behind. If protests were
uttered, and even written and printed, against the
senselessness of these frenzied proceedings, such
protests were either hushed up or shouted down.[1]

[1] I know, for example, of the following protest made by
Russian students and sent to Paris, but not accepted by a
single newspaper:

'An open letter to French students.

'A group of Moscow law students with the University
Inspector at their head has recently had the audacity to speak
in the name of all Moscow students regarding the Toulon
festivities.

'We, the representatives of the Moscow Union of students of

To say nothing of the millions of working days wasted on these festivities or the wholesale drunkenness (connived at by all the authorities)

various provinces, protest most emphatically against that group's assumption of authority, and against the exchange of greetings that has taken place between it and the French students. We too regard France with warm affection and profound respect, but we so regard her because we see in her a great nation which has in the past constantly been the mouthpiece and herald to the whole world of the great ideals of liberty, equality, and fraternity, and which was foremost in courageously attempting to incorporate those great ideals in life. The best part of the youth of Russia has always been ready to acclaim France as leader in the struggle for the future welfare of humanity. But we do not regard festivities like those of Kronstadt and Toulon as appropriate occasions for such greetings.

'On the contrary, these festivities represent a sad, though we hope temporary, condition—the desertion by France of her former great historic role. The country which once called upon the whole world to break the chains of despotism and offered its fraternal aid to any people fighting to be free, is now burning incense before the Russian Government, which systematically impedes the normal, organic growth of a people's life, and relentlessly and unscrupulously crushes every aspiration towards enlightenment, freedom, and independence. The Toulon demonstrations are one act of the drama of antagonism created between the two great nations of France and Germany by Napoleon III and Bismarck. That antagonism keeps all Europe under arms and makes Russian absolutism (that absolutism which has always been the support of arbitrary power and despotism against freedom, and of exploiters against the exploited) the arbiter of the political destinies of the world. These festivities evoke in us a feeling of pain for our own country and of regret at the blindness of so considerable a part of French society.

'We are convinced that the younger generation of France will not be carried away by national chauvinism, but that, ready to struggle for the better social conditions towards which humanity advances, it will know how to interpret the present events and what attitude to adopt towards them. We hope our ardent protest may find a sympathetic response in the hearts of the youth of France.

'Union of the Council of the Twenty-four Federated Societies of Moscow Students.'—L.T.

of those who took part in them, to say nothing
of the senselessness of the speeches that were delivered, most insane and cruel things were done
and no one paid any attention to them.

Thus some dozens of people were crushed to
death and no one found it necessary to refer to it.
A correspondent wrote that a Frenchman told
him at a ball that there was now hardly a woman
in Paris who would not betray her duty to satisfy
the desire of any of the Russian sailors. And all
this passed unnoticed as though it ought to be so.
There were even cases of unmistakable insanity.
One woman for instance put on a dress of the
colours of the French and Russian flags, and
having waited for the arrival of the sailors, cried:
'*Vive la Russie!*' and jumped from the bridge into
the river and was drowned.

In general the women played a conspicuous
part in all these celebrations and even directed
the men. Besides throwing flowers and various
ribbons and presenting gifts and addresses, French
women flung themselves on the Russian sailors
in the streets and kissed them; others for some
reason brought their children to them to be
kissed, and when the Russian sailors gratified
their wish, all those present were moved to
ecstasy and wept.

This strange excitement was so infectious that
as one of the correspondents relates, an apparently
quite healthy Russian sailor, after witnessing for
a fortnight all that was going on around him,
leapt from his ship into the sea in broad daylight
and swam about shouting: 'Vif lya Frantz!'
When he was pulled out and asked why he had

done it, he replied that he had taken a vow to swim round the ship in honour of France.

In this way the excitement grew and grew quite unchecked, like a rolling snowball, and at last not only those on the spot, and not only those who were predisposed and of weak nerves, but even strong and normal people succumbed to the general mood and reached an abnormal condition.

I remember that when carelessly reading one of the descriptions of the triumphal reception of the sailors, I suddenly became aware that a feeling of emotion was being communicated to me and that I was even on the verge of tears. And I had to make an effort to resist that feeling.

III

In the Kiev University Records a Professor of Psychiatry, Sikórsky by name, recently gave an account of a psychical epidemic of Malevanism—as he calls it—which he had investigated in certain villages of the Vasilkóvsky district of the province of Kiev. In Sikórsky's words, that epidemic consisted essentially in the fact that some people in those villages under the influence of a leader named Malevánov, imagining that the world would soon come to an end, altered their whole manner of life and began giving away their possessions, dressing themselves up, eating and drinking nice things, and ceased working. The Professor found the condition of these people abnormal. He says: 'Their extraordinary complacency often passed into exaltation—a joyful condition lacking external cause. They were sentimentally disposed, courteous to an extreme, very talkative, active in their movements, and apt to shed facile tears of joy that disappeared as easily as they came. They sold necessities to buy parasols, silk kerchiefs, and the like; and the kerchiefs served them only as toilet adornments. They ate many sweetmeats. Their state of mind was always joyous, and they led an idle life, visiting one another and walking about. When the evident foolishness of refusing to work was pointed out to them they always replied with the stereotyped phrase: "If I want to work I'll work: if I don't want to, why should I force myself?" '

The learned professor considers that the condition of these people constitutes a clear case of a psychopathic epidemic, and advises the government to take measures to prevent its spreading. He concludes his article with the words: 'Malevanism is the cry of an ailing population. It is its prayer for deliverance from intoxicants, and for an improvement in educational and sanitary conditions.'

But if Malevanism is the cry of an ailing population and a prayer for deliverance from intoxicants and harmful social conditions, what a much more terrible cry from an ailing population, and what an entreaty to be rescued from intoxicants and false social conditions, is this new malady that has broken out in Paris, and that with frightful rapidity has mastered the greater part of the urban population of France and almost the whole of the governmental and privileged classes of Russia!

And if it is admitted that the mental derangement of the Malevanists is dangerous, and that the government would do well to follow the professor's advice and arrange for the confinement of some of their leaders in lunatic asylums and monasteries and the banishment of others to remote regions; how much more dangerous should we consider this new epidemic which has appeared in Toulon and Paris and spread all over France and Russia, and how much more necessary must it be, if not for the government then for society, to take resolute measures to prevent the diffusion of such epidemics.

The resemblance between the one and the other epidemic is complete. There is the same extraordinary complacency passing into spontaneous and joyful exaltation, there is the same sentimentality, exaggerated courtesy and loquacity, the same frequent tears of emotion that come and go without reason, the same holiday mood, the same festivities, the same promenading and paying calls, the same dressing up in showy clothes, the same fancy for choice food, the same senseless speeches, the same idleness, the same singing and music, the same direction by the women, and the same clownish poses in *attitudes passionelles* which Sikórsky observed among the Malevanists, and which I understand as meaning those unnatural poses assumed during ceremonious meetings, receptions, and the delivery of speeches at banquets.

The resemblance is complete! The only difference—and it is a very important one for the society in which these things occur—is that in the one case the madness is confined to some dozens of poor peaceful villagers living on their own small means and therefore unable to do violence to their neighbours, and infecting others only by the personal and vocal transmission of their mood; while in the other case it is the madness of millions of people who control vast sums of money and have the means of doing violence to other people (rifles, bayonets, fortresses, ironclads, melinite and dynamite), having moreover at their disposal most powerful means of spreading their madness—postal services, telegraphy, enormous numbers of newspapers, and all sorts of publications which vie with one another in spreading the infection to all ends of the earth. And there is another difference: the first set of people, far from drinking to excess, make no use of intoxicating drinks, while the second set keep themselves in a constant state of semi-intoxication. And therefore, for the society in which such phenomena occur, the difference between the Kiev epidemic (during which, according to Sikórsky's information, no acts of violence or murders were committed) and the one that prevailed in Paris (where twenty women were crushed to death during one procession) is as great as that between a cinder that falls from the grate and lies smouldering on the floor which it will obviously not set alight, and a fire which has already reached the doors and walls of a house. The results of the Kiev epidemic, in the worst case, will be that the peasants of a millionth part of Russia will spend what they have earned by their toil and will not be able to pay the State taxes. But the consequences of the Toulon-Paris epidemic which has seized upon people who wield terrible power, enormous sums of money, weapons of violence, and means of spreading their madness, may and must be terrible.

IV

When a feeble and unarmed old idiot in cap and dressing-gown is mouthing nonsense one may listen to him with compassion without contradicting him, and even humouring him in jest; but when a whole crowd of sturdy madmen armed from head to foot with sharp daggers, swords, and loaded revolvers, have broken out of confinement and are excitedly brandishing their deadly weapons, one cannot humour them, or even feel at ease for an instant. And so it is with the excitement aroused by the French receptions in which French and Russian society is now involved, for those who have succumbed to this epidemic of insanity are in possession of terrible weapons of murder and destruction.

It is true that in all the speeches and toasts uttered during those festivities, and in all the articles about them, it was constantly proclaimed that the object of what was happening was to secure peace. Even the partisans of war spoke not of hatred for those who had seized the lost provinces, but of some sort of love which somehow hates.

The cunning of the mentally afflicted is however well known, and this constant repetition of

the sentence: 'We don't want war, we want
peace!' and the silence about what is in everyone's mind, is a most menacing symptom.

In his answering toast at the banquet in the
Elysée, the Russian ambassador said: 'Before proposing a toast to which not only all within these
walls will respond from the very depth of their
hearts, but to which all those far and near whose
hearts are beating at this moment in unison with
ours in all parts of great and beautiful France
as well as in all Russia, will respond with equal
ardour, allow me to convey to you the expression
of our profound gratitude for the words of greeting addressed by you to the Admiral authorized
by the Tsar to return the Kronstadt visit. The
lofty station you occupy has given emphasis
to your words concerning the true significance
of the splendid, *peaceful* triumph that is being
celebrated with such remarkable unity, loyalty,
and sincerity.'

The same quite irrelevant reference to peace
is found in the speech of the French President:

'The bonds of love which unite Russia and
France,' said he, 'strengthened two years ago by
the touching manifestations of which our fleet
was the object at Kronstadt, are becoming closer
every day, and the honest interchange of our
friendly sentiments must inspire all who have
at heart the blessing of *peace*, confidence and
security'—and so on.

In both speeches the blessings of peace and
peaceful celebrations are alluded to quite un-
expectedly and irrrelevantly.

It is the same with the telegrams exchanged

between the Russian Emperor and the French President. The Russian Emperor telegraphed:

'*Au moment où l'escadre russe quitte la France, il me tient à cœur de vous exprimer combien je suis touché et reconnaissant de l'accueil chaleureux et splendide que mes marins ont trouvé partout sur le sol français. Les témoignages de vive sympathie qui se sont manifestés encore une fois avec tant d'éloquence, joindront un nouveau lien à ceux qui unissent les deux pays et contribueront, je l'espère, à l'affermissement de la paix générale, objet de leurs efforts et de leurs vœux les plus constants.*'

The French President in his reply telegram said:

'*La dépêche dont je remercie votre majesté m'est parvenue au moment où je quittais Toulon pour rentrer à Paris. La belle escadre sur laquelle j'ai eu la vive satisfaction de saluer le pavillon russe dans les eaux françaises, l'accueil cordial et spontané que vos brave marins ont recontré partout en France affirment une fois de plus avec éclat les sympathies sincères qui unissent nos deux pays. Ils marquent en même temps une foi profonde dans l'influence bienfaisante que peuvent exercer ensemble deux grandes nations devouées à la cause de la paix.*'

Again in both telegrams without rhyme or reason there is a reference to peace which has nothing to do with the reception of the sailors.

There was not a speech or an article in which it was not said that the object of all these orgies was the peace of Europe. At the dinner given by the representatives of the Russian Press everyone spoke of peace. Zola, who recently wrote that war was necessary and indeed beneficial, and M. de Vogüé who has more than once expressed the same opinion in print, did not say a word about war but spoke only of peace. The sittings of the Chamber were opened with speeches about the late celebrations, and the speakers declared that these festivities were the declaration of peace to Europe.

It is just like a man coming into a peaceable company and at every opportunity eagerly assuring those present that he has no intention whatever of knocking anyone's teeth out, blacking their eyes, or breaking their arms, but only wants to pass the evening peaceably. 'Nobody doubts it,' one wishes to say: 'Even if you had such horrible intentions, at any rate don't dare to mention them.'

Many articles about the celebrations actually contained a plain and naïve expression of pleasure that during the festivities no one expressed what, *tacitu consensu*, it had been decided to conceal from everybody, and that only one incautious man (who was promptly removed by the police) shouted aloud what everyone was thinking: '*A bas l'Allemagne!*' In the same way children sometimes are so delighted at having concealed their mischief that their delight betrays them.

Why be so pleased that no one has said anything about war if we really are not thinking of it?

V

No one thinks of war, but milliards of money are spent on warlike preparations, and millions of men are under arms in Russia and in France. 'But this is all done to ensure peace. *Si vis*

*pacem, para bellum. L'empire c'est la paix, la républ-
ique c'est la paix.'*

But if so, why is it that among us in Russia the
military advantage of our alliance with France
in case of war with Germany is explained not
only in all the newspapers and periodicals published for people supposed to be educated, but
even in the *Rural News*, a paper published by the
Russian Government for the peasants? There
it is impressed on this unfortunate folk, deluded
by the government, that 'to be friendly with
France is also useful and advantageous for Russia
because if, contrary to expectations, the Powers
we have mentioned (Germany, Austria, and
Italy) decided to violate the peace with Russia,
then (though she might, by God's help, hold her
own unaided and deal successfully with the very
powerful alliance of her enemies) it would not be
an easy task, and even a successful struggle would
involve great sacrifices and losses'—and so on.
(*Rural News*, No. 43, 1893.)

And why is history taught in all French high
schools from a primer compiled by Monsieur
Lavisse (21st edition, 1899) in which there is the
following statement:

*Depuis que l'insurrection de la Commune a été
vaincue, la France n'a plus été troublée. Au lendemain
de la guerre, elle s'est remise au travail. Elle a payé
aux Allemands sans difficultés l'énorme contribution
de guerre de cinq milliards. Mais la France a perdu sa
renommée militaire pendant la guerre de 1870. Elle a
perdu une partie de son territoire. Plus de quinze cent
mille hommes qui habitaient nos départements du Haut-
Rhin, du Bas-Rhin et de la Moselle, et qui étaient de bons*

Français, ont été obligés de devenir Allemands. Ils ne sont pas résignés à leur sort. Ils détestent l'Allemagne; ils espèrent toujours redevenir Français. Mais l'Allemagne tient à sa conquête, et c'est un grand pays dont tous les habitants aiment sincèrement leur patrie et dont les soldats sont braves et disciplinés. Pour reprendre à l'Allemagne ce qu'elle nous a pris, il faut que nous soyons de bons citoyens et de bons soldats. C'est pour que vous deveniez de bons soldats que vos maîtres vous apprennent l'histoire de la France. L'histoire de la France montre que dans notre pays les fils ont toujours vengé les désastres de leurs pères. Les Français du temps du Charles VII ont vengé leurs pères vaincus à Crécy, à Poitiers, Azincourt. . . . C'est à vous—enfants élevés aujourd'hui dans nos écoles—qu'il appartient à venger vos pères, vaincus à Sedan et à Metz. C'est votre devoir, le grand devoir de votre vie. Vous devez y penser toujours. . . and so forth.

At the foot of the page there is a series of questions on the above: 'What did France lose as well as a part of her territory? How many Frenchmen were turned into Germans by the loss of that territory? Do those Frenchmen love Germany? What should we do in order some day to regain what Germany has taken from us? . . .'

There are also some *Réflexions sur le livre VII,* in which it is said that 'the children of France should remember our defeats in 1870' and that 'they should feel the burden of that recollection in their hearts', but that 'this recollection should not discourage them: it should, on the contrary, arouse their valour.'

So that if in official speeches peace is talked of with great insistence, the common people, the rising generation, and the Russian and French people in general, are quietly and constantly impressed with the necessity, righteousness, advantageousness, and even the heroism of war.

'We do not think of war. We are only concerned about peace.'

One would be inclined to ask: *Qui diable trompe-t-on ici?* if that question were worth asking, and if it were not all too evident who is the unfortunate victim who is being deceived.

That victim is always and ever the deceived, foolish, working folk—those who with blistered hands have built all those ships, fortresses, arsenals, barracks, cannon, harbours, steamers, and moles, and all these palaces, halls, platforms, and triumphal arches; who have set up and printed all these newspapers and pamphlets, and have procured and brought all these pheasants and ortolans, oysters, and wines that are consumed by the men who are fed, brought up, and kept by them, and who are deceiving them and preparing the most fearful calamities for them. It is always the same kindly, foolish folk, who stand open-mouthed like children, showing their healthy white teeth, naïvely delighted by dressed-up admirals and presidents with flags waving above them, and by fireworks and bands of music; and for whom, before they have time to look round, there will be neither admirals nor presidents nor flags nor bands, but only a desolate battlefield, cold, hunger, and anguish—before them murderous enemies and behind them relentless officers preventing their escape—blood, wounds, suffering, putrefying corpses, and a senseless unnecessary death.

And men like these who are now feasting at the celebrations in Toulon and Paris will sit in a dark cloth tent after a good dinner, with unfinished glasses of good wine before them and with cigars between their teeth, and will indicate, with pins stuck into a map, the spots where such-and-such a quantity of cannon-fodder (made up of these same simple people) must be expended in order to capture such-and-such a position or to obtain this or that ribbon or Order.

VI

'But there is nothing of the kind, there are no warlike intentions,' we are told. 'It is only a case of two nations feeling mutual sympathy and expressing that feeling to one another. What is there wrong in the representatives of a friendly nation being received with special celebrations and honour by the representatives of another nation? What is there bad in that—even if one admits that the alliance may have significance as a defence against a dangerous neighbour who threatens the peace of Europe?'

It is bad because it is a most obvious and shameless falsehood, lacking any justification. This sudden exceptional love of Russians for French and French for Russians is false. Our implied dislike and distrust of the Germans is also false. And it is still more false to say that the aim of all these unseemly and senseless orgies is to preserve the peace of Europe.

We all know that we have not previously experienced and do not now experience any special love for the French; just as we have not previously experienced and do not now experience any special enmity for the Germans.

We are told that Germany has designs against Russia, that the Triple Alliance threatens our own peace and the peace of Europe, and that our alliance with France equalizes the forces and is therefore a guarantee of peace.

This assertion is so obviously silly that one is ashamed to refute it seriously. For such an alliance to ensure peace all the forces would have to be mathematically equal. If the preponderance is now on the side of the Franco-Russian alliance the danger is still there. It is even greater, for if there was a danger that Wilhelm at the head of a European alliance would disturb the peace, there would be a much greater danger that France—who cannot reconcile herself to the loss of her provinces—would do so. Why, the Triple Alliance called itself the peace-league, though to us it seemed a league of war. And in just the same way the Franco-Russian Alliance cannot appear other than it really is—a league of war.

How then, if peace depends on the balance of power, can one define the units between which an equilibrium must be established? The English are now saying that the alliance of Russia and France threatens them, and that they must form a new alliance. Into how many alliances must Europe be divided to establish an equilibrium? Why, if that is how things are, then the strongest man in any society of people is a danger, and the others should form alliances to counterbalance him.

People ask: 'What is there bad in France and Russia expressing their mutual sympathy in order to ensure peace?'

It is bad because it is a lie, and a lie can never be uttered without doing harm.

The devil is a murderer and the father of lies. Lies always lead to murder, and especially in such a case as this.

Before the Turkish war,[1] just as is the case now, a sudden love was supposed to have sprung up between us Russians and certain Slavonic brethren of ours to whom no one had paid any attention for some hundreds of years; whereas the Germans, French, and English had always been, and still are, incomparably nearer and more akin to us then any of those Montenegrins, Serbians, or Bulgarians. Then, too, similar enthusiasms, receptions, and celebrations were started, fanned by the Aksákovs and Katkóvs who are now mentioned in Paris as models of patriotism. Then, as now, they only spoke of the mutual love that had suddenly sprung up between the Russians and the Slavs. At first, just as now in Paris so then in Moscow, they ate, drank, said silly things to one another and were touched by their exalted feelings, spoke of union and peace, and kept silent about the chief matter —the designs against Turkey. The newspapers worked up the excitement and gradually the government began to take part in the game. Serbia revolted. There were diplomatic notes and semi-official articles. The newspapers lied more and more, invented, and grew heated. And

[1] The Russo-Turkish war of 1877-8.—A.M.

in the end Alexander III, who did not really want war, was unable to avoid consenting to it, and that occurred which we already know: the destruction of hundreds of thousands of innocent people, and the brutalizing and stupefying of millions. And what has been done in Toulon and Paris and is still being done in the newspapers, is obviously leading the same way, or to still worse calamities. Various Generals and Ministers will drink to France, to Russia, to different regiments, armies, and fleets, in just the same way to the strains of *God Save the Tsar* and *la Marseillaise*. The papers will print their lies, the idle crowd of rich people who do not know what to do with their time and their energy will babble patriotic speeches and stir up enmity towards Germany. And however peacefully inclined Alexander III may be, events will so shape themselves that he will be unable to refuse his assent to a war which will be demanded by everyone around him, by all the newspapers, and (or so it always seems in such cases) by the public opinion of the whole nation. And before we have time to look round the usual ominous and senseless proclamation will appear in the columns of the press:

'We, by the grace of God autocratic Emperor of all the Russias, King of Poland, Grand Duke of Finland, &c., &c., announce to all our faithful subjects that for the good of our beloved people entrusted to us by God we have deemed it our duty before God to send them to the slaughter. May God be with them.'—and so on.

The bells will peal and long-haired men will

dress themselves in gold-embroidered sacks and begin to pray on behalf of murder. The familiar, age-old, horrible business will recommence. The editors of newspapers will set to work to arouse hatred and murder under the guise of patriotism and will be delighted to double their sales. Manufacturers, merchants, and contractors for army-stores, will hurry about joyfully in expectation of doubled profits. Officials of all sorts will busy themselves in the hope of being able to steal more than usual. Army commanders will bustle here and there, drawing double pay and rations and hoping to receive various trinkets, ribbons, crosses, stripes, and stars, for murdering people. Idle ladies and gentlemen will fuss about, entering their names in advance for the Red Cross and getting ready to bandage those whom their husbands and brothers are setting out to kill— imagining that they will be doing a most Christian work thereby.

And hundreds of thousands of simple kindly folk, torn from peaceful toil and from their wives, mothers, and children, and with murderous weapons in their hands, will trudge wherever they may be driven, stifling the despair in their souls by songs, debauchery, and vodka. They will march, freeze, suffer from hunger, and fall ill. Some will die of disease, and some will at last come to the place where men will kill them by the thousand. And they too, without themselves knowing why, will murder thousands of others whom they had never before seen, and who had neither done nor could do them any wrong.

And when there are so many sick, wounded, and killed that there are not hands enough to pick them up, and when the air is so infected by that rotting cannon-fodder that it becomes unpleasant even to the commanders, then they will stop for a while, the wounded will somehow be picked up, the sick brought in and dumped in heaps where chance may decide, and the dead dug into the ground and sprinkled over with lime. And then once more the whole crowd of deluded men will be led on and on, till those who started the mischief are weary of it, or until those who thought it necessary have got what they wanted.

And so once again men will have been made savage, ferocious, and brutal; and love will wane in the world, and the Christianizing of mankind which had begun will be retarded again for scores or hundreds of years. And once again those for whom it is profitable will declare with assurance that since there was a war, that proves war to be necessary, and they will again begin to prepare future generations for it, perverting them from childhood upwards.

VII

Hence, when such patriotic demonstrations as the Toulon festivities take place, people's wills are bound in advance, though apparently only for the distant future, and they are pledged to the accustomed iniquities that are always the result of patriotism. And everyone who realizes the significance of those festivities cannot but protest against their tacit implication. Thus when those gentlemen, the journalists, assert that every Russian sympathizes with what took place at Kronstadt and Toulon and Paris and that this alliance for life and death is confirmed by the will of the whole people, and when the Russian Minister of Education assures the French ministers that all under his command (the children, scholars, and writers of Russia) share his feelings, and when the commander of the Russian squadron assures the French that all Russia will be grateful for the reception given them, and when the chief priests answer for their flocks with assurances that the prayers of the French for the welfare of the Imperial family are joyfully echoed in the hearts of the Tsar-loving Russian people, and when the Russian ambassador in Paris, who is regarded as the representative of the Russian people, declares, after a dish of *ortolans à la soubise et logopèdes glacées* and with a glass of Grand Moët champagne in his hand, that all Russian hearts beat in unison with his own, which is brimming over with sudden and exceptional love for *la belle France*—then we who are free from that insanity consider it our sacred duty, not only for ourselves but also for tens of millions of Russians, to protest most emphatically against such a statement, and to affirm that our hearts do not beat in unison with those of these gentlemen—the journalists, ministers of education, commanders of squadrons, chief priests, and ambassadors—but on the contrary are filled with indignation and disgust at the pernicious falsehood and wrong which they, consciously or unconsciously, are spreading around by their words and deeds. Let them drink Moët as much as they please, let them write articles and make speeches, but let them do so for themselves alone. We who regard ourselves as Christians cannot allow ourselves to be bound by what these gentlemen are saying and writing.

We cannot allow it because we know what lies hidden under all these drunken ecstasies, speeches, and embraces, which do not look like a confirmation of peace as they assure us, but rather like the orgies and drunkenness criminals indulge in when preparing to co-operate in crime.

VIII

About four years ago the first swallow of the Toulon spring—a French agitator[1] well known as an advocate of war with Germany—came to Russia to pave the way for a Franco-Russian alliance and visited us in the country. He arrived while we were mowing the hay. On returning to the house for lunch we made our visitor's acquaintance, and he immediately told us how he had fought in the war of 1870, had been taken prisoner and had escaped, and how he had sworn a patriotic oath—of which he was evidently proud—not to cease agitating for war with Germany till the integrity and honour of France was restored.

Our circle did not share his conviction that an alliance of Russia with France was necessary for the recovery of France's former frontiers and

[1] Paul Déroulède (1846–1914). Author of *Chants du Soldat.* —A.M.

the restoration of her power and glory and to safeguard ourselves from Germany's evil designs. To his plea that France could not rest satisfied until she recovered her lost provinces, we replied that neither could Prussia rest satisfied until she had avenged herself for Jena, and that if a French *revanche* should now succeed, the Germans would have to re-avenge it and so on without end.

To his plea that the French were in duty bound to rescue their brothers who had been torn from them, we replied that the position of the working-class inhabitants of Alsace-Lorraine under German rule was, for the most part, hardly worse in any respect than it had been under French rule, and that because it would be pleasanter for some Alsatian to be reckoned as French rather than German, and because he, our visitor, wished to vindicate the glory of French arms, it was not worth while to incur the terrible miseries war occasions, and not right even to sacrifice a single human life.

When he said that it was all very well for us to talk like that, since we had not endured what France had, but that we should speak differently if the Baltic Provinces or Poland had been taken from us, we replied that even from a political point of view the loss of Poland or the Baltic Provinces could not be considered a calamity, but might rather be regarded as a benefit, since it would spare us the military force and the political expenditure they require; while from a Christian point of view we could in no case assent to war, since war demands the murder of men, and

Christianity not only forbids all murder, but requires the doing of good to all men, accounting them all as brothers without distinction of nationality. A Christian Government when engaging in war should, we said, to be consistent, not only remove the crosses from the churches, convert the church buildings to other purposes, give the clergy other duties, and above all suppress the Gospel—it should also renounce all the precepts of morality that result from the Christian doctrines. *C'est à prendre ou à laisser*, we told him. Until Christianity is abolished people can only be drawn into war by cunning and deception, as is done now.

But we see this cunning and deception and therefore cannot yield to it.

And since we had no band, no champagne, nor anything to befog our senses, our visitor merely shrugged his shoulders and with characteristic French politeness said that he was very grateful for the hospitable reception he had met with in our house, but much regretted that his views had not met with a similar welcome.

IX

After this conversation we went with our guest to the hay-field, and there, hoping to find more sympathy for his ideas among the people, he asked me to translate to my fellow-worker, Prokófy, an old, sickly, ruptured peasant, but still a persistent worker, his plan of action against the Germans, which was to squeeze them between the Russians and the French from both sides. The Frenchman explained this graphically to

Prokófy by pressing each side of the man's sweat-soaked hempen shirt with his white fingers, and I remember Prokófy's good-natured surprise and derision when I explained to him the meaning of words and gesture. He evidently took the proposal about squeezing the Germans from both sides as a jest—unable to believe that a grown-up educated man could calmly and soberly speak of war as being desirable.

'Why, if we squeeze them from both sides,' said Prokófy, replying by a jest to what he took to be a jest, 'there would be nowhere for them to move. We must let them out somewhere.'

I translated that reply to my visitor.

'*Dites-lui que nous aimons les Russes,*' said hé.

These words evidently surprised Prokófy even more than the proposal to squeeze the Germans, and aroused a certain feeling of suspicion.

'Who does he belong to?' asked Prokófy, distrustfully indicating my visitor with his head.

I said that he was a wealthy Frenchman.

'And what business has he come about?' asked Prokófy.

When I explained that he had come in the hope of getting the Russians to form an alliance with France in case of war with Germany, Prokófy evidently retained his suspicions, and turning to the peasant women who were sitting among the hay-cocks, involuntarily expressed his feeling by shouting to them in a stern voice to go and rake up the loose hay.

'Hey, you crows, you're all asleep! Get to work! Here's a time to deal with the Germans! The hay's not in yet and it looks as if we may

have to begin reaping[1] the corn on Wednesday,'
said he. And then, as if afraid of having offended
the foreign visitor, he added, with a good-natured
smile that showed the stumps of his worn teeth:
'You'd better come and work with us and bring
the Germans along too, and when we've done
work we'll have some merry-making together.
The Germans are men too, like ourselves.'

And having said this, Prokófy drew his sinewy
arm from between the prongs of the pitchfork
on which he was leaning, threw the fork on his
shoulder and went over to the women. '*Oh, le
brave homme!*' exclaimed the polite Frenchman,
laughing, and so ended for the present his diplomatic mission to the Russian people.

The sight of those two men, so different from
one another—the well-fed elegant Frenchman,
in a top-hat and the long overcoat that was then
very fashionable, radiant with freshness and self-
confidence, with his white hands, unused to
work, energetically showing how the Germans
must be squeezed; and the shaggy figure of
Prokófy, shrivelled up by constant labour, always
tired but always at work despite his enormous
rupture, with fingers swollen by toil, with wisps
of hay in his hair, with slack home-made breeches
and down-trodden bark shoes, striding along
with an enormous fork of hay on his shoulder,
with that step, not lazy but economical in movement, with which a working man always moves
—the strong contrast presented by those two men
made much clear to me then, and now, after
the Toulon-Paris festivities, vividly recurs. One

[1] Or 'go squeezing'.—A.M.

of them personified all those who, fed by the people's toil, afterwards use those same people for cannon-fodder; while the other personified that very cannon-fodder which feeds and protects the others who afterwards so dispose of it.

X

'But two provinces have been taken from France, children torn from a beloved mother. And Russia cannot permit Germany to dictate to her and deprive her of her historic mission in the East, nor risk the chance of being deprived, like the French, of her territory—the Baltic provinces, Poland, and the Caucasus.'

'And Germany cannot tolerate the possibility of losing the advantages she has gained at such cost! And England will not yield her naval supremacy to anyone!'

When such words are uttered it is usually taken for granted that the French, the Russians, the Germans, and the English, ought to be ready to sacrifice everything to regain their lost provinces, to maintain their influence in the East, to preserve their unity and power, or their supremacy on the sea, and so on.

It is taken for granted that the feeling of patriotism is, in the first place, a feeling innate in every man; and secondly that it is such a lofty moral feeling that it should be infused into those in whom it is absent. But neither the one assumption nor the other is correct. I have lived half a century among the Russian people, and during all that time I have never seen or heard a manifestation or expression of patriotism among the great mass of real Russian peasants, with the exception of patriotic formulas learnt in military service or repeated from books by the more superficial and degraded of the people. I have never heard expressions of patriotic feeling expressed by our people. On the contrary, I have constantly heard, from the most serious and respected of the country folk, expressions of complete indifference to, and even contempt for, any kind of patriotic manifestation. I have observed the same thing among the working people of other countries, and educated Frenchmen, Germans, and Englishmen, have repeatedly told me the same thing.

The working people are too much taken up with the task of earning a living for themselves and their families to be able to interest themselves in the political questions that figure as the chief motives of patriotism. The question of Russia's influence in the East, the unification of Germany, the return of France's lost provinces, of the cession of this or that part of one State to another, and so on, does not interest them—not only because they hardly ever know the conditions under which these questions arise, but because the interests of their life are quite apart from national and political interests.

To a man of the people it is always a matter of complete indifference where a frontier is drawn, to whom Constantinople may belong, whether Saxony or Brunswick shall, or shall not, be a member of the German Union, whether Australia or Matabeleland shall belong to England— or even to what government he has to pay his taxes and into which army he must send his sons. The important thing for him is to know how much tax he will have to pay, whether the army service will be a long one, whether he will have to pay for the land over many years, and whether he will get much for his work—all questions quite apart from national and political interests. That is why—despite the intensive efforts made by governments to instil a patriotism into people that is not innate in them, and to suppress the ideas of socialism that are developing among them—socialism is penetrating more and more into the masses of the people, while patriotism, with which they are so carefully inoculated by the government, not only fails to spread, but is disappearing more and more and is only maintained among the upper classes to whom it is profitable.

If it does happen that patriotism takes possession of the crowd, as has now occurred in Paris, it only happens when the masses are subjected to intensive hypnotism by the governments and ruling classes, and such patriotism is only maintained among the people as long as that hypnotic influence is maintained.

So for instance in Russia, where patriotism, in the form of love and devotion to the Faith, the Tsar, and the Fatherland, is grafted onto the Russian people with extraordinary intensity by every instrument in the hands of the government: the Church, the schools, the Press, and all kinds of ceremonies—the Russian working class, the hundred-million Russian people, despite the undeserved reputation bestowed on them as being particularly devoted to their Faith, Tsar, and

R

Fatherland, are in fact the freest of all people from the deception of patriotism and from devotion to Faith, Tsar, and Fatherland. For the most part the Russian peasant knows nothing about the Faith—that Orthodox State faith to which he is supposed to be devoted—and as soon as he recognizes it he rejects it and becomes a rationalist, that is, he adopts a belief which can be neither attacked nor defended. And towards his Tsar (in spite of incessant, intensive attempts to instil a feeling of devotion) his attitude is the same as to all authorities employing violence, that is one if not of condemnation then of complete indifference. While as to his Fatherland (unless one understands it to mean his own village or his own district) he is either completely ignorant of it or, if he knows it, he makes no distinction between it and other countries. Russians now settle quite indifferently in Russia or outside it, in Turkey or in China, just as they formerly emigrated to Austria or to Turkey.

XI

My old friend D—[1] who lived alone in the country during the winter while his wife was in Paris, where he visited her occasionally, often conversed with his steward—an illiterate but wise and venerable peasant—who came in the long autumn evenings to bring his report. Among other things, my friend used to tell him of the advantages of the French system of government as compared with our own. This was on the eve

---

[1] This no doubt was D. A. Dyákov, from whom the character of Dmítri in *Boyhood* and *Youth* was drawn.—A.M.

of the last Polish insurrection (of 1863-4) and the interference of the French Government with our affairs. At that time the patriotic Russian Press was burning with indignation at this interference, and so stirred up the ruling classes that our political relations became very much strained and there was talk of a war with France.

My friend having read the papers, told his steward of the relations between Russia and France, and influenced by the tone of the Press and being an old military man, said that if there were a war he would re-enter the army and go to fight the French. At that time patriotic Russians considered a *revanche* on the French for Sevastopol necessary.

'Why should we fight?' asked the steward.

'Well, how can we allow France to dictate to us?'

'But you yourself say that they are better governed than we are,' said the steward quite seriously. 'Then why not let them arrange things for us too?'

And my friend told me he was so taken aback by this comment that he did not know what to reply, and only laughed as one does on awakening from a deceptive dream.

Such opinions may be heard from every sober Russian working man who is not under the hypnotic influence of the government.

People speak of the love of the Russian peasantry for their Faith, their Tsar, and their Fatherland, and yet there is not a single Russian peasant community which would hesitate for a moment if they had to choose which of two places to settle

in: one in Russia under their 'Little Father the
Tsar' (as he is termed in books), with their holy
Orthodox Faith, in their adored Fatherland, but
with less and poorer land; and one anywhere outside Russia, in Prussia, China, Turkey, or Austria,
without their Father, the white Tsar, and without the Orthodox Church, but with more and
better land. They would all choose the latter!
This we have often seen before and still see to-day.

For every Russian peasant the question under
what government he will live (since he knows
that whichever it is he will be plundered just the
same) has infinitely less importance than—I
won't even say whether the water is good, but
whether the clay is soft and cabbage grows well.

It might be supposed that this indifference
arises from the fact that any government under
which they might come would be better than the
Russian, since there is none worse in Europe.
But that is not so, for as far as I know, the same
attitude prevails among English, Dutch, and
German peasants who emigrate to America, and
among others who come to Russia.

The shifting of the European population from
one rule to another, from Turkish to Austrian
or from French to German, makes so little difference to working-class conditions that it cannot
in any case arouse discontent among the workers
unless they are subjected to suggestion from
governments and the ruling classes.

XII

In proof of the existence of patriotism, people
usually point to manifestations of it on various

ceremonial occasions: in Russia during the coronation,[1] and after the attempt on the Tsar's life on October 17th;[2] in France when war was declared on Prussia; in Germany when victory was celebrated; or during these Franco-Russian festivities.

But one has to know how these manifestations are prepared. In Russia, for instance, during every journey made by the Tsar, men from the peasant communities and the factories are prepared to meet and welcome him.

The enthusiasm of the crowd is for the most part artificially prepared by those to whom it is necessary, and the degree of enthusiasm displayed merely indicates the degree of art of the organizers of that enthusiasm. That art is an old one and its specialists have consequently reached great virtuosity in preparing these ecstasies.

When Alexander II was still heir to the throne and in command of the Preobrazhénsk Regiment, as the heir-apparent usually was, he once drove after dinner to the regiment, which was then in camp. As soon as his carriage was seen, the soldiers, it is recorded, ran out to meet him just as they were in their shirt-sleeves, and greeted their august commander with such enthusiasm that they all raced after the carriage and many of them crossed themselves as they looked up at the Tsetsarévich. All who saw this reception were touched by the naïve devotion and love of the Russian soldiers for the Tsar and his heir, and

---

[1] Of Alexander III in 1883, two years after his accession.—A.M.

[2] A terrorist attempt to blow up the train in which Alexander III was travelling was made at Bórki, near Khárkov, in 1888. One of his children was injured.—A.M.

by the unaffected and evidently spontaneous religious enthusiasm their faces and gestures expressed, and especially by the way they crossed themselves. Yet it was all artificial and had been prepared in the following way.

After parade the day before, the Tsetsarévich mentioned to the commander of the Brigade that he would drive over next day.

'When may we expect your Imperial Highness?'

'Probably in the evening. But please let there be no preparations.'

As soon as the Tsetsarévich had gone, the commander called the company commanders together and gave instructions that the soldiers were all to be in clean shirts the next day and that as soon as the Tsetsarévich's carriage (for which signalmen were to be on the look-out) was seen, they were all to run out to meet it just as they were, with cries of 'Hurrah!' and were to run after the carriage, each tenth man in the company crossing himself as he ran. The sergeant-majors paraded the companies, and counting each man stopped at the tenth: 'One, two, three, four . . .eight, nine, ten. Sidorénko, you'll cross yourself! One, two, three, four . . .Ivánov, cross yourself!' It was all done to order, and the impression of enthusiasm produced on the Tsetsarévich and on all who were present, even on the soldiers and officers and the brigade-commander who had arranged it all, was complete. And it is done in just the same way, though less crudely, wherever there are patriotic manifestations. The Franco-Russian celebrations which appeared to us as spontaneous expressions of popular feeling did not occur of themselves, but were on the contrary very skilfully and pretty obviously prepared and evoked by the French government.

'As soon as the arrival of the Russian sailors became known'— [I am again citing the *Rural News*, a government organ which collects its information from all the other papers] 'committees were immediately formed to organize celebrations not only in all large and small towns on the rather lengthy route from Toulon to Paris, but even in many towns and villages quite a distance away from it. Subscription lists were opened everywhere towards the expenses of these festivities. Many towns sent deputations to our ambassador in Paris with requests that the Russian sailors should visit them if only for a day, or even for an hour. The municipal councils of all the towns where it was arranged for our sailors to stay, assigned enormous sums, more than a hundred thousand rubles, for the organization of various fêtes and festivities, and announced their readiness to spend still larger sums if only the receptions and festivities might be as splendid as possible.

'In Paris itself, besides the sums allotted by the municipality for this purpose, a large amount was collected by a private committee for the arrangement of festivities, and the French Government allotted more than a hundred thousand rubles to Ministers and other officials as entertainment expenses for the reception of the Russian visitors. In many towns where our sailors did not show themselves at all, it was nevertheless

decided to arrange all sorts of festivities on
October 1st in honour of Russia. Many towns
and provinces decided to send special deputations to Toulon or Paris to greet the Russian
visitors and take them presents as souvenirs of
France, or to send them addresses and telegrams
of welcome. It was decided that the 1st of
October should be regarded everywhere as a
national holiday and that the pupils of all educational establishments should be given a holiday
on that day, and those in Paris two days. It was
decided to remit all fines incurred by officials of
the lower ranks, that they might remember the
1st of October with gratitude as a day of rejoicing
for France.

'To make it easier for the public to visit Toulon
and take part in the welcome to the Russian
squadron, the railways reduced their fares by
half and special trains were provided.'

And then when a whole series of simultaneous
measures (such as a government can always take
thanks to the power in its hands) has been taken
everywhere, and a certain portion of the people,
chiefly the scum of the town rabble, has been
brought to an abnormally excited condition,
people say: 'Look! This is a spontaneous expression of the will of the whole nation.'

Such manifestations as those that have lately
taken place in Toulon and Paris, which take
place in Germany at receptions of the Emperor
or of Bismarck, at the manœuvres in Lorraine,
and that are constantly repeated in Russia on
every ceremonial occasion, only prove that the
means existing for exciting the crowd are so

powerful that the government and the ruling classes which control them can always evoke at will whatever manifestation they please. On the other hand nothing so clearly proves the absence of patriotism in the people as these intense efforts now employed by the governments and the ruling classes to arouse it artificially, and the smallness of the results obtained despite all these efforts.

If patriotic feelings were really so innate in the people, they would be left to appear freely of themselves and would not have to be worked up continually by artificial means as well as on special occasions.

Let them cease if but for a while to force the whole Russian people to swear allegiance to each Tsar on his coronation, as is now done, let them cease solemnly pronouncing the customary prayers for the Tsar at every Church service, let them cease making holidays of his birthday and name-day—with the ringing of bells, illuminations, and the prohibition of work; let them cease displaying his portrait everywhere, give up printing his name and the names of his family, and even the pronouns relating to them, in enormous letters in prayer-books, calendars, and school books; let them cease glorifying him in special books and gazettes devoted entirely to that purpose, and let them cease prosecuting and imprisoning men for the slightest disrespectful word about the Tsar; let them cease doing these things if but for a while, and we should see in how far it is natural for the people—the real working people like Prokófy and the village elder Iván, and all the Russian peasants—to feel (as people assure us and as foreigners believe) adoration for the Tsar, who in one way or other delivers them over into the hands of the landowners and the rich people generally.

So with Russia. And in the same way let them in Germany, France, Italy, England and America, cease doing all that is being strenuously done there too in the same way by the ruling classes to arouse patriotism and devotion and submission to the existing government, and then we should see in how far this supposed patriotism is characteristic of the peoples of our time.

As it is, people are constantly hypnotized from childhood in one and the same direction by all possible means: school books, Church services, sermons, speeches, books, newspapers, poems, and monuments. Some thousands of people are brought together, forcibly or by bribery, and when they have been joined by the loafers who are always glad to see any spectacle, they begin to shout what is shouted before them to the accompaniment of cannon and bands and glitter and brilliance of all kinds, and we are told that this is the expression of the feelings of the whole nation. But in the first place these thousands, or at most tens of thousands, who shout at such celebrations, form but a tiny ten-thousandth part of the whole population. And in the second place, of these tens of thousands of shouting and hat-waving people, the greater part, if not assembled by force as is done among us in Russia, have been artfully lured there by some bait or other. Thirdly, among all those thousands there are scarcely a few dozen who know what it is all about: they would shout and wave their hats in just the same way if the very opposite of what is happening were taking place. And fourthly, the police are present who promptly silence and remove all who shout anything the government does not wish and demand—as was strenuously done during the Franco-Russian celebrations.

In France they acclaimed with similar enthusiasm Napoleon the First's war with Russia, Alexander I, against whom that war was fought, then Napoleon again, then again the Allies, the Bourbons, the Orleans,[1] the Republic, Napoleon III, and Boulanger; while in Russia they acclaim with equal enthusiasm to-day Peter,[2] to-morrow Catherine, afterwards Paul, Alexander, Constantine,[3] Nicholas, The Duke of Leuchtenberg,[4] our brother-Slavs, the King of Prussia, the French sailors, and anyone whom the authorities wish welcomed. And the same thing takes place in England, America, Germany and Italy.

What is called patriotism is merely, in our day, on the one side a certain frame of mind constantly produced and supported among the people by the schools, the Church, and a venal press, for purposes required by the government; and on the other side a temporary excitement aroused in the classes of the lowest mental and moral level by

[1] King Louis-Philippe.—A.M.
[2] Peter III who was assassinated.—A.M.
[3] A brother of Alexander and of Nicholas II. He was proclaimed Emperor by the Decembrist conspirators in 1825.—A.M.
[4] Maximilian Eugène Joseph Napoleon, Duke of Leuchtenberg (son of Eugène de Beauharnais who bought the dukedom of Leuchtenberg). He married Márya Nikoláevna, a sister of Alexander II.—A.M.

special means adopted by the ruling classes and afterwards given out as an expression of the permanent will of the whole nation. The patriotism of oppressed nationalities is no exception to this. That too is unnatural in the labouring masses, and is artificially fostered in them by the upper classes.

XIII

'But if the working people do not experience patriotic emotions, that is because they have not yet reached the level of that lofty emotion natural to every educated man. If they have not yet reached it, it should be developed in them, and that is just what the government is doing.'

People of the ruling classes say that with such complete conviction that patriotism is a lofty sentiment, that common folk who have not experienced it acknowledge themselves to blame for not feeling it, and try to persuade themselves that they do feel it, or at least pretend to do so.

But what is this lofty feeling the ruling classes think should be developed in the people?

That sentiment, in its most precise definition, is nothing but putting one's own kingdom or people before every other kingdom or people—a feeling fully expressed by the patriotic German song: *Deutschland, Deutschland über alles*, in which it is only necessary to substitute *Russland, Frankreich, Italien*, or any other kingdom, in place of *Deutschland*, to obtain the clearest formula for the lofty feeling of patriotism. No doubt that feeling is very useful and desirable for governments and for the unity of a State, but one cannot help seeing that it is not at all a lofty sentiment, but on the contrary a very stupid and immoral one: stupid because if each kingdom is to consider itself better than any other, it is evident that they will all be wrong; and immoral because it inevitably impels every man who feels it to seek advantages for his own State and people to the detriment of other States and peoples—an impulse directly contrary to the fundamental moral law recognized by all, not to do to others what we do not wish done to us.

Patriotism may have been a virtue in the ancient world when it demanded of a man devotion to the highest ideal then attainable—that of his fatherland. But how can it be a virtue in our time, when it demands what is contrary to the ideal of both our religion and morality, and is a recognition not of the equality and brotherhood of men but of the predominance of one State and one people over all others? But more than that, this sentiment is no longer a virtue in our time but is certainly a vice. Patriotism in its true meaning cannot exist in our time, for there are no material or moral grounds for it.

Patriotism had a meaning in the ancient world when each nation was more or less homogeneous professing one national religion and subject to the absolute power of its divinely appointed ruler, and appeared to itself to be as it were an island in the midst of an ocean of barbarians constantly striving to submerge it.

It is understandable that in such a case patriotism—that is the desire to withstand the attacks of the barbarians, who were not only ready to destroy the social order of the nation but threatened it with plunder, wholesale murder, captivity, enslavement, and the violation of its women—was a natural feeling. It is understandable that to preserve himself and his fellow-countrymen from such disaster a man might put his own people before all others, entertain a hostile feeling for the surrounding barbarians, and kill them to defend his own people.

But what meaning can such a feeling have in our Christian times? On what grounds and for what object can a Russian of our time go and kill Frenchmen and Germans, or how can a Frenchman kill Germans, when—however ill-educated he may be—he knows very well that the men of other kingdoms and peoples against whom his patriotic enmity is aroused are not barbarians but Christians, just such people as he is, often of the same creed and profession as he, desiring peace and a peaceful exchange of labour, and who are for the most part united with him either by the common interests of work, that is by trade, by spiritual interests, or by both of these? So that very often men of one kingdom are nearer and more necessary to men of another kingdom than to their own countrymen, as is the case with commercial folk, with workmen connected with employers of other nationalities, and especially with learned men and artists.

Besides, the very conditions of life have so changed now that what we call our country—which we are supposed to distinguish in some way from all the rest—has ceased to be as clearly defined as it was in ancient times when the people forming one nation belonged to one race, one State, and one religion: the patriotism of the Egyptians, Jews, or Greeks, for instance, who when defending their fatherland were also defending their religion, their nationality, their native land and their State.

But how can an Irishman in the United States express his patriotism to-day, when by his religion he belongs to Rome, by his birth to Ireland, and as a citizen to the United States? And the Czech in Austria, the Pole in Russia, Prussia, and Austria, the Hindu in the British Empire, and the Tartar and the Armenian in Russia and Turkey, are in a similar position. But leaving aside these several subject nationalities, even men of the most homogeneous States, such as Russia, France, and Prussia, can no longer feel the sentiment of patriotism which was natural to the ancients, for very often the chief interests of their lives (sometimes domestic, when their wives are of another nation, sometimes economic, when their capital is invested abroad, sometimes spiritual, scientific, or artistic) are not in their own country but outside it, in that State against which their patriotic enmity is being aroused.

And above all, patriotism is impossible in our time because however we have tried during nineteen hundred years to conceal the meaning of Christianity, it has nevertheless permeated our life, and controls it to such a degree that even the coarsest and most stupid people cannot now fail to see the complete incompatibility of patriotism with the moral principle by which they live.

XIV

Patriotism was a necessity in the formation and consolidation of strong States composed of heterogeneous populations and needing defence against barbarians. But when Christian enlightenment had transformed those States from within, giving to them all the same basic principles, patriotism became the sole obstacle to that union among nations for which Christian consciousness had prepared them.

Patriotism in our day is a cruel tradition surviving from an outlived past. It is maintained only by inertia and because governments and the ruling classes, feeling that their power and even their existence is bound up with it, persistently excite and maintain it among the people by cunning and by violence. Patriotism in our time resembles scaffolding which was needed for the erection of the walls of a building, and which though it now obstructs the use of the building is still not removed because its existence is profitable to certain people.

For a long time past Christian nations have not had, nor could have had, reasons for quarrelling. One cannot even imagine how or why Russian and German workmen, working peacefully together on their frontiers and in their cities, should begin to quarrel with one another. Still less can one imagine enmity between a Kazán peasant supplying grain to a German, and the German who supplies him with scythes and machines. It is the same with French, German, and Italian workmen. And it is absurd even to speak of a quarrel between learned men, artists, and writers of different nationalities, absorbed in the same general interests independently of nationality and politics.

But the governments cannot let the people be quiet—that is, in peaceful relations with one another—for the chief, if not the sole, justification for the existence of governments lies in pacifying and adjusting their hostile relations. And so the governments provoke those hostile relations under the guise of patriotism, and then make a show of pacifying them. It is like a gypsy who, having sprinkled pepper under his horse's tail and lashed him in his stall, leads him out hanging onto his halter and pretending that he can hardly control the excited animal.

We are assured that the governments are anxious to preserve peace between the peoples. But how do they preserve it?

Men live on the banks of the Rhine in peaceful intercourse with one another, when all at once, in consequence of various disputes and intrigues between kings and emperors, war begins, and it seems necessary to the French government to declare some of those inhabitants to be French. Centuries pass: the people have grown used to the position, when enmity again arises between the governments of the great nations and a war is started on very empty pretexts, and it seems necessary to the Germans to declare these men Germans again, and ill will is aroused between all the French and the Germans.

Or Germans and Russians are living quietly on their frontier, peaceably exchanging services and the products of labour, and all at once those same institutions which exist for the purpose of maintaining peace between nations begin quarrelling, commit one folly after another, and can find nothing better to do than the childish trick of punishing themselves merely to get their own way and mortify their opponents (in this case very conveniently for themselves, for those who institute a tariff war do not suffer from it themselves—others have to do that). A customs war is started, such as was recently waged between Russia and Germany. And by the help of the newspapers ill will is aroused between Germans and Russians, which is further inflamed by the Franco-Russian festivities, and may at any moment lead to a bloody war.

I have cited these last two instances of how governments influence the people and arouse their hostility to other nations, because they are modern instances. But there is not a single war in all history which has not been evoked by governments and by governments alone, quite independently of the advantage of the people, for whom a war, even a successful one, is always harmful.

The governments assure their peoples that they are in danger of being attacked by other nations or by foes in their midst, and that the only way to escape that danger is by slavish obedience to their governments. This is seen very plainly during revolutions and dictatorships, and it occurs always and everywhere where there is arbitrary rule. Every government explains its existence and justifies all its violence on the ground that if it were not there things would be worse. Having convinced the people that they are in danger, the governments dominate them. And when the peoples are dominated by governments the latter compel them to attack each other. And in this way a belief in the governments' assurance of the danger of attacks by other nations is confirmed among the peoples.

Divide et impera.

Patriotism in its simplest, clearest, and most indubitable meaning is nothing but an instrument for the attainment of the government's ambitious and mercenary aims, and a renunciation of human dignity, common sense, and conscience by the governed, and a slavish submission to those who hold power. That is what is really preached wherever patriotism is championed.

Patriotism is slavery.

The advocates of peace by means of arbitration reason thus: two animals cannot divide their prey except by fighting: children act thus also, and so do barbarians and the barbarous nations. But rational men settle their disagreements by discussion, persuasion, and by referring the decision of the question to disinterested and reasonable people, and the nations of our day ought to act so. These arguments seem quite correct. The peoples of our time have reached a period of enlightenment and have no enmity towards one another and could settle their differences in a peaceful manner. But the argument is only correct in so far as it applies to the people alone, and only if the people are not under the sway of their governments. People in subjection to their governments cannot be rational, for subjection to government is already an indication of the utmost irrationality.

What use is it to talk of the reasonableness of men who promise in advance to fulfil everything (including the murder of men) commanded by government—that is, by men who have happened to get into the position of rulers?

Men who can undertake to fulfil with unquestioning submission all that is decreed by men they do not know, living in Petersburg, Vienna, or Paris, cannot be rational; and the governments—that is, the men wielding such power—can still less be reasonable. They cannot but misuse such insensate and terrible power and cannot but be crazed by wielding it. For this reason peace between nations cannot be attained by the reasonable method of conventions and arbitrations so long as that submission of the peoples to governments, which is always irrational and pernicious, still continues.

But the subjection of men to government will always continue as long as patriotism exists, for every ruling power rests on patriotism—on the readiness of men to submit to power for the sake of the defence of their own people and country, that is, their State, from the dangers supposed to threaten them. The power of the French kings over their people before the Revolution rested on such patriotism, and so did the power of the Committee of Public Safety after the Revolution, and on that same patriotism the power of Napoleon (both as Consul and Emperor) was built up, and the power of the Bourbons after the overthrow of Napoleon, and then of the Republic and of Louis-Philippe, and then again of the Republic and again of Napoleon III, and then once more of the Republic; and on that same patriotism the power of Boulanger was all but established.

It is terrible to say that there is not, and has never been, any act of collective violence by one set of people upon another that has not been perpetrated in the name of patriotism. In the name of patriotism the Russians have fought against the French and the French against the Russians. In the name of patriotism the Russians and the French are now preparing to fight against the Germans, and in the name of patriotism the Germans are preparing to fight on two fronts. And it is not wars alone. In the name of patriotism the Russians are oppressing the Poles and the Germans the Slavs, and in the name of patriotism the Communists slaughtered the men of Versailles and the men of Versailles the Communists.

XV

It would seem that the spread of education, improved means of transport, and increased intercourse between different nations, the growth of the public Press, and above all the decreasing danger from other nations, should make it more and more difficult, and at last impossible, to maintain the deception of patriotism.

But the fact is that those very means of general superficial education, increased facilities for travel and intercourse, and especially the growth of the Press, more and more controlled by the governments, give them nowadays such possibilities of exciting feelings of mutual hostility between the nations that though the uselessness and harmfulness of patriotism has become increasingly obvious, the influence exerted by governments and the ruling classes to arouse patriotism among the people has increased to an equal extent.

The only difference between past and present is, that as many more people now share in the advantages afforded by patriotism to the upper classes, many more people take part in spreading and keeping up that amazing superstition.

The more difficult governments find it to retain their power, the more people they share it with.

Formerly a small group of rulers held the power: emperors, kings, dukes, and their officials and warriors. But now that power and the advantages it affords are shared not only by the officials and clergy, but also by large and even small capitalists, landowners, bankers, members of the legal professions, teachers, rural functionaries, learned men, artists, and especially writers for the Press. And all these people, consciously or unconsciously, spread the deception of patriotism necessary for the maintenance of their advantageous position. And thanks to the fact that the means of deception have become greater and that an ever greater number of people now participate in it, it is so successfully carried out that despite the greater difficulty of the deception the people are as much deceived as ever.

A hundred years ago the illiterate masses, having no conception of whom their government consisted, or of the nations that surrounded them, blindly obeyed the local officials and nobles by whom they were enslaved. And it was enough for the government to keep those officials and nobles under its control by means of bribes and rewards, for the masses obediently to fulfil what was demanded of them. But now, when the masses can for the most part read and know more or less of whom their government consists and what nations surround them; when men of the people continually and easily move from place to place carrying news of what is being done in the world, mere demands that people shall fulfil the government's orders are no longer sufficient. It is necessary also to befog the just ideas which the people have of life, and to instil into them other conceptions of the conditions of their life and of the attitude of other nations towards them.

And thanks to the development of the Press, of education, and of the facilities for travel, the governments, having their agents everywhere, by means of decrees, Church teaching, schools and newspapers, instil into the people the wildest and most perverse conception of their interests, and of the mutual relations of the peoples and their characteristics and intentions. And the people are so oppressed by toil that they have neither time nor opportunity to understand the significance and test the justice of the ideas instilled into them, and submit implicitly to the demands thus imposed upon them in the name of their welfare.

And those of the people who have freed themselves from constant toil and secured some

education, and who it would seem might therefore understand the deception to which they had
been exposed, are submitted to such threats,
bribes, and hypnotization by the government,
that almost without exception they promptly
pass over to its side, and obtaining advantageous
and well-paid posts as teachers, priests, officers,
or officials, begin to share in spreading the deception which ruins their fellows. It is as if at
the doors of education snares were placed in
which all who in one way or other escape from
amid the masses crushed by toil, are inevitably
caught.

At first when one understands all the cruelty of
this deception one feels indignant with those who
from personal, covetous aims, or from vanity,
promote this cruel deception which ruins not
only men's bodies but also their souls, and one
wishes to expose these cruel deceivers. But the
fact is that the deceivers act as they do not because they wish to deceive but because they can
hardly act otherwise. And their deception is not
Machiavellian—not done with a consciousness
of the deception they are producing—but for the
most part with a naïve conviction that they are
doing something good and elevated—in which
conviction they are continually supported by the
sympathy and approval of all those around them.
It is true that dimly feeling that their power and
advantageous position depends on that deception
they are involuntarily attracted to it, but they
act as they do not from a wish to cheat the people,
but because they think that what they are doing
is of use to them.

So the emperors and kings with their ministers, perform their coronations, manœuvres, reviews, and visits to one another during which, dressed up in various uniforms, they move from place to place and consult together with serious faces how to keep peace between supposedly hostile people (to whom it would never occur to fight), and are fully convinced that all they are doing is extremely valuable and reasonable.

In just the same way all the ministers, diplomats, and officials of all sorts, dressing themselves up in their uniforms with various ribbons and crosses and anxiously writing their obscure, involved, and useless communications, reports, instructions, and projects, on fine paper all carefully docketed, are fully convinced that without their activity the whole life of the people would cease or fall to pieces.

The military too, attired in their ludicrous costumes and seriously discussing what rifles and cannon kill people best, are fully convinced that their manœuvres and parades are very important and necessary for the people.

The clergy who preach patriotism, and the journalists and writers of patriotic poems and school-books who receive a generous remuneration for them, have the same conviction, and the organizers of festivities such as the Franco-Russian ones share it also and are sincerely moved when they pronounce their patriotic speeches and toasts. All these people perform their role unconsciously, because it is necessary or because their whole life is built on that deception and they can do nothing else. Meanwhile those very actions evoke sympathy and approval from all those among whom they are performed. Being all bound up with one another they not only approve and justify one another's actions and activity —emperors and kings justifying the doings of the military, the officials, and the clergy; and the military, officials, and clergy, the doings of the emperors and kings and of one another—but the common crowd (especially in towns) seeing no intelligible meaning in all that is being done by these people, involuntarily attribute to it a peculiar and almost supernatural significance. The crowd see, for instance, that triumphal arches are erected, that men dress up in crowns, uniforms, and sacerdotal vestments, that fireworks are displayed, cannon are fired, bells are rung, regiments march with bands playing, papers and telegrams fly about, and couriers rush from place to place, while anxious men in strange attire ride incessantly from place to place, say and write something, and so on; and not being in a position to ascertain that all this is being done (as is actually the case) without the least necessity, the crowd attribute to it a special, mysterious, and important significance, and greet all these shows with ecstatic cries or silent respect. And these expressions, sometimes of delight and always of respect, strengthen the confidence of those who are doing all these silly things.

Not long ago Wilhelm II ordered himself a new throne with some special ornamentation, and having dressed himself up in a white uniform with a cuirass, tight breeches, and a helmet with a bird on it, and having also put on a red mantle, came out to his subjects and sat down on that new throne, fully convinced that this was a necessary and very important affair. And his subjects not only saw nothing ridiculous in it but considered the sight a very solemn one.

XVI

For a very long time past the power of the governments over the peoples has not rested on force, as it did in the days when one people conquered another and held it in subjection by force of arms, or when the rulers had legions of armed janissaries, *oprichniki*, and armed guards amid an unarmed people. For a long time past the power of the governments has rested on what is called public opinion.

There is a public opinion that patriotism is a great moral sentiment, and that people should consider their own nation and State as the best in the world; and this results in a public opinion that it is right and proper to acknowledge the authority of the government and to submit to it, that it is right and proper to serve in the army and submit to its discipline, that it is right and proper to give one's earnings to the government in the form of taxes, that it is right and proper to accept the decisions of the courts, and that it is right and proper to accept as divine truth whatever the emissaries of the government deliver to us.

And once such a public opinion exists, a mighty power is established, controlling in our days milliards of money, an organized mechanism of administration, the postal services, telegraphy, telephones, disciplined armies, the law courts, the police, a submissive clergy, schools, and even newspapers; and this power maintains among the people the public opinion needed for its own maintenance.

The power of the governments rests on public opinion, and possessing power they can always support the sort of public opinion they require by their whole organization, officials, law courts, schools, the Church, and even the Press. Public opinion produces the power, power produces public opinion; and it seems as if there were no escape from this position.

And that would really be the case if public opinion were something fixed and unchanging and if governments could always produce the public opinion they desired.

But fortunately that is not so. In the first place, public opinion is not something constant, unchanging and stagnant, but on the contrary is something continually changing and moving with the movement of mankind. And secondly, public opinion not only cannot be produced at will by governments, but is what produces governments and gives or deprives them of power.

If public opinion seems to remain stationary, and is now what it was decades ago, or if it oscillates in some particular respects as though returning to a former state (now, for instance, abolishing a republican government and replacing it by a monarchy, and now again destroying a monarchy and replacing it by a republic)—this only seems so when we look at the external manifestations of public opinion which are artificially produced by the governments. We need only regard public opinion in relation to the whole life of the people to see that public opinion, like time, never stands still, but is always moving, always going persistently forward along the path by which humanity is advancing, just as the spring moves steadily forward along the way the sun leads it, despite delays and fluctuations. So that, though in its external aspects the position of the peoples of Europe is almost the same to-day as it was fifty years ago, the peoples' relation to it is quite different. Though there are the same rulers, armies, wars, taxes, luxury and poverty, Catholicism, Orthodoxy, and Lutheranism as before, in the old days they existed because public opinion demanded them, whereas now they exist only because the governments artificially keep up what was once a living public opinion.

If we often fail to notice this movement of public opinion, just as we fail to notice the movement of the river when we are swimming with the current, that is because the unnoticed changes of public opinion which constitute its movement take place within ourselves.

Public opinion is by its nature a constant and irresistible movement. If it seems to us to stand still, that is because there are everywhere people who at a certain phase of public opinion have secured for themselves an advantageous position and afterwards use every effort to give it permanence and prevent the emergence of what is new and real and what, though not as yet fully expressed, is already alive in people's consciousness. And such men, retaining an outlived public opinion and concealing the new one, are those who now constitute the governments and the ruling classes, and who profess patriotism as a necessary condition of human life.

The means these people control are enormous, but as public opinion is something ever fluid and growing, all their efforts cannot but be in vain: what is old decays and what is young grows.

The longer nascent public opinion is checked the more does it grow and the more strongly will it find expression. The governments and the ruling classes try with all their might to keep up the old patriotic public opinion on which their power rests and to restrain manifestation of the new opinion which will destroy it. But to retain the old and stop the new is possible only within certain limits, just as a dam can only hold running water back to a certain extent.

However much the governments may try to excite in people the old public opinion of the heroism of patriotism—now no longer natural to them—men of our time no longer believe in it, but believe ever more and more in the solidarity and brotherhood of all nations. Patriotism does not now offer men anything but a most terrible future; while the brotherhood of all the people is an ideal which becomes ever more and more intelligible and desirable to mankind. And so the transition from the old, outlived public opinion to the new one must inevitably be accomplished. That transition is as inevitable as the fall of the last dry leaves in spring and the opening out of the young ones from the swollen buds.

And the longer that transition is postponed the

more insistent it becomes and the more obvious is its inevitability.

Indeed, it is only necessary to consider what we profess both as Christians and simply as men of our time—to think of those moral principles by which we are guided in our social, family, and personal life, and of the position in which we have placed ourselves in the name of patriotism—to realize what a degree of contradiction there is between our consciousness and that which, through the intensive efforts of the government, is still considered to be our public opinion. It is only necessary to reflect on the most ordinary demands of patriotism, which are presented to us as something very simple and natural, to realize to what an extent those demands contradict that real public opinion which we all share. We all consider ourselves free, educated, humane men, and even Christians; yet we are in such a position that if Wilhelm takes offence at Alexander to-morrow, or Mr. N. N. writes a lively article on the Eastern question, or Prince So-and-so plunders some Bulgarians or Serbs, or some Queen or Empress takes offence at something, we—educated, humane Christians—must all go to kill people whom we do not know and towards whom, as towards all men, we are well disposed.

If that has not yet happened we are indebted, so people assure us, to Alexander the Third's pacific disposition or to the fact that his son Nicholas Alexándrovich[1] is to marry Victoria's

---

[1] In November 1894 he ascended the throne of Russia as Nicholas II. A month later he married Princess Alexandra of

granddaughter. But were someone else in Alexander's place or should Alexander's disposition change, or should Nicholas Alexándrovich marry Amelia instead of Alex. then we shall rush to rip out each other's guts as if we were wild beasts.

Such is the supposed public opinion of our time, and opinions of that kind are calmly repeated in all the most progressive and liberal organs of the Press.

If we, Christians for a thousands years, have not yet cut one another's throats, it is only because Alexander the Third does not allow us to do so.

Surely that is terrible!

XVII

No feats of heroism are needed to bring about the greatest and most important changes in the life of humanity; neither the arming of millions of men, nor the construction of new railways and machines, nor the organization of exhibitions or Trades Unions, nor revolutions, nor barricades, nor dynamite outrages, nor the perfection of aerial navigation, and so forth. All that is necessary is a change of public opinion.

And for that change no effort of thought is demanded, no refutation of any existing thing, and no planning of anything new and extraordinary. All that is necessary is to cease acquiescing in the public opinion of the past, now false and already defunct and only artificially induced by governments. It is only necessary for each individual to say what he really thinks

Hesse, the daughter of Queen Victoria's second daughter, the Princess Alice.—A. M.

and feels or at least to refrain from saying what he does not think.

If only men—even a few—would do that, the out-worn public opinion would at once and of itself fall away and a new, real, and vital public opinion would manifest itself. And with this change of public opinion all that inner fabric of men's lives which oppresses and torments them would change of its own accord. One is ashamed to say how little is needed to deliver all men from the calamities which now oppress them. It is only necessary to give up lying! Only let men reject the lie which is imposed upon them; only let them stop saying what they neither think nor feel, and at once such a change of the whole structure of our life will be accomplished as the revolutionaries would not achieve in centuries even if all power were in their hands.

If only men believed that strength lies not in might but in truth, and if they spoke that truth boldly, or at least did not go back on it in word or deed; if only they would cease saying what they do not think and doing what they regard as bad and stupid!

'What does it matter if one shouts: "*Vive la France*" or "Hurrah!" to some emperor, king, or conqueror, or puts on a uniform embroidered with a courtier's key and goes to wait in his ante-chamber, there to bow and address him by strange titles, and then impresses on all—especially on the young and the uneducated—that this is very praiseworthy? What does it matter if one writes an article in defence of the Franco-Russian Alliance or the tariff war, or in condemnation

of the Germans, Russians, French, or English?
What does it matter if one goes to patriotic
festivities and drinks to the health of, and addresses laudatory speeches to, men one does not
like and with whom one has nothing in common?
What does it matter even, if in conversation one
admits the value and utility of treaties and alliances
or remains silent when our own people and State
are praised while other races are maligned and
abused, or when Catholicism, Orthodoxy, or
Lutheranism is extolled, or heroes of war or
rulers, such as Napoleon and Peter, or in our day
Boulanger and Skobelev?'

All that may seem very unimportant. But yet
in these apparently unimportant actions—in our
indicating to the extent of our powers the unreasonableness of what we clearly see to be irrational and refraining from taking part in it—
lies our great and irresistible power: the power
which constitutes that unconquerable force which
makes up real genuine public opinion—that
opinion which with its own advance moves all
humanity. Governments know this. They tremble before that force and strive in every possible
way to counteract and overcome it.

They know that strength lies not in force but
in the action of the mind and in its clear expression. And they fear that expression of independent thought more than an army. So they
establish censorships, bribe newspapers, and seize
control of the Churches and schools. But the
spiritual force which moves the world eludes
them. It is not in a book or a newspaper: it
cannot be trapped but is always free, for it lies in

the depths of man's consciousness. This most powerful, elusive, and free force shows itself in man's soul when he is alone and reflects on the phenomena of the world and then involuntarily expresses his thoughts to his wife, his brother, his friend, and to all from whom he accounts it a sin to conceal what he considers to be the truth. No milliards of rubles, or millions of troops, or any institutions, or wars, or revolutions, can or will produce what a free man can produce by the simple expression of what he considers right, independently of what exists and what is impressed upon him.

One free man says frankly what he thinks and feels in the midst of thousands who by their actions and words maintain just the opposite. It might be supposed that the man who has frankly expressed his thought would remain isolated, yet in most cases it happens that all, or the majority, of the others have long thought and felt the same as he, only they have not expressed it. And what yesterday was the novel opinion of one man becomes to-day the general opinion of the majority. And as soon as this opinion is established, at once by imperceptible degrees but irresistibly, the conduct of mankind begins to alter.

As it is each man, even if free, says to himself: 'What can I do alone against this ocean of evil and deception that overwhelms us? What is the use of expressing my opinion? Why indeed even form one? Better not think about these obscure and involved questions. Perhaps these contradictions are an inevitable condition of our existence. And why should I struggle alone with all

the evil of the world? Is it not better to go with
the stream that carries me along? If anything
can be done it must be done in association with
others and not alone.' And abandoning that
mighty instrument of thought and its expression
which moves the world, each individual man
takes to the instrument of social activity, not
noticing that all forms of social activity rest on
the very foundations against which he ought to
struggle, and that when entering on the social
activity which exists in our world, every man is
obliged at least to some extent to deviate from
the truth and make concessions which destroy
the force of the powerful weapon that has been
given him. It is as though a man who has been
given a blade with so keen an edge that it will
cut through anything, should begin to use that
edge to hammer nails.

We all complain of the senseless order of our
life which is at variance with our whole being,
and yet we neglect to use the unique and powerful instrument in our hands—the consciousness
of truth and its expression. On the contrary,
under pretext of struggling against evil we actually
destroy that instrument and sacrifice it to the
exigencies of an imaginary conflict with the
existing order.

One man does not assert the truth he knows,
because he feels himself bound to people with
whom he is engaged; another because that truth
might deprive him of a profitable position which
enables him to support his family; a third because
he wants to attain fame and power to be used
afterwards in the service of mankind; a fourth

because he does not wish to break with an ancient and sacred tradition; a fifth because he does not wish to offend people; and a sixth because the utterance of the truth would arouse persecution and interfere with some excellent social activity he is pursuing or intends to pursue.

One man serves as an emperor, a king, a minister, a government official, or an army officer, and assures himself and others that the deviations from truth that are unavoidable in his position are amply redeemed by the good he does. Another in the office of a spiritual pastor does not in the depth of his soul believe all he teaches, but permits himself a deviation from truth in consideration of the good he does. A third instructs men by means of literature, and despite the necessity of not telling the whole truth in order not to stir up the government and society against him, has no doubt that he is doing good. A fourth struggles openly with the existing order as a revolutionary or an anarchist, and is fully persuaded that the aims he pursues are so beneficial that the suppressing of the truth, or even the falsehoods necessary for the success of his activity, do not destroy the utility of his work.

That the order of life opposed to the conscience of men should be changed and replaced by one accordant with their consciences, it is necessary that the old outlived public opinion should be replaced by a new and living one.

And for the old, outlived public opinion to make way for the new and living one, it is necessary that men who recognize the new demands of life should express them clearly. Yet those who are conscious of these new demands, not only pass them over in silence—one for the sake of one thing, another for the sake of another—but both by word and deed attest their direct opposites. Only the truth and its free expression can establish that new public opinion which will reform the out-of-date and harmful order of life; and yet we not only fail to utter the truth we know but often give direct expression to what we ourselves regard as false.

If only free men would not rely on what has no power and is never free, that is, external force; but would trust in what is always powerful and free, that is, the truth and its expression!

If only men would boldly and clearly express the truth already manifest to them (of the brotherhood of all nations and the crime of exclusive devotion to one's own) that defunct, false, public opinion on which rests the power of governments and all the evil they produce, would slough off of itself like a dead skin and reveal that new, living, public opinion which now only awaits the shedding of the old husk that has confined it, in order to announce its demands clearly and powerfully and establish new forms of existence in conformity with the conscience of mankind.

XVIII

Men have only to understand that what is given out to them as public opinion and is maintained by such complicated, strenuous, and artificial means, is not public opinion but a dead relic of what once was public opinion; they have only, above all, to believe in themselves—in the fact that what they are conscious of in the depths of their souls and what craves expression in each of them and remains unexpressed only because it runs counter to existing social opinion, is that force which transforms the world and to express which is man's vocation—they have only to believe that the truth lies not in what is said by the people around them but in what is said by their conscience, that is, by God—and the false and artificially maintained public opinion will instantly vanish and a true public opinion establish itself.

If only people would say what they think and refrain from saying what they do not think, all the superstitions bred by patriotism would fall away at once with all the evil feelings and acts of violence that are based upon them. The hatred and enmity of one country for another that is fanned by the governments would cease, and so would the glorification of warlike exploits, that is, of murder; and above all there would be an end of respect and subservience towards those in power and of the surrender to them of men's labour—for these things have no foundation but patriotism.

If that were done, the vast mass of weak people who are always guided by outside influences would instantly pass over to the side of the new public opinion. And a new public opinion would predominate in place of the old.

The governments may control the schools, the Church, the Press, milliards of rubles and millions of disciplined men made into machines, but all that apparently terrible organization of brute force is nothing before the recognition of the truth which surges in the soul of each man who knows its power, and from whom it is communicated to a second and a third, as one candle can light an infinite number of others. That light need only be kindled, and all that seemingly mighty organization will melt away like wax before the fire and be consumed.

If only men understood the mighty power given them in the word which expresses truth; if only they would refuse to sell their birthright for a mess of pottage, if only they would use the power they possess, their rulers would not only not dare, as now, to threaten at their caprice to plunge or not plunge men into universal slaughter, but they would not even dare to hold their reviews and manœuvres of disciplined murderers before the eyes of a peaceful population. Nor would they dare to arrange or upset tariff agreements in their own interest and for the advantage of their assistants, and they would not dare to take from the people the millions of rubles which they distribute to their assistants and which they spend on preparations for murder.

And so a change is not only possible but inevitable. That such a change should not take place is as impossible as that a dead tree should not decay and fall, and a young one grow up.

Peace I leave with you; my peace I give unto you. Let not your heart be troubled, neither let it be afraid, said Christ. And that peace is already with us and it depends on us to secure it.

If only the hearts of individual men would not be troubled by the temptations which assail them every hour, and would not be frightened by the imaginary terrors that alarm them; if only men recognized in what their mighty and all-conquering power lies, the peace which they have always desired—not the peace obtained by diplomatic negotiations, by visits of emperors and kings from one town to another, by banquets, speeches, fortresses, artillery, dynamite and melinite, by exhausting the people by taxation or tearing the flower of the nation from toil and corrupting it, but the peace which is secured by the free advocacy of the truth by each individual man—would long since have been established among us.

Moscow.
   March 17th 1894.

LA MARSEILLAISE

Allons enfants de la patrie,
Le jour de gloire est arrivé.
Contre nous de la tyrannie,
L'étendard sanglant est levé,
L'étendard sanglant est levé.
Entendez-vous dans les campagnes
Mugir ces féroces soldats?
Ils viennent, jusque dans nos bras,
Égorger nos fils, nos compagnes!
Aux armes, citoyens!
Formez vos bataillons.
Marchez, marchez! qu'un sang impur,
Abreuve nos sillons.

Que veut cette horde d'esclaves,
De traîtres de rois conjurés!
Pour qui ces ignobles entraves,
Ces fers, dès longtemps préparés?
Ces fers, dès longtemps préparés?
Français! pour nous, ah! quel outrage!
Quels transports il doit exciter!
C'est nous qu'on ose menacer,
De rendre à l'antique esclavage.

Aux armes, &c.

Tremblez, tyrans et vous perfides,
L'opprobre de tous les partis!
Tremblez, vos projets patricides
Vont enfin recevoir leur prix,
Vont enfin recevoir leur prix.
Tout est soldat pour vous combattre,
S'ils tombent, nos jeunes héros,

La France en produit de nouveaux,
Contre vous tous prêts à se battre.

Aux armes, &c.

Français, en guerriers magnanimes,
Portez ou retenez vos coups;
Épargnez ces tristes victimes,
A regret s'armant contre nous;
A regret s'armant contre nous;
Mais le despote sanguinaire,
Mais les complices de Bouillé
Tous ces tigres qui sans pitié
Déchirent le sein de leur mère.

Aux armes, &c.

Amour sacré de la patrie,
Conduis, soutiens nos bras vengeurs.
Liberté, Liberté chérie,
Combats avec tes défenseurs:
Combats avec tes défenseurs:
Sous nos drapeaux que la victoire
Accoure à tes mâles accents,
Que tes ennemis expirants
Voient ton triomphe et notre gloire.

Aux armes, &c.

THE MARSEILLAISE

COME children of our Fatherland
Her day of glory now draws nigh.
Of tyranny the cruel hand
Uplifts its gory standards high,
Uplifts its gory standards high.
D'you hear how in the fields out there
Those infuriated soldiers yell?

They're coming in our very arms
Our women and our sons to slay.

Come seize your arms, men!
Your battalions form.
March on, march on! their blood impure
Shall soon into our footprints flow.

What seeks that slavish horde
Of traitors and conspiring kings?
For whom have been these fetters,
These chains forged long ago?
These chains wrought long ago?
For us, O men of France. Outrageous!
What fury 'twill in us inspire!
It is ourselves they dare to threaten
With ancient slavery again.

Come seize, &c.

You tyrants tremble! Tremble you
Perfidious dregs of every party.
Your patricidal projects
At last will pay their price,
At last will pay their price.
To fight you each will be a soldier,
And if they fall—our youthful heroes—
Our France will soon find new ones
All ready to face you.

Come seize, &c.

O men of France, highminded warriors,
You'll deal or will withold your blows.
And you will spare those piteous victims
To fight us armed against their will.
But do not spare those gory despots,
Accomplices of de Bouillé,

Those tigers who remorselessly
Would rend their mother's breast.

Come seize, &c.

O sacred love of Fatherland,
Support thou our avenging arms.
O liberty, dear liberty,
Help thou in thy defenders' fight.
Beneath our flag may victory
Come hurrying at thy virile call,
And may our dying enemies
Our glory and our triumph see.

Come seize, &c.

PATRIOTISM AND GOVERNMENT

'The time is fast approaching when to call a man a patriot will be the deepest insult you can offer him. Patriotism now means advocating plunder in the interests of the privileged classes of the particular State system into which we have happened to be born.'—E. BELFORT BAX.

I

I HAVE already several times expressed the thought that in our day the feeling of patriotism is an unnatural, irrational, and harmful feeling, the cause of a great part of the ills from which mankind is suffering, and that consequently this feeling should not be cultivated, as it now is, but should on the contrary be suppressed and eradicated by all rational means. Yet strange to say—though it is undeniable that the universal armaments and destructive wars which are ruining the peoples result from that one feeling—all my arguments showing the backwardness, anachronism, and harmfulness of patriotism have been and still are met either by silence, by intentional misinterpretation, or by a strange unvarying reply to the effect that only bad patriotism (Jingoism, or Chauvinism) is evil, but that real good patriotism is a very elevated moral feeling to condemn which is not only irrational but wicked.

What this real, good patriotism consists in, we are never told. If anything is said about it we get declamatory, inflated phrases, instead of explanation, or else some other conception is substituted—something which has nothing in common with the patriotism we all know and from the results of which we suffer so severely.

It is generally said that the real, good patriotism consists in desiring for one's own people or State such real benefits as do not infringe the well-being of other nations.

Talking recently to an Englishman about the present war,[1] I said to him that the real cause of the war was not avarice, as was generally said, but patriotism, as the whole temper of English society showed. The Englishman did not agree with me, and said that even were it so it merely showed that the patriotism at present inspiring Englishmen is a bad patriotism; but that good patriotism, such as he was imbued with, would cause his English compatriots to act well.

'Then do you wish only Englishmen to act well?' I asked.

'I wish all men to do so,' said he, indicating clearly by that reply the characteristic of true benefits whether moral, scientific, or even material and practical—which is that they spread out to all men. But to wish such benefits to everyone is evidently not only not patriotic but the reverse.

Neither do the peculiarities of each people constitute patriotism, though these things are purposely substituted for the conception of patriotism by its defenders. They say that the peculiarities of each people are an essential condition of human progress, and that patriotism, which seeks to maintain those peculiarities, is therefore a good and useful feeling. But is it not quite evident that if, once upon a time, these peculiarities of each people—these customs, creeds, languages—were conditions necessary for the life of humanity,

---

[1] The South African War of 1899-1902.—A. M.

in our time these same peculiarities form the chief obstacle to what is already recognized as an ideal—the brotherly union of the peoples? And therefore the maintenance and defence of any nationality—Russian, German, French, or Anglo-Saxon, provoking the corresponding maintenance and defence not only of Hungarian, Polish, and Irish nationalities, but also of Basque, Provençal, Mordvá,[1] Tchouvásh, and many other nationalities—serves not to harmonize and unite men but to estrange and divide them more and more from one another.

So that not the imaginary but the real patriotism which we all know, by which most people to-day are swayed and from which humanity suffers so severely, is not the wish for spiritual benefits for one's own people (it is impossible to desire spiritual benefits for one's own people only), but is a very definite feeling of preference for one's own people or State above all other peoples and States, and a consequent wish to get for that people or State the greatest advantages and power that can be got—things which are obtainable only at the expense of the advantages and power of other peoples or States.

It would therefore seem obvious that patriotism as a feeling is bad and harmful, and as a doctrine is stupid. For it is clear that if each people and each State considers itself the best of peoples and States, they all live in a gross and harmful delusion.

---

[1] The Mordvá (or Mordvinian) and Tchouvásh tribes are of Finnish origin, and inhabit chiefly the governments of the Middle Volga.—A.M.

II

One would expect the harmfulness and irrationality of patriotism to be evident to everybody. But the surprising fact is that cultured and learned men not only do not themselves notice the harm and stupidity of patriotism, but resist every exposure of it with the greatest obstinacy and ardour (though without any rational grounds) and continue to belaud it as beneficent and elevating.

What does this mean?

Only one explanation of this amazing fact presents itself to me.

All human history from the earliest times to our own day may be considered as a movement of the consciousness both of individuals and of homogeneous groups from lower ideas to higher ones.

The whole path travelled both by individuals and by homogeneous groups may be represented as a consecutive flight of steps from the lowest, on the level of animal life, to the highest attained by the consciousness of man at a given moment of history.

Each man, like each separate homogeneous group, nation, or State, always moved and moves up this ladder of ideas. Some portions of humanity are in front, others lag far behind, others again—the majority—move somewhere between the most advanced and the most backward. But all, whatever stage they may have reached, are inevitably and irresistibly moving from lower to higher ideas. And always, at any given moment, both the individuals and the separate groups of people—advanced, middle, or backward—stand in three different relations to the three stages of ideas amid which they move.

Always, both for the individual and for the separate groups of people, there are the ideas of the past, which are worn out and have become strange to them and to which they cannot revert: as for instance in our Christian world, the ideas of cannibalism, universal plunder, the rape of wives, and other customs of which only a record remains.

And there are the ideas of the present, instilled into men's minds by education, by example, and by the general activity of all around them; ideas under the power of which they live at a given time: for instance, in our own day, the ideas of property, State organization, trade, utilization of domestic animals, and so on.

And there are the ideas of the future, of which some are already approaching realization and are obliging people to change their way of life and to struggle against the former ways: such ideas in our world as those of freeing the labourers, of giving equality to women, of ceasing to use flesh food, and so on; while others, though already recognized, have not yet come into practical conflict with the old forms of life: such in our times are the ideas (which we call ideals) of the extermination of violence, the arrangement of a communal system of property, of a universal religion, and of a general brotherhood of men.

And therefore every man and every homogeneous group of men, on whatever level they may stand, having behind them the out worn

remembrances of the past and before them the
ideals of the future, are always in a state of
struggle between the moribund ideas of the
present and the ideas of the future that are
coming to life. It usually happens that when an
idea which has been useful and even necessary in
the past becomes superfluous, that idea, after a
more or less prolonged struggle, yields its place to
a new idea which was till then an ideal, but which
thus becomes a present idea.

But it does occur that an antiquated idea,
already replaced in people's consciousness by a
higher one, is of such a kind that its maintenance
is profitable to those who have the greatest influence in their society. And then it happens that
this antiquated idea, though it is in sharp contradiction to the whole surrounding form of life
which has been altering in other respects, continues to influence people and to sway their
actions. Such retention of antiquated ideas always
has occurred, and still does occur, in the region of
religion. And it occurs because the priests, whose
profitable positions are bound up with the antiquated religious idea, purposely use their power
to hold people to this antiquated idea.

The same thing occurs in the political sphere,
and for similar reasons, with reference to the
patriotic idea on which all arbitrary power is
based. People to whom it is profitable to do so
maintain that idea by artificial means though it
now lacks both sense and utility. And as these
people possess the most powerful means of influencing others, they are able to achieve their
object.

In this, it seems to me, lies the explanation of the strange contrast between the antiquated patriotic idea and that whole drift of ideas making in a contrary direction which has already entered into the consciousness of the Christian world.

III

Patriotism as a feeling of exclusive love for one's own people and as a doctrine of the virtue of sacrificing one's tranquillity, one's property, and even one's life, in defence of one's own people from slaughter and outrage by their enemies, was the highest idea of the period when each nation considered it feasible and just for its own advantage to subject to slaughter and outrage the people of other nations

But already some two thousand years ago humanity, in the person of the highest representatives of its wisdom, began to recognize the higher idea of a brotherhood of man; and that idea penetrating man's consciousness more and more, has in our time attained most varied forms of realization. Thanks to improved means of communication and to the unity of industry, of trade, of the arts, and of science, men are to-day so bound to one another that the danger of conquest, massacre, or outrage by a neighbouring people has quite disappeared, and all peoples (the peoples, but not the governments) live together in peaceful, mutually advantageous, and friendly commercial, industrial, artistic, and scientific relations, which they have no need and no desire to disturb. One would think therefore that the antiquated feeling of patriotism—being super-

fluous and incompatible with the consciousness
we have reached of the existence of brotherhood
among men of different nationalities—should
dwindle more and more until it completely disappears. Yet the very opposite of this occurs:
this harmful and antiquated feeling not only continues to exist, but burns more and more fiercely.

The peoples without any reasonable ground
and contrary alike to their conception of right
and to their own advantage, not only sympathize with governments in their attacks on other
nations, in their seizures of foreign possessions and
in defending by force what they have already
stolen, but even themselves demand such attacks,
seizures, and defences: are glad of them and take
pride in them. The small oppressed nationalities
which have fallen under the power of the great
States—the Poles, Irish, Bohemians, Finns, or
Armenians—resenting the patriotism of their
conquerors which is the cause of their oppression,
catch from them the infection of this feeling of
patriotism—which has ceased to be necessary
and is now obsolete, unmeaning, and harmful—
and catch it to such a degree that all their
activity is concentrated upon it, and though
they are themselves suffering from the patriotism
of the stronger nations, they are ready for the
sake of patriotism to perpetrate on other peoples
the very same deeds that their oppressors have
perpetrated and are perpetrating on them.

This occurs because the ruling classes (including not only the actual rulers with their officials
but all the classes who enjoy an exceptionally advantageous position: the capitalists, journalists,

and most of the artists and scientists) can retain their position—an exceptionally advantageous one in comparison with that of the labouring masses—thanks only to the government organization which rests on patriotism. They have in their hands all the most powerful means of influencing the people, and always sedulously support patriotic feelings in themselves and in others, more especially as those feelings which uphold the government's power are those that are always best rewarded by that power.

The more patriotic an official is, the more he prospers in his career. The war produced by patriotism gives the army man a chance of promotion.

Patriotism and its resulting wars give an enormous revenue to the newspaper trade and profits to many other trades. The more every writer, teacher, and professor preaches patriotism the more secure is he in his place. The more every emperor and king is addicted to patriotism the more fame he obtains.

The ruling classes have in their hands the army, the schools, the churches, the press, and money. In the schools they kindle patriotism in the children by means of histories describing their own people as the best of all peoples and always in the right. Among adults they kindle it by spectacles, jubilees, monuments, and by a lying patriotic press. Above all they inflame patriotism by perpetrating every kind of injustice and harshness against other nations, provoking in them enmity towards their own people, and then in turn exploit that enmity to embitter their people against the foreigner.

The intensification of this terrible feeling of patriotism has gone on among the European peoples in a rapidly increasing progression, and in our time has reached the utmost limits beyond which there is no room for it to extend.

IV

Within the memory of people not yet old an occurrence took place showing most obviously the amazing intoxication caused by patriotism among the people of Christendom.

The ruling classes of Germany excited the patriotism of the masses of their people to such a degree that, in the second half of the nineteenth century, a law was proposed in accordance with which all the men had to become soldiers: all the sons, husbands, fathers, learned men, and godly men, had to learn to murder, to become submissive slaves of those above them in military rank, and be absolutely ready to kill whomsoever they were ordered to kill; to kill men of oppressed nationalities, their own working men standing up for their rights, and even their own fathers and brothers—as was publicly proclaimed by that most impudent of potentates, William II.

That horrible measure, outraging all man's best feelingsin the grossest manner, was acquiesced in without murmur by the people of Germany under the influence of patriotism. It resulted in their victory over the French. That victory excited the patriotism of Germany yet further, and by reaction that of France, Russia, and the other Powers; and the men of the European countries unresistingly submitted to the introduction of general military service—i.e., to a state of slavery involving a degree of humiliation and submission incomparably worse than any slavery of the ancient world. After this servile submission of the masses to the calls of patriotism, the audacity, cruelty, and insanity of the governments knew no bounds. A competition in the usurpation of other peoples' lands in Asia, Africa, and America began—evoked partly by whim, partly by vanity, and partly by covetousness—and was accompanied by ever greater and greater distrust and enmity between the governments.

The destruction of the inhabitants of the lands seized was accepted as a quite natural proceeding. The only question was who should be first in seizing other peoples' land and destroying the inhabitants? All the governments not only most evidently infringed, and are infringing, the elementary demands of justice in relation to the conquered peoples and in relation to one another, but they were guilty, and continue to be guilty, of every kind of cheating, swindling, bribery, fraud, spying, robbery, and murder; and the peoples not only sympathized and still sympathize with them in all this, but rejoice when it is their own government and not another government that commits such crimes.

The mutual enmity between the different peoples and States has latterly reached such amazing dimensions that, notwithstanding the fact that there is no reason why one State should attack another, everyone knows that all the governments stand with their claws out and their teeth bared, and only waiting for someone to be in trouble or become weak, in order to tear him to pieces with as little risk as possible.

All the peoples of the so-called Christian world have been reduced by patriotism to such a state of brutality that not only those who are obliged to kill or be killed desire slaughter and rejoice in murder, but all the people of Europe and America, living peaceably in their homes exposed to no danger, are at each war—thanks to easy means of communication and to the press—in the position of the spectators in a Roman circus, and like them delight in the slaughter, and raise the bloodthirsty cry, '*Pollice verso*.'[1]

And not only adults, but children too, pure, wise children, rejoice, according to their nationality, when they hear that the number killed and lacerated by lyddite or other shells on some particular day was not seven hundred but a thousand Englishmen or Boers.

And parents (I know of such cases) encourage their children in such brutality.

But that is not all. Every increase in the army of one nation (and each nation, being in danger, seeks to increase its army for patriotic reasons) obliges its neighbours to increase their armies, also from patriotism, and this evokes a fresh increase by the first nation.

And the same thing occurs with fortifications and navies: one State has built ten ironclads, a neighbour builds eleven; then the first builds twelve, and so on to infinity.

---

[1] In the Roman amphitheatres the sign given by the spectators who wished a defeated gladiator to be slain was the turning out of thumbs (*pollice verso*).—A.M.

'I'll pinch you.' 'And I'll punch your head.' 'And I'll stab you with a dagger.' 'And I'll bludgeon you.' 'And I'll shoot you.' . . . Only bad children, drunken men, or animals, quarrel or fight so, but yet it is just what is going on among the highest representatives of the most enlightened governments, the very men who undertake to direct the education and the morality of their subjects.

V

The position is becoming worse and worse, and there is no stopping this descent towards evident perdition.

The one way of escape believed in by credulous people has now been closed by recent events. I refer to the Hague Conference, and to the war between England and the Transvaal which immediately followed it.

If people who think little or only superficially were able to comfort themselves with the idea that international courts of arbitration would supersede wars and ever-increasing armaments, the Hague Conference and the war that followed it demonstrated in the most palpable manner the impossibility of finding a solution of the difficulty in that way. After the Hague Conference it became obvious that as long as governments with armies exist, the termination of armaments and of wars is impossible. That an agreement should become possible it is necessary that the parties to it should *trust* each other. And in order that the Powers should trust each other they must lay down their arms, as is done by the bearers of a flag of truce when they meet for a conference.

So long as governments continue to distrust one another, and instead of disbanding or decreasing their armies always increase them in correspondence with augmentations made by their neighbours, and by means of spies watch every movement of troops, knowing that each of the Powers will attack its neighbour as soon as it sees its way to do so, no agreement is possible, and every conference is either a stupidity, or a pastime, or a fraud, or an impertinence, or all of these together.

It was particularly becoming that the Russian rather than any other government should be the *enfant terrible* of the Hague Conference. No one at home being allowed to reply to all its evidently mendacious manifestos and rescripts, the Russian Government is so spoilt that—having without the least scruple ruined its own people with armaments, strangled Poland, plundered Turkestan and China, and being specially engaged in suffocating Finland—it proposed disarmament to the governments in full assurance that it would be trusted!

But strange, unexpected, and indecent as such a proposal was—coming at the very time when it was preparing an increase of its own army—the words publicly uttered in the hearing of the people were such, that for the sake of appearances the governments of the other Powers could not decline the consultation, comical and evidently insincere as it was. The delegates met—knowing in advance that nothing would come of it—and for several weeks (during which they drew good salaries) though laughing in their sleeves, they all conscientiously pretended to be much occupied in arranging peace among the nations.

The Hague Conference, followed up as it was by the terrible bloodshed of the Transvaal War which no one attempted or is now attempting to stop, was nevertheless of some use, though not at all in the way expected of it—it was useful because it showed in the most obvious manner that the evils from which the peoples are suffering cannot be cured by governments; that governments, even if they wished to, cannot terminate either armaments or wars.

To have a reason for existing, governments must defend their people from other people's attack. But not one people wishes to attack or does attack another. And therefore governments, far from wishing for peace, carefully excite the anger of other nations against themselves. And having excited other people's anger against themselves and stirred up the patriotism of their own people, each government then assures its people that it is in danger and must be defended.

And having the power in their hands the governments can both irritate other nations and excite patriotism at home, and they carefully do both the one and the other. Nor can they do otherwise, for their existence depends on their acting thus.

If in former times governments were necessary to defend their people from other people's attacks, now on the contrary governments artificially disturb the peace that exists between the nations and provoke enmity among them.

When it was necessary to plough in order to sow, ploughing was wise, but it is evidently absurd and harmful to go on ploughing after the seed has been sown. But this is just what the governments are obliging their people to do: to infringe the unity which exists and which nothing would infringe were it not for the governments.

VI

What really are these governments without which people think they could not exist?

There may have been a time when such governments were necessary, and when the evil of supporting a government was less than that of being defenceless against organized neighbours; but now such governments have become unnecessary and are a far greater evil than all the dangers with which they frighten their subjects.

Not only military governments but governments in general could be, I will not say useful but at least harmless, only if they consisted of immaculate, holy people, as is theoretically the case among the Chinese. But then, by the nature of their activity which consists in committing acts of violence,[1] governments are always composed of elements quite contrary to holiness—of the most audacious, unscrupulous, and perverted people.

A government therefore is the most dangerous

[1] The word *government* is frequently used in an indefinite sense as almost equivalent to management or direction; but in the sense in which the word is used in the present article, the characteristic feature of a government is that it claims a moral right to inflict physical penalties and by its decree to make murder a good action.—A.M.

organization possible, especially when it is entrusted with military power.

In the widest sense the government, including capitalists and the Press, is nothing but an organization which places the greater part of the people in the power of a smaller part who dominate them. That smaller part is subject to a yet smaller part, that again to a yet smaller, and so on, reaching at last a few people or one single man who by means of military force has power over all the rest. So that all this organization resembles a cone of which all the parts are completely in the power of those people, or that one person, who happen to be at the apex.

The apex of the cone is seized by those who are more cunning, audacious, and unscrupulous than the rest, or by someone who happens to be the heir of those who were audacious and unscrupulous.

To-day it may be Borís Godunóv,[1] and to-morrow Gregory Otrépyev.[2] To-day the licentious Catherine, who with her paramours has murdered her husband; to-morrow Pugachév;[3] then Paul the madman, Nicholas I., or Alexander III.

To-day it may be Napoleon, to-morrow a Bourbon or an Orléans, a Boulanger or a Panama

[1] Borís Godunóv, brother-in-law of the weak Tsar Fëdor Ivánovich, succeeded in becoming Tsar, and reigned in Moscow from 1598 to 1605.—A.M.

[2] Gregory Otrépyev was a pretender, who passing himself off as Dmítrj, son of Iván the Terrible, reigned in Moscow in 1605 and 1606.—A.M.

[3] Pugachév was the leader of a most formidable insurrection in 1773–5, and was executed in Moscow in 1775.—A.M.

Company; to-day it may be Gladstone, to-morrow Salisbury, Chamberlain, or Rhodes.

And to such governments is allowed full power not only over property and lives, but even over the spiritual and moral development, the education, and the religious guidance of everybody.

People construct this terrible machine of power, they allow anyone to seize it who can (and the chances always are that it will be seized by the most morally worthless)—they slavishly submit to him, and are then surprised that evil comes of it. They are afraid of anarchists' bombs, and are not afraid of this terrible organization which is always threatening them with the greatest calamities.

People found it useful to tie themselves together in order to resist their enemies, as the Circassians[1] did when resisting attacks. And they still go on tying themselves together though the danger is quite past.

They carefully tie themselves up so that one man can have them all at his mercy. Then they throw away the end of the rope that ties them and leave it trailing for some rascal or fool to seize and to do them whatever harm he pleases.

And when people set up, submit to, and maintain an organized and military government, what are they doing but just that?

VII

To deliver men from the terrible and ever-increasing evils of armaments and wars, we want

[1] The Circassians, when surrounded, used to tie themselves together leg to leg, that all should die fighting and none escape. Instances of this kind occurred when their country was being annexed by Russia.—A.M.

neither congresses nor conferences nor treaties nor courts of arbitration, but the destruction of those instruments of violence which are called governments and from which humanity's greatest evils flow.

To destroy governmental *violence* only one thing is needed: it is that people should understand that the feeling of patriotism which alone supports that instrument of violence is a rude, harmful, disgraceful, and bad feeling, and above all immoral. It is a rude feeling because it is natural only to people standing on the lowest level of morality and expecting from other nations such outrages as they themselves are ready to inflict. It is a harmful feeling because it disturbs advantageous and joyous peaceful relations with other peoples, and above all produces that governmental organization under which power may fall and does fall into the hands of the worst men. It is a disgraceful feeling because it turns man not merely into a slave but into a fighting cock, a bull, or a gladiator, who wastes his strength and his life for objects which are not his own but his government's. It is an immoral feeling because, instead of confessing himself a son of God (as Christianity teaches us) or even a free man guided by his own reason, each man under the influence of patriotism confesses himself the son of his fatherland and the slave of his government, and commits actions contrary to his reason and conscience.

It is only necessary that people should understand this, and the terrible bond called government by which we are chained together will fall to pieces of itself without a struggle, and with it the terrible and useless evils it produces will cease.

And people are already beginning to understand this. For instance, a citizen of the United States writes:

'We are farmers, mechanics, merchants, manufacturers, teachers, and all we ask is the privilege of attending to our own business. We own our homes, love our friends, are devoted to our families, and do not interfere with our neighbours—we have work to do and wish to work.

'Leave us alone!

'But they will not—these politicians. They insist on governing us and living off our labour. They tax us, eat our substance, conscript us, draft our boys into their wars. All the myriads of men who live on the government depend upon the government to tax us, and in order to tax us successfully standing armies are maintained. The plea that the army is needed for the protection of the country is pure fraud and pretence. The French Government frightens the people by telling them that the Germans are ready and anxious to fall upon them. The Russians fear the British. The British fear everybody. And now in America we are told we must increase our navy and add to our army because Europe may at any moment combine against us.

'This is fraud and untruth. The plain people in France, Germany, England, and America, are opposed to war. We only wish to be let alone. Men with wives, children, sweethearts, homes, aged parents, do not want to go off and fight someone. We are peaceable and we fear war. We hate it.

'We should like to obey the Golden Rule.

'War is the inevitable outcome of the existence of armed men. The country which maintains a large standing army will sooner or later have a war on hand. The man who prides himself on fisticuffs is going some day to meet a man who considers himself the better man, and they will fight. Germany and France have no issue save a desire to see which is the better man. They have fought many times—and they will fight again. Not that the people want to fight, but the superior class fan fright into fury and make men think they must fight to protect their homes.

'So the people who wish to follow the teachings of Christ are not allowed to do so, but are taxed, outraged, and deceived by governments.

'Christ taught humility, meekness, the forgiveness of one's enemies, and that to kill was wrong. The Bible teaches men not to swear; but the superior class make us swear on the Bible in which they do not believe.

'The question is: How are we to relieve ourselves of these cormorants who toil not, but who are clothed in broadcloth and blue, with brass buttons and many costly accoutrements—who feed upon our substance and for whom we delve and dig?

'Shall we fight them?

'No, we do not believe in bloodshed. Besides they have the guns and the money and can hold out longer than we.

'But who composes this army that they would order to fire upon us?

'Why, our neighbours and brothers—deceived into the idea that they are doing God's service by protecting their country from its enemies. When the fact is our country has no enemies save the superior class that pretends to look out for our interests if we will only obey and consent to be taxed.

'In this way they siphon our resources and turn our true brothers upon us to subdue and humiliate us. You cannot send a telegram to your wife, or an express package to your friend, or draw a cheque for your grocer, until you first pay the tax to maintain armed men who can quickly be used to kill you; and who will imprison you if you do not pay.

'The only relief lies in education. Educate men that it is wrong to kill. Teach them the Golden Rule, and yet again teach them the Golden Rule. Silently defy this superior class by refusing to bow down to their fetish of bullets. Cease supporting the preachers who cry for war and spout patriotism for a consideration. Let them go to work as we do. We believe in Christ—they do not. Christ spoke what he thought. They speak what they think will please the men in power—the superior class.

'We will not enlist. We will not shoot at their order. We will not "charge bayonet" upon a mild and gentle people. We will not fire upon shepherds and farmers fighting for their firesides, at the suggestion of Cecil Rhodes. Your false cry of "Wolf! wolf!" shall not alarm us. We pay your taxes only because we have to, and we will pay no longer than we have to. We will pay no pew-rents, no tithes to your sham charities, and we will speak our minds upon occasion.

'We will educate men.

'And all the time our silent influence will be making itself felt, and even the men who are conscripted will be half-hearted and refuse to fight. We will educate men into the thought that the Christ Life of Peace and Goodwill is better than the Life of Strife, Bloodshed, and War.

'"Peace on earth!"—it can only come when men do away with armies and are willing to do unto other men as they would be done by.'

So writes a citizen of the United States. And from various sides, in various forms, such voices are sounding.

This is what a German soldier writes:

'I went through two campaigns with the Prussian Guards (in 1866 and 1870), and I hate war from the bottom of my soul for it has made me inexpressibly unfortunate. We wounded soldiers generally receive such a miserable recompense that we have indeed to be ashamed of having once been patriots. I, for instance, get ninepence a day for my right arm which was shot through at the attack on St. Privat, August 18, 1870. Some hunting dogs are allowed more for their keep. And I have suffered for years from my twice wounded arm. Already in 1866 I took part in the war against Austria and fought at Trautenau and Königgrätz, and saw horrors enough. In 1870, being in the reserve, I was called out again, and as I have already said I was wounded in the attack at St. Privat: my right arm was twice shot through lengthwise. I had to leave a good place in a brewery and was unable afterwards to regain it. Since then I have never been able to get on my feet again. The intoxication soon passed and there was nothing left for the wounded invalid but to keep himself alive on a beggarly pittance eked out by charity. . . .

'In a world in which people run round like trained animals and are incapable of any other idea than that of overreaching one another for the sake of mammon—in such a world let people think me a crank, but for all that I feel in myself the divine idea of peace which is so beautifully expressed in the Sermon on the Mount. My deepest conviction is that war is only trade on a larger scale—the ambitious and powerful trade with the happiness of the peoples.

'And what horrors do we not suffer from it! Never shall I forget the pitiful groans that pierced one to the marrow!

'People who never did each other any harm begin to slaughter one another like wild animals, and petty slavish souls implicate the good God, making Him their confederate in such deeds.

'My neighbour in the ranks had his jaw broken by a bullet. The poor wretch was mad with pain. He ran about like a lunatic and could not even get water to cool his horrible wound in the scorching summer heat. Our commander, the Crown Prince (who was afterwards the noble Emperor Frederick), wrote in his diary: "War is an irony on the Gospels." . . .'

People are beginning to understand the fraud

of patriotism, in which all the governments take such pains to keep them involved.

VIII

'But,' it is usually asked, 'what will there be instead of governments?'

There will be nothing. Something that has long been useless and therefore superfluous and bad will be abolished. An organ that being unnecessary has become harmful will be abolished.

'But,' people generally say, 'if there is no government people will violate and kill each other.'

Why? Why should the abolition of the organization which arose in consequence of violence and which has been handed down from generation to generation to do violence—why should the abolition of such an organization, now devoid of use, cause people to outrage and kill one another? On the contrary, the presumption is that the abolition of the organ of violence would result in people ceasing to violate and kill one another.

Now some men are specially educated and trained to kill and to do violence to other people —there are men who are supposed to have a right to use violence, and who make use of an organization which exists for that purpose. Such deeds of violence and such killing are considered good and worthy deeds.

But then people will not be so brought up, and no one will have a right to use violence to others, and there will be no organization to do violence, and—as is natural to people of our time —violence and murder will always be considered bad actions no matter who commits them.

But should acts of violence continue to be committed even after the abolition of the governments, such acts will certainly be fewer than they are now when an organization specially devised to commit acts of violence exists, and we have a state of things in which acts of violence and murders are considered good and useful deeds.

The abolition of governments will merely rid us of an unnecessary organization which we have inherited from the past, an organization for the commission of violence and for its justification.

'But there will then be no laws, no property, no courts of justice, no police, no popular education', say people who intentionally confuse the use of violence by governments with various social activities.

The abolition of the organization of government formed to do violence does not at all involve the abolition of what is reasonable and good, and therefore not based on violence, in laws or law courts, or in property, or in police regulations, or in financial arrangements, or in popular education. On the contrary, the absence of the brutal power of government which is needed only for its own support, will facilitate a more just and reasonable social organization, needing no violence. Courts of justice, and public affairs, and popular education, will all exist to the extent to which they are really needed by the people, but in a form which will not involve the evils contained in the present form of government. Only that will be destroyed which was evil and hindered the free expression of the people's will.

But even if we assume that with the absence of governments there would be disturbances and civil strife, even then the position of the people would be better than it is at present. The position now is such that it is difficult to imagine anything worse. The people are ruined, and their ruin is becoming more and more complete. The men are all converted into war-slaves, and have from day to day to expect orders to go to kill and to be killed. What more? Are the ruined peoples to die of hunger? Even that is already beginning in Russia, in Italy, and in India. Or are the women as well as the men to go as soldiers? In the Transvaal even that has begun.

So that even if the absence of government really meant anarchy in the negative disorderly sense of that word—which is far from being the case—even then no anarchical disorder could be worse than the position to which governments have already led their peoples, and to which they are leading them.

And therefore emancipation from patriotism and the destruction of the despotism of government that rests upon it, cannot but be beneficial to mankind.

IX

Men, bethink yourselves! For the sake of your well-being, physical and spiritual, for the sake of your brothers and sisters, pause, consider, and think of what you are doing!

Reflect, and you will understand that your foes are not the Boers, or the English, or the

French, or the Germans, or the Finns, or the Russians, but that your foes—your only foes—are you yourselves, who by your patriotism maintain the governments that oppress you and make you unhappy.

They have undertaken to protect you from danger and they have brought that pseudo-protection to such a point that you have all become soldiers—slaves—and are all ruined, or are being ruined more and more, and at any moment may and should expect that the tight-stretched cord will snap and a horrible slaughter of you and your children will commence.

And however great that slaughter may be and however that conflict may end the same state of things will continue. In the same way and with yet greater intensity, the governments will arm, and ruin, and pervert you and your children, and no one will help you to stop it or prevent it if you do not help yourselves.

There is only one kind of help possible—the abolition of that terrible cone of violence which enables the person or persons who succeed in seizing the apex to have power over all the rest, and to hold that power the more firmly the more cruel and inhuman they are, as we see by the cases of the Napoleons, Nicholas I, Bismarck, Chamberlain, Rhodes, and our Russian Dictators who rule the people in the Tsar's name.

There is only one way to destroy the binding together of this cone—it is by shaking off the hypnotism of patriotism.

Understand that you yourselves cause all the evils from which you suffer, by yielding to the suggestions by which emperors, kings, members of Parliament, governors, officers, capitalists, priests, authors, artists, and all who need this fraud of patriotism in order to live upon your labour, deceive you!

Whoever you may be—Frenchman, Russian, Pole, Englishman, Irishman, or Bohemian—understand that all your real human interests, whatever they may be—agricultural, industrial, commercial, artistic, or scientific—as well as your pleasures and joys, in no way run counter to the interests of other peoples or States, and that you are united with the folk of other lands by mutual co-operation, by interchange of services, by the joy of wide brotherly intercourse, and by the interchange not merely of goods but also of thoughts and feelings.

Understand that the question as to whether your government or another manages to seize Wei-hai-wei, Port Arthur, or Cuba does not affect you, or rather that every such seizure made by your government injures you by inevitably bringing in its train all sorts of pressure by your government to force you to take part in the robbery and violence by which alone such seizures are made, or can be retained when made. Understand that your life can in no way be bettered by Alsace becoming German or French and Ireland or Poland being free or enslaved—whoever holds them. You are free to live where you will, even if you be an Alsatian, an Irishman, or a Pole. Understand too, that by stirring up patriotism you will only make the case worse, for the subjection in which your people are kept has resulted simply from the struggle between patriotisms, and every manifestation of patriotism in one nation provokes a corresponding reaction in another. Understand that salvation from your woes is only possible when you free yourself from the obsolete idea of patriotism and from the obedience to governments that is based upon it, and when you boldly enter into the region of that higher idea, the brotherly union of the peoples, which has long since come to life and from all sides is calling you to itself.

If people would but understand that they are not the sons of some fatherland or other, nor of governments, but are sons of God and can therefore neither be slaves nor enemies one to another —those insane, unnecessary, worn-out, pernicious organizations called governments would cease, and with them all the sufferings, violations, humiliations, and crimes which they occasion.

[May 10, o.s., 1900.]

INTRODUCTION TO A SHORT BIOGRAPHY OF WILLIAM LLOYD GARRISON

(A Letter to the Editors: Vladimir Chertkov and Florence Holah.)

I THANK you very much for sending me the biography of Garrison.

Reading it, I recalled the spring of my awakening to true life. Garrison's speeches and articles bring vividly back to me the spiritual joy I experienced twenty years ago when I learnt that the law of non-resistance had been recognized and proclaimed by him even as far back as the eighteen forties (I learnt later about Ballou) and that he had made it the basis of his practical activity for the emancipation of the slaves. I myself had been inevitably brought to the law of non-resistance by recognizing the full meaning of the Christian teaching, which disclosed to me the great and joyful ideal to be realized in Christian life.

At that time my joy was mingled with bewilderment as to how it was that this great Gospel truth, explained by Garrison fifty years ago, could have been so hushed up that I then had to express it as something new.

My bewilderment was increased by the fact that not only men antagonistic to the progress of mankind, but also very advanced and progressive men, were either completely indifferent to this law, or were actually opposed to the promulgation of what lies at the foundation of all true progress.

But as time went on it became clearer and clearer to me that the general indifference and opposition then expressed, and that still continues to be expressed, towards this law of non-resistance—especially amongst political workers—are merely an indication of the great importance of that law.

'The motto upon our banner', wrote Garrison in the midst of his activity, 'has been from the commencement of our moral warfare: "OUR COUNTRY IS THE WORLD; OUR COUNTRYMEN ARE ALL MANKIND." We trust that it will be our only epitaph. Another motto we have chosen is, "UNIVERSAL EMANCIPATION". Up to this time we have limited its application to those who in this country are held by Southern taskmasters as marketable commodities, goods and chattels, and implements of husbandry. Henceforth we shall use it in its widest latitude—the emancipation of our whole race from the dominion of man, from the thraldom of self, from the government of brute force, from the bondage of sin, and the bringing it under the dominion of God, the control of an inward spirit, the government of the law of love. . . .'

Garrison, a man enlightened by the Christian teaching, having begun with the practical aim of striving against slavery, soon understood that the cause of slavery was not the casual temporary seizure by the Southerners of a few millions of negroes, but the ancient and universal recognition, contrary to Christian teaching, of the right of coercion by some men in regard to others. A pretext for recognizing this right has always been that men regarded it as possible to eradicate or diminish evil by brute force, that is, by evil. Having once realized this fallacy, Garrison put forward against slavery neither the suffering of slaves nor the cruelty of slaveholders nor the social equality of men, but the eternal Christian law of refraining from opposing evil by violence, that is, 'non-resistance'. Garrison understood what the most advanced of the other fighters against slavery did not understand: that the only irrefutable argument against slavery is a denial of any man's right over the liberty of another under any conditions whatsoever.

The Abolitionists endeavoured to prove that slavery was unlawful, disadvantageous, cruel: that it depraved men, and so on; but the defenders of slavery in their turn proved the untimeliness and danger of emancipation and the evil results liable to follow it. Neither the one nor the other could convince his opponents. But Garrison, understanding that the slavery of the negroes was only a particular example of universal coercion, put forward a general principle with which it was impossible not to agree—the principle that no man, under any pretext, has the right to dominate his fellows, that is, to coerce them. Garrison did not so much insist on the right of negroes to be free, as deny the right of any man, or any body of men, to coerce any man in any way by force. For the purpose of combating slavery he advanced the principle of a struggle against all the evil of the world.

This principle put forward by Garrison was irrefutable, but it affected and even overthrew all the foundations of established social order, and so those who valued their position in that existing order were frightened at its announcement and still more at its practical application to life; they endeavoured to ignore it, to elude it; they hoped to attain their own objects without a declaration of the principle of non-resistance to evil by violence and its application to life, which would they thought destroy all orderly organization of human life. The result of this evasion of the recognition of the unlawfulness of coercion was the fratricidal war which, externally solving the slavery question, introduced into the life of the American people the new and perhaps even greater evil of that corruption which accompanies every war.

Meanwhile the substance of the question remained unsolved, and the same problem, though in a new form, now confronts the people of the United States. Formerly the question was how to free the negroes from the violence of slaveholders; now it is how to free the negroes from the violence of the whites and the whites from the violence of the blacks.

The solution of this problem in its new form can certainly not be accomplished by lynching negroes, nor by any skilful and liberal measures of American politicians, but only by the application to life of the principle Garrison proclaimed half a century ago.

I read the other day in one of the most progressive periodicals the opinion of an educated and intelligent writer, expressed with complete assurance of its validity, that my recognition of the principle of non-resistance to evil by violence is a lamentable and rather comic delusion which, taking into consideration my old age and certain merits, can only be passed over in indulgent silence.

I encountered exactly the same attitude towards this question in a conversation I had with the remarkably intelligent and progressive American, W. J. Bryan. He also, with the evident intention of gently and courteously showing me my delusion, asked how I explained my strange principle of non-resistance to evil by violence, and as usual he brought forward the argument, which seems to everyone irrefutable, of a brigand who kills or violates a child. I told him that I recognize non-resistance to evil by violence because, having lived seventy-five years, I have never, except in discussions, encountered that fantastic brigand who before my eyes desired to kill or violate a child, but that I perpetually did and do see not one but millions of brigands using violence towards children and women and men and old people and all the labourers, in the name of a recognized right to do violence to their fellows. When I said this my kind interlocutor, with his naturally quick perception, without giving me time to finish, laughed and recognized that my argument was satisfactory.

No one has seen that fantastic brigand, but the world groaning under violence lies before everyone's eyes. Yet no one sees or desires to see that the strife that can liberate man from violence is not strife with a fantastic brigand, but with those actual brigands who now practice violence on men.

Non-resistance to evil by violence really only means that the mutual interaction of rational beings on one another should consist not in violence (which should be only admitted in relation to lower organisms deprived of reason) but in rational persuasion; and that, consequently, all who desire to further the welfare of mankind should strive towards this substitution of rational persuasion for coercion.

It would seem clear that during the last century fourteen million people were killed, and that the labour and lives of millions of men are now spent on wars necessary to no one; that the land is mostly in the hands of those who do not work on it, and that the produce of human labour is mostly consumed by those who do not work, and that the deceits which reign in the world exist only because violence is allowed for the sake of suppressing what to some people seems evil, and that we should therefore endeavour to replace violence by persuasion. That this may become possible it is first of all necessary to renounce the right of coercion.

Strange to say the most progressive people of our circle regard it as dangerous to repudiate the right of violence and to endeavour to replace it by persuasion. These people, having decided that it is impossible to persuade a brigand not to kill a child, think it also impossible to persuade working men not to take the land and the produce of their labour from those who do not work, and they find it necessary to coerce the labourers.

So that, sad as it is to say so, the only explanation of the failure to grasp the significance of the principle of non-resistance to evil by violence is this: that the conditions of human life are so distorted that those who consider the principle of non-resistance, imagine that its adaptation to life and the substitution of persuasion for coercion would destroy all possibility of that social organization and those conveniences of life which they enjoy.

But the change need not be feared; the principle of non-resistance is not a principle of coercion but of concord and love, and therefore cannot be made coercively binding upon men. The principle of non-resistance to evil by violence, which consists in the substitution of persuasion for brute force, can only be accepted voluntarily; and to whatever extent it is freely accepted by men and applied to life—that is, to the extent to which men renounce violence and base their relations on rational persuasion—to that extent alone will true progress be accomplished in the life of men.

Therefore, whether men desire it or not, they can only free themselves from enslaving and oppressing one another in the name of this principle. Whether men desire it or not this principle is at the root of all true improvement that has taken place and is still taking place in the life of man.

Garrison was the first to proclaim this principle as a rule for the organization of man's life.

That is his great merit. If he did not at the time obtain pacific liberation of the slaves in America, he indicated the way in which to free all men from the power of brute force.

Therefore Garrison will for ever remain one of the greatest reformers and promoters of true human progress.

I think that the publication of this short biography will be useful to many people.

Yásnaya Polyána, January 1904.

ADDRESS TO THE SWEDISH PEACE CONGRESS IN 1909

DEAR BROTHERS:

We have met here to fight against war. War, the thing for the sake of which all the nations of the earth—millions and millions of people—place at the uncontrolled disposal of a few men or sometimes only one man, not merely milliards of rubles, talers, francs, or yen (representing a very large share of their labour), but also their very lives. And now we, a score of private people gathered from the various ends of the earth, possessed of no special privileges and above all having no power over anyone, intend to fight—and as we wish to fight we wish also to conquer—this immense power not of one government but of all the governments, which have at their disposal these milliards of money and millions of soldiers and who are well aware that the exceptional position of those who form the governments rests on the army alone: the army which has a meaning and purpose only if there is a war, the very war against which we wish to fight and which we wish to abolish.

For us to struggle, the forces being so unequal, must appear insane. But if we consider our opponents' means of strife and our own, it is not our intention to fight that will seem absurd but that the thing we mean to fight against can still exist. They have millions of money and millions of obedient soldiers; we have only one thing, but that is the most powerful thing in the world—Truth.

Therefore, insignificant as our forces may appear in comparison with those of our opponents, our victory is as sure as the victory of the light of the rising sun over the darkness of night.

Our victory is certain, but on one condition only—that when uttering the truth we utter it all, without compromise, concession, or modification. The truth is so simple, so clear, so evident, and so incumbent not only on Christians but on all reasonable men, that it is only necessary to speak it out completely in its full significance for it to be irresistible.

The truth in its full meaning lies in what was said thousands of years ago (in the law accepted among us as the Law of God) in four words: *Thou Shalt Not Kill*. The truth is that man may not and should not in any circumstances or under any pretext kill his fellow man.

That truth is so evident, so binding, and so generally acknowledged, that it is only necessary to put it clearly before men for the evil called war to become quite impossible.

And so I think that if we who are assembled here at this Peace Congress should, instead of clearly and definitely voicing this truth, address ourselves to the governments with various proposals for lessening the evils of war or gradually diminishing its frequency, we should be like men who having in their hand the key to a door, should try to break through walls they know to be too strong for them. Before us are millions of armed men, ever more and more efficiently armed and trained for more and more rapid slaughter. We know that these millions of people have no

wish to kill their fellows and for the most part
do not even know why they are forced to do that
repulsive work, and that they are weary of their
position of subjection and compulsion; we know
that the murders committed from time to time
by these men are committed by order of the
governments; and we know that the existence of
the governments depends on the armies. Can
we, then, who desire the abolition of war, find
nothing more conducive to our aim than to propose to the governments which exist only by
the aid of armies and consequently by war—
measures which would destroy war? Are we to
propose to the governments that they should
destroy themselves?

The governments will listen willingly to any
speeches of that kind, knowing that such discussions will neither destroy war nor undermine
their own power, but will only conceal yet more
effectually what must be concealed if wars and
armies and themselves in control of armies are
to continue to exist.

'But', I shall be told, 'this is anarchism; people
never have lived without governments and States,
and therefore governments and States and military forces defending them are necessary for the
existence of the nations.'

But leaving aside the question of whether the
life of Christian and other nations is possible without armies and wars to defend their governments
and States, or even supposing it to be necessary
for their welfare that they should slavishly
submit to institutions called governments (consisting of people they do not personally know),

and that it is necessary to yield up the produce of their labour to these institutions and fulfil all their demands—including the murder of their neighbours—granting all that, there yet remains in our world an unsolved difficulty.

This difficulty lies in the impossibility of making the Christian faith (which those who form the governments profess with particular emphasis) accord with armies composed of Christians trained to slay. However much you may pervert the Christian teaching, however much you may hide its main principles, its fundamental teaching is the love of God and one's neighbour; of God—that is of the highest perfection of virtue, and of one's neighbour—that is of all men without distinction. And therefore it would seem inevitable that we must repudiate one of the two, either Christianity with its love of God and one's neighbour, or the State with its armies and wars.

Perhaps Christianity may be obsolete, and when choosing between the two—Christianity and love or the State and murder—the people of our time will conclude that the existence of the State and murder is so much more important than Christianity, that we must forgo Christianity and retain only what is more important: the State and murder.

That may be so—at least people may think and feel so. But in that case they should say so! They should openly admit that people in our time have ceased to believe in what the collective wisdom of mankind has said, and what is said by the Law of God they profess: have ceased to believe in what is written indelibly on the heart of each man, and must now believe only in what is ordered by various people who by the accident of birth have happened to become emperors and kings, or by various intrigues and elections have become presidents or members of senates and parliaments—even if those orders include murder. That is what they ought to say!

But it is impossible to say it; and yet one of these two things has to be said. If it is admitted that Christianity forbids murder, both armies and governments become impossible. If it is admitted that the government acknowledges the lawfulness of murder and denies Christianity, no one will wish to obey a government that exists merely by its power to kill. And besides, if murder is allowed in war it must be still more allowable when a people seeks its rights in a revolution. And therefore the governments, being unable to say either the one thing or the other, are anxious only to hide from their subjects the necessity of solving the dilemma.

And for us who are assembled here to counteract the evil of war, if we really desire to attain our end, only one thing is necessary: namely to put that dilemma quite clearly and definitely both to those who form the governments and to the masses of the people who compose the army. To do that we must not only clearly and openly repeat the truth we all know and cannot help knowing—that man should not slay his fellow man—but we must also make it clear that no considerations can destroy the demand made by that truth on people of the Christian world.

Therefore I propose to our Meeting to draw up

and publish an appeal to all men, and especially to the Christian nations, in which we clearly and definitely express what everybody knows but hardly anyone says: namely that war is not—as most people now assume—a good and laudable affair, but that like all murder, it is a vile and criminal business not only for those who voluntarily choose a military career but for those who submit to it from avarice or fear of punishment.

With regard to those who voluntarily choose a military career, I would propose to state clearly and definitely in that appeal that notwithstanding all the pomp, glitter, and general approval with which it is surrounded, it is a criminal and shameful activity; and that the higher the position a man holds in the military profession the more criminal and shameful is his occupation. In the same way with regard to men of the people who are drawn into military service by bribes or by threats of punishments, I propose to speak clearly and definitely of the gross mistake they make— contrary to their faith, morality, and common sense—when they consent to enter the army; contrary to their faith, because by entering the ranks of murderers they infringe the Law of God which they acknowledge; contrary to morality, because for pay or from fear of punishment they agree to do what in their souls they know to be wrong; and contrary to common sense, because if they enter the army and war breaks out they risk having to suffer consequences as bad or worse than those they are threatened with if they refuse. Above all they act contrary to common sense in that they join that caste of people which deprives them of freedom and compels them to become soldiers.

With reference to both classes I propose in this appeal to express clearly the thought that for men of true enlightenment, who are therefore free from the superstition of military glory (and their number is growing every day) the military profession and calling, notwithstanding all the efforts to hide its real meaning, is as shameful a business as an executioner's and even more so. For the executioner only holds himself in readiness to kill those who have been adjudged harmful and criminal, while a soldier promises to kill all whom he is told to kill, even though they be those dearest to him or the best of men.

Humanity in general, and our Christian humanity in particular, has reached a stage of such acute contradiction between its moral demands and the existing social order, that a change has become inevitable, and a change not in society's moral demands which are immutable, but in the social order which can be altered. The demand for a different social order, evoked by that inner contradiction which is so clearly illustrated by our preparations for murder, becomes more and more insistent every year and every day. The tension which demands that alteration has reached such a degree that, just as sometimes only a slight shock is required to change a liquid into a solid body, so perhaps only a slight effort or even a single word may be needed to change the cruel and irrational life of our time—with its divisions, armaments, and armies—into a reasonable life in keeping with the consciousness of contemporary humanity. Every such effort, every such word, may be the shock which will instantly solidify the super-cooled liquid. Why should not our gathering be that shock? In Andersen's fairy tale, when the King went in triumphal procession through the streets of the town and all the people were delighted with his beautiful new clothes, a word from a child who said what everybody knew but had not said, changed everything. He said: 'He has nothing on!' and the spell was broken and the King became ashamed and all those who had been assuring themselves that they saw him wearing beautiful new clothes perceived that he was naked! We must say the same. We must say what everybody knows but does not venture to say. We must say that by whatever name men may call murder—murder always remains murder and a criminal and shameful thing. And it is only necessary to say that clearly, definitely, and loudly, as we can say it here, and men will cease to see what they thought they saw and will see what is really before their eyes. They will cease to see the service of their country, the heroism of war, military glory, and patriotism, and will see what exists: the naked, criminal business of murder! And if people see that, the same thing will happen as in the fairy tale: those who do the criminal thing will feel ashamed, and those who assure themselves that they do not see the criminality of murder will perceive it and cease to be murderers.

But how will nations defend themselves against their enemies, how will they maintain internal order, and how can nations live without an army?

What form the life of men will take if they repudiate murder, we do not and cannot know; but one thing is certain: that it is more natural for men to be guided by the reason and conscience with which they are endowed, than to submit slavishly to people who arrange wholesale murders; and that therefore the form of social order assumed by the lives of those who are guided in their actions not by violence based on threats of murder but by reason and conscience, will in any case be no worse than that under which they now live.

That is all I want to say. I shall be very sorry if it offends or grieves anyone or evokes any ill feeling. But for me, a man eighty years old, expecting to die at any moment, it would be shameful and criminal not to speak out the whole truth as I understand it—the truth which, as I firmly believe, is alone capable of relieving mankind from the incalculable ills produced by war.